Shea Butter Republic

Shea Butter Republic

State Power, Global Markets, and the
Making of an Indigenous Commodity

Brenda Chalfin

ROUTLEDGE
NEW YORK AND LONDON

Published in 2004 by
Routledge
29 West 35th Street
New York, NY 10001
www.routledge-ny.com

Published in Great Britain by
Routledge
11 New Fetter Lane
London EC4P 4EE
www.routledge.co.uk

Routledge is an imprint of the Taylor & Francis Group.

Printed in the United Stated of America on acid-free paper.

10 9 8 7 6 5 4 3 2 1

Library of Congress Cataloging-in-Publication Data

Chalfin, Brenda.
    Shea butter republic : state power, global markets, and the making of an indigenous
commodity / Brenda Chalfin.
        p. cm.
Includes bibliographical references and index.
    ISBN 0–415–94460–0 (HC : alk. paper) — ISBN 0–415–94461–9 (pbk. :
alk. paper)
    1. Shea butter industry—Ghana. 2. Shea butter industry—Africa,
West. I. Title.
    HD9490.5.S483G43 2004
    338.4'76643—dc21

                                                              2003014613

Contents

List of Figures and Maps

Figures

Maps

List of Illustrations

All photographs by author unless otherwise indicated.

Acknowledgments

This study of the West African shea economy has had a long gestation, leading me from graduate school in Philadelphia to Bawku District in Ghana's far northeast corner, and remaining with me in Denver, Gainesville and finally, Princeton.

I first traveled to northern Ghana in 1985, before I knew about shea. Due to petrol and spare-parts shortages—the lingering effects of economic crisis—few passenger vehicles were available for the journey from Tamale to Bolgatanga. Like other travelers, my companion and I "begged" a ride on whatever vehicles passed our way. We found space on a flatbed State Transport maintenance truck. Driving by miles of lush green rice fields dotted with red and yellow birds and inundated by an August rain, I was transfixed by the vastness of the northern horizon. Interrupted only by scattered compounds and distant rock outcroppings, the setting contrasted sharply with the hills and dense forests and cocoa plots of Asanti Region where I had spent the previous two months working as a development volunteer. As we approached Bolga, we passed the junction for Tongo, the village made famous by Meyer Fortes in his pioneering study of the Tallensi. Though the nearness of a place so sacred to the history of anthropology told me I had "arrived" as a student of African culture, there were no visible markers of its significance other than a few guinea fowls, accustomed to the paucity of traffic, sunning themselves in the middle of the road. Disappointed despite the achievement of physical proximity to a site of long-standing anthropological import, I wondered if it might still be possible to glean new insight from this place and the many lives and histories it contained.

After the two weeks I spent visiting Peace Corps volunteers in Bolga and Navrongo and wandering through towns, villages, homesteads, farms and roadsides, replete with shrines, pito-bars, and, even at that time, a host of international development agents, I was convinced that there was much to learn. I was immediately intrigued by issues of ethnicity, economy and domesticity. In a region inhabited by a multitude of ethnic groups, I wondered how ethnic differences were managed and maintained in the face of frequent interaction. I was drawn to the marketplace, a site determining the spatio-temporal rhythms of life and organizing the interaction of people from different locales and economic positions. Finally, I was fascinated by elaborate displays of domestic order conveyed by labyrinthine compound houses. These mud-brick structures were built and rebuilt to reflect changing family composition, most especially the household's accumulation of wives and their shifting status in the household.

Although I had already traveled widely in both East and West Africa, in graduate school at the University of Pennsylvania several years later, it was to Northern Ghana that my mind returned when I thought about possible sites and topics for field research. The composite of gender roles, ethnicity, and trade that I recalled struck me as particularly relevant to issues at the fore of my graduate education in anthropology and African political economy: most significantly, the explosion of interest in the informal economy. With this topic in mind, I began to reconsider my experience in the north and to think about markets in Ghana's Upper East Region as a multiplex interface, providing a space for the negotiation of female autonomy and ethnic difference as well as the mediation of relations between society and the state. Situated just a few miles from Ghana's border with both Burkina Faso and Togo and with a heavy presence of police officers and border guards and a host of other government agents, the town of Bawku appeared to be a ideal venue for the investigation of these concerns. In 1990, I returned to northern Ghana to pursue a ten-week dissertation feasibility study in Bawku District focusing on the social organization of trade. In the short time I was there, it became apparent that relationships among traders, whether cooperative or competitive, were shaped by the presence or absence of state regulation and surveillance.

A few years later, my proposals for dissertation research sought to incorporate an additional level of analysis into the study of commercial life in Bawku: that of global economic shifts. At the time, not only were many African economies in throes of international-financial-institution mandated economic reforms, new global markets and modes of multinational intervention were opening up for African products. With Ghana considered a structural adjustment success story and ripe for both foreign investment and export diversification, it seemed relevant to consider the impact of all of these trends on economic conditions in the northeast, an area physically marginal from national centers of power and long neglected in the country's development agenda. In particular, I wondered about the implications of these policies, with their focus on market reform—a shorthand for privatization and market-promotion—for the extensive commercial matrix already in place. I was especially curious about their effects on the place of the state, for long an impetus to rural resistance rather than incorporation, in northern economic life. Would this new market-oriented agenda bring northern commerce back into the fold of the official national economy? Would it provide the impetus for further independence? The shea economy seemed a perfect candidate for this line of inquiry. Firmly rooted in the domestic economy and with a long history of circulation within regional markets spanning several neighboring states, shea was also the target of export promotion efforts driven by both the government of Ghana and the international financial regime of the World Bank and International Monetary Fund.

When I arrived in Ghana early in 1994 I could little anticipate the opportunity I would have to witness the dynamics of commercial transformation in northern Ghana firsthand. Not long before, the government mandated the privatization of shea export, opening the market to private formal sector firms (both local and international), all the while maintaining its own role as market overseer. My time in the field was spent tracking the effects of this policy shift at all levels of the shea economy. My research took me from the board rooms of the Ghana's monolithic parastatal, the Cocoa Marketing Board, and its subsidiary, the Produce Buying Company, to the offices of both established and fledging private export firms in Ghana's national and regional capitals, and into the rural communities of the northeast where shea was procured, refined, traded and consumed. I tagged along on private-company purchasing expeditions, accompanying representatives on forays into rural markets and households.

In addition to tracing the way shifts in national policy and international standards were interpreted and implemented by state agents and formal sector entrepreneurs, I researched the forms and reforms of local, regional and export markets for shea from the vantage point of the rural women whose livelihoods depended on shea processing and trade. Based in Bawku District, I inserted myself in the daily routines of these economic actors, first with awkwardness and later with more ease. I roamed the markets near and far to Bawku town, searching out women who picked and processed shea. We sat together as I collected data on shea nut supply, prices, consumption habits and customer relations. Building on these relationships, I began to make regular trips to the homes of butter processors in

Saabon, Boubuilla, and Gozense where I sought to be employed and educated in the fine art of butter-making. Women in each community were gracious enough to let me try my hand in what was for them a major source of income. I pounded nuts and mixed vats of unguent shea nut emulsion, seeking to master the techniques of butter extraction and listen carefully to my preceptors.

In Accra and Tamale I combed colonial records for mention of shea, uncovering detailed maps of shea cover in the Northern Territories. I came across tallies (calculated in head-loads) of shea's carriage across the tributaries of the Volta River on the way to forest zone markets, and I found dozens of district officers' reports on the status of trade in Bawku during the first few decades of the twentieth century. All convinced me of the importance of shea to the building of the colonial apparatus in Ghana's northern savanna and state-building in Ghana more generally. Cued by this contemporaneous record, I reread Fortes Tallensi research—this time the work of both Meyer and Sonia—searching for observations of economic life and colonial engagement.

When I returned to the U.S. in late 1995, after nearly one and a half years in the field, and sought to convey my experiences in Ghana, I quickly realized that my own re-entry had been preceded by that of shea itself. Although the people whom I met knew little of northern Ghana, many were aware of shea, whether from their sampling of the cosmetics market, shopping in natural food stores, visits to elite boutiques and Afro-centric salons, or the perusal of health, beauty and life-style magazines. I became the recipient of shea products from around the country—soaps, lip-balms, massage lotions—as well as the target of requests for the 'real-stuff' that I hauled home from Ghana in Milo tins and Bournevita jugs. With this sort of exposure, I knew it was necessary to extend my research to encompass the receiving-end of the shea commodity chain and the different ways shea has moved into metropolitan markets and cosmopolitan lifestyles: how shea is distributed and refined, marketed and consumed. I began to surf the web, looking for new shea vendors. I visited shopping malls in order to survey the latest array of shea products, studying labels, interviewing salespeople and querying shoppers. I read cosmetics and confection trade magazines and called the corporate headquarters of firms buying or selling shea on the international market.

Forged from the vantage point of these many interests and individuals and grounded in the political and economic history and ethnography of northeast Ghana, this book is an account of the contested and contingent dynamics of shea commercialization. Highlighting the resilience and ongoing revision of African states and social institutions, it seeks to expose the forceful yet decidedly non-hegemonic character of global political and economic conditionalities.

None of these explorations, nor the time, knowledge and concentration necessary to analyze and account for them would be possible without the aid and inspiration of many.

At Amherst College, Deborah Gewertz and Don Pitkin introduced me to the world of anthropology, and Jack Pemberton drew me to Africa through the study of art and ritual. I made my first trip to northern Ghana in 1985 with Laura Fry, who, with her undogged sense of humor, adventure and politesse, was a perfect companion. Funding from the Anthropology Department and Graduate School of Arts and Science at the University of Pennsylvania allowed me to return to northern Ghana in 1990 to pursue a dissertation feasibility study in Bawku District. By way of Gracia Clark, I was lucky enough to meet Sulaiman Abudulai, a native of the area, who put me in contact with many of his friends and relatives. Dr. Abudalai's introductions provided the foundation for the friendships that would sustain me throughout my time in the field, both in 1990 and when I returned in 1994 and 1995 for my dissertation research with the support of a Fulbright and Wenner-Gren Foudation grant, and on later visits in 1996 and 2000. Most importantly, I gained the acquaintance of Mary Abugri who insightfully arranged for me to live with the Nimbo family in Missiga, a few miles outside of Bawku town.

In Missiga, Moses and Mary Nimbo and their children, Deborah, Elisha, Dorcas, Susie, Miriam, Keren, Silas, Paul and Aki-wele, provided a home for me during the over two-year period I resided in Bawku. Without their support and care, and the ease with which they integrated a stranger into their household, it would have been difficult to carry-out my research. Not only did they provide a space for emotional respite, the entire family was responsible for educating me about Kusasi culture and the joys and hardships of family and community life in northeast Ghana. The Nimbo household was truly a home away from home during my time in the field. My relationships with each family member anchor both my memories of and on-going personal and intellectual commitment to the northeast.

As my time in Bawku increased, so did the range of persons to whom I grew indebted. Nachinaba Bugri was a perfect field assistant in 1990. In 1994 and 1995, and briefly again in 1996 and 2000, I was lucky enough to work closely with Seidu Mumini whose patience, endurance and social finesse made it possible for me to move in and out of many research contexts in Bawku Districts and beyond. Deftly navigating gender and ethnic divides, Seidu helped me establish ties to shea-butter makers (including his own household in Tesh-Natinga) and shea traders. I am grateful to all of these women for their help, their openness and their incredible generosity. I would like to thank in particular, Limmatta Zabrim, Alabugril Sumaila, Asom Zabrim, Maimuna Issaka, Barkisu Asuor, Ramatu Asuar, Apoasaan Asuor, Maimuna Hamidu (pictured on the cover), Mariama

Ayisa, Ayi Haruna, Atiawin Belko and Mary Anaba. Without their cooperation and willingness to answer my many questions and incorporate me into
their work routines at home and in the market, I could not have completed
this study. The personal and physical strength and grace with which each one
of these women manage a tremendous work load, matched by an unfailing
dedication to their children and families, will always impress and inspire me.

Outside of Bawku, I benefited from the aid of many others in Ghana. In
Accra, I was affiliated with the Institute of African Studies at the University
of Ghana. Facilitated by Professor Kwame Arhin in his capacity as Director,
this allowed me to gain access to resources on campus and, most of all, research clearance. I am especially appreciative of the on-going intellectual
support provided by Takyiwaah Manuh, also at the Institute of African
Studies, as well as Baffour Agyeman-Duah, at the Center for Democratic
Development.

Intermittent visits to Accra enabled me to become familiar with the
working of the several private export companies involved in the shea trade
as well as the Cocoa Marketing Board (CMB) and the Produce Buying
Company (PBC). With the permission of Flt. Lt. Joe Atieno, I was able to
undertake extensive interviews with Ben Manor in the PBC Accra office as
well as with PBC managers Luke Malaku in Tamale and Norbert Abilla in
Bolgatanga. Paul Kassardjian, Ousman Hamza, Anthony Sikpa, Joseph
Binney, Tehuru Ibrahim, Tawia Akyea, and Ampofo Twumasi all gener-
ously educated me about the working of private export firms and granted
me an open invitation to work with their agents in the north. Leslie Flagg
at Technoserve and Mr. Bugbilla at FASCOM also provided much valued
information and assistance. Collection managers and clerks at the The National Archives helped me uncover dusty files on Bawku and shea, sending
me home with stacks of photocopies.

On my visits to Accra I was always warmly welcomed by Patrick and
Fortune Fiachey who helped to accommodate me at the flats on Okudan
Road in Osu. The staff at USIS also deserves great thanks. Mike and Jan
Orlansky did not hesitate to invite me into their home for rest and relax-
ation. Sarpai Nunoo and Nancy Keteku never failed to provide help, advice
and good conversation.

In Tamale I found respite at the Catholic Guest House as well as Tamale
Institute of Cross-Cultural Studies run by Jon Kirby, a fellow anthropologist and student of the north. I also met faculty from the then new University of Development Studies, led by Professor Raymond Bening. In every
conversation with these scholars, I was always deeply educated and impressed by their knowledge of and commitment to understanding the history, needs and life-ways of the savanna zone.

As a graduate student at the University of Pennsylvania, Sandra Barnes,
Tom Callaghy and Lee Cassenelli were a source of tremendous intellectual

energy and support. They always provided valuable guidance even as they encouraged me to forge my own intellectual trajectory. Also at Penn, Janet MacGaffey, Arjun Appadurai and Webb Keane, each in different ways, introduced me to the theories of markets, commodities and global economies which inform this book. Sara Berry and Gracia Clark enlightened me to the possibilities of working in Ghana and the promise of historically informed economic research. In each and every book, article, lecture and conversation, Jane Guyer convinced me again and again of the importance of investigating the situation of rural lives and livelihoods, especially those of women, within wider political and economic orders.

Many friends in Philadelphia, both within the Anthropology Department and outside of it deserve tremendous thanks. Julie Sisskind, Rachel Tolen, Amy Trubek, Sharon Nagy, Sarah Diamond, Jen Goodman, Robyn Spero, Ruth Sullivan and Dina Schlossberg all helped me begin and finish this project and provided the necessary respite from it. In Denver, Robin Calland, Imelda Mulholland, Tracy Ehlers and Angelique Haugerud provided a great source of intellectual exchange and encouragement. More recently, at the University of Florida, my efforts have been supported by my many colleagues in Anthropology and African Studies. I am especially grateful to Steve Brandt, Allan Burns, Peter Schmidt, and Anita Spring, who brought me to UF, and to Dean Neil Sullivan, Michael Heckenberger, Kesha Fikes, Tony Oliver-Smith, Ken Sassaman, and Luise White for appreciating and encouraging the possibilities of an ethnographic approach to state power and global processes.

I finished this book while on leave at the Institute for Advanced Study in Princeton, NJ. The profound humanism of the faculty of the School of Social Science, Albert O. Hirschman, Clifford Geertz, Joan Scott and Michael Walzer, created an unusually receptive environment for new scholars such as myself. Membership at the Institute provided a crucial opportunity to embed my ethnographic research within an analysis of the global determinations of the shea economy. I especially appreciate the support and open-mindedness of Joao Beihl, Jennifer Hasty, Madeline Kochen, Rachel Neis and Neil Englehart.

I would like to thank the editorial staff at Routledge, Priti Gress, Eric Nelson, Angela Chnapko, and Donna Capato, for seeing this project to fruition. Robert Lopez of Gainesville, Florida used his excellent cartography and research skills to produce the maps. The book also draws on material I published previously in "Risky Business: Economic Uncertainty, Market Reforms and Female Livelihoods in Northeast Ghana," *Development and Change*, November 2000, 31, 5: 987–1008; "The Changing Face of 'One-Mouth': Household Labor and Commercial Intensification in Northern Ghana," *At the Interface: The Household and Beyond*, Society for Economic Anthropology Annual Proceedings, D. Small and N. Tannenbaum eds., University Press of America, 1999; and "Market Reforms and the State: The Case of Shea in Ghana," *Journal of Modern African Studies*, September 1996, 34, 3: 421–439.

Other debts are more personal and enduring. Helping me to keep my ambitions in perspective, my parents, Leita and Robert Chalfin, have always approached my work in Africa with curiosity and encouragement. Daniel Smith, my husband, has been a source of incredible support and enthusiasm throughout my time in Ghana and during the many years it has taken to complete this project. His many trips to Ghana and willingness to integrate himself into my research as assistant, sounding-board, photographer, and traveling companion enabled me to bring together my life and identity in Ghana with that in the U.S. I am infinitely grateful to him for his encouragement, humour and wisdom. This book, however, belongs most of all to my son Eliot and daughter Safi, who continually inspire me with their own curiosity about the world and openness to the connections among all of us.

I.1 Shea trees, shea nuts, and shea butter.

West African Shea

From Indigenous Commodity to Postindustrial Luxury

This book, an economic biography of a sort, is about a West African commodity known as shea (*Butyrospermum parkii*) and the challenges its commercial history poses to conventional pathways of tropical commoditization. Focused on the shea economy of the West African nation of Ghana, the book is fundamentally concerned with the logics of economic engagement: the way global economic shifts are brought to bear on, altered, or kept at bay by states and rural economic actors and institutions. Two concerns setting shea apart from other tropical commodities frame the analysis presented here. First, how do we account for the persistence of a domestic market for shea geared to rural provisioning in the face of a long history of export promotion? Second, how can we explain shea's changing status on the global market from an inexpensive and little-noticed industrial raw material to a much-discussed and high-priced consumer item?

Shea trees are indigenous to Africa and grow wild throughout the vast west African savanna zone stretching from Cameroon to Senegal and encompassing Ghana, Cote d'Ivoire, Nigeria, Togo, Benin, Mali, Niger, and Burkina Faso. Shea may also be found further east in Uganda and Sudan. Resistant to plantation cultivation, shea thrives in the savanna's ever-receding forests and on farms where the trees are left to grow whenever land is cleared or returned to fallow. Shea nuts are crushed to produce a thick yellow cream known in Anglophone areas as "shea butter" and as "karite" within the Francophone states.[1] The primary source of edible oil in the savanna, shea nuts and shea butter are sold in rural and urban markets

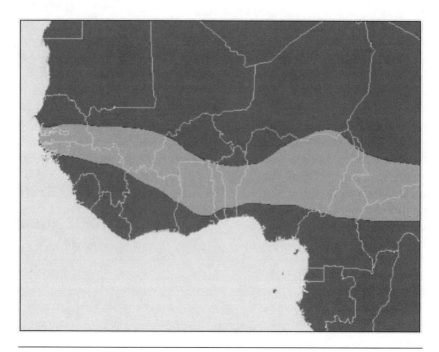

Map 1 The Savanna Zone of West Africa, where Shea Trees Grow in Abundance

throughout West Africa, where they have been enmeshed in the region's commercial circuitry since the medieval period, if not earlier.

Shea's circulation is by no means confined to Africa. For most of the twentieth century, shea was traded on the world market in response to the demands of the North Atlantic states for tropical oils. Yet even with the rise of the export market, shea—in marked contrast to other tropical commodities—remains a staple of the West African economy, widely consumed and central to the livelihoods of rural women who collect, process, and sell it. Faced with such an anomaly of economic survival, this book explores the foundations of the domestic shea economy and the conditions shaping its longevity and resilience despite the pressures of export development.

The paradoxes posed by shea's commercial trajectory not only lie at the intersection of the domestic and export markets but are also located within the export market itself, at the intersection of two streams of global demand. Marketed as a low-priced and little-noticed industrial raw material, shea, for most of its history on the world market, has had a relatively nondescript commercial identity. Breaking away from this long-standing and largely generic categorization, shea moved into a wholly different economic niche in the late 1980s. Sold in exclusive shops at exorbitant rates

and incorporated into a wide array of products geared to self-care, this savanna staple holds a position at the cutting edge of global capitalism at the
turn of the millennium, catering to the desire of cosmopolitan consumers
around the world—from Paris and Tokyo to São Paulo and Dubai—for a
self-indulgent exoticism. Like the survival of the domestic shea economy
in the face of a growing export market, shea's movement from industrial
input to luxury consumer item confounds a much more typical path of
tropical commoditization characterized by the gradual popularization of
goods initially construed as rare and difficult to afford or attain. This book
is concerned with uncovering the factors accounting for this seemingly
novel sequence of commercial bifurcation, from a common and low-cost
commodity in Africa and a cheap raw material in the industrial economies
of the North Atlantic to an expensive luxury good within a truly global
market.

Centered on the specifics of the shea commodity chain (see Figure 1),
the book takes these two lines of inquiry—one focused on rural economies, the other focused on export trends—to gain insight into wider shifts
in tropical economies and global markets. Throughout, politics and history are kept at the fore, conveying the forceful and enduring, though ever-
changing, role of the state and of social struggle more generally in
processes of market reproduction and restructuring, whether within tropical economies or outside them.

Central Arguments: Global Markets, Rural Livelihoods, and the State

Focusing on the complex contours of shea's pathway from the forests,
farms, and markets of the West African savanna to the realms of transnational capital and cosmopolitan consumption, the study of shea serves to
complicate prevailing characterizations of globalization and tropical commoditization. The journey along shea's commercial trajectory moves
between northern Ghana—a landscape of millet, mud brick homes, harmattan winds, intense physical labor, and deep environmental knowledge—and the corporate headquarters, trade associations, international
blocs, and postindustrial lifestyles that comprise the architecture of the
global economy. By looking deeply at the connections and disjunctures
marking shea's route from pre- to postindustrial commodity, the book
challenges widely held assertions about power relations within and between global markets, states, and rural communities. Rather than portray-
ing export promotion policies as necessarily or easily privileging private
capital and international markets over national institutions and interests,
or treating rural economic institutions as a conservative force in the face of
capitalist development, a more complicated scenario is revealed.

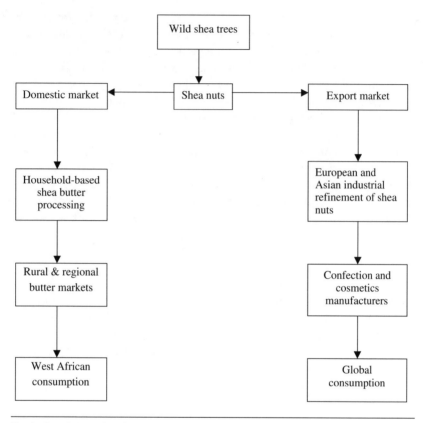

Fig. 1 Foundations of the Shea Commodity Chain

Most of all, this study calls into question the hegemonic character of global economic regimes and patterns of commoditization. Confounding presumptions regarding the coherence of market forces or the social settings where they originate and unfold, the book instead suggests that all are better understood as uneasy configurations of knowledge, actors, and material resources. It shows how economic directives crafted in tandem by multilateral and state institutions are pulled into social fields as much as they are imposed upon them, and that these encounters are iterations of relationships and understandings already in motion—of alliances, enmities, and ideologies built, dissolved, and reconfigured. The ever-dynamic character of global economic processes is evident in the diverse and shifting commitments of institutions of international finance and governance, multinational corporations, and First World consumers to tropical commoditization. It is also apparent in the forceful role played by the offices and agents of the postcolonial state, neither overwhelmed nor undermined

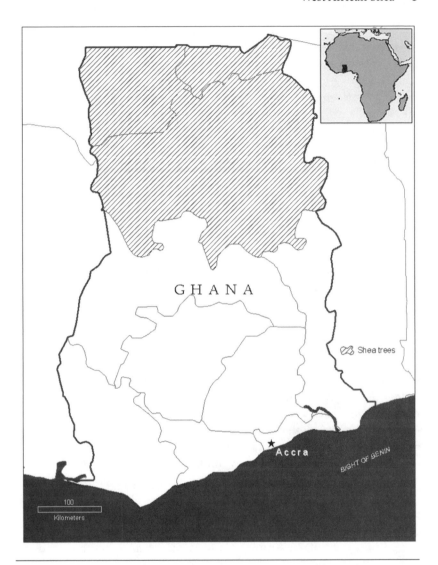

Map 2 Distribution of Shea Trees in Ghana's Northern Sector

by global agendas. At once innovative and conservative, rural communities likewise contain within them a mosaic of divisions and ties and offer no singular set of responses to policies and pathways of global economic restructuring. Although they seek to engage new economic opportunities and changing market conditions, rural economic actors involved in the shea economy remain committed to the provisioning of the domestic market, albeit in different ways.

This book argues that the movement of tropical commodities into the world market is neither a simple nor an automatic process through which global capital draws tropical products and producers into its lair and demand dictates and overwhelms the terms of supply. On the contrary, from the perspective presented here, the global market—while forceful—is neither coordinated nor consistent within, nor does it command consent from without. Rather, the process of market formation is a highly contingent one, emerging out of a compendium of heterogeneous forces. What's more, the case of shea makes it evident that global initiatives must contend with highly resilient domestic markets and niche economies providing rural producers with an alternative to involvement in export initiatives. Even as these economic forms may be altered by their engagement with policies of export promotion, they nevertheless provide a basis for the refusal and reworking of them.

Equally significant to the development of export markets are the interventions and predilections of states—colonial and postcolonial. Within the West African colonies and protectorates that came to constitute the nation of Ghana, the apparatus of the state—its agents, institutions, and strategies of rule—had a profound influence on the character and potential of the export economy. More than a source of resources, markets were consistently used by states as a means to assert authority, create constituencies, and forge territorial claims. The persistence of this dynamic of state-building challenges the widely held assumption that globalization necessarily obviates state institutions and authority. It also undercuts the neoliberal argument that the streamlining of state operations leads to greater efficiency and accountability.

A call for the recognition of these multiple engines and anchors of commercial transformation is not to suggest that the foundations of the market are so aleatory as to be only an effect or source of disorder. Rather, the aim is to replace models of tropical commoditization founded on notions of subsumption with a more conjunctural conceptualization. From this perspective, the shifting form of the shea market is driven not by overwhelming forces but by *forceful intersections* of distinct economic formations. This, then, is a refutation of a largely taken-for-granted sense of global demand and of markets more generally, as ever-expanding and encompassing everything in their path—what Appadurai (1986: 17) describes as the "tendency of all economies to expand the jurisdiction of commoditization." Marking a historical shift as much as an analytic one, the study of shea presents a much more fractured commercial vision. No doubt the proliferation and acceleration of global commercial flows characteristic of this moment is made effective through a process of economic extension—locating new sites and sorts of labor, raw materials, capital, consumers, and consumer goods. However, the circulation of shea is equally shaped by the imperatives of the domestic economy, geared to a different realm of demand, and enabled by different relations of production and exchange.

By relinquishing the optic of encompassment and instead turning to the spaces of engagement where distinct economic and political orders intersect, we can maintain a hold on the intertwined dynamics of integration and differentiation. By no means is this to advocate a return to older models of articulation (Meillassoux 1981; Wolpe 1980) in which export promotion relies on domestic economies only to sustain the labor power of export producers. Where the domestic, in the articulation model, was valued for its reproductive potentials and ultimately undermined by the extractive tendencies of export initiatives, the domestic market for shea operates as a much more autonomous realm, with its own expansive dynamic and own capacity to shape—and even initiate—the terms of interface with the export market. These, then, are parallel commercial realms, not dominant and subordinate ones.

Shea in Ethnographic Perspective: The Rural Foundations of the Shea Economy

Providing an alternative to studies of African economies that focus largely on agriculture, the case of shea sheds new light on the predominant axes of labor and resource control within rural communities. Most important, the examination of shea raises important questions about the political economy of gender. This is because throughout the West African savanna, shea is an inextricable feature of the female domain. Women gather the nut, process it, and share and sell the oil they make. The scent of shea is an undercurrent of women's space, whether the market, kitchen, bedroom, or bath. Women cover their abdomens with shea butter during and after pregnancy and massage it over their infants from head to toe. In northeast Ghana, women around the time of delivery may sit over basins of warm water and shea oil to facilitate parturition. Whether to celebrate marriage or childbirth, shea is what one woman gives another. When a pregnant woman comes to market to buy a large pot of butter, you know her time is near. No woman's kitchen is complete without a store of shea butter tucked in the larder—at least a few balls of the butter wrapped in greasy paper, if not a calabash-full.

It is women who hold knowledge of shea location, tree history, and maturation. This is so even though men typically own the farms on which the trees stand, and male lineage heads are the designated overseers of the bush where shea trees are found. It is women who wake before dawn during the

I.2 Shea butter for sale in Bawku Market.

rainy season, when the shea fruits mature, and walk together to field and forest to fill their basins with nuts before returning home to cook and cultivate. Women know that it is better to gather nuts from the ground rather than from the tree and that smaller nuts may be richer than larger ones. They know to watch for snakes hidden in the early morning underbrush. They are the ones who can recite the requisite charms and prayers to appease the dwarfs and spirits of the forest when they go to gather nuts. They know which neighbors are lenient when they discover you on their property searching for nuts, and which ones will exact a fine or cause embarrassment.

Shea, most of all, is central to women's livelihoods. For savanna women, especially those who reside in rural towns and villages, the sale of shea, processed or unprocessed, is integral to the generation of cash income. Likewise, if a woman can pick and process nuts for home consumption, she can avoid spending cash, conserving an otherwise scarce resource. Indeed, as a wild crop—a sort of found object of the rural landscape with gender-restricted access—shea is essentially free to any woman who has the time and labor power to pick it. Even nuts left to rot on the market floor after the tasty fruit is eaten can be gathered, dried, and sold. In the marketplace, it is not uncommon for elderly women to enlist the aid of young children to scavenge for discarded nuts. When nuts are collected from farm and forest, any income from their sale is pure profit, and once value is added through processing, the profit rises considerably.

Shea is all-purpose. It is an essential ingredient in savanna cuisine. Relatively inexpensive, shea is the most desired oil for food preparation. It is the base of most soups; mixed with onion and pepper, it is a popular condiment. Combined with millet flour, water, and savory spice, it is used in beverages shared with guests at weddings, funerals, and work parties. Shea serves a myriad of uses outside food production. It is widely employed in soap-making, both industrial and artisanal. Factories in Burkina and Mali produce a distinctive soap with a shea butter base, as do household-based soap-makers throughout the region. Shea is also essential to many craft activities such as dying and leatherworking, both long-standing modes of livelihood in the savanna zone. Poured on a pot-sherd and ignited, it is a popular illuminant. Predating kerosene, it continues to be used in rural villages where cash is short and electrification nonexistent. Shea is used to temper and preserve the calabash bulbs of the locally made xylophone and guitar and to anoint corpses before burial. It is the prime ingredient in many medicines, human and veterinary, both as a vehicle for other substances and because of its own antibacterial properties. It is applied topically as a beauty aid to combat the harsh climes of the savanna, heal the cracks of hard work, and draw out a smooth and shiny complexion. In the dry savanna environment, children's skin and hair glisten with shea on the early morning walk to school and after the evening bath. Among the Beng of the Ivory Coast, mothers "rub shea butter all over their babies' skin after the bath" in order to make "the skin glow and show off the baby to great advantage" (Gottlieb 2000: 81). In the Gambia, the use of shea on a newborn's umbilicus is known to prevent infection (Leach et al. 1999).

Processing shea nuts to extract the rich kernel oil is arduous, requiring tremendous strength and finesse. As a result, those engaged in large-scale butter-making typically restrict their efforts to butter production and purchase rather than pick the bulk of their nut supplies. They scour rural and urban markets and the courtyards and storerooms of family and friends for high-quality and low-priced nuts. Once nuts are procured, in order to realize their value, butter processors must tap the full range of female economic knowledge and labor networks. To extract butter, nuts are shelled and dried and then cracked by hand with a stone or wooden mallet. The nuts are then pulverized. If the cost is low and the location convenient, they may be brought to a fuel- or electric-powered grinding mill. It is equally common for rural women to crush nuts between stones or with mortar and pestle. Once the nuts are ground to a fine paste, they are combined with water, and the paste is mixed rapidly to aerate it, creating a creamy emulsion. Warm water is added to help the fat dissolve, and the mixture is whipped again. Cool water is sprinkled over the viscous compound, causing the separated fat to harden. More mixing is required, along with a series of rinses, and a heavy white mass—not quite solid, not quite liquid—is extracted handful by handful, leaving a chalky brown bath with its own set of uses. The shiny white suspension must now be drained, boiled, and filtered. It is then left to set for a few days. Ranging in color from white to a golden yellow, and semisolid at room temperature, the resulting shea butter can last for several years if properly dried and stored.

The slow progress from nut to butter requires the input of many heads and hands. Except in the smallest of quantities, it is physically too difficult to process nuts by oneself. Efficient extraction, moreover, requires expert knowledge. The exact steps involved in butter processing depend on the age and quality of nuts and even on weather conditions. Knowing exactly what to do and when comes with years of observation and experience. Supervision is the purview of older women no longer strong enough to involve themselves in the physical rigors of butter production. It is younger women, however, who have the energy to crush and pound nuts and beat the slurry of oil and water, bending from the waist to the ground in order to reach their arms deep into the processing pot. Other hands are needed to fetch water, start the fire, wash bowls, raise and lower basins, and spell a tired mixer. Butter production, consequently, is a group and usually intergenerational effort. The youngest women—daughters, daughters-in-law, and junior wives—are the source of labor, middle-aged women, the source of capital, and older women, the source of expert knowledge.

The conditions of shea collection, processing, and exchange push us to rethink the terms conventionally used to understand rural political economy, especially the character of gender roles and relations. In a perspective now taken for granted, scholarship on rural economic life in Africa has long identified gender as the primary axis of socioeconomic differentiation and entitlement (Baumann 1928; Boserup 1970; Burton and White 1984; Guyer 1988, 1991). From this vantage point, not only do women and men pursue different economic roles, occupying themselves with different tasks and working in different domains (e.g., weeding versus harvesting; subsistence versus cash-crop production), but these differences are considered to be thoroughly embedded in hierarchy. Research on the gender division of labor in Africa reveals time and again that, within rural society, the work of women is thought of as subordinate to that of men, despite the tremendous—and often greater—contribution it makes to material provisioning and well-being as well as the inordinate contribution of females to the tasks of reproduction (Davison 1988; Stichter and Parpart 1988; Whitehead 1984c, 1984d). According to this analytic, women's economic disablement derives from the uneven terms of resource access and control, limiting their rights to land, labor, and livestock compared to men, while allowing men to make claims on female labor and output. So positioned, with few resources and little authority, women share a common status as an underclass.

I.3 Crushing shea nuts with a wooden mallet. (Photo by Daniel Smith).

I.4 Three generations of shea butter processors in the Sumaila household of Saabon. (Photo by Daniel Smith).

The recognition of the pervasiveness of these patterns across regions and over time is unassailable, providing powerful insight into the gendered foundations and effects of economic differentiation. Yet the study of shea suggests that this model of gender relations may be specific to the agricultural pursuits from which it is derived and that there are other productive domains that also make a critical contribution to rural provisioning and in which different production relations are evident. Hence the assumption that the conditions of agriculture set the standard terms of entitlement and inequality within all aspects of rural livelihood obscures the full picture of rural economic life. Not only is the recognition of alternatives outside agriculture important for understanding the strategies women forge to counter prevailing conditions of subordination. These alternatives alert us to the character of economic domains and activities that are likely to grow in significance as communities across the continent contend with the legacy of overproduction, population pressure, environmental degradation, and the possibilities of agricultural decline, along with the growing demand for nontraditional and nonagricultural exports such as shea.

Specifically, the conditions of shea commercialization call into question assumptions about the character of female economic practice within the household-based economies that lie at the foundation of rural life. For women in Africa's agrarian economies, the domestic domain is typically held to be a site of female obligation where women gain recognition for their contribution to the support of others (Davison 1988; Stichter and Parpart 1988; Whitehead 1984c, 1984d). In contrast, with regard to shea, the household operates as foundation for women's commercial endeavors where they exercise substantial control over resources, including their own labor and the labor of other females. The work of shea processing and trade enables women to gain status and recognition—not to mention material rewards—within both the domestic context and the public realm beyond it. These are by no means atomized efforts haphazardly forged or occasionally pursued as a temporary counter to the inequalities of agricultural livelihoods. Enlisting the ongoing participation of female residents of rural households and communities, they are widespread, well institutionalized, and regularly carried out alongside agricultural endeavors.

The Shifting Currents of Shea Commercialization

Though the presence and accessibility of shea, along with its many uses, contribute to the self-support of savanna communities and savanna women in particular, at the same time shea links savanna residents to much wider economic circuits and distant locales. Contrary to popular representations of shea as newly or only partially commoditized and conveyed to consumers in the markets of the global North, shea has a very long history of commercialization within Africa and outside it. There are records of shea's movement across the Sahel and into the forest and coastal zones of West Africa dating from the Middle Ages—evidence suggesting an even more extensive and earlier unrecorded history (Lewicki 1974: 107). Shea's long history of extralocal circulation is by no means confined to the African continent. Starting in the eighteenth century, shea, alongside other tropical oils, found its way into European and even Brazilian markets. There are records as well of stubborn Dahomean chiefs resisting European traders' demand for shea for fear of it supplanting the commodities (slaves and palm oil) under their control (Denham and Clapperton 1926).

Caught in this long-established web of tropical commoditization, shea has maintained a presence—sometimes great, sometimes small—in the landscape of metropolitan consumption and industry throughout the twentieth century. As a consequence, shea export has served as one of the few means for savanna residents to engage the currents of the global economy, not simply as consumers—and at second or third hand at that— or targets of policy-makers and economic lobbyists, but as suppliers to those at the center of the economic vortex that is global capitalism. The extension of shea's commercial web has always brought political entailments. In the late nineteenth century, shea's commercial potential as a raw material for European industry provided the impetus for colonial occupation of

Ghana's northern savanna (Ferguson 1974). From that time forward, shea's value as an export provided a foundation for state engagement of savanna communities. Waxing and waning with the proclivities of the reigning government as much as the vicissitudes of the world market, the nature and extent of state involvement in the shea export market may well be considered a gauge of state interest in the savanna region more generally.

Comparing the transformations of the shea economy during the colonial era with the dynamics of shea commercialization during the 1980s and 1990s, this book explores the patterning of and relationship between changes occurring on the global, state, and domestic levels. The aim is to convey the highly dynamic and disjunctive character of global economic change by tracing the metamorphosis of one epoch of tropical commoditization into another. As in the colonial period, the 1980s and 1990s were marked by powerful changes in the terms of state involvement in the export of shea and in turn, in the restructuring of the domestic shea economy. In the 1980s, after a long period of state control of but only limited state interest in shea that began in the late 1940s, shea export became a target of excessive state involvement. Government agents set up thousands of cooperatives known as Shea Nut Farmer Societies throughout Ghana's northern savanna with the exclusive charge of collecting and marketing shea nuts for export. Only state agents were authorized to buy these nuts for export or sell them on the world market. This unprecedented agenda of state control reflected the desire of the newly installed Provisional National Defence Council (PNDC) government to rally and sustain popular support in the north after years of neglect and disengagement (Mikell 1991). Control of shea export was an important tactic used by the state to reinsert the country's savanna zone into the national political map and reestablish the flow of resources to and from centers of power (Azarya and Chazan 1987). So strong was this imperative that it directly contravened the very conditionalities of liberalization that the new government, headed by J. J. Rawlings, promised to embrace in return for a massive loans package from the World Bank and the International Monetary Fund (IMF) on which its fiscal survival depended.

In the early 1990s, overturning the reforms of the previous decade, government policy with regard to shea was thoroughly reworked once again. At this time, the export market was opened to private formal-sector buyers, and the state sought to divest itself from the shea sector. A wide range of private firms applied for licenses to buy Ghanaian shea nuts and sell them on the world market. While some of these firms were based in Ghana, all were multinational in scope and tied in some way to European and Asian companies and capital. These firms sent agents to rural markets and communities in northern Ghana and sought to take over the state's place in the shea market, even as the state strived—often surreptitiously—to maintain a stake in the shea economy. As in the 1980s, this move was driven by political motives rather than any singular economic logic. With little choice but to acknowledge finally and more fully the mandates of international donors on which the country continued to rely, the Rawlings government was able, by privatizating shea, to temporarily satisfy the World Bank and IMF representatives. Yet the liberalization of the shea market worked to deflect attention from a more substantial mandate to which the government hesitated to commit. Holding at bay the government's most important political constituency—Ghana's huge class of cocoa farmers—this was the privatization of the cocoa market.

As state policy with respect to shea was changing during the 1980s and 1990s, shea was also being repositioned on the global front. For most of the twentieth century, shea's presence on the world market derived from its use in a spectrum of everyday goods, from soap, candles, and animal feed to margarine, cakes, and a wide range of confections (Irvine 1961: 587; McPhee 1926). Most of all, shea served as a key ingredient in a commodity that epitomizes the breadth and continuity of patterns of tropical commoditization taking root during the height of European imperialism: chocolate. This is because shea's primary use on the world market was as a cocoa butter substitute in chocolate production. Indeed, chocolate manufacture depends on two of the oldest of tropical exports whose sourcing spans nearly the entire Southern Hemisphere: cocoa and sugar (Mintz 1985; Wolf 1982). Not only have the mass production and export of cocoa and sugar transformed tropical labor flows and labor processes around the globe, but the mass consumption of chocolate has gone hand in hand with transformations in production and lifestyles in the industrialized economies of the Northern Hemisphere (Bailleux 1996; Brenner 1999; Coe 1996).

Cocoa butter substitutes such as shea helped make possible the mass production and marketing of chocolate (Minifie 1989). Because shea is cheaper than cocoa butter, its use makes chocolate more affordable and available to a wider range of consumers. Shea also has a lower melting point than cocoa butter, making it easier to work with and especially good for the creation of hard candy coatings. This single difference facilitated the conversion of chocolate confection from small-scale to factory-based production and heightened the durability of chocolate products, all contributing to their mass-marketability. As such, shea is widely favored by those companies engaging in large-scale industrial manufacture of chocolate. This is the realm of American firms such as Mars (Brenner 1999), Cadbury in the United Kingdom (Smith 1990), and the Swiss firm Lindt, all makers of low- and middle-brow chocolate. Mass-produced, inexpensive, quickly consumed, and lacking status appeal, this chocolate bears little resemblance to the much purer and more expensive artisanal chocolate of the Belgians and the French, by whom it is disdained on ground of both quality (due to its high filler or fat [*gras*] content) and low price (Terrio 1996). Incorporated into a commodity, highly processed, low in prestige, and rarely drawing attention to its tropical origins (in favor of a quintessentially modern image), the presence of shea or any other cocoa butter substitute in mass-made and mass-marketed chocolate is hardly noticed by either manufacturers or consumers. If at all, it is marked only by a fine-print reference to vegetable fat on a candy wrapper.

Shea's long-established use as a cocoa butter substitute is in striking contrast to the new economic niche it moved into in the late 1980s. Shea's standing in the world market was fundamentally altered by the emergence of new patterns of work and consumption within the late-industrial economies of North America, Europe, and Asia. At this time, shea gained a new role as a luxury item catering to middle- and upper-middle-class cosmopolitan consumers' desires for leisure, status distinction, and the exoticism of a distant world beyond the reach of corporate capitalism. Rather than an unnamed component of cheap commodities with mass appeal, shea became the featured component of a range of high-status goods consumed by a relatively elite class of shoppers over the course of a decade. By the mid-1990s, shea was a dominant presence in the market for natural cosmetics, an industry worth $2.5 billion in 1997 (Brown 1998) and growing as it sets the pace for leisure consumption in the most powerful economies of the northern hemisphere. Hence, after nearly a century of obscurity on the international market, shea has come to hold a recognized place in the minds and shopping carts of a powerful group of cosmopolitan consumers, defining a market that is profitable, well known, and on the cutting edge of global capitalism.

Marketed as much for their curative properties as for the promise of self-renewal they offer, cosmetics made from shea are presented to consumers as embodying the essential qualities of a faraway and wholly natural landscape along with the labor power of those who inhabit it. Catering to shoppers' desires for self-indulgence, caretaking, and relief from the distresses of postindustrial life, it is the increasingly global and fluid economic order of the late-capitalist age that makes such consumption patterns and concomitant modes of imagining self and other possible (Chalfin 1997). Presented within this rubric of signification, shea is the featured ingredient of a variety of makeups and skin preparations, from baby ointments and massage creams to soaps and muscle toners. In its many permutations, shea is bought, sold, refined, and concocted by a spectrum of companies and concerns. They include The Body Shop and Estée Lauder's Origins, two of the leading firms in the international cosmetics trade; older or more specialized firms such as Crabtree & Evelyn and Smith & Hawken, as well as newer firms with the same image such as Bare Escentuals; and firms with greater market share and mass appeal such as Bath & Body Works, now a fixture in nearly every U.S. shopping mall. This trend is by no means restricted to American companies. The Body Shop, now multinational, has British roots. A French perfume company, L'Occitane, with a line of cosmetics devoted to shea, has opened a series of seemingly exclusive shops across the United States, yet they cater to a truly global clientele. The company is well represented not only in nearly every European capital but also across East Asia and the Middle East, from South Korea to Kuwait and the United Arab Emirates as well as in North and South Africa. A tremendous range of smaller firms, "green" in orientation, feature products made with shea.

Shea also holds a place in a well-established but long-obscured "ethnic" market serving African-American consumers. Originally posed as an alternative to corporate-styled commoditization, this market was for many years organized around privately owned Afrocentric boutiques and home-based mail-order sales. Recognizing the growing spending power and consumer consciousness of African Americans, larger and well-established firms are now incorporating shea into their products, from the prestigious Bobbi Brown cosmetics line to widely marketed hair preparations from Revlon. Indeed, with corporate backing this market has returned to Africa itself. Coming full circle, in Ghana, imported hair treatments in urban salons feature shea. Even Unilever, for years an exporter of shea from Ghana and well known across the continent for its near-monopoly of the soap trade (Burke 1996), markets a perfumed Vaseline brand of shea butter in several African cities. Nearly twenty times the price of the locally extracted and refined oil, it appeals to upper-class and upwardly mobile urban consumers. Demonstrating the increasingly common character of such reversals, a report from the West Africa International Business Linkage program noted that an entrepreneur from Guinea who was in the United States for a conference on the promotion of African exports purchased hair relaxer kits to bring home from the Shea Butter Company of Illinois (WAIBL 2003). Manufactured abroad, products such as these are now being emulated by African firms, which mimic styles of packaging and similarly represent a familiar substance in a foreign guise.

Globalization and Tropical Economies:
New Commodities and Modes of Consumption

The accelerated commercialization of shea during the 1980s and 1990s and its gradual movement into a new niche economy at the cutting edge of

I.5 Luxury cosmetics that feature shea. These include soap, body lotions and scrubs, lip balms, perfume (shown left to right), shaving cream, diaper ointment, shampoo, suntan lotion, massage oil, and hair treatments (not shown).

global capitalism may best be understood within the broader context of global economic restructuring. The expansion of the sort of globalized luxury market now occupied by shea says everything about a tremendous wave of change impinging upon the economies of the Northern and Southern hemispheres alike. Facilitating the emergence of global economic networks under the control of no single state, this period of transformation began with the dismantling in the 1970s of the Bretton Woods system, which had established the U.S. dollar as the world monetary standard. This shift set in motion the breakdown of institutions of national coordination and propelled the emergence of multinational corporations, a trend that continues into the present (Schaffer 2002: 52–56). Marked by the rise of postindustrial economies in the North and new forms of agroindustrialization in the South (McMichael 1994), this economic configuration is predicated on new forms and relations of labor, capital, communication, governance, and culture, with overwhelming effects on tropical commodity flows.

Rather than supplying a few primary products such as cocoa, cotton, or coffee to metropolitan markets and consumers as in the past, tropical economies like that of Ghana are now sources of myriad goods (Jaffee 1994). Primarily natural resources with little value-added processing, these so-called "nontraditional exports" (Barham et al. 1992) run the gamut from native species and long-indigenized ones to bioengineered and synthetic hybrids. The novelty of these tropical commodity regimes is not simply a function of product type since many of these goods—like shea—are not especially new to the market. Their newness derives equally from the changing character of production, distribution, and, not least, consumption (Mintz 1985; Roseberry 1996). Facilitated by the extension and acceleration of distribution (McMichael 1994: 5; Friedland 1994: 213) and the intensification and standardization of production patterns, a tremendous range of tropical products is now available on the world market, accessible to and desired by more people in more places and more often. Reflecting a much broader economic trend of mass-marketing of commodities formerly considered "restricted" in terms of both price and cultural capital (from croissants at McDonald's to Starbucks baristas at the Safeway supermarket), tropical goods once thought of as luxury items, rare and difficult to procure, can now be easily purchased by metropolitan consumers and other "cosmopolitans"[2] with the requisite knowledge and means of access.

The tremendous impact of this wave of economic restructuring on tropical commodity markets over the past two decades has been most evident in the transformation of the fresh fruit and vegetable sector (Friedland 1994; Gereff and Korzeniewicz 1994). In this market, the expansion of tropical production now guarantees a steady supply of both familiar and exotic goods to Europe and North America. In Africa, for example, french beans, strawberries, sunflowers, and florals such as chrysanthemums, carnations, and roses, in addition to a variety of Asian vegetables—all nonindigenous—are grown for European export (Little and Dolan 2000; Jaffee 1994). Central and South America are likewise leading sources of fresh fruit and vegetables for the United States. Brazilian grapes (Collins 2000), Chilean apples, pears, peaches, and nectarines (Goldfrank 1994), and Guatemalan snow peas (Von Braun et al. 1989) supplement an already steady stream of Mexican produce, including tomatoes, cantaloupe, honeydew, cucumber (Stanford 2000), broccoli, and asparagus (Watts 1992), destined for export to North America year-round. Virtually obviating notions of seasonality or regional specialization, all of these products are reaching metropolitan consumers in record volumes.

The creation and continued satisfaction of these new patterns of consumption are founded upon an array of changes in realms of production and distribution. In order to stimulate and control new tropical-commodity flows in a manner that meets the demands of markets both large and refined in taste, multinational firms and their agents are now increasingly involved in rural production in ways different from the past. Foreign investors and their local brokers, concerned with product quality, production margins, and the timing of output, have begun to dictate and closely monitor production patterns, often relying on contract farming or other outgrower schemes (Little and Watts 1994; Jaffee 1994). Placing new sorts of liability on rural suppliers (Little and Dolan 2000), short-term commitments are the norm as investors, wholesalers, and foreign distributors aim to remain flexible enough to respond to the vagaries of the world market. All of this is closely linked to the extension of global technoscapes (Appadurai 1990), making available bigger and more cargo jets and runways to support them and facilitating financial transfers and high speed of communication (Bestor 2001).

The expanding web of tropical commoditization is by no means restricted to temperate transplants or products long familiar to and favored by Northern consumers. Side by side with the large and firmly established flows of indigenous products such as Caribbean Basin bananas and African pineapples, a wide range of other native or "nativized" species now circulate within the global market. Tropical fruits such as avocado, mango, and papaya, along with a variety of vegetables such as okra, chilies, yam, and sesame, are now well known in the markets of the North and are hardly considered foreign in character or origin by consumers. The steady growth of this market has paved the way for the development of a much newer class of tropical exports—products such as carambola (star fruit) and kiwano melon (Cook 1994)—which retain an aura of exoticism yet are gradually gaining recognition and popularity on the mass market. Even these goods—despite marketing campaigns which promote their distinctive origins and traits, from taste to appearance and use—are enmeshed in increasingly generic production regimes. Invoking classic "Fordist" production tactics, cultivation and harvesting techniques for these so-called "exotics" are more and more standardized and controlled by investors and distributors. The object is to decrease labor costs and unify product quality, all the while preserving the perceived artisanal character which makes the product desirable in the eyes of consumers (Friedland 1994: 219).

As this strand of capitalist development has spun its own mutations, to paraphrase Pred and Watts (1992), reaching into new locales and product types and consumption niches, the restructuring and reorientation of tropical sourcing has lost its exclusive anchoring in the world of fruit and vegetables and classic horticulturals. The growing popularity of shea, along with an emerging class of commodities loosely labeled "botanical" or "essential," from jojoba to calendula, neem, seaweed—neither horticultural in the traditional sense nor predominantly marketed as foodstuffs—signals a new instantiation of the increasingly variegated wave of late-twentieth century tropical commoditization. Among these goods is a wide variety of nontimber forest products akin to shea: tree and nut oils, medicinal plants, wild seeds, honey, gums, rattan, and more, used in foodstuffs and beauty and health aids (Carr et al. 2000: 134). Once obscure components of tropical livelihoods and landscapes, yet now objects of popular, albeit refined, consumption and appreciation among middle- and upper-class consumers, these products may certainly be characterized as new outposts of a global economic landscape. Running the gamut from medicinals to food supplements or "nutraceuticals," including a wide array of self-care products, and presented in a seemingly unadulterated form, they represent an emergent tropical commodity niche, both distinctive from and related to what came before.

Taking shea as a prime representative of a new sort of global commercial circuit, the book traces the development and implications of this emergent form of tropical commoditization in terms of the political economy of Ghana and the broader precedent of tropical commercial restructuring described above. The careful investigation of this single trajectory of economic reform makes it possible not simply to track the implications of new modes of commercialization for rural communities in the West African savanna, the Ghanaian state, or the producers and manufacturers of luxury cosmetics, but to say something about the overall shape and direction of global capitalism and the place of tropical commodities in lives and livelihoods at the start of a new millennium more generally. This study, in short, uses the distinctive dynamics of shea market reform as they are experienced by rural residents and state actors in Ghana as a foundation to reconsider the character of global economic change.

The Fault Lines of Globalization and Rural Political Economy

Despite the spectacular growth and transformation of tropical commodity regimes occurring during the 1980s and 1990s, their ascendance is neither uncomplicated nor guaranteed. The pathway of the global market, though it may be vast, is neither seamless nor inevitable. As Appadurai (1986: 17) reminds us, the circuit of any commodity is perpetually threatened by diversion—by takeoffs, spin-offs and breakdowns. In today's global economy, this is all the more so. In an era marked by the increasing span of economic institutions and their necessary flexibility, each and every market is perched on a delicate constellation of forces. Though some institutions and relationships are undoubtedly stronger than others, in an age where tastes, political alliances, and financial markets are unstable, all are prone to dissolution. As the case of shea makes clear, such fracturing cannot be read as a simple indication of resistance to global hegemony; such a singular world order does not exist. Rather, the fault lines of globalization are internal to it. Global economic forces, far from being unified, are driven by distinct, and not always compatible, agendas. Likewise, the numerous and diverse entities engaging the globalization process, whether states, international financial institutions, farmers cooperatives, rural households, or cosmopolitan consumers, are divided in their aims and inconstant in their capacities.

The fractured character of the globalization process is starkly apparent in the multiple institutions and agendas engaged in making shea into a new sort of global commodity. Rooted in divergence as well as conjuncture, shea market growth is spurred by the intersection of several supranational trends. These range from the neoliberal reforms of the IMF and World Bank, the restructuring of European governance through the European Union, the negotiating capacity of international commodity lobbies, and the dynamism of corporate capital, to the emergence of new forms of status consciousness among cosmopolitan consumers. Each of these trends is characterized by different goals and origins and contains considerable internal contradiction.

The tensions of globalization are not restricted to market forces—consumer, corporate, or financial. This is because global directives, while dominant, are not isolated from the objectives of other bodies, notably the state, as mentioned above. Not only does the success of global initiatives depend on the cooperation of states (Sassen 1996, 2000), but states also manipulate global processes for their own ends. As a consequence, political concerns often override strictly economic imperatives in the process of market restructuring. At the same time, states are themselves beset by shifting and contradictory tendencies as they manage disparate constituencies and the diverse agendas of their agencies and officers. This applies equally to the West African states where shea is sourced and the European, American, and Asian nations where it is consumed, and this is true whether states have little or great clout in the international realm and applies to the colonial era as well as the present. Nor are the directives of international institutions immune from state influence. International financial bodies rely heavily on states to implement their agendas. Hence, national governments not only influence the formulation of neoliberal reform policies (Callaghy and Ravenhill 1993), but also exercise even greater control over their outcome. In the case of shea market restructuring in

Ghana, state agents determined the course of shea market privatization, forcefully illustrating what Watts (1994: 15) calls "the fallacy of a simple public-private dichotomy." Likewise, in the global arena, individual states worked to influence the standards of chocolate production affecting the market for shea and their own political standing at home and abroad.

In addition to challenging presumptions about the state's easy submission to global agendas, the wide-ranging and often contradictory character of the many forces and entities engaged in making shea a new type of global commodity raises many questions about the course of social and economic transformation within the rural communities where shea is sourced. From the shifting international economic environment to the unsteady conditions of cosmopolitan consumption and demand and the concerted yet precarious quest of the state to survive liberalization, all of these dynamics have a discernable impact on socioeconomic order within Ghana's northern savanna. Confounding the widely held assertion that export promotion necessarily advantages males and disadvantages women (Boserup 1970; Carney 1994; Etienne 1980; Mackintosh 1989), despite shea's status as a distinctly female commodity, the enlargement of shea's commercial trajectory precipitates an array of responses among rural women reflecting the prerogatives of kinship, class, and political affiliation as much as gender.

Allying males and females and sustaining a select group of women at the expense of another, the conditions of export promotion underwriting shea's circulation on the world market during the 1980s and 1990s induced new processes of differentiation within savanna communities at the same time as they intensified old ones. In the face of export initiatives, large-scale traders (both male and female) with the requisite wealth and political ties usurped the role of smaller players (all of them women) who had maintained a long-standing commitment to the provisioning of the domestic market. This was accompanied by growing stratification among women positioned in the market as nut traders versus those devoted to the processing and sale of shea butter. Rendering access to capital increasingly important for market engagement, the promotion of shea export also induced new hierarchies among butter-makers themselves, heightening their dependence on resources gleaned outside the shea economy itself, whether the profits from cash-cropping, savings, or ties to better-capitalized investors. Butter-makers who could not cultivate these sources of wealth had little choice but to withdraw from the market altogether.

At the same time as the shifting contours of commercialization fostered differentiation, they also caused rural residents to broaden the scope of collective endeavor. These cooperative strategies involved males and females and tempered the tendencies of stratification. Butter-makers formulated new collective modalities geared to conserving capital, expanding the range of the regional market, and complementing already existing strategies of labor concentration. They likewise pursued kin-based reciprocities as they sought to glean productive capital from husbands and far-flung family members. Confounding the widespread characterization of West African households as nonpooling (Roberts 1988), in the face of changing market conditions, husbands invested in raw materials for their wives' shea processing endeavors. Family assets—from means of transport to work spaces and even the labor of junior males—were made available to female household members despite the prerogatives of male ownership.

Regardless of the strategic character of the adjustments made by rural residents involved in the shea economy, export initiatives exposed them to tremendous uncertainty. Export programs were constantly being imposed, withdrawn, and reformed. Within an environment of such enormous flux, rural nut traders and butter-makers worked assiduously to maintain the regional market, even as its context of operation was constantly reconfigured. Yet in the midst of the extreme unpredictability of the export market on the one hand, and the apparent conservatism of the domestic market on the other, new and more enduring economic forms nevertheless were taking shape. These productions were not only about the making of a market but equally about the making of economic subjects. For at the same time as class and capital were emerging as increasingly important arbiters of one's place and potential in the shea economy, another sort of economic consciousness—perhaps less coherent but nonetheless equally concrete in its effects—was brought into being. In the face of the commercial interventions of the 1980s and 1990s, savanna butter-makers and shea traders plotted an agenda in a manner that acknowledged the persistent interventions of the state agents and private firms even as it refused or resisted them, and employed these acquired sensibilities in the pursuit of alliances and ideals of economic order. Speaking and acting against and in relation to the agendas of a new export market, these individuals realized their own possibilities and positionalities as a new sort of economic actor, sometimes to their economic benefit, but often not.

In sum, an examination of the shifting currents of shea commercialization reveals much about the disparities of globalization and the complex and constantly reconfigured institutional foundation of states and rural livelihoods in West Africa. By tracing how economic directives, global in scale and origin, gain a presence in rural communities and are received and reworked by rural residents, state actors, and representatives of private firms, it becomes possible to forge a new understanding of the globalization process. Rather than coordinated and monolithic, from the perspective of those individuals whose livelihoods are centered in (though by no means restricted to) the social and physical landscape of Ghana's northern savanna, globalization appears contingent, contradictory, and uncertain—a compendium of multiple initiatives rather than a singular force. This perspective likewise sheds new light on those "middle forms" mediating the linkage between the global and the local. Whether emanating from the state or the private sector, these entities are engaged in their own project of transformation as they seek authority, resources, and legitimacy at a time when established boundaries offer neither the restrictions nor the security of the past.

Finally, by drawing attention to hidden spaces and modes of commoditization, the study of shea's shifting commercial trajectory provides insight into the character of the rural economy itself. Rather than domains of female obligation, with respect to shea butter production, rural households emerge as sites where women control and concentrate labor, allowing them to endow resources with value and to accumulate wealth. From nut collection and butter processing to the nut trade, the many aspects of shea commercialization in which rural women involve themselves are highly resilient, allowing them to forge a path between otherwise restricted economic domains. The forms of work that surround shea are too specialized to be considered housework yet not specialized enough to be considered handicraft; shea is found at the margins of forests and farms, fruiting at the end of the dry season, and it is sold, processed, and picked throughout the year, placing it at the interstices of rural economic life. Drawing upon resources from a wide array of social relationships and economic pursuits, this positioning enables rural women to engage new market conditions at the same time as it provides a buffer against the most onerous dislocations. However, the embeddedness of shea work and the resources that sustain it—whether time, labor, or nuts—does not override the tendencies toward rural stratification brought about by export initiatives that make access to capital a prerequisite of market participation. As the amassing of cash increasingly emerges as the arbiter of success in both the nut and butter trade, the possibilities of part-time shea work become threatened for those without access to capital and more exclusive and professionalized for those who can claim, hold, and concentrate money wealth.

Chapter Outlines

Encompassing the entirety of the shea commodity chain, the book is organized into six chapters drawing on original and comparative ethnographic research, archival sources, macroeconomic data, and policy documents. Based on twenty months of fieldwork in 1990, 1994, 1995, 1996, and 2000 carried out in rural households and markets and alongside state agents and the employees of formal-sector export firms, the book tells the story of market and state restructuring primarily from the vantage point of the men and women who work and reside in Bawku District, located in Ghana's far northeast corner. Multilocal in nature, these data also include the experiences of merchants, state personnel, and formal-sector employees based in Ghana's national capital, Accra, and other regional centers. This is supplemented by ethnographic observation and interviews in the United States carried out among those who sell and purchase shea as a luxury commodity in addition to library and Internet research on international economic policy, corporate strategy and marketing, and consumption trends.

Countering the idea that shea is new to the market in West Africa or beyond, Chapter 1 explores the status of shea as an indigenous commodity native to the savanna region, embedded in culturally specific beliefs and practices, and, most of all, produced specifically for exchange. The chapter challenges assumptions about the individualized character of commercial endeavor and discusses the place of shea collection and butter production within the household economy and the cooperative character of work that goes into make shea a commercial good. Calling into question the idea that rural African women's household roles center only on reproductive goals and obligations to others, the chapter shows how commercial shea processing is crucial to the cultivation of female identities and relationships at the same time as it is a source of livelihood and independent income.

Moving back in time, Chapter 2 traces shea's evolution from an indigenous commodity to a world-market export during the era of colonial expansion in the early and mid-twentieth century. The chapter describes how colonial interventions aimed at export market promotion and rural responses to them spurred a shift in shea's commercial status within the northern savanna. Prior to colonial engagement, shea was primarily a prized long-distance trade item within the West African subregion, on the one hand, and an item produced primarily for home consumption within savanna communities, on the other. Colonial initiatives both directly and indirectly fostered the development of a different commercial stream, rendering locally produced shea nuts and butter widely available within the markets of the rural savanna. The chapter points to the close connection between policies of market development and state-building not just in terms of supplying resources to the colonial regime but in relation to a deeper political project of defining political subjects, controlling labor, and territorializing state power. This would lay the foundation for later policies of export promotion on the part of the state and responses to them on the part of the rural populace.

Shifting the lens from the colonial period to the present, the next chapters trace the dynamics of shea commercialization during the 1980s and

1990s and continue to argue for a thoroughly political reading of processes of market-building, whether on the domestic or international front. Chapter 3 focuses on the 1980s—a period of political transition and insecurity in Ghana. It explores the reemergence of shea as a charged site for the negotiation of state-society relations in the northern savanna as well as the state's obligations to international bodies. The chapter surveys the state's attempts to reclaim the rural shea economy, promoting export-market development over and above domestic markets and rural provisioning along with new terms of economic citizenship in the savanna zone. Increasing demand for shea and making participation in the rural shea market a means of gaining access to the state, this policy agenda would give new value to shea within the rural economy, with both positive and negative consequence. For the rural women long involved in the rural shea economy as nut collectors and traders, this dynamic would bring new status to their work at the same time as it threatened their control of a market they had previously dominated. Yet, as in the colonial era, the politicization of the shea market inspired rural residents overall to maintain a hold on the market for shea as a means of opposing the exactions and abuses of the national government.

Moving from the rural savanna to the global market, chapter 4 examines the changing commercial profile of shea taking form during the 1990s and tracks the forces responsible for the shea's bifurcated identity on the world market as a luxury commodity and cheap industrial raw material. In unpacking these dynamics, the chapter explores the interface of state institutions and supranational bodies in the battle over standards of chocolate production, with profound effect on the commercial prospects of shea as an industrial input. At the same time, the chapter investigates the roles of consumer taste, corporate capital, and private development initiatives in creating new possibilities for the consumption of shea as a luxury item. In considering the conditions responsible for the duality of shea's commercial trajectory, the chapter argues that the processes of global economic transformation in which shea is embedded remain largely uncoordinated, making them both powerful and unstable.

Chapter 5 probes the effects of the changing face of global demand for shea along with the implementation of neoliberal economic reforms on processes of economic and political restructuring within Ghana during the 1990s. It focuses on the interactions of state agents, rural entrepreneurs, and representatives of the private firms finally allowed to participate in the shea export market. The chapter traces the specific ways in which new forms of commercial capital enter into the domestic shea economy and how this is guided by past state initiatives and the survival of old power blocs within and outside the state. By honing in on contests among rural suppliers to maintain ties to the state, the chapter identifies an only partial process of state withdrawal from the shea market. It looks closely at this combined dynamic of regulation and liberalization accompanying privatization, which allowed shea suppliers in some rural areas to gain control over the terms of export sales and purchasing even as other markets and communities were rendered increasingly vulnerable to and dependent on the incursions of private buyers. Like the export agendas of earlier eras, these interventions, whether direct or indirect, altered the character of rural economic institutions even in the most remote areas of northern Ghana. Most of all, the incursions of state agents and private firms over the course of the 1990s contributed to the emergence of new sorts of boundaries within the rural economy, from the geographic delimitation of state and private-company activity to the conventions of market-based trade and the protection and expectation of exclusive contracts and investments on the part of both nut suppliers and nut buyers.

Chapter 6, delving further into the rural economy, considers the implications of privatization and shea market restructuring during the 1990s not for the export market but for rural provisioning. Focusing on rural nut traders and shea butter producers, the chapter investigates the rising capital requirements of shea butter production accompanying export promotion and the challenges this presents to enterprise reproduction for the women involved in these endeavors. Turning once again to the discussion of cooperative work forms, the chapter compares women's capacity to mobilize labor with their capacity to mobilize capital, showing how the latter is a highly uneven and insecure process. It becomes apparent that although cooperative efforts are increasingly vital to the mobilization of capital for commercial butter production, rural women must at the same time engage in diverse economic pursuits to secure the cash, credit, and social ties necessary to purchase shea nuts. As a result, the collective potentials of butter-making are increasingly crosscut by more individualized trajectories of economic loss and gain. Although individual economic biographies have always shaped a woman's place in the collective, as the capital requirements of butter processing increase, so do such processes of differentiation, posing new threats to the reproduction of the domestic shea economy and its future as a widespread source of livelihood for rural women.

The Conclusion reiterates the central findings of the book: the globalization process is vast, heterogeneous, and rife with contradiction. Tropical commodity regimes, as a force of late capitalism and postindustrial economic change, are in a process of restructuring. Rather than singular in form, they contain within them multiple trajectories, both expanding long-established modes of tropical commercialization and moving into new areas, generating new types of products, values and types of consumer. In the process, postcolonial states are not being undermined by the ascendance of global economic forces, but they are being altered. In the case of Ghana, we see a two-sided process by which state power is consolidating and "going underground," diffusing its influence through new coalitions and modes and sites of operation. Rural economic identities and institutions are also being transformed by processes of global economic change. In the case of shea, these shifts have been most dramatic for rural women. However, even for women within a single community and a single industry, there is a great deal of variation in their experience of these dynamics, demonstrating the salience of class, kinship, and individual strategy in explaining the currents of rural economic change. Rural women, whether seeking to preserve core economic institutions from which they derive value and identity or altering them in concert with the shifting economic environment, are only partially successful given the increasingly diversified tactics of export market development shaping shea's profile on the global market.

Establishing the ethnographic frame for all of these discussions, the character of economic life in Bawku District is described in the following section, entitled The Setting.

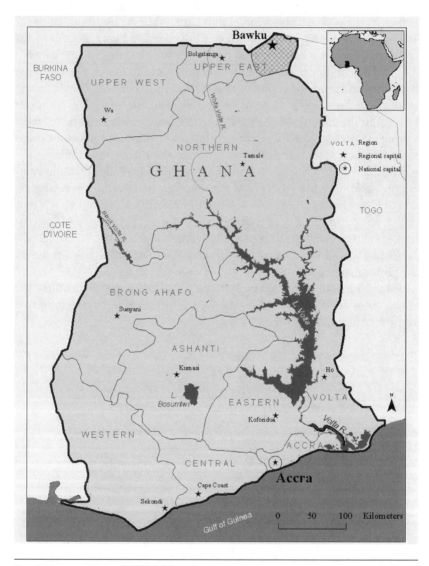

Map 3 Ghana and Bawku East District

The Setting

The portrait of rural livelihoods presented here is drawn from the study of Bawku East District in Ghana's far northeast corner. Bordering Togo to the east and Burkina Faso to the north, Bawku East is an international and ethnic border zone encompassing the trading center of Bawku and numerous smaller towns, villages, and satellite markets. Whitehead aptly describes the district as "an ethnically mixed area which has functioned as a refuge area for many generations of rural migrants" (1984a: 3). The inhabitants of Bawku are primarily Kusasi, an ethnic group related to the Tallensi and exhibiting a similar acephalous social structure (Manoukian 1951). Bawku also hosts a large population ethnically identified with the Mamprussi state, a polity sharing a common origin with the Mossi and Dagomba (Manowkian 1951). With much social interchange and cultural overlap (including intermarriage and mutually intelligible languages), and at the same time a history of animosity, Kusasi and Mamprussi ethnic differentiations are not always clear-cut—but are sometimes all too clear (Bening 1975b: 130; Drucker-Brown 1988–1989; Smith 2001).[1]

Bawku is also home to people of Busansi and Bimoba heritage. Concentrated in the district's northern and eastern edges, respectively, they are also integrated into the district's population. The area is inhabited in addition by Hausa, Mossi, and Zaberma peoples. Tracing their history to northern Nigeria, Burkina, and Niger, members of these groups found their way to Bawku during the early twentieth century through the allure of the long-distance trade routes that crossed the district and to escape the exactions of French colonial rule in neighboring territories (Hart 1978).

Economic life in Bawku East is representative of that of rural savanna communities more generally. Population density in this district of 300,000

(Ghana Statistical Service 1998) is among the highest in the country and growing. Combined with environmental degradation and limited investments by the state in economic development and infrastructure, this makes Bawku East among the poorest areas of Ghana as a whole, with 97 percent of the population below the national poverty line (Sarris and Shams 1991: 67). According to the Ghana Statistical Service, in 1999 poverty levels in the Upper East Region where Bawku is located were the deepest in the country (2000b: 13, 40). Per capita cash income is nearly 40 percent below the national average (Ghana Statistical Service 2002a: 102) and 80 percent of residents live in "extreme poverty" (Ghana Statistical Service 2000b: 13, 40). Within this context of impoverishment, Bawku's economy, as in many other rural savanna communities across West Africa, is beset by the intertwined processes of agricultural decline and commercial intensification. Because these conditions take an extreme form in Bawku, the case study of the district makes apparent widespread trends that are powerfully determinative of savanna communities' experiences of and responses to national and international economic policies—such as those related to shea commercialization.

Bawku's economy is fundamentally shaped by the ecology and geography of the savanna environment. As in much of the surrounding area—whether southern Mali, Burkina Faso, and Niger, or northern Togo, Benin, Nigeria, and Côte d'Ivoire—the savanna ecosystem determines the rhythms and possibilities of agriculture, the foundation of the local economy. Bawku's agricultural economy has a marked seasonality reflecting the sharp distinction between the single rainy season, running from May or June through September or October, and the dry season that spans the rest of the year. This yearly divide between wet (*seug*) and dry (*u'un*) is further fractured into four climatic periods: the heart of the farming season, running from June through August (*budug sasa*); the harvest season, from September through November (*kyi kyeob wen*—literally "millet cutting time"); the harmattan, the season of wind and dust (*si-siem sasa*), from December through February; and the hot season (*tulug sasa*), from March through May. This cycle in its most basic form progresses from the plenty of the harvest season to the scarcity and hunger of the rainy season, and conditions parallel shifts in the form and context of work. While the harvest season initiates a surge in trade and decline in farmwork once the crops are in, the rainy season marks a return to the farm and a retreat from the market.

In Bawku East, rural residents as well as those at the perimeter of the district's several towns typically reside in homes made from mud brick roofed with thatch or corrugated zinc. The sprawling complexes, built on land to which the household head holds inherited rights, house multiple generations of a single family, as is common among many patrilineal and patrilocal peoples in West Africa. Containing an array of rooms ringing an inner courtyard and surrounded by a high mud wall, these compound homes can easily be altered to reflect changing family needs, wealth, and composition. Due to kin ties and for convenience, the houses are often loosely clustered to form village and neighborhood hamlets.

Agricultural production in Bawku East District centers on intensive cultivation carried out on fields near to residential areas as well as on distant plots. The right to farm, like the right to build, is typically inherited through paternal kin but may also be ceded to individuals and their descendants by community leaders, a practice that is supplemented by shorter-term loan and rental agreements. Farming is generally a low-tech endeavor, with the handheld hoe the single critical instrument of production. The burning of plots to regenerate the soil and clear the previous year's debris is a common practice. When possible, farmers manure their plots, especially those close to home and livestock corrals, and, if they can afford it, apply chemical fertilizer. While the hiring of bullock and plow teams is widespread, the purchase of fertilizer is beyond the reach of most rural budgets.

The staple food crops are millet, sorghum, and, more recently, maize. These grains are supplemented by the cultivation of pulses, most importantly cowpeas (*Vigna unguiculata*), bambara beans (*Voandzeia subterranea*) and peanuts (*Arachus hypogaea*). These are grown as both food and cash crops, along with rice and sweet potatoes in a few well-watered parts of the district. A variety of vegetables, usually *neri* (*Colocynthis citrullus*, a seed-producing gourd) and okra (*Hibiscus esculentus*), may be intercropped or cultivated in kitchen gardens close to the compound that consist primarily of leafy greens (Cleveland 1980: 267–8). Given the limitations on land and fertility, people do their best to double-crop staple grains, planting early millet in April or May and a second round of grains several weeks later. With the exception of early millet, which is ready to eat by mid-July, harvesting begins in September and continues through November.

Grain stands are considered family fields. They are designated for household consumption and all able-bodied family members—male and female, child and adult—are expected to apply their labor to them. This is achieved through a division of labor locally perceived as age-and gender-appropriate. Youths help seniors, women usually plant and harvest, and men as well as women weed. A similar division of labor is pursued on cash-crop plots held by individual male household members. Although women may oversee plots of their own, the assistance of their male relatives is by no means guaranteed or expected. Given their limited command of family labor, women seek other sources of aid. Extrahousehold labor takes a variety of forms, ranging from reciprocal work groups and invited work parties compensated "in kind" to waged labor compensated in cash. All may be employed both on household and on individually managed plots (Cleveland 1980: 275). In addition to the standard repertoire of rainy season crops, dry season gardens of onion and tomatoes, largely cultivated by men, are increasingly popular (Roncoli 1994). An important supplement to agricultural incomes, wild resources like shea are collected during the early part of the rainy season and serve as an immediate and future source of cash or food. Shea procurement and the agricultural economy lie in a delicate balance, however, as agricultural intensification limits the length of fallows and increases land under cultivation (Peiler 1994). These conditions work against the preservation and regenerative capacities of wild tree stands at the same time as they cut into the labor available for nut collection and processing.

Although agriculture is a focus for the investment of substantial land and labor geared to food production and self-sustaining cultivation of staple foods remains the goal of most households (Devereux 1993b), non-agricultural and off-farm pursuits are becoming increasingly important to economic survival in Bawku due to a persistent dynamic of agricultural decline. Bawku, like many other savanna communities, is subject to the twin pressures of population growth and land degradation. With population density approaching more than 300 people per square mile in 1989 (Webber 1996: 441; Roncoli 1994: 226), pressure on land is considerable. Not only have fallows been abandoned and nearly all available land used for farming, but increasingly intensive cultivation methods have also been employed by local farmers, resulting in a decline in soil fertility and crop yields (Webber 1996: 446). These declines are exacerbated by the use of inappropriate technology and inputs, such as tractors, inorganic fertilizers, and new seed varieties, that occurred in the 1950s, sixties, and seventies as part of the high-tech economic development agenda of the postcolonial state (Roncoli 1994: 240). Climatic factors, namely anomalous rainfall patterns including periodic drought and overall desiccation, have further aggravated the agrarian deterioration brought about by social, political, and technical factors (Webber 1996: 439; Whitehead 1984a). These dynamics have had two major effects: first, increasing the labor requirements of agricultural production; and second, increasing the importance of off-farm modes of income generation (Roncoli 1994: 459; Webber 1996: 449).

Given these conditions, remarks by Tomich, Kilby, and Johnson regarding the "hidden extent of rural non-farm activities" are appropriate to Bawku. Challenging the conventional equation of rural livelihoods with agriculture, they assert that:

> apart from agricultural processing, a large share of the rural population is engaged in full- or part-time jobs in manufacturing, repair, construction, retail and wholesale trade, restauranting, transport, personal services, and salaried

employment. Part-time activities carried on in the homestead, typically by women, include brewing, garment making, and traditional crafts. Petty trading and repair are also frequently part-time. (Tomich et al. 1995: 44)

In Bawku, this pattern of economic diversification is well elaborated as residents pursue and increasingly depend on a wide array of nonagricultural work year-round that is oriented to self-provisioning as well as the market.

For those who reside in Bawku, the decline in agricultural productivity contributes to the increasing centrality of trade to economic life. Capturing the importance of the market even in a largely subsistence-oriented agricultural economy like that of Bawku, Whitehead remarks:

> Although a high proportion of food consumed by self-provisioning farmers does not enter or derive from the market, markets are important in the self-provisioning sector. In the conditions of agricultural production in sub-Saharan Africa, self-provisioning has normally been met by consuming own grown product plus that obtained on local market exchanges. Perhaps more importantly, most self-provisioning farmers . . . sell food. There should be no suggestion that subsistence needs are met before surplus is marketed, nor that the divide between market and non-market is the same as the divide between production for self-consumption and production for exchange. (Whitehead 1990: 435)

Such dependence on the market obtains not only during the rainy season, when food stores are generally low, but throughout the year. In Bawku, trade occurs on multiple levels, encompassing agricultural produce along with handicrafts and factory-made goods both new and used. Situating Bawku within an expansive and diverse economic field, some of these products originate and are consumed within Bawku District itself; others flow to and from the savanna subregion, the wider Ghanaian economy, and an extended international economy linking Bawku to neighboring West African states as well as the economies of Asia, Europe, and North America.

Upon arriving in Bawku, one is immediately impressed by the town's commercial vigor, which contrasts with the backdrop of agricultural decline. The two, however, are thoroughly intertwined and attest to the scope and significance of expansive commercial circuits within the livelihoods of residents of this seemingly remote border area.

Bawku market, for decades located in the town's central square and under renovation in the late 1990s, snakes through the town in a vast patchwork occupying every available open space. The market's tightly formed aisles, packed with shoppers and traders sitting on the ground or beside wooden tables and sheds, leave little room to maneuver, especially every third day, when market is in full session. On market days, the roads and paths leading to town are awash with rural women trekking in from the surrounding villages and neighborhoods to trade. Wearing faded tops, printed cloth wrapped around their waists, and well-worn rubber slippers, women stream into town from all directions, balancing on their heads enamel basins heavily loaded with their wares. Holding agricultural produce (millet, maize, sorghum, rice, groundnuts), garden vegetables, foods and medicines gathered in the bush, and a variety of indigenous commodities processed at home for resale (shea, dawa dawa, malt, clay pots, cotton thread), the basins contain the bounty of female and familial labors produced in the face of land shortage, population pressure, and environmental decline. Staking a place for herself in the town's marketplace, each woman sells whatever she is able: from hundred-kilo bags of rice right after harvest to meager bowls of dried okra once the bounty of harvest is gone.

Men come to market too. Some on foot and more on bikes and motorcycles, they bring small and large livestock to sell: cattle, sheep, goats, and fowl, as they have for decades (Hart 1978). Others convene in the wholesale market, bargaining over lots of kola, beans, and groundnuts. Elderly men come to town wearing handwoven cotton smocks and leather-bound straw hats. Younger men come in trousers and T-shirts purchased secondhand or, if more prosperous, tailored "up-and-down" suits in serge or khaki. Those who come from surrounding villages remain in town to socialize once they have finished trading, like their female counterparts, stopping for a drink at the *pito* (millet beer) bars on the outskirts of town or visiting friends and family members who live or work in the concrete-block and mud-brick structures that surround the town's commercial core.

The trade in foodstuffs—grains, pulses, livestock, and indigenous commodities like shea—caters to local consumption needs at the same time as it ties the Bawku to neighboring states and the broader Ghanaian economy. There is an extensive regional market for agricultural produce connecting Bawku, Burkina Faso to the north, and Niger to the northeast. This is accompanied by a southern trade circuit connecting Bawku to Ghana's Northern Region as well as the markets of Accra and Kumasi in southern and central Ghana (Chalfin 2001). Depending on the market, local residents search for income within these networks. While the local trade is dominated by loosely knit associations of those native to or long resident in the district, long-distance commerce is managed by a complex network of middle people, some residing in Bawku, others based further a field. Shea figures into all of these commercial circuits. Butter made in Bawku is purchased by local residents for consumption. Butter from Ghana's Northern Region is brought to Bawku and purchased for local use or bulked and sent to Burkina and Niger. Shea nuts likewise move into Bawku from satellite markets in surrounding villages and small towns. The nuts may be sold to local butter-makers or traders from the Northern Region, who themselves occasionally bring nuts to sell. These buyers face competition from

II.1 Bawku Market on a crowded market day.

representatives of Ghana-based parastatals and private firms, as well as buyers from Togo and Burkina Faso.

The market for agricultural goods in Bawku is situated within a broader complex of economic connections, rendering the district a repository of a wide array of imports and manufactures and further shaping livelihoods in the area. Attesting to these ties and the economic opportunities gleaned from them, the town's main street is lined with storefronts, kiosks, and shipping containers turned shops, full of manufactured goods from Ghana, Europe, Asia, and a host of African countries. Hajias and El Hajis sit by their wares dressed in expensive wax prints and flowing embroidered bubus of imported damask cotton. Shop attendants sport the latest imported fashions. Goods spill over storefront display areas and onto the sidewalk and street. There are piles of mattresses and plush upholstered furniture, grinding mills and electric generators, lines of bicycles, motorcycles, and scooters and accompanying accessories and spare parts. Cartons and containers of processed foods—powdered and tinned milk, MILO, infant formula, sardines, tuna, tomato paste, macaroni, cooking oil, baked beans, oats, and cornflakes—are piled high alongside crates of soft drinks, bales of bottled and packaged water, and a wide variety of Lever-made soaps.

Household goods abound—plastic, Pyrex, and enamel bowls and basins of all styles and sizes, insulated coolers, flasks and food containers, cooking pots, plastic mats and carpets. Some shops specialize only in textiles, wax prints from Ghana, Nigeria, and Holland, others offer T-shirts, poly-blend prints, baby clothes and accessories, ready-made outfits from Thailand, and Muslim veils in dozens of patterns and colors. Many of these items can be found in Bawku due to the town's proximity to Burkina Faso and Togo, which are Francophone nations with economic policies and histories entirely different from Ghana and much easier access to European and Asian imports as well as goods from Nigeria, the economic hub of West Africa.

Despite the commercial bounty on display in town's center, the economic inventory of rural households remains meager. Rural women own clothes, cooking pots, and serving bowls. Their bedrooms are likely to contain a few plastic or straw sleeping mats, a suitcase for storage, and a few stools. Men are likely to own a bicycle and, if more prosperous, a donkey and donkey cart. Water is collected from boreholes and deep wells, and access to electricity is limited. Even when power is available, households often lack the funds necessary to pay for connection, just as they struggle to pay school fees and buy uniforms and notebooks for school-age children. For members of most rural households, the extravagant displays of goods in Bawku town are largely inaccessible. While some of the town's and district's residents—salaried workers such as teachers, nurses, and state functionaries

II.2 A typical storefront in Bawku town displaying an array of manufactured goods, from cooking pots to insecticides.

and the families of better-off merchants—can afford these goods, to most they represent the possibilities of trade, not consumption.

The documented and undocumented flow of goods across the border into Bawku is widespread, giving the town and its residents a reputation for *kalabule* (a popular Hausa slang for black-market trade). Participation in cross-border trade (both legal and illegal) is a major source of revenue and economic advantage for a good number of Bawku's inhabitants. This is the case whether one takes part in the petty carriage of undeclared items for consumption or participates in complex smuggling networks that bring large quantities of goods into the district and neighboring regions for purposes of trade. Indeed, even shea may enter the realm of illicit commerce, as traders and butter-makers in the border zone seek to evade tariffs and price controls in one country or another (Chalfin 2001).

Shaped by the interplay of political geography and agricultural ecology, Bawku's status as a regional trading center both heightens and lessens economic insecurity in the district. On the one hand, Bawku's border-zone location, drawing traders and agricultural commodities from elsewhere, makes its market attractive to the district's rural producers, whether they choose to sell their wares or to purchase food supplements on the cheap. Likewise, the district's proximity to neighboring states offers easy access to a wide range of imports and manufactures, improving standards of rural consumption and providing an array of commercial opportunities beyond subsistence production.

Reflecting the "double edge" of commercial linkage, these enticements, however, carry their own risks that threaten rural livelihoods. Because markets in Burkina to the north and the urbanizing areas of Ghana's Northern Region to the south both typically offer higher prices for food staples, these goods are progressively siphoned out of the district after harvest and end up in urban grain stores outside the region itself (Whitehead 1984a: 11–12). Not only does this diminish much-needed local food stores, but it also undermines access to manufactures and imports circulating through the district. On this issue Cleveland (1980: 295–96) remarks:

> Since Kusaok is on the border with both Upper Volta [sic] and Togo there is a flourishing black market which works to the extreme disadvantage of local subsistence farmers. Many manufactured items from the south meant for local consumption pass across the border, pulled by a ten to one or greater black market rate. To some extent this is also true of agricultural goods, including food shipped in for famine relief.

Thus poised between an increasingly marginalized agricultural sector demanding greater investment only to produce less, and the expansion of commercial opportunity only to risk more, Bawku residents, like other rural savanna dwellers, must contend with these intertwined trajectories of agricultural decline and commercial connection as they confront both subtle and profound shifts in national and international economic policy, whether related to shea or otherwise.

CHAPTER 1

Making Butter
*Indigenous Patterns of Commoditization
in Northern Ghana*

Beyond Agriculture: Commerce
and Cooperation in the Shea Economy

In northern Ghana, as elsewhere in West Africa's savanna belt, shea is a
ubiquitous feature of the economic landscape. On agricultural plots, shea
is among the few woody species left standing when the land is put into production, and shea trees remain and propagate when the land is farmed or
left fallow. Shea is ever-present in the marketplaces of the savanna. The
green shea fruits are sold at the beginning of the rainy season, and shea
nuts flood the market at its end. Displayed in clay and enamel pots, baskets, and calabashes or shaped into loaves and lozenges, shea butter is sold
throughout the year. In the urban trading centers, shea butter traders clus-
ter together in designated aisles; they may be dispersed throughout rural
markets, occupying every available space and protecting their butter from
the sun with damp leaves and pieces of worn-out cloth. The scent of shea is
everywhere. Cooked-food sellers use it to fry and season the snacks sold
from roadside stands or trays head-loaded through crowded marketplaces
and truck stops. Shea is a fundamental ingredient of savanna cuisine, especially those dishes made from indigenous products—native pulses, finger
millets, and leafy greens.

Rubbed into the hair and skin on a daily basis as both medicinal and
beauty preparation, shea's presence is constant and embodied. Shea most
of all pervades the female domain. It is women who devote their time to

1.1 Shea fruits for sale in Pusiga Market. (Photo by Daniel Smith).

nut picking, butter preparation, and nut and butter sales. They are the ones who prepare sauces rich in shea butter and who use the butter to care for themselves and their children, massaging postpartum and newborn bodies with shea for comfort, protection, and proper self-presentation.

In the savanna region, shea butter processing is a task familiar to most women, one that they perform from time to time throughout their lives. Many women, especially those who live in less densely populated areas where shea trees are plentiful, produce shea butter for home consumption on an annual basis after amassing sufficient nuts from the bush or their own property. In sharp contrast to the promotional material accompanying shea in the cosmopolitan cosmetics sector, which presents it as newly commoditized and produced largely for subsistence, almost all households purchase the bulk of the shea butter they need from the market—whether for food preparation, medicine, adornment, or otherwise. Accordingly, there are women who are entirely commercially oriented in their butter-making endeavors. Living in households, neighborhoods, and villages with reputations for large-scale and skilled butter-making, they cater to the needs of the wider community as well as the demands of more distant markets and consumers, processing large quantities of butter on a weekly basis and purchasing rather than picking nuts. For these women, shea butter extraction is a vocation to which they devote tremendous effort and from which they derive the basis of their livelihood. Indeed, shea producers are thoroughly embedded in the market, and the market is embedded in their relationships and identities.

This chapter takes the work of such professional butter-makers as its focus, highlighting the strongly commercial character of the indigenous butter industry and the intersecting processes of butter production and social reproduction. The chapter pays close attention to the labor forms associated with commercial butter-making and their implications for the social and economic standing of rural women. Given the extraordinarily high labor demands of butter extraction, in northern Ghana a woman's ability to concentrate labor is the prime determinant of her potential and performance in the butter market. Women meet the labor demands of commercial shea production through various processes of labor pooling. Cooperative rather than waged and built upon ties of kinship and coresidence, these productive arrangements are firmly rooted in the domestic domain, rendering the circulation of female labor within and between domestic units essential to sustaining and intensifying market-oriented butter production. Obviating the need for cash to pay for labor, these work routines are complemented by loose credit arrangements between nut suppliers and butter-makers that allow them to invest in and expand their butter-making enterprises with little capital.

Bringing to the fore the combined commercial and cooperative character of the shea industry, examination of the labor forms surrounding shea butter processing reveals the strong market orientation of shea producers. In doing so, the chapter engages a larger debate about the characterization of the rural African economy and women's place within it. Specifically, the study of commercial shea butter production—a decidedly nonagricultural endeavor—provides a fuller picture of the political economy of gender in contrast to prevailing portraits of rural women's economic standing based on the study of agriculture alone. Although agriculture is certainly the dominant productive endeavor in rural economies, the tendency to treat it as definitive of women's overall economic position is problematic when other economic pursuits are characterized by different forms of labor and property. These distinctions are especially critical in savanna areas such as northeast Ghana, where labor migration and the declining conditions of agricultural production render investment in nonagricultural endeavors increasingly prevalent among women and crucial to their survival.[1]

African women's role in agriculture is typically portrayed as a situation of constraint and obligation to others by virtue of their subordination on the basis of gender, age, and kinship (Boserup 1970; Davison 1988; Guyer 1980, 1988, 1991; Hafkin and Bay 1976; Meillassoux 1981; Roberts 1988;

Whitehead 1984b, 1990). Disabled in all such status hierarchies, women in West Africa, much more than men, are considered to have little authority to command the labor of others for the expansion of their productive efforts. Speaking of the Kusasi, the predominant ethnic group in Bawku District, Whitehead explains the ideologies underpinning women's lack of social power to command labor:

> [C]alling farmers to work for you, despite the language of helping or "begging," is an act of social superordination. It is associated with having the social position, the power or the resources, to command others. For women to do this would be to contravene the marked gender based hierarchy of authority and deference within households and kin groups. (Whitehead 1984b: 39)

It is argued, moreover, that in agriculture the impairments of women's low status are most obvious when the work is geared to women's own gain rather than that of the wider domestic group. Roberts, for example, states:

> It is rare to find reference to systems in which women are perceived to initiate the process of production through the mobilization of labor from household, kin, or the socio-political networks of the community. . . . As far as women outside the household are concerned, the ability to mobilize their labor appears to be very restricted. (Roberts 1988: 99, 106)

In contrast, in shea processing, women control their own labor along with productive resources within and beyond the household, including the labor of other women. Calling into question the appropriateness of the agricultural model to the study of nonagricultural pursuits, the case of shea makes evident the varied positioning of women within the proclaimed hierarchies of resource control and the alternatives they forge outside them. The labor forms engaged in butter production, moreover, confound the common assumption that the cooperative and nonmonetized nature of women's work is indicative of a limited commercial orientation and low individuation of economic goals and gains (Roberts 1988; Whitehead 1984b). On the contrary, in the case of shea, the pooling of labor provides the foundation for the initiation, sustenance, and expansion of women's participation in the market. This is worthy of note because the cooperative and nonwaged character of these labor arrangements along with their domestic location makes it easy to misrecognize them as only forms of reproductive work rather than directly productive efforts in their own right (Whitehead 1990: 448; Blackden and Morris-Hughes 1993: 24).

Both productive and reproductive—a potential that is occluded by the analytic myopia of paradigms that assess women's economic situation in terms derived from the study of males and in relation to them (Elson 1995)—not only does household-based work make possible the concentration and coordination of female labor necessary for market-oriented butter production, the exercise of such labor power is also integral to cultivation of female social identities and solidarities, contributing to rural women's "self-making." This self, forged in the process of cooperative work, is not "self-less," nor is the collective from which it emerges entirely egalitarian. For at the same time as they cultivate and further a commitment to one another, shea butter processors unabashedly engage in reciprocal labor exchanges for the sake of individual enterprise and accumulation.

Exploring these several themes, the portrait of commercial shea butter production presented here draws from the extended study of butter processing households in a number of communities in and around the town of Bawku. Three communities where commercial butter processing forms the foundation of female livelihood—Saabon, Boubuilla, and Gozense—provide the core of the material. Women in the periurban community of Saabon have only limited access to agriculture but find opportunity in trade, in Boubuilla, women engage in both agriculture and commerce, and in the largely rural village of Gozense, the imperatives of agriculture override commercial opportunity. In all of these communities, butter processors purchase shea nuts from the market. Discussion of these communities is supplemented by research performed in shea processing and shea nut collecting households in the villages of Kolpeleg, Koltaamse, Ninkongo, Tesh-Natinga, and Nisbulaga—all located in areas where shea nuts may be procured from trees on farms and fallows and in the forest. Providing a foundation for the analysis of the commercial orientation of shea butter processing, its counterposition to modes of agricultural production, and the resilience of rural women's cooperative work routines, the chapter begins with a discussion of the ecology of shea trees and shea nut collection.

The Natural and Human Ecology of Shea

The counterpoint provided by shea to the dominant agricultural economy—both distinct from yet coordinated with it—derives from shea's unique ecology. A wild species indigenous to the African savanna (Boateng 1970: 52), shea trees are able to withstand drought and the drying winds of the harmattan due to their deep root structure. The trees are found among the grass and shrubs of savanna parklands and at the edge of farms, where they are left uncut due to their economic value when land is cleared (Division of Agriculture 1962: 364). In environments where shifting cultivation is the norm, shea trees are one of only a few species that remain in the high canopy when farms are cleared (Food and Agriculture Organization 1981: 201; Benneh 1987: 165; Meek 1925: 142, Peiler 1994).[2] Even when cultivation methods are intensified, shea trees are not cut down by farmers, allowing the trees to live for centuries and grow up to twenty meters high (Podeba 1999).

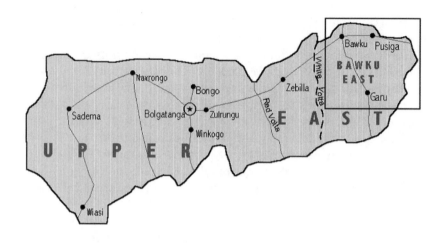

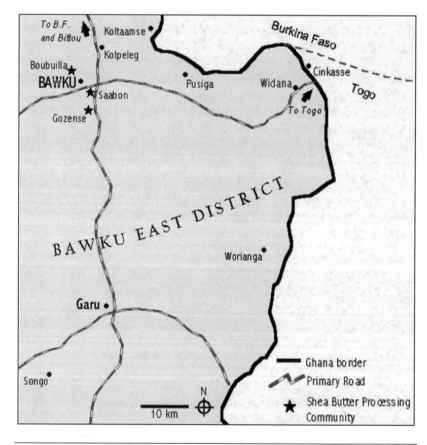

Map 4 Commercial Shea Butter Processing Communities in Bawku East District

This form of passive and protective silvaculture appears to have a long history in the West African savanna. Traveling in "Bambara country" in the late eighteenth century, Mungo Park remarks "in clearing wood for cultivation, every tree is cut down but the shea" (1971: 202). Although shea trees are highly resistant to any sort of plantation-based cultivation, their presence near settlements and areas of active farming appears to be symbiotic, promoting the trees' development and productivity (Peiler 1994). In these areas, shea trees may grow to fifty feet due to protection from fire and "possibly the kraaling of cattle within their root range and the dumping of village refuse" (Division of Agriculture 1962: 365).[3] In fallow areas, in contrast, shea trees rarely reach more than twenty feet. Likewise, in the forest or bush the growth of shea trees may be stunted due to the shading effect of more rapidly growing plants and trees (Imperial Institute 1912b: 285).

Because shea trees bear fruit during the hungry season and their produce enters the market while other crops are still in the field, the shea economy offers relief from the overarching seasonal rhythms of agriculture, providing a distinct set of possibilities in the realm of consumption and trade. Shea flowers appear as early as December and January, while the rest of the landscape is dry and barren, and become increasingly prevalent in March and April.[4] Several weeks later appear the shea fruits, light-green berries with a thick, soft pericarp two or three inches in diameter like that of a fig. These fruits contain in their center a large brown seed consisting of an inner kernel—from which shea butter is extracted—covered by a hard shell (Peiler 1994: 51). In some parts of northern Ghana, shea fruits can be collected almost year-round ("Field Report," 1994), although most trees bear in May and June—the early part of the rainy season, when the first crops are planted—and into July and August.

Access to shea trees and tree produce is embedded in several distinctive tenure systems, depending on whether the trees are located on farm land or in forested areas that are considered common property. During the colonial era in northern Ghana, especially in areas with a strong tradition of political hierarchy, access to shea trees growing in the forest zones was often regulated by a chief or the person holding the post of land-priest, known as the *tendaana* (Roncoli 1994: 233–34).[5] Under these circumstances, an individual was obligated to seek permission to gather shea produce and pay the chief a user fee in cash or kind (McPhee 1926: 187; Cardinall 1920: 61). Based on information from 1948, Skinner records a similar situation within the neighboring Mossi area of Burkina Faso. There chiefs exercised considerable discretion over trees located on uncultivated community lands and could grant exclusive access to particular people as rewards for service (Skinner 1964: 117).[6]

However, more recently in northeast Ghana, access to trees and tree products growing on communal lands and forests has been relatively free from political obligation. In these cases, exploitation of sylvan produce—whether fruit, firewood, or medicinals—is self-regulated and, unlike many other sorts of resources, open to women. Speaking of common-property systems elsewhere in Africa, Rocheleau's (1987: 91) remarks are appropriate to shea: "While the commons is rarely the exclusive domain of women, it is often a major source of subsistence and commercial products for women. As village development cycles and land-use conversion and intensification proceeds, the commons may become a residual domain, left to women by default."

Whatever the developmental trajectory of common property and forest resources in the region, women maintain a firm hold on shea. Pockets of bush are a popular source of shea supplies because they contain trees of a wide range of ages and tree density is high, even if the shea fruits are not readily accessible. It is not uncommon for women to walk for several miles in order to collect shea from these areas. Women from the village of Pialago a few miles from Garu, for example, will make a ten mile trip by foot several times during the shea season to collect nuts from the forest zone at the western edge of the district, a supply zone that is also popular with other women in the area. The Pialago women, though they frequent it, fear the forest, which they regard as a hiding place for wild animals and dangerous spirits. To protect themselves from these hazards, women prepare medicines and incantations to fortify themselves before entering the forest.

In contrast, when shea trees are on cultivated land—including formerly cultivated land that is lying fallow—they are subject to more exclusive property rights. Overall, in northeast Ghana, agricultural property is allocated on the basis of lineage membership. In Bawku, rights to trees and tree crops on a parcel of land are the purview of a lineage member granted the right to farm that land by the lineage or family head. If that land is ceded to another lineage member, rights to the trees revert to the person ceding the land. Likewise, if land is otherwise loaned or rented, the tenant has no guaranteed or probable right to the trees and tree crops it contains. Whoever the specific recipient is, once these rights to sylvan resources are allocated, it is assumed that whoever holds them will automatically cede these rights to his wife or wives, as the collection of shea produce is the preserve of women. A woman has no obligation to give the husband a share of her product or the profit she derives from collecting shea fruit and nuts from trees on her husband's farms, or to share it with others. If a man has several wives, they all have an equal right to pick the nuts from the family farm. Occasionally, a woman may be granted permission to pick nuts from someone else's farm, but such extension of collection rights is relatively rare. In the village of Koltaamase, for instance, where shea trees are plentiful, during years when yields are high, women from neighboring communities are allowed to pick shea fruit from local farms. Nevertheless, they are

1.2 Collecting shea nuts.

prohibited from picking directly from the shea trees—the prerogative of the farmer owner and his immediate family—and can only collect fruit that has fallen on the ground.

As much to fit in with the exigencies of women's work as to avoid notice, nut collection is often restricted to marginal times of the day. Most shea collection takes place at dawn, sometimes as early as four or five o'clock in the morning. In addition to facilitating the coordination of shea collection and other work or a round-trip trek to a faraway forest in a single day, furtive incursions into neighboring farms are also possible at this time. Roaming fields and forests before first light exposes women to all the hazards that come with darkness and poor visibility. This is compounded by a whole series of risks particular to shea collection, whenever it is undertaken. Because fallen shea fruit are a favorite food of snakes that feed in the early morning in the grass underneath trees, shea collectors frequently encounter snakes, and snakebites are usually fatal. Women also take risks by climbing shea trees to shake limbs or pluck fruit. Although women may be adept at this, accidents are quite common, causing health personnel from clinics and hospitals in northern Ghana to attribute women's broken bones to the dangers of climbing shea and other fruit trees.

Shea collection is an arduous endeavor requiring an ongoing investment of time and energy that delivers incremental returns rather than windfall gains. During shea season, women gather fruit on a daily basis. As only a few pieces of fruit may be available from each tree each time they go out, it may take weeks to fill a basin with fruit and even longer to obtain the same volume of nuts. One Kolpeleg woman explained how she went out at dawn to look for nuts "every blessed day" during the rainy season, despite all the other work for which she was responsible. Another reported how her efforts to gather shea nuts every day for a month resulted in the collection of only a single bag of shea nuts, a relatively good harvest compared to the three weeks it took another woman to collect only a fraction of that amount.

Even where trees are plentiful, nut collection does not produce substantial returns in the short term. In Koltaamse, where a large family farm can contain up to a hundred trees, three women working six hours on each of two consecutive days harvested only a few gallons of fruit each. Though many or all of the women in a household may collect shea from the same farm or forest plot, the gathering of fruit and nuts is largely an individualized task. While a woman may receive assistance from her children, each woman collects her own nuts. Especially when traveling to faraway forest zones, women will gather shea in a group for company and safety. Nevertheless, each one collects her own stock. A Pialago woman explained that even if they wanted to, coordinating collective shea gathering would be nearly impossible during the rainy season, when each woman faces different and not always predictable obligations to their own and family farms.

Nut sales are an important way for women to turn their labor and property rights, however residual, into cash. Because nuts are considered the property of the person who gathers them, women have complete control over the disposal of their nut harvests, and the majority of women who gather shea nuts sell some of the nuts they collect. Indeed, nut collection is widely pursued by rural women whether they intend to process butter or not, as the very opportunity to earn cash from the sale of shea fruits and nuts collected without monetary cost is a great incentive to rural women. Saul (1989: 184) describes the situation in southern Burkina Faso, where shea is also an importance source of female livelihood: "Unlike processing activities which require some capital, gathering requires little more than effort and time and can be undertaken by anybody. The sale of shea nuts brings important revenues."

Women's capacity to use nuts as a store of wealth is especially important during the rainy season, when household food and cash stores are low. Rural women frequently sell the shea nuts they gather at the start of the rainy season in order to get the money necessary to buy foodstuffs—both grain and soup ingredients. In this manner, rural women's shea nut stores, converted to cash in small increments, serve as a sort of bank of wealth from which value is gradually withdrawn and reinvested. Moreover, because their price tends to rise as the rainy season progresses, stored nuts accrue value over time. In addition, the nuts, unlike cash, are considered a woman's exclusive property and are therefore protected from the incursions and demands of others. Throughout northern Ghana, women aggressively pursue the opportunity to store and generate cash from the collection of shea nuts. Because of this, from the end of the hot season in May and June and well into the rainy season, the site of women head-loading basins or calabashes of green shea fruit through farms and forests and along the roadside in the early morning and evenings is widespread.

As the high population of Bawku town and its environs has forced the clearing of many formerly forested areas and the shortening if not the complete override of fallows, shea tree cover is increasingly sparse anywhere near this urban core. Trees remain abundant at the perimeters of the district due to lower population density, a less intensive agricultural regime, and a more favorable physical geography, marked by the prevalence of water courses. Hosting trees at a range of stages of growth and productivity on farms and in uncultivated forest, this shea zone extends from the western edge of the district (near the villages of Kugri, Atuba, and Kusalnaba) to its southern boundary with Mamprussi District (close to the villages of Songo and Denungo). The villages of Worianga and Basiyunde mark out the eastern edge of the shea zone. It reemerges much further north close to the Burkina border, taking the form of pockets of older trees in Koltaamse and Kolpeleg.[7] Although butter-makers who live in areas where shea trees are plentiful are able to collect a portion of nuts for their own use, butter-makers residing in or nearby Bawku town, where trees are scarce—such as the women of Saabon, Boubuilla, and Gozense—are almost entirely dependent on the market for nut supplies, indicating the fundamentally commercial character of butter production for them. These women typically purchase nuts in rural or urban markets directly from nut collectors or, more often, from professional nut traders who bulk nuts from household and market-based purchases. Most butter-makers have regular suppliers who provide them with nuts through extended credit arrangements, allowing them to process and sell butter before paying for the nuts they use.

Learning to Labor in Butter-Producing Households: From Merged Identities to Independent Capacities and Claims

While the purchase of shea nuts and the sale of shea butter are centered in the marketplace, in the Kusasi and Mamprussi communities of Bawku East, the production of shea butter takes place in the domestic domain. In Bawku, as elsewhere in Ghana's northern savanna zone, commercial butter production is the purview of women living in specific households, neighborhoods, and communities. Butter-making families and households are well known and well recognized by others. They are easily identified by the tools, raw materials, and by-products of butter production that occupy and surround them and the overall ambiance of female work—from the scent of boiling butter to the sound of nuts being pounded early in the morning and late at night and the sight of shea nuts spread to dry on the courtyard floor or the clusters of waist-high clay pots used for extracting oil splashed with the deep-red residue of ground shea nuts.

The domestic location of butter processing has everything to do with its labor requirements. The control, exchange, and reproduction of the labor necessary for butter-making are rooted in the household. Thoroughly intertwined with household capacities and the norms of household membership, the transmission and amalgamation of butter-processing skills is anchored in wider rubrics of intrahousehold training, rendering participation in shea processing a means of impressing and expressing butter-makers' social status within the domestic group. Typically, the specialized skill necessary for butter production is conveyed by senior women to their daughters, daughters-in-law, and cowives. Invoking a well-known Lever Brothers advertisement depicting a mother, daughter, and grandmother, a Saabon woman explained that butter-making was a largely inherited craft conveyed "from generation to generation." Not only does intergenerational knowledge transmission foster cooperation and the codification of female labor, of equal import is that it also enables the exercise of control over that labor, as senior women direct and extract the work capacity of their trainees. These expropriations, however, gradually give way to independent capacities and autonomous claims, preparing junior women to contribute to and share in the collective endeavors and resources of a household's female members.

The Training and Labor of Girls

Girls are likely to take up the work of the women in the household where they are raised, and it is not unusual for shea butter-makers to learn and begin to practice their trade as children. Receiving training in butter production from her mother or other female kin in the household, a girl learns to make butter through direction and observation. She does so by emulating the efforts of her female guardians and responding to their expectation that she carry out as much work as she can physically bear—usually the tedious and exhausting labors of head-loading, mixing, and beating shea nuts and butter in various stages of preparation. Not only does this endow a girl or young woman with the skills necessary for independent income generation even before she marries, but, equally important, it also enables married women to shape and gain access to an additional source of labor—that of girls—over which they have nearly full discretion. Their labor power thus disciplined, girls in shea-processing households make a significant contribution of physical effort to the hard work of butter production. Almost every woman who makes butter utilizes the assistance of her own daughter, that of another girl in the household, or the daughter of friends or kin living nearby.

In shea processing, girls' labor, in addition to supplementing a woman's own, may also serve as a surrogate for it. When Anombod, a Gozense butter-maker, injured her foot and could not work, she recalled her daughter from where she was temporarily residing the home of relatives in order for the daughter to take over her own role in butter processing. Even if a woman produces butter without the aid of other adults, she rarely does so without the assistance of a girl. *In Danku the Soup Is Sweeter* (Beital 1993), a film on women living in northwest Ghana, about one hundred miles from Bawku, highlights the essential contribution of girls to commercial shea production. In the film, a butter processor describes her heavy reliance on her daughters' input, noting that the volume of butter she produces drops sharply when they leave for school. In many households, girls may be kept out of school for this among other reasons.[8]

Due to the common practice of both long- and short-term fostering in northern Ghana (Goody 1982), premarital occupational training and labor obligations are not restricted to a girl's natal household or the tutelage of her mother. Many girls are brought up by senior female relatives, typically the sisters or aunts of their mothers or fathers. Gaining access to the labor of the daughters of kin, especially when a woman has no qualified daughters of her own, or none coresident, can be crucial for enterprise viability and reproduction. Butter producers accordingly seek out and hold onto such sources of assistance. In the village of Ninkongo, for example, Hadiza, a widowed woman in her fifties, moved to her brother's house after her husband died. There she established a butter-making business relying on the aid of the brother's three teenage daughters. Too old to do much of the heavy labor of mixing, Hadiza closely supervised the girls' labor, processing butter once a week with their assistance. In return for their services, she allowed the girls to use as much of the butter as they needed for household food preparation, reserving the larger part for her own trade in the market.

In Boubuilla, Maimuna, one of the leading butter-makers in the community, relied on the aid of her senior sister's daughter. The young woman resided with her as both a domestic charge and domestic assistant since Maimuna's own small daughter—only four years old—was much too young for the task of butter-making. The cultivation of skill simultaneously with labor extraction may also be extended to "structural" daughters—nonrelated or remotely related girls who enter a household to receive economic training and support in return for the provision of domestic service. This was the situation of a teenage girl, Amata, whose own mother was very poor and without a steady source of income. Regularly lending a hand in two neighboring butter-producing households, Amata gained experience in butter processing, occasionally receiving a small quantity of nuts from her sponsors to make and sell butter for herself.

Grants-in-aid from real or surrogate mothers like the one received by Amata are not unusual for girls in their midteens. Already experienced in butter production and with the likelihood of marriage not far off, a daughter may be given the opportunity by her mother to make butter on her own and keep the profits. Like Amata's benefactors, Ashata, a Kolpeleg buttermaker, regularly gave her fifteen-year-old daughter Anaatu money to buy nuts to make and sell butter independently, even though this arrangement diverted labor from the mother's enterprise. From Ashata's point of view, of equal importance to any immediate material gain her daughter's butter processing might engender were the entrepreneurial skills this experience prepared her to bring to her future husband's home. With these interests in mind, Ashata mandated that Anaatu use her profits to invest in cloth and other items for her trousseau. So common is the initiation of economic independence during a girl's teenage years that most girls in butter-making household eventually come to divide their time between assisting their mothers with processing and trade and pursuing their own butter business. Hence, while girls are obliged to comply with the exactions of their mothers and the other women with whom they work and live, ongoing cooperation paves the way for the receipt of economic support and a try at commercial independence.

Given the training and commercial experience they gain during childhood and adolescence, the large majority of women brought up in shea-processing households pursue butter production as their primary source of income upon marriage. This situation obtains even if the other members of a woman's husband's household have no prior involvement in butter-making. Such a dynamic demonstrates the importance of intergenerational knowledge transmission for the reproduction of commercial shea processing as a specialized vocation. Indeed, today as in the past, women involved in butter production since childhood frequently operate as vectors of economic knowledge and skill, mobilizing other women in their marital homes and even the wider community to engage in commercial butter-making.

The Training and Labor of Brides

If a woman has not learned about butter processing during childhood, she is likely to be introduced to the requisite techniques as an adult if she marries into a household or community where commercial butter production is considered the female norm. Once familiar with butter-producing techniques and integrated into a household work routine, a young bride often comes to adopt shea work as her own. Even if a new wife does not pursue butter production as a primary mode of income generation, she is still expected to participate to some extent in butter production and sale. In areas where butter production is widespread as well as profitable, adoption of the trade is all but mandated by a woman's cowives.

The training of a new wife, or *amariya* (a Kusaal adaptation from Hausa), like that of a daughter, embeds the transfer and practice of butter-processing skills in domestic relations of authority and dependence. Just as a daughter must abide by the requests of her mother, eventually enabling her to master a trade and gain autonomy, a new wife is expected to defer to her mother-in-law and more senior cowives, gradually acquiring economic expertise and a place of her own among them. A junior wife's economic person is largely merged with that of her mother-in-law, whom she is obligated to assist with all of her work, whether for immediate domestic benefit, the market, or the wider community. This labor contract is implicit; as a Saabon woman in her fifties, put it: "How can you help someone besides the mother-in-law?" This economic relationship is nevertheless not one-sided: just as the junior woman is obliged to work with the senior, the senior is responsible for the junior.

A mother-in-law invests in a young wife in several ways. Not only does she support her charge through the provision of food while the young woman is under her tutelage, she also trains her to provide adequate domestic services to her husband and other household members as well as to support herself eventually through income-generating activities that extend beyond the household. For those senior women engaged in market-oriented butter production, attention to shea processing and trade forms a centerpiece of this relationship. Although it is likely that a young wife will already be familiar with most forms of domestic work (cooking, cleaning, water carrying, house-building, etc.) as result of her own upbringing, in order to integrate herself as fully as possible into her husband's household she is expected to adopt the particular standards and needs of her husband's home as well as the specialized work of the mother-in-law.

During the early stage of domestic training, a young wife is truly in limbo, straddling the identities of girl and woman. Embodying this uncertain status, one new bride in Gozenze spent the first few months in her husband's home allied with the husband's junior sisters, working and socializing with them, rather than the other wives in the compound. The young woman demonstrated her new status as a married woman only in a few tasks, such as when she wore a veil—a practice at which she was still somewhat awkward—when she went to town to shop. It is not surprising that a new wife may feel more comfortable spending time with girls close

1.3 Two women from Boubuilla with their children. As is customary, the woman on the right has returned to her natal home to receive help caring for her infant.

to her age, since her economic status is nearly parallel to theirs during the period of training. In the same way that the allocation of a daughter's labor is completely at the discretion of her mother, a newly married woman's economic autonomy is still highly circumscribed.

A young wife's fealty to her mother-in-law is well illustrated by the common practice of sharing her bedroom, kitchen, and yard.[9] A woman who has been married for thirty years considered this a tacit fact of marital duty. As she saw it: "A young wife is put into the mother-in-law's yard in order to help her." Although a new wife may visit her husband in his private room, the mother-in-law's sleeping room (*duug*), yard (*zakin*), and kitchen (*da'ang*) remain the wife's primary domestic residence—the place where she performs the bulk of her domestic duties—for the first few years or more of her marriage. The relationship between a new wife and her husband is not overlooked when women explain a bride's economic dependence. As a shea butter-maker from Gozense put it: "You have to enjoy with your husband for some time before you start to work." Among the Tallensi, fifty miles to the west of Bawku, Fortes (1936: 239) documented identical codes of marital conduct more than half a century ago: "A newly married wife has a room in the quarters of her husband's mother, if she is alive or his senior wife. In due course, however, whether it be a man's first wife or a later wife, he must build her separate quarters."

As the relationship between a bride and her mother-in-law functions as a form of domestic training, it simultaneously enables senior women to extract labor from junior women, as does a mother from a daughter. It is not usual for an older woman to transfer much of her labor burden onto the junior, giving her the most taxing tasks to carry out. When processing shea, a junior woman will be burdened with the onerous duties of crushing nuts and beating the pureed shea nuts with water. The older woman, in contrast, will oversee butter extraction and engage in the lighter work of collecting and boiling the oil once it has been extracted. In the past such labor discipline was an explicit element of household work relations among junior and senior women, though today it may be somewhat mitigated. Alabugril, an elderly shea butter producer from Saabon, vividly described her own experience as a young wife in the household of the Zagabo chief nearly half a century ago: "When we helped the old ladies with the *dawa dawa* [a condiment made from fermented seeds] we would step on the *dawa dawa* as if we were dancing and if we were lazy the old ladies would push and verbally abuse us." She added, "If you did that to a young wife now, she would run away." Even though such threats are no longer so overt, a young woman still has little grounds on which to refuse or challenge her mother-in-law's exactions, and the mother-in-law has every right to pursue them.

Despite this element of exploitation, in the course of investing time and energy in her mother-in-law's work, a young wife gradually gains skill on her own part and is afforded increasing autonomy and compensation for her efforts. As a first step in this process, she begins preparing meals for her husband in his mother's kitchen, often buying soup ingredients with money supplied by the senior woman. Eventually, this increase in independence will spill over into the young woman's activities outside the household, and she will be considered eligible to engage in market-oriented butter production in her own right. Yet in order to get her own work off the ground, a new wife typically requires financial assistance from her mother-in-law.

The provision of financial support may take different forms. Sometimes the older woman gives a share of her work and profits to the younger woman. Alternatively, the two women may continue to work together processing butter and each will claim the profit on alternate market days. A mother-in-law might also present her daughter-in-law with a gift of cash or nuts in order to endow her with the means for independent butter production. Just as the younger woman relies on the older for financial support during this phase of domestic training, she remains in need of the older woman's butter-making tools and work space as well as her expert guidance in butter production. As a consequence, even as a new wife gains a modicum of economic autonomy, the older woman retains a claim on her labor. Occasionally a young women with previous butter experience will use the wealth she saved from her natal household to finance her work as a married woman, somewhat mitigating the older woman's influence over her butter-making efforts but not escaping the older woman's authority over the disposal of her time and energy more generally.

In terms of both domestic responsibility and extrahousehold income generation, a woman usually remains in a position of dependence for the first several years of her marriage. It is only after a new wife achieves a requisite level of social maturity, marked by the birth of one or more children, that she will move into her own room, replete with private yard and cooking and work space, both equipping and qualifying her to work for herself. Indeed, for a woman in northern Ghana, the receipt of a room, yard, and kitchen of one's own signals a significant shift in marital and social status, affording her the privileges, responsibilities, and recognition of a fully adult female.[10] It is only by having this trio of domestic spaces (room, kitchen, and yard) that a woman can carry out her full domestic responsibilities of child care, cooking, and home-based work and gain recognition for her efforts. Once these markers of full female adulthood are achieved, a wife will be afforded control of her income-generating activities, including butter production, and be able to negotiate her economic obligations to her husband without her mother-in-law's interference.

The Work of Wives

Once a woman completes her domestic apprenticeship and has attained the requisite skill and social standing, she is free to establish a commercial butter-making enterprise of her own. She will hold full and exclusive rights in her product, along with any profits. However, because butter production is largely a cooperative endeavor, drawing on assets that are collectively held or the property of someone other than the butter-maker, a butter-maker's economic independence depends on her domestic cohorts. Even as a woman preserves her exclusive rights in the butter she makes with the nuts she has picked or purchased, each butter-maker in a given household will draw on the assistance of others, and they will draw on hers. In this way, the hierarchies of domestic training pave the way for both economic autonomy and economic cooperation.

The expression of mutual aid among household members in the course of butter processing is premised on a loosely defined moral economy. Described as a disposition to help one another and receive help in return (*son taba*), it gets played out in a wide range of ways, depending on the interests and situation at hand. One informant explained, "there is a feeling that 'house people' should help each other so their work is not spoiled. [Accordingly], 'house people' can beg each other for assistance with their work." Compliance is more voluntary than compulsory, though refusal to assist someone else is likely to limit a person's future receipt of aid. "Somebody can refuse to help you. There's nothing wrong with refusing and you can't be angry with them. Even if a person never helps, you can't talk about them. But when that person's time to request help comes, you can refuse them too."

Not only may female butter processors from the same household, whether young or old, share labor and tools in the spirit of *son taba*, they may also share capital, enhancing their commercial potential. Yacubu-ma described the system of cash pooling and circulation she became familiar with as a young wife and which she still employs today as the most senior woman in a Saabon butter-making household. She explained that women in the household maintain a common fund for purchasing nuts, which they access on a rotating basis. Once a woman sells the butter she has made from the nuts purchased with the joint funds, she returns the nut capital to the next person in the roster, saving whatever remains as her own as profit. Even in situations where mutuality runs high, individual claims to product and profit are maintained. This is the case among cowives from a butter-producing household in the village of Nisbulaga a few miles south of the marketing center of Garu. Sharing all of the work and expenses entailed in shea processing, these women go to their husband's farm to pick nuts together, decorticate, and crack the nuts together, pool money to send the nuts to the grinding mill, and extract the shea butter together. If their own store of nuts is depleted, they will pool their funds to purchase nuts. With each one producing in turn, however, the wives in this household are able to maintain an exclusive claim on the butter they collectively produce.

According to the women who participate in them, the success of such financial arrangements depends on the strong loyalties that common household residence and responsibilities engender. They argue that only women from a single household will be committed to repaying a group loan in a timely manner and maximizing their profit so as to assure the return of sufficient funds. As one resident put it, pointing out the individual commercial benefit shea butter producers derive from the moral solidarity and investment in *son taba* that obtains in a household: "If the women are from the same 'yard,' they will all profit from each other's gains."

Discussion

These intersections of kinship and economy underwriting household-based butter production in northern Ghana bring a number of points to the fore. The first is that the cultivation of skills geared to extrahousehold income generation is a basic component of domestic relations. Muting the distinction between productive and reproductive aims, in northern Ghana commercial endeavors such as butter production are integral to the definition of female social roles and identities in the domestic domain. Not only does the acquisition of commercial knowledge and skill via domestic training enable a woman to provide for herself and others, but more fundamentally, it also authorizes her to envision herself in this capacity, thus effecting a change in social status in addition to economic performance. In this manner, the conventions of female domestic apprenticeship produce and reproduce categories of identity at the same time as they entrain labor power. These dynamics make a crucial contribution to the social and material reproduction of the domestic unit.

Confounding a strict divide between cooperation and individuation, the second observation emerging from this example of combined commercial and familial endeavor in shea processing is that the relationships of authority and expropriation upon which domestic training is based pave the way for eventual economic independence and autonomy. As the final stages of domestic apprenticeship make apparent, this independence is only partially and incompletely marked by individuation. Remaining anchored in domestic networks of support, shea butter production for individual gain is tied instead to the equalization of women's economic rights and responsibilities in the household. For shea butter-makers, economic independence is about producing for oneself, but neither by oneself nor for oneself alone. As we have seen, junior women establish economic autonomy not by withdrawing support for their more senior precept but through the ongoing provision of that support. By augmenting or subsidizing the work of her mother, mother-in-law, or senior rivals, a junior woman eventually gains recognition in her own right and receives the same assistance in return. In this way, junior women are afforded economic independence only by entering into and sustaining their participation in a context of mutual aid. As will be discussed below, this brand of economic autonomy—grounded as it is in both hierarchy and reciprocity—remains a fundamental feature of commercial butter production and is subject to elaboration as women mature and their enterprises grow. Indeed, among shea producers in northeast Ghana, cooperation is integral to both individual commercial success and industrywide commercial growth.

Finally, just as Berry (1988) identifies a dynamic of "concentration of property rights without privatization" occurring in African land transactions, the organization of commercial shea butter production reflects a related yet significantly different amalgam of cooperation and individuation. While the economic actors Berry describes cultivate exclusive rights in collectively held assets, butter-makers cultivate the collective potentials of butter processing for individual benefit. Despite their obvious self-interest and market orientation, here they eschew telescoped transactions or assistance in favor of ongoing and diffuse obligations. If Berry's landowners attempt to unbundle amalgamated property rights, shea butter processors, in contrast, try to aggregate them in order to secure their claims in the present and over the long run. With the goal of maximizing access to labor and minimizing the capital requirements of their work, among the many common resources upon which butter-makers depend, the pooling of labor is most important. Cooperative labor exchanges are essential if butter-makers are to meet the sheer energy requirements of commercially oriented production. Like the extended terms of credit typically made available by nut sellers, which help butter-makers avoid having to buy nuts outright, these arrangements allow rural women to avoid squandering their meager cash incomes on hiring labor.

Labor Processes beyond the Household: Collective Endeavors and Identities

Reflecting rural women's imperatives of labor concentration and capital conservation, the collective resources necessary for butter-making may be drawn from beyond the boundaries of a single household, bringing together the material endowments of daughters, cowives, kin, and neighbors. Facilitating such collective endeavors, commercial shea butter producers come together to create reciprocal work groups known by the term *Nyoor Yinii*, a Kusaal term meaning "one-mouth." Facilitating larger-scale production and greater production frequencies than other sorts of inter- or intrahousehold cooperation, as well as guaranteeing reliable access to labor and other means of production, Nyoor Yinii work groups enable women to mobilize the resources necessary for commercial butter processing and even intensification in the face of the many other demands on their time and labor with which they must contend.

Nyoor Yinii Work Groups: The Face of Extrahousehold Cooperation

Shea butter processors involved in Nyoor Yinii associations work together, sharing tools, knowledge, work space, and labor, and may even sell butter for one another in the market. Working en masse or in smaller clusters, they regularly participate in joint butter-making efforts, coming together on a weekly or biweekly basis, if not more often. Nyoor Yinii associations are diverse and flexible in form, and individual shea butter-makers express an enduring commitment to these collectivities upon which their commercial success depends. Nyoor Yinii are centered not so much on the interests of any one individual but on the common concerns and needs of group members. Above all, Nyoor Yinii represent a partnership among a group of women—their numbers ranging from just a few to community-wide associations with several dozen members—for the express purpose of sharing work, even as the product and profits from that work are individually claimed. The institutional features of Nyoor Yinii groups vary widely; they may be strictly organized, with a roster and dues and even state sanction, or grow out of a more implicit alliance among friends and neighbors who consider the provision of mutual support a taken-for-granted aspect of their social identity. Not restricted to shea, Nyoor Yinii work groups are instituted in whatever contexts women need or seek material support, from agricultural work and house-building to funerals, weddings, and community celebrations.

Despite their wide-ranging variation, Nyoor Yinii work groups have a distinctive character premised on a set of core sentiments and practices. In their practical instantiation, Nyoor Yinii work groups invoke a number of organizational parameters. Geared to the accomplishment of specific tasks and formed for that purpose, Nyoor Yinii is more goal-directed than the diffuse intrahousehold alliances of *son taba*. Yet like *son taba*, Nyoor Yinii is based on ongoing rather than momentary ties and multiple instances of working together. With the potential to span several work contexts, these efforts may be directed to a single type of task or many different ones. Whatever the case, each Nyoor Yinii member is expected to make an equal contribution to and have equal share in the group's labor. While the Nyoor Yinii work process is predicated on joint efforts and obligations, the outcome of that work is typically the purview of an individual.

The definitive values surrounding Nyoor Yinii may be located in the discourses attached to its practice. To participate in Nyoor Yinii is to be "as one" in work: to act as a group in cooperation and empathy. Lahdi, a middle-aged Saabon butter-maker, well describes women's wide-ranging institution of this sentiment, both within a discreet work context and beyond it in any context where material aid is relevant: "You have a group; someone delivers [a child], you go and greet and give money. Someone has a farm, you go and work on the farm. Someone has a funeral, you go and greet them. Someone is building, you go and beat the yard . . . that is Nyoor Yinii." Ideally, participation in Nyoor Yinii is not motivated by practical expediency alone but based on a moral commitment. It is this interest of group members in one another's concerns that distinguishes and empowers Nyoor Yinii. As Barkisu, the leading butter-maker in Gozense, put it: "'Nyoor Yinii' means 'united work'; unless you are in unity, you cannot do anything." Participation in a Nyoor Yinii work group is considered by women as an essential means of increasing their own economic potential, of making their work "go higher" (*fun tuma ken tuon*, "may your work go higher," being a common greeting exchanged by women) by compounding their own economic capacity. It is the benefit gained from the whole being greater than the sum of its parts that women in a Nyoor Yinii work relationship provide for and share with each other.

The structural features of Nyoor Yinii—that is, how women work together—are premised on particular conceptions of women's labor. In the course of working together, Nyoor Yinii actualizes, in the words of Azara, a fifty-year-old Saabon woman, "*poab pang*" ("women's strength and skill"), a term that encompasses not only labor power in the strict sense but also women's embodied capacities more generally. Likewise, the metaphor of consumption invoked by the term "one-mouth" refers not so much to the provision of food (a standard feature of extrahousehold work parties) as to the act of eating as one and thus being of one body: a single laboring body both suffering and enjoying together.

Recognizing that Nyoor Yinii is not just about labor but is evocative of female solidarity more generally is essential to capturing its fundamentally performative aspects. Women's collective work practices are highly choreographed displays of physical and vocal knowledge and coordination, encompassing a corpus of women's songs and task-specific patterns of movement. Some Nyoor Yinii associations may be singularly devoted to the collective demonstration of these skills and knowledge and only secondarily economic in orientation. As such, they function to produce not simply material effects but sentimental ones related to the affirmation of collective identities and ideals. Activated in the course of labor—whether economic or ritual—these material and sentimental outcomes are mutually reinforcing, with working together fostering a common vision and the sense of empathy facilitating the coordination of work.

Such an activation and display of embodied capacities in connection with female "self-making" is nowhere more evident than in the case of the many women's performance groups identifying themselves as Nyoor Yinii. Dancing and singing for funerals, weddings, locally based yearly celebrations such as *Saaman paad* (the Kusasi Harvest/New Year's festival), and other public gatherings such as the opening of a school or a community development project, performance groups are a fixture of women's lives in nearly every rural community in Bawku District. The songs of these women's associations make frequent reference to Nyoor Yinii, as do the songs performed by Nyoor Yinii work groups engaged in the laborious work of plastering mud walls and pounding the large interior courtyards of local compound homes.[11] Taking place during the dry season and requiring the intensive and coordinated efforts of at least a dozen women, yard-beating proceeds through a series of highly choreographed stages, each entailing a different work motion, musical accompaniment, and configuration of leaders and followers.

1.4 Members of the Gozense Nyoor Yinii Association perform at a community celebration. (Photo by Daniel Smith).

Of all the forms of extrahousehold labor that women may access and perform, Nyoor Yinii is largely preferred. Waged labor, known by the term "by-day," is an entrenched feature of rural livelihoods in northeast Ghana. Carried out by men and women, children and the elderly, it is widely employed in agriculture and other endeavors such as house construction or the transport of goods to market via donkey cart. Based on different sorts and sources of labor value from "by-day," participation in Nyoor Yinii work groups is one of the few ways women can guarantee access to labor beyond their immediate households. Nyoor Yinii, of course, is not "cost"-free, but rather than requiring payment in cash—a resource rural women find hard to replace or conserve—Nyoor Yinii can be repaid with a woman's own labor.

Because it is subject to numerous and irrefutable claims, women's labor is highly circumscribed. A woman nevertheless makes the most of her own labor capacity and that of other women, whether within or outside Nyoor Yinii. Masters of the art of "self-exploitation," in Chayanovian (1986) terms, women utilize and invest their labor power whenever they can. Their interests in doing so, grounded in the unique exchange value of work as compared to cash and other commodities, are manifold. Paying for labor with labor, an essential feature of Nyoor Yinii, enables women to minimize their expenditure of cash, thus reserving it for needs that cannot otherwise be satisfied, such as the purchase of medicine or building materials, payment of school fees, and so on. The instantiation of Nyoor Yinii exchanges affirms Moore's claim that: "A widespread reason for the choice of exchange labor arrangements is that they obviate the need for cash" (1975: 279). In addition, the investment of labor in a Nyoor Yinii work group ensures a future return on that labor, a long-term claim that the payment of wages or even the provision of food for work by no means guarantees. While the premises of Nyoor Yinii mandate that labor is properly exchanged for labor among its members, a butter-maker participating in a Nyoor Yinii labor exchange, by selling the product of that labor, has the opportunity to earn money outside of that exchange. Facilitated by associations such as Nyoor Yinii, butter-makers are able to satisfy their desire to keep any semblance of paid labor out of the household yet may still use the household as a foundation for individual gain and market participation.

True to the characterization of the labor of butter processing as noncommoditized despite the long-standing commoditization of its product, in only one instance did a woman remunerate her cowife for assistance with butter production. An exception that proves the rule, the incident was set apart from the usual pattern of labor exchange in several ways even as it tried to replicate it. In this unusual case, Hadiza, a Boubuilla woman who had just returned home after several years living and working in southern Ghana, borrowed two bags of shea nuts to process and sell quickly in order to reestablish herself and her means of income generation in the north. Removed from the household for many years, she could not expect to be privy to the circuits of mutual aid. Her ability to command such assistance was further compromised by the fact that two bags of nuts represented an inordinate amount of processing work. To get help with processing, Hadiza enlisted the assistance of Asana, a junior cowife in the household. Although she was a cloth trader and not a professional butter-maker, Asana was well versed in butter production due to her experience helping other women in the household. The fact that Asana did not process butter of her own also limited Hadiza's capacity to receive help from her in the spirit of *son taba*. Consequently, Hadiza promised to pay her cowife for her help. This transaction, however, was couched in the trappings of reciprocity and common interest, approximating features of mutual aid. Rather than giving Asana a cash sum once the processing was over, Hadiza waited until after the butter was sold and she had made her profit. She then presented the money to Asana as a "thank you" for her work and a contribution toward her own business.

Despite their highly performative and affective aspects, not to mention the decidedly nonmonetized character of Nyoor Yinii labor, Nyoor Yinii associations should not be considered a throwback to a premarket economy. On the contrary, through their participation in Nyoor Yinii, women

1.5 Kolpeleg women working together on a groundnut farm. (Photo by Daniel Smith).

thoroughly and strategically engage in the market, operating in a decidedly for-profit and individualized basis. Women who rely on the market for income generation participate in Nyoor Yinii to conserve capital and concentrate labor power. This market orientation may be both organizational and individual. Not only do individual women engage in Nyoor Yinii labor exchanges in the pursuit of independent gain, but Nyoor Yinii groups as a whole are involved in profit-making endeavors.

In agriculture, for example, as is the case in Saabon, a collection of half a dozen women will work together on a regular basis tending to the tasks of sowing, weeding, and harvesting (or one phase in this task sequence) each other's cash-crop groundnut and rice plots in turn. The same Nyoor Yinii group will make itself available to work on nonmembers' farms for hire. In the past, according to the recollections of the most senior women in the community, rewarding such a Nyoor Yinii work group with a meal was sufficient recompense. Today, however, a monetary payment is required. Obscuring its potential resemblance to a wage for labor, this compensation is paid to the group rather than each worker. Responding to such commercial opportunities coming with cooperation, women who do not farm for themselves or cultivate only a small cash-crop plot of their own and need little additional labor may, as a supplementary source of income, devote themselves to Nyoor Yinii work for others during the farming season. This is true of a Nyoor Yinii group organized by Kolpeleg women who hired themselves out, finding work together on ten different farms over the span of a few months.

Even women's Nyoor Yinii performance groups may be geared to income generation. Nyoor Yinii performance groups vie for invitations to perform in other communities. In return for their efforts, they receive a meal, transportation, and a performance fee. The fee is usually divided among the performers, with a portion reserved for a common savings fund to which group members make weekly contributions. Often this money will be used to purchase performance uniforms—nowadays two cloths and a white T-shirt printed with the group's name or other commemorative event, such as the portrait of deceased elder. Enlarging the group's economic orientation, the money may also be parlayed into collective economic ventures, such as joint groundnut or rice production. Such a merging of social interests and economic investments is not restricted to traditional Nyoor Yinii dance groups; it is also apparent in the less traditional women's associations, such as the case of a women's prayer group from an Assemblies of God Church whose members identified themselves as Nyoor Yinii and who used their collective orientation and savings funds to invest in groundnut farming.

Although commercial butter producers involved in Nyoor Yinii do not engage the market as a group, butter-makers' Nyoor Yinii associations reflect and respond to the possibilities for commercial growth and gain. Shea butter processors employ Nyoor Yinii as a principle means of sustaining and intensifying commercial production on both an individual and a group level. The way in which this is done varies widely, attesting to the flexibility of Nyoor Yinii as an institutional form and to the diverse histories, capacities, and interests of different butter-makers and butter-making communities, along with the range of economic opportunities and obligations they face. The constellation of conditions bearing upon the forms or functions of Nyoor Yinii work groups involved in the shea economy, along with the significant role played by Nyoor Yinii associations in engaging and enlarging commercial opportunity, is evident in portraits of female cooperation in the three different communities—Saabon, Boubuilla, and Gozense—where butter-making is a mainstay of women's livelihood.

Saabon: Nyoor Yinii as Commercial Potential

Saabon, more a neighborhood than a discrete village, is located on the outskirts of Bawku town, less than a mile from the town's central square. It is more urban and commercial in orientation than Boubuilla and Gozense. The community is primarily Muslim and Mamprussi, with a few houses claiming ties to chiefly lineages. Residents of Saabon rely on a mix of trade, government employment, and private enterprise (including agriculture) for their income. With a small number of male household heads involved in business as contractors and transport owners, and others receiving government salaries, a few Saabon families enjoy relative prosperity. Their homes are built from concrete blocks and contain private wells and adjoining mosques—signs of self-sufficiency and an attraction to others. Children in these households are well provided for, receiving parental support from primary school through postsecondary training. The remainder of the community, however, is decidedly working class. Families occupy mud-brick homes, some roofed with thatch rather than the more costly zinc. These households struggle to obtain the funds necessary to sustain their children's education and depend on their more prosperous neighbors and relations for work and financial support.

Whether wealthy or impoverished, women in a wide range of Saabon households are invested in commercial butter production. Indeed in this community, age is a better indicator of a woman's involvement in butter processing than is household income. Butter-making is more prevalent among older and middle-aged women than among young women, who find themselves drawn to the trade in cloth and other manufactures due to their proximity to Bawku town and the ease of traveling across the border to Togo to procure goods for sale. Many of the more senior women involved in commercial butter processing are former residents of the village of Zagabo, which they fled in the mid-1980s after a series of what are considered to be anti-Mamprussi attacks. Once relocated to the perimeter of Bawku town, they had to contend with the loss of both property and possessions and the decline of agricultural opportunity. Despite their new economic environment and the labor and capital constraints they face within it, these women, to whatever extent they can, strive to replicate the patterns of rural livelihood they practiced prior to their exodus, including shea butter production. Doing so involves recruiting the aid and interests of younger women, even if on only a temporary and occasional basis.

For the middle-aged and older generation of women who once resided in Zagabo, Nyoor Yinii alliances shape their work patterns and social relations. Although butter production is restricted in scale due to the limited assets of butter-makers, Nyoor Yinii is nevertheless a widespread feature of commercial butter-making. These work groups, organized on an extra-household level, recreate for the older women in the community the kind of labor pool that was once available in the large compound houses of their former village but which was dissolved in the course of resettlement. Nyoor Yinii groups in Saabon operate as multipurpose networks of female cooperation. Often localized in scope and subtly activated, Nyoor Yinii associations in this community are not always readily apparent or fully engaged. Hence they serve as an embedded structure rather than an obvious or sustained institutional form. While women in Saabon occasionally come together to perform during communitywide celebrations to express their solidarity overtly, more common are small and diffuse networks of cooperation such as those mobilized in farming and butter production. The remarks of Azara, a Saabon butter-maker, articulate this situation well:

> Shea work is hard and you need strength and group work to help you carry water, mix, and pound. If I had enough nuts I could get four or five Nyoor Yinii people to help with the work, but after getting burned out and losing my possessions in the 1985-to-1986 conflict, I don't have enough wealth to produce on a large scale the way I used to.

Despite the obstacles to engaging in large-scale commercial endeavors, the activation of NyoorYinii alliances is essential to sustaining and expanding commercially oriented production, even on a reduced scale. In farming, where membership in each Nyoor Yinii group numbers not more than five, women annually provide labor for each other's small cash-cropping plots. Asom, an aged widow who moved into the home of her husband's brother's son after leaving Zagabo, has for several years worked with a group of three other women, rotating labor from one woman's rice or groundnut plot to another's. Two cowives, Hadiza and Zelisha, also participate in a small Nyoor Yinii farming roster with two women from different households, while their own cowives concentrate on trade rather than cash-cropping as a source of income.

Similarly compensating for the loss of capital, economic opportunity, and household labor, the activation of Nyoor Yinii networks in Saabon for shea butter processing may be irregular in timing and configuration. In Saabon, most butter-makers involved in Nyoor Yinii alliances rarely work together on a regular schedule or as a group. Asom and her Nyoor Yinii cohorts circulate their labor on a casual and reduced basis, with group members visiting each other from time to time to exchange greetings and lend a hand in butter processing. Yet it is the apparently casual nature of these exchanges that is important to understanding the character of Nyoor Yinii in Saabon. These sorts of Nyoor Yinii ties are as much a source of potential help—a contingent source of effort—as are the actual mobilization and maximization of that aid.

Also diffuse but not as decentralized as these more informal exchanges, Nyoor Yinii alliances in Saabon less frequently embed themselves in other sorts of social networks. Signaling a sort of "reabsorbtion" of Nyoor Yinii back into the domestic group, female members of an extended family may decide to congregate in a single household for the purpose of butter production. If their own cowives lack the skills or initiative necessary for butter production, women may chose to return to their natal home—or that of a close relation—to tap into the networks of labor and knowledge required to make butter. This was the case, for example, in the Sumaila household, where married daughters and former cowives permanently residing in other houses regularly came together to make butter. Supporting commercial endeavors on a modest scale, Nyoor Yinii networks in Saabon were poised to engage greater commercial opportunity when and if it arose.

Boubuilla: Enlarging Cooperation and Engaging Multiple Markets

Situated among millet and maize fields, Boubuilla is a largely agricultural community located two miles northeast of Bawku town. Slightly above average in its material endowments, Boubuilla is within easy walking distance of Bawku market. It is also near the many bush paths that radiate from Bawku into southern Burkina Faso, making trade a preoccupation of Boubuilla residents. As is common in villages throughout the region, Boubuilla residents also rely on labor migration. Whether in the long or short term, the flow of people in and out of the community results in an infusion of knowledge and resources, with significant implications for economic interests and capacities at home.

Shea butter processors in Boubuilla, as in Saabon, use Nyoor Yinii ties to bolster the commercial potential of their butter-making enterprises. Yet in contrast to Saabon, Boubuilla women explicitly and maximally engage Nyoor Yinii's collective and commercial possibilities. In doing so, the productive arrangements mobilized by Boubuilla butter-makers facilitate commercial intensification by heightening the scale of production and supplying a wide array of markets. Indeed, so dominant are Boubuilla butter-makers' Nyoor Yinii associations in size and presence that they have begun to replace intrahousehold production routines.

The effective organization of commercial shea butter processors in Boubuilla derives from a tradition of collective aid and the superior resource endowments of the community compared to Saabon. Most Boubuilla women participate in a dance group that performs at funerals and other observances within the community as well as public celebrations in Bawku town. A large number of Boubuilla women also work together during the dry season to perform architectural labor beating compound yards from hard-packed gravel, mud, and cow dung. So proficient are Boubuilla women at this arduous task that they are often invited to apply their efforts to the homes of friends and relatives in other communities. Requiring the coordination of work schedules and the labor process, Nyoor Yinii dance and building associations are overseen by a designated leader known as the *tuon-gaad*. In Boubuilla, this is the role of an animated and hard-working middle-aged woman named Asana, who is well-known for her skill and energy. Boubuilla women come together for agricultural work as well. Not only do they assist with the cultivation of one another's cash-crop plots, they also help each other manage domestic obligations, contributing labor to the weeding of family farms. The coordination of commercial shea butter production in this community hence occurs in a context where patterns of cooperation are widespread and well established.

Overcoming the limits posed by reliance on intrahousehold assistance, nearly three quarters of the butter-makers in Boubuilla process butter together in a collective work space. Consisting of grass-roofed shelters bordered by log benches and the massive clay mixing pots necessary for butter-making, the work space is located in an open area between several homes. All of the community's butter-makers are free to make butter here. They may also use the butter pots and other tools contained in the communal work space, though these implements are considered the private property of individuals, and not all butter-makers have their own. This work arrangement was conceived by two of Boubuilla's leading and seniormost butter-makers, Mariama and Ashata, the leaders of the butter-makers' Nyoor Yinii association. Assembled with the aid of the other butter processors on land controlled by Mariama's and Ashata's household head, these common butter processing sites had been in existence by the mid-1990s for nearly thirteen years. They were first established when the two women and several other families in the community returned to Boubuilla to settle after residing for a decade in southern Ghana as migrant agricultural laborers. Attesting to the innovative and adaptable character of

1.6 Mariama, leader of the Boubuilla women's group, cools shea butter in clay pots before taking it to market.

1.7 Boubuilla shea butter processors' collective work space.

Nyoor Yinii, the concept of a common work space outside the bounds of any one house and with tools available for all to use was modeled after the palm oil processing workshops in Ghana's oil palm belt, where the Boubuilla women worked while in the south.

Having learned to process butter for home use as children, Ashata and Mariama resumed and expanded upon this line of work when they resettled in Boubuilla. Though butter-making was already practiced in the community, the return of several experienced butter-makers from the south fostered its revival, giving younger women moving into the community increasing opportunity to learn and practice the craft with their cowives and in-laws. As butter processing gained renewed popularity as a common occupation in Boubuilla through this development, some women pursued butter-making skills through extrahousehold means, defying the usual pattern of intrahousehold skill transfer (whether natal or marital). Afuse, for example, learned to make butter from women living in the household next door to her marital home. First helping her neighbors process and sell butter, she eventually received assistance from them once she was able to buy nuts on her own. Having mastered the skills necessary for independent processing, Afuse shared her expertise with a cowife, who eventually took up the trade.

Heightening the significance of extrahousehold ties, such a transfer of knowledge and labor between two households on an individualized basis was part of an overall reorientation of butter-making underway in Boubuilla. With labor and other productive resources pooled among several households on an increasingly generalized basis and a common work space established, collective butter processing under the rubric of Nyoor Yinii helped butter-makers intent on sustaining or expanding their commercial enterprise to overcome the limits of intrahousehold assistance—an issue of particular concern to Boubuilla residents. In Boubuilla, because rates of labor migration are high, women as well as men frequently go south for both brief and extended visits. As a consequence, household composition and hence the membership of any household-based production team are inherently unstable. Given these circumstances, the cultivation of permanent and extended extrahousehold sources of assistance such as Nyoor Yinii work groups was one way women could compensate for the unreliable nature of mutual aid on an intrahousehold level.

Moreover, the pooling of productive resources beyond the household also enabled Boubuilla butter-makers to manage their commitments to a diverse array of markets without compromising their access to productive aid. This was important because, as their commercial endeavors grew, the butter-makers geared their trade to a wide range of markets in and around Bawku and southern Burkina Faso. These included Bawku's central market, markets of the Ghana-Burkina borderlands, such as Kulungungu and Garinga, as well as Bittou, a more distant regional trade center in southern Burkina. Some butter-makers attended a single market regularly, while others shifted their market orientation according to market conditions and their own economic situation. Because these markets meet on different days and have different seasonalities of demand, it was difficult for women from a single household or even a few women from different households to coordinate their production schedules. Having a common work space where all butter-makers were welcome at any time solved this dilemma.

As butter production increasingly moved out of the house and the collective practices of Nyoor Yinii moved into butter production, these arrangements worked to eclipse intrahousehold processing patterns With butter-makers abandoning household-based processing for extrahousehold collective processing in the public work area, it became necessary to construct a second work space to accommodate new members. This system of collective production was also harnessed by women who continued to make their own butter at home but who were attracted to the joint resources and other perks of group membership. Spending several hours a week providing assistance to other women in the collective work space, they received help in their own home from other group members, in this manner "internalizing" extrahousehold work patterns. Other women combined participation in Nyoor Yinii butter production with additional forms of intra- and extrahousehold labor exchange. Zuwira, for example, lent a hand in the collective work area, continued to work with her cowives at home, and participated in her friend Maimuna's butter-producing enterprise in a neighboring household.

Given the already widespread nature of cooperative work in Boubuilla, it is not surprising that women combined these ways of working together, undermining the priority of intrahousehold relations of butter production. The fluid and varied character of women's commitments to any one shea processing routine likewise echoed the multiple and crosscutting networks of cooperation characteristic of women's collective endeavors in Boubuilla more generally. For butter processors in Boubuilla, the collective potential of Nyoor Yinii alliances as well as their flexibility was crucial to engaging the full range of commercial opportunities available to them. Indeed, far from commercialization contributing to individualization, for Boubuilla women, entry into the butter business, increased butter production, and movement into a wide array of markets all relied on the enlargement and formalization of practices of cooperation within the productive realm.

Gozense: Cultivating Extrahousehold Alliances and Expanding the Purview of Nyoor Yinii

Five miles from Bawku town, the village of Gozense is more remote than either Saabon or Boubuilla. Inaccessible by public transportation due to its location along a road made up of flooded culverts and stretches of rock and sand, Gozense is most often reached by foot or bicycle. Given the lack of convenient access to trade routes and neighboring commercial centers, agriculture, supplemented by labor migration more than trade, is the mainstay of rural livelihoods in Gozense. Without the amenities enjoyed by communities more proximate to Bawku—from schools and shops to grinding mills and electricity—and with the bulk of the male population absent from home due to the lure and necessity of labor migration, in Gozense the imperatives of female self-support run high. The tendency of community residents—especially its female population—towards self-reliance, however, operates within a wider context of rural mobilization. In response to the community's low standard of living, combined with the efforts of a handful of well-educated and well-connected "native sons," Gozense has been the target of a number of development initiatives introducing community members to new resources, aspirations, and forms of organization.

For women in Gozense women, like their counterparts in Saabon and Boubuilla, the mobilization of Nyoor Yinii ties provides the foundation for commercial intensification among shea butter-makers. But although commercial butter production is not new to Gozense, the formal mobilization

1.8 Interior courtyard of Gozense household where women are engaged in commercial butter production. Crushed shea nuts are drying on the floor, along with the dross from butter extraction shaped into briquettes for use in cooking fires.

of Nyoor Yinii work groups is, not only in the case of shea processing but in women's lives overall. Attesting to the inherent adaptability of Nyoor Yinii work patterns, the organization of shea processing in Gozense exhibits a form significantly different from that employed elsewhere. This is a result of the specific history of butter-making in the community, which was previously marked by limited extrahousehold cooperation and only recently by a concerted effort to maximize commercial opportunity. Prior to the appearance of the Nyoor Yinii work groups in butter production, Gozense women's sustained coordination of work was quite limited. While Gozense women may have "begged" women from other households for help with farming and construction from time to time, these efforts were generally haphazard. Neither did the Gozense women participate in formally organized dance groups. As a result, butter-makers' institution of Nyoor Yinii marks a major shift in Gozense women's economic relations in general. This shift was dramatic, as butter-makers quickly enlarged the realm of their cooperative and commercial endeavors, simultaneously innovating the overall structure and function of Nyoor Yinii.

Even though the trend toward sustained cooperation and formalized work groups is recent, commercial butter production is a practice of long standing in Gozense. Adubo, a woman well into her seventies, spent most of her married life making clay pots for butter-makers in Gozense and neighboring villages. Introduced to the art of large-scale butter processing by her cousin in Zagabo half a century ago, she occasionally engaged in commercial butter production as a means of income generation, first making it in small quantities to sell in the neighborhood before she married and the in larger quantities to sell in the market after she moved to her husband's home in Gozense. Never considering butter production her singular occupation, Adubo pursued it alongside the production and sale of pottery, *pito* (millet beer), and preground millet flour. Adubo's buttermaking skills were replicated by other women in Gozense as she shared her knowledge of processing techniques with her daughters as well as women marrying into the community. Although women from different households occasionally pooled their labor in the course of butter processing, these work groups were small, informal, and highly localized, neither identifying themselves nor being identified by others as Nyoor Yinii.

Since Adubo's time, commercial butter processing has come to occupy an increasingly central place in the livelihoods of Gozense women. Treated as a primary means of income generation and a skill in which they are expert, butter production in Gozense is by now the common occupation of women in the households of Adubo's husband's brothers and sons. Due to their shared knowledge and commercial orientation, levels of intrahousehold cooperation among butter-makers are fairly high, with women in individual households working together or in teams. Not restricted to the circulation of labor, this cooperation extends as well to the sharing of productive means. Cowives, such as Akimsa and her rivals, for instance, contribute the purchase of butter mixing bowls, to which they have equal access. In other households, all the butter-makers may use the equipment owned by one person—typically the senior wife.

In the early 1990s a concerted shift in processing patterns came into play as Gozense butter-makers formed a Nyoor Yinii work group known as the Gozense Kwatuodib (literally, "Gozense Butter Making People"), and began to circulate labor and other forms of economic aid on an extrahousehold level. The formation of the Gozense butter-makers association was initiated by Barkisu, now the community's leading butter-maker. Hailing from an area where women have engaged in large-scale commercial butter production for several decades and where extrahousehold work patterns are not uncommon, Barkisu's instigation of collective butter-making in Gozense can be interpreted simply as a replication of an already familiar production pattern. Her promotion of the exchange of labor and other economic services may also be considered self-interested, since she, given the size of her butter-making enterprise, could surely take advantage of the assistance provided by Nyoor Yinii group members. However, in rallying

Gozense butter-makers to her cause, Barkisu introduced an array of practices having no single precedent and conveying widespread benefit. This was to have a notable affect on Gozense women's economic identities, activities, and potentials related to butter-making and more generally.

As labor exchanges on a household-to-household basis took shape, a few or all of the butter-makers from one household would provide assistance to butter-makers in another household and receive help from them in return. While intrahousehold aid centered on the pooling of labor for the arduous task of beating the ground shea nut paste with water to release the oil, women from other households devoted their aid to water carrying, occasionally assisting with cracking shea nuts in preparation for grinding, and less frequently, beating the pulverized shea nuts with water. Reducing both the toil and time necessary for butter processing, these interhousehold labor exchanges made it possible for butter-makers to increase their productive capacity.

In addition to helping one another with butter production, members of the Gozense Kwatuodib also extended the scope of mutual aid to encompass butter marketing. Unlike the Boubuilla women, all the Gozense butter-makers regularly attend Bawku central market, facilitating groupwide coordination of trade. If a Gozense woman is unable to attend the market, butter-makers in other houses help her cowives carry her butter to market and oversee its sale and delivery to customers. Similarly, once in the market, the other group members help to collect the debts of the absent woman. This sort of aid, conducted after the fact of production, is essential to enterprise reproduction and expansion, not to mention income generation. Only if a woman can get her butter to market and collect money for it can she recoup the capital necessary for sustaining or enlarging her buttermaking enterprise and meeting her cash needs.

Also expanding the group members' commercial orientation, under Barkisu's guidance the Gozense Kwatuodib organized itself according to a widely known pattern introduced by government and nongovernmental organizations' (NGO) personnel for the administration of community development projects. Conforming to this model, the Gozense Kwatuodib established an executive board with Barkisu at the helm and Awin, another leading butter-maker in the community and among the more senior women still actively engaged in butter processing, as second in command. They were joined by a secretary/treasurer, the literate son of Ramatu, the group's most senior member. In keeping with this model, members of the Gozense Kwatuodib were expected to attend monthly meetings as well as pay dues with accounts and records to be maintained by the secretary. In organizing their finances, the Gozense Kwatuodib members replicated the popular practice of group saving known as *susu*, where women make a

1.9 In Gozense, Salamatu (background) works with her cowife's daughter to process shea butter. In the foreground is the elderly Adubo, who introduced shea butter processing to the community.

small contribution to a common fund each market day. The money saved may be withdrawn by individual members or used for a common investment. The Gozense butter-makers elected to do the latter; after paying dues for several months, they used their funds to purchase T-shirts emblazoned with the group's name as well as matching cloths for themselves.

In the context of northern Ghana, such material investments have important social and material effects. Women dress alike, a practice known as *yayi* (Hausa for "to do"/"to do it"), on any public occasion when they wish to demonstrate their cohesion: from the weddings and funeral of kin to communitywide celebrations like *Saaman pad*. In the case of the Gozense Kwatuodib, "making *yayi*" announced and affirmed their identity and solidarity not just as women of a community, but as women doing a certain type of work, thereby conveying a commitment to butter-making as central and definitive aspect of their social identity. In this manner, the Gozense Kwatuodib members' strategies of collective resource management, as evidenced in their performance of *yayi*, where both an end expressing the group's solidarity and collective accomplishments and a means for their future cooperation.

The cooperative endeavors carried out by the Gozense butter-makers during the first several months of the Kwatuodib group's existence, at once a sign of existing cohesion and of future economic potential, both intensified the group's involvement in commercial butter production and extended its economic purview beyond butter-making. First, displays of economic strength helped the group to attract new members, raising the ranks of the Gozense Kwatuodib from fifteen to twenty-two members in less than a year. This committed more butter-making households and more butter-makers in each household to Nyoor Yinii labor exchanges and the group's common fund. These initial accomplishments also provided a foundation for Gozense Kwatuodib members to pool and circulate labor and other material resources in contexts outside butter production. Group members, for example, began to assist on one another's groundnut and rice farms. The group as a whole also pooled resources to make a substantial contribution of foodstuffs—five bowls of rice and cooking oil—to the wedding celebration of the group's secretary. Ongoing contributions to the group's savings funds gave members control over substantial financial assets: nearly four hundred dollars by July 1995, just a year and a half after the group was formed. As group members planned to use the money to purchase nuts in bulk to share at the beginning of the next season, these resources provided a basis for Gozense Kwatuodib to invest in new means of supporting and expanding their involvement in commercial butter production. This strategy would prove crucial for sustaining commercial butter production as market conditions changed.

In enlarging the range of the group's commercial pursuits, members of the Gozense Kwatuodib were clearly striving to increase their own economic standing. Their efforts, however, were not solely a form of self-help. Rather, group members aimed to improve their economic capacities in order to gain external recognition and access to external sources of material aid. The leader, Barkisu, frequently alluded to the necessity of being a group in order to obtain external economic assistance, as did other group members when quizzed about the purpose of their organization. Though the specific route pursued by the Gozense butter-makers may have been unprecedented, organizing a group as a means of eliciting externally based material support was by no means an unusual economic strategy in Bawku District or even in the village of Gozense itself. In northern Ghana, both state-based and nongovernmental organizations dispensing material assistance expected to work through community organizations rather than individuals or the community as a whole. Gozense residents had direct experience with this practice. In the early 1990s an NGO sponsored the construction of a primary school near the village, requiring provision of labor and the formation of a steering committee. The Ghana Water and Sewerage Corporation (GWSC) a few years earlier, after a water pump was installed, similarly required the community to establish a water committee to oversee pump use and repair.

Expressing a recent pan-African trend of increasing government support for women's groups in particular (Wipper 1995: 183), the 31st December Women's Movement, a quasi-governmental organization dedicated (on a rhetorical level at least) to enhancing women's economic standing as part of its larger agenda of political mobilization, had established a program in Bawku District. Although they did not visit Gozense directly, 31st December representatives toured a large number of communities, instructing women to form organized groups in order to qualify for guidance and possible financial assistance from the nationally based association. The representatives in fact advised these groups to model themselves on Nyoor Yinii, due to the already established salience of this cooperative form in the lives of local women.[12] Given the widespread publication and inevitable circulation of these strategies for tapping externally based economic support, it is not surprising that Gozense women would adapt them to their own economic agenda. So successful were Gozense women at doing so that in 1997 they received a grinding mill from the International Development Exchange, a U.S.-based NGO. In the eyes of the Gozense Kwatuodib, installation of a grinding mill could foster members' commercial endeavors by relieving the drudgery of carrying shea nuts back and forth to town for grinding and by providing income from the provision of grinding services to women in their own and surrounding villages.

Gozense women, in sum, used the mandate of Nyoor Yinii to do much more than expand commercial efforts through the concentration of labor. Although labor pooling was certainly important for engaging commercial opportunity, it was only one of many collective strategies pursued by the Gozense Kwatuodib in the name of commercial gain. In addition to assisting one another with production, members of this association assisted one another with marketing. They also engaged in the pooling of capital. Not only did these practices enable them to participate in the market on a larger and more efficient scale than before, but they were also integral to the forging of new solidarities. These solidarities themselves, by qualifying the group for development support, were the source of additional economic aid and opportunity, further enhancing the commercial potentials of the Gozense butter-makers.

Discussion

As these three examples demonstrate, though Nyoor Yinii is grounded in deep-rooted sentiments of female solidarity and moral economy, the work patterns emerging out of these alliances are by no means conservative. On the contrary, they enable women to respond to new experiences, circumstances, and interests, including commercial opportunity. Nyoor Yinii alliances facilitate women's commercial endeavors in a number of ways. Most of all, the concentration of labor afforded by Nyoor Yinii allows women to meet the energy requirements of regular and large-scale butter processing, requisites of sustained market participation. Similarly, the sorts of labor exchange at the heart of Nyoor Yinii facilitate the conjuncture of the different types of skill—from sheer muscle power to intellectual expertise—necessary for successful oil extraction. Bringing together women of different ages, status, and backgrounds, these encounters are equally important for the transfer and preservation of the specialized knowledge. Even when the frequency and scale of butter production is relatively modest, as in the case of Saabon, the circulation of labor characteristic of Nyoor Yinii also makes it possible for butter-makers to compensate for the limited aid that may be available at the household level. Overcoming the need for all women in a household to partake in butter processing, as in Saabon, or the need to coordinate butter processing efforts, as in Boubuilla, this allows for greater specialization and individuation among butter-makers. While some Saabon women may chose to pursue butter production through Nyoor Yinii, others may opt out. An individual Boubuilla woman, may in turn use the parameters of generalized reciprocity characteristic of Nyoor Yinii in community to forge an independent path of market engagement, making butter when she deems appropriate for the market of her choice.

Nyoor Yinii alliances also foster commercial participation and gain due their capacity to conserve capital. The pooling of labor characteristic of Nyoor Yinii mitigates the need to exchange cash for labor, allowing women with low cash reserves to enter the market. In addition, Nyoor Yinii alliances can provide a foundation for pooling, saving, and investing cash, as in Gozense. As is also the case of Gozense, Nyoor Yinii alliances may attract financial support from sources outside the market. In this manner, group efforts and identification provide a foundation for financial gain on both the organizational and the individual level, increasing the marketability of female labor and its product.

Nyoor Yinii work patterns, moreover, are flexible, enabling butter-makers to respond swiftly and effectively to the unstable market conditions characteristic of the economy of northern Ghana. The enduring character of Nyoor Yinii associations allows for sudden expansions and contractions of collective efforts. Even if these ties have been dormant or minimized, as in the case of Saabon, this makes it possible to engage the assistance of others whenever necessary. Nyoor Yinii associations can also easily be extended to encompass new personnel, as occurred in Boubuilla and Gozense, as well as new markets. Whether under the leadership of charismatic individuals such as Gozense's Barkisu or the two Boubuilla butter-makers who learned about palm oil processing as migrant laborers, the activities and parameters of Nyoor Yinii organization are likewise amenable to innovation, enabling them readily to engage new commercial opportunities while preserving their jointly individual and collective character. Indeed, Nyoor Yinii, as a productive dynamic invested in the creation of value, seems to thrive on the new ideas and opportunities that outsiders may bring to the domestic economy.

It is instructive to compare Saul's (1989: 185) description of the organization of shea production among rural Bobo women based on research in southern Burkina Faso with that of Bawku's butter-makers. Like the situation in northern Ghana, shea processing among the Bobo is a labor-intensive exercise requiring the contribution of females from beyond a single household. These configurations parallel those of the Bawku women in that they are typically multigenerational and dominated by older women who are considered to be the repositories of expert skill and knowledge. However, much more than in northern Ghana, senior Bobo women, due to the formal recognition of matrilineal principles and uterine alliances, dominate women's work groups and serve as the arbiters of resource distribution. Such a hierarchy, though present to some degree in the early training of daughters, brides, and cowives, is little replicated in Bawku, where more egalitarian principles of cooperation prevail. This may well reflect not only the absence of institutionalized matrilines but also a much less hierarchical social order overall, in keeping with the classification of the Kusasi and other ethnic groups predominant in Bawku's rural communities as "stateless societies." Nevertheless, as in the Bobo case, butter-makers in northern Ghana activate specifically female principles of alliance and economic organization that differ from the dominant patriarchal order.

The comparison of the Nyoor Yinii cooperative work groups of northeast Ghana with several other African examples makes it possible to specify some of the political-economic conditions that promote or undermine women's cooperative labor arrangements. In contrast to the Ghanaian example, the Liberian case discussed by Bledsoe (1980: 112) points to a decline in cooperative work groups with the rise of market participation and opportunities for wage employment. Similarly, in southern Malawi, Davison (1995: 194) identifies a decline in female cooperative work with the production of cash crops under conditions of land shortage and goes so far as to suggest that "women are disinclined to engage in activities that require an additional labor contribution when they have limited control of the output." In the Gambia (Carney 1994), however, the opposition between waged labor—and cash income generation more generally—and cooperative work is not as clear-cut, even when women's access to land is severely limited. Carney's (1994: 179) research reveals that cooperative work provides the very possibility of wage earning as groups hire themselves out to work on farmers' cash-crop plots for fixed wages. In fact cooperative organization, as opposed to individual sale of labor, enables women to exercise greater control over the terms of the cash payment for their work. Here again, cooperative labor is well embedded in the market and cash earning.

In a variation on the same theme, in the case of Bawku, women participate in Nyoor Yinii as way to access cash, but they do this by means of the market for commodities rather than the market for labor. This may well be because Nyoor Yinii—as a more reliable source of work than either hiring labor or being hired—provides a more secure foundation for entering the market and earning cash through commodity exchange. A similar arrangement—likely for the same reasons—is found among female beer-brewers in southern Burkina Faso (Saul 1981: 747). Here, the cash-conservative cooperative labor arrangements attached to market-oriented beer production underwrite the possibility of female wealth accumulation in rural communities. Taken together, these examples point to a possible correlation between poor labor markets and the prevalence of collective work patterns in commodity production. They suggest more generally the importance of looking closely at the nature of factor markets—whether for land, labor, or other productive inputs—as well as markets for the commodities produced when trying to comprehend the persistence or decline of cooperative work forms in commercially oriented rural economies with limited industrialization, like those in much of Africa.

Conclusion

To conclude, the preceding discussion makes it apparent that in northern Ghana shea butter production is highly commercial in orientation. The large majority of women engaged in butter processing do so to earn income via market-based trade. They engage the market in manner that minimizes the capital requirements of production and guarantees access to substantial labor with an eye toward maximizing profit and preserving scarce resources. Indicative of their strong commercial orientation, butter processors are highly aware of and responsive to shifts in market conditions, constantly modifying their production and marketing strategies. They approach the market as individuals, selling butter for their own gain and organizing their butter-making enterprises in a manner that suits their own needs.

Notwithstanding the butter-makers' commercial savvy however, the parameters of butter production pursued by women in northern Ghana do not conform to classic models of market mentality. As we have seen, despite the highly individuated outcomes of shea butter production and trade, shea processing is a largely collective enterprise, whether involving the female residents of a single household or drawing on the joint efforts of women from a wider community. Indicating the close connection between commercialization and collective work patterns, as butter-makers' commitment to the market intensifies, so does the scope and scale of cooperation. The circumstances of shea butter processing in northern Ghana thus confound the assertion that cooperative work is incompatible with a commercial orientation, whether as a refuge from the market or an obstacle to it.

The nexus of commercialization and cooperation among butter processors calls into question other presumptions regarding the character and relation of African social and economic structures, especially the connection between gender and work and, in turn, reproduction and production. With regard to Africa's largely rural and agrarian societies, the domestic domain has typically been characterized as an arena in which women are engaged in productive activities for others and reproductive endeavors for all (Guyer 1995). Shifting the lens beyond agriculture complicates this conception, for the case of butter production proves the domestic a realm of female enablement where women exercise control over their own and others' labor to engage productive opportunities in their own right. In addition, the case of shea makes clear that these independent productive activities are neither secondary to nor separate from reproductive roles. Rather, they are integral to the development and demonstration of core female social identities and solidarities, a phenomenon Clark (1999) also identifies in female traders among the matrilineal Asante in central Ghana. As we have seen, the insertion of individuals within *son taba* and Nyoor Yinii networks and the concomitant circulation of resources among them—whether raw labor power, specialized knowledge, or productive capital—contribute to the realization of fundamental female statuses of daughter, wife, and mother at the same time as they underwrite commercial success. These statuses are thus actualized via commercial activity, not prior to it.

These insights regarding the commercial character of the domestic shea economy are important for a number of reasons. On a most basic level, they stand to correct the images of shea as non- or newly commercialized and of shea butter producers as new to the market—images that are promoted in much of the marketing material accompanying the repositioning of shea as a new type of global commodity. They also suggest the indigenous modes of commoditization surrounding the production and sale of shea butter in northern Ghana are enduring because of their very flexibility. Although the provisioning of the domestic market remains a priority of rural butter-makers, the way they accomplish this aim varies considerably. The flexible work forms of Nyoor Yinii and *son taba* allow shea butter-makers to tailor their work routines to the ever-changing exigencies of rural economic life. One reason this is possible is that butter-makers can harness relationships already in existence on the household and community level. By the same token, butter-makers' activation of these ties serves to strengthen and reproduce them, contributing to their availability for future endeavors. Despite their collective character, these productive arrangements nevertheless allow rural women to claim individualized rewards, further guaranteeing investment in the preservation of these arrangements.

Finally, and of broader significance, the productive arrangements sustaining the commercial shea economy in northern Ghana suggest the relevance of continuing a wider analytic project of theorizing the overlap and interplay of production and reproduction within household-based economies and concomitant patterns of gender-based entitlement and doing so in a manner that overcomes the agricultural myopia of prevailing theorizations. This seems especially pressing given the conditions of agricultural decline occurring in many parts of Africa, including the vast midsection of the continent that makes up the savanna zone. In light of the concurrent process of commercial reform taking place throughout Africa and carrying with it new sorts of demand for tropical products, such an endeavor is all the more timely. As subsequent chapters will make evident, the collective arrangements of commercial butter processing—however long-lived or emancipatory—situate rural butter-makers within a much larger political economy created by state institutions and global commercial forces beyond the immediate control of savanna residents, male or female.

CHAPTER 2

Shea and the Colonial State
Commodity Rule in Northern Ghana

Although shea is firmly embedded in the livelihoods and lifestyles of rural women residing in West Africa's savanna, it is also situated in a much wider web of meanings and economic relationships. In the 1990s, following nearly a century of steady but silent incorporation into metropolitan industry, shea gained a visible presence in the centers of cosmopolitan consumption and commerce—an economic arena far removed from the markets, farms, and forests of northern Ghana. At the turn of the millennium, shea is as likely to be found in the shopping districts of any of the world's global cities or even less central places as it is in the markets of West Africa.

In New York, London, Hong Kong, Mexico City, Paris, Tokyo, Tunis, and Johannesburg, shops abound specializing in goods from around the world touted for their luxury and aesthetic of good taste ("Lush hour," 2002).[1] Among the wares are an array of body tonics, cosmetics, soaps, and essential oils that include shea. Presented to the consuming public as extraordinarily pure with only the barest imprint of mass manufacture, they are packaged with natural materials and labels noting their exotic origins and restorative qualities. Shea products occupy a small area in some of these settings and in others, like the Body Shop, take up a few aisles or even whole shops, as in the case of L'Occitane, which has over three hundred outlets devoted to shea product lines (White 2002).

Even if one moves out of the elite consumption zone, shea can still be found in department stores, drug chains, and more out-of-the-way places such as health food and ethnic specialty shops. Shea is marketed by the world's leading cosmetic firms—Estée Lauder, Clarins ("Treatment cosmetics," 1998), Lancôme ("Handy work," 2001), Helena Rubinstein ("Master sculptors," 2000), and Revlon ("Hair care," 1999)—as well as much smaller ones, many devoted to shea alone. Often sold in pure form, shea finds its way into a tremendous range of cosmetic formulations from lipstick to sunscreen, diaper creams, foundation, massage oil, and hair relaxer. Shea may be found in combination with an endless list of ingredients such as fruit extracts ("Treatment cosmetics," 1998), beeswax ("Marketing news: Body," 2001), mushrooms (ibid.), apricot oil, and the list goes on. Columns on shea abound in ordinary newspapers, and shea is written about in magazines as varied as *Essence, Working Women, Mother and Baby, Mirabella, Time Out, Pride, Today's Black Woman, Community Pharmacy* and *Business Week.* Shea can be found circulating within the full range of consumption sites of late-modern life, from the mass markets of Lever Brothers and Vaseline to mail-order catalogs such as Smith and Hawken and Real Goods, and shopping malls and Internet vendors with names like Mode de Vie, Mistrall, the African Shea Butter Company, Karite Gold, Body ButterZ, and Ébène.

Despite the apparent newness of shea's image as a global commodity, shea's journey from the savanna zone to shopping center—from nonindustrial to postindustrial—began more than a century ago, as the economic and political architecture of European—specifically British—colonialism moved into the West African savanna. Since that time shea has been caught in the ever-shifting integuments of global commerce and cosmopolitan taste—processes intimately tied to the configuration of power within and between the tropics and the polities of the Northern hemisphere. As a consequence, shea has long been present on the world market, but unevenly, with its form and visibility changing with the tides of much wider material and political transformations.

This chapter focuses on the conditions surrounding the emergence of shea as an export commodity during the colonial period and its implications for the domestic shea economy. It details the pervasive yet often hidden mechanisms of colonial state-making surrounding the movement of tropical commodities out of Africa and into the metropole. Highlighting the struggles over resources emerging in the course of market-building and restructuring as well as the way market reform served as a vehicle for the imposition of a wider logic of state rule—that is, the terms of political belonging and exclusion along with the conventions of labor and territorial control—this chapter argues for a thoroughly political reading of processes of market reform with respect to shea and more generally over the course of British imperial rule in West Africa and in its aftermath.

The chapter describes the powerful role played by shea in the orientation of colonial state penetration in northern Ghana. Yet these state interventions, however constant, were also unsteady, indicating the shifting agendas of the colonial regime and its uneasy relationship to both colonial territories and private capital at home. As a result of these ongoing efforts to impose and revise an imperialist commercial version, the market for shea was repeatedly rendered a site of struggle between state agents and rural residents. With the export market little able to provide a viable alternative to rural shea traders and producers given this wholly unstable environment, these policy shifts nevertheless subjected the indigenous shea economy to a constant stream of adjustments and repositionings even as they failed to fully engage it.

Commodity Paths and the Theorization of Colonial Rule

In the spring of 1892, George Ekem Ferguson, an African official of the Gold Coast's British colonial administration, embarked on a journey throughout the area that today constitutes the northern part of the West African nation of Ghana. Trained at the Royal School of Mines and an expert cartographer and geologist, Ferguson was experienced in both diplomacy and exploration, with over a decade of service in the colonial government (Sampson 1956: 36). In his reports to the governor of the Gold Coast, Ferguson commented on the tremendous resource base of the savanna territories to the north of the Gold Coast colony. He noted the commercial vitality of the area and the host of goods—from shea, gold, and ivory to horses, cattle, and gum arabic—already circulating in the regional economy. He wrote to his superiors: "We must develop the resources of those countries by showing the tribes articles such as gum, shea butter and other products that will be acceptable to us as exports" (Ferguson 1974: 78). Intrigued in particular by the commercial promise of shea, Ferguson described its use and preparation in detail:

> The fruit of the shea butter tree is edible, very sweet, and of a peculiar flavor. The recipe for obtaining the butter is as follows: Clear the flesh away from the fruit, dry in sun, boil in water and dry again. Separate seed inside from shell and testa surrounding, beat seed in mortar and grind to fineness, and put into hot water, stirring well. When cold, take off butter from top, leaving residue at bottom, which if not fine enough is again dried and mixed with others for a second operation. Melt the butter till foreign matters settle in bottom and decant. (1974: 68)

Ferguson was not the first outsider to note the unique character or commercial potential of shea. In the centuries preceding colonial rule and well into the colonial era, shea held a prominent place in the West African economy. Medieval Arabic and European sources document the prevalence of shea butter in marketplaces and households throughout the West African savanna and the Sahel. The famous Muslim scholar Ibn Battuta, in the course of his 1352-to-1353 expedition, received a calabash of shea butter while traveling in the empire of ancient Mali (Lewicki 1974: 106). In 1477 Malfante, a Genoese explorer, found shea butter imported from the Sudan in the Tuat Oasis on the road from Gao (in northern Mali) to Morocco (Lewicki 1974: 108).

Centuries later, travelers continued to remark on the substantial value of shea products in the West African region. Mungo Park noted the presence of shea butter among the Bambara, referring to it as the "the main article of their inland commerce" (1971: 203). Other accounts from this era record the production and sale of shea products over a wide geographic area spanning from Senegal and Guinea in the west to Nigeria in the east (Lewicki 1974: 107). In 1892, a French traveler, "Andre Rancon met a westbound caravan of ninety-three people in Dentila (now in southeast Senegal), of whom seventy-nine were carrying shea butter, nearly two metric tons in all, from Konkadugu for sale at MacCarthy's Island on the Gambia" (Curtin 1975: 230). Heinrich Barth (1890) likewise described shea butter as one of the principle articles in the marketplace in Timbuktu.

Long-distance traders plying the length and breadth of West Africa incorporated shea products into their marketing networks. Diahanke merchants traveling from the Upper Niger to Senegambia in the eighteenth century carried shea butter (Curtin 1971: 233); and during the mid-nineteenth century, shea butter was brought north to Mali along with slaves by Jula caravans (Meillassoux 1971: 186). Shea products were equally important in the forest and coastal markets as they were in the northern savanna. The presence of shea butter, handwoven cotton cloth, and other savanna commodities within the regional markets of the forest-based Akan during the seventeenth century is well documented (Daaku 1971: 177). The Yarse, a Mossi subgroup who gathered trade goods from the region now encompassing southern Burkina Faso and northern Ghana, specialized in shea butter, livestock, and slaves, which they exchanged for kola in Asante markets in the forest zone (Lovejoy 1980: 126). Hausa traders coming from further north and east purchased sheep, cattle, slaves, shea butter, and salt in the savanna zone, which they imported into northern Asante centers (Lovejoy 1980).

Not only was shea was an important source of cooking oil within the expanding Asante economy (Lovejoy 1980: 13) but also, symbolizing its status as a luxury good, high-quality butter was stored in finely decorated pots of beaten brass and used as a skin conditioner and adhesive for the

2.1 Decorative brass containers known as *forowa* (Twi) used in the early decades of the twentieth century by people in Ghana's forest zone to store shea butter, which they considered a luxury item.

ceremonial ornamentation of the body with gold dust (Ghana Museums and Monuments 1970: 23, 39; McLeod 1981: 135; Ross 1974). Catering to the demand for shea along the coast, Volta River salt traders based in Ada, on the eastern edge of the Gold Coast colony, went as far north as Kratchi and Yapai to sell their wares and filled their canoes with shea butter on the return journey to trade in southern markets (Sutton 1981: 52). Elsewhere along the West Atlantic Basin, Park comments: "Negro slave merchants, besides slaves and the merchandise they bring for sale to the whites, supply the inhabitants of the maritime districts with native iron, sweet smelling gums and frankincense, and a commodity called shea-toulou which literally translated, signifies tree-butter. (1971: 26)"

Paving the way for the extension of these long-standing commercial circuits into European markets, Ferguson's forays into the hinterlands of the Gold Coast initiated a chain of events that were to affect dramatically the shea economy and in turn the larger political and economic landscape of the northern savanna. The changes set in motion by the patterns of colonial engagement driving Ferguson's mission were both profound and highly unstable. As in other cases of colonial resource extraction, this instability was no doubt due in part to fluctuations in world market conditions as well as indigenous resistance to colonial policy (Berry 1993a; Shenton 1986). In accounting for these inconsistencies, however, what seems less noted is the contingent character of imperial rule. Emerging out of competing interests and ideologies within the colonial administration as well as between the colonial administration and private European capital, these contingencies were inherent in the colonial order itself (Lonsdale and Berman 1979). Hence, due to the vagaries of imperial state interests

and capacities, colonial markets and the policies undergirding them—
even for a single commodity such as shea—were rarely consistent in structure, function, or intent.

Exemplifying the ever-dynamic integuments of imperial power, shea
commercialization throughout the era of British rule shifted in and out of
the optic and toolbox of colonial administration. Sometimes central, sometimes peripheral, attractive at one moment for its export potential, at another for its value within the domestic economy, and at yet another time for
its role in regional markets, the place of shea within colonial policy and
practice depended on the shifting proclivities of the colonial state. Reflecting the rise and fall of markets, paradigms of statecraft, and political coalitions, the nature and extent of shea commercialization at any given
time—both during the colonial era and more recently—may be taken as a
barometer of the intensity and orientation of state engagement in Ghana's
northern savanna zone more generally. Hence, despite the long-term significance of shea within the West African economy and the apparent resilience
of indigenous patterns of production, consumption, and distribution, since
the end of the nineteenth century the terms of shea commercialization—
for both domestic and export markets—have been profoundly shaped by
processes of state-building and restructuring.

Indicative of the pervasive politicization of colonial economies, the unstable nature of shea commercialization well illustrates Mahmoud Mamdani's characterization of markets as "historically created through social
struggle" (1991: 457). In the northern hinterlands of the Gold Coast, such
a politicization of commerce took a range of forms, both subtle and overt.
Right from the start, for the colonial administration the development of
the shea market was not an end in itself but a means of statecraft—of asserting control over persons and resources and forging and sustaining an
exclusive territorial presence. Yet state interests were themselves unsteady,
further contributing to the political character of market-building and reform. Bound up in different ways with the control of labor, loyalty, and
space, this was due to the diverse agendas of different colonial offices and
the differential positioning of colonial officials within them.

The colonial administration, rife with contradiction, pursued a plethora of competing aims when it came to shea: supporting itself and supporting metropolitan commercial interests; imposing order and fostering
internal cooperation; controlling people and populations and promoting
social mobility; extracting resources at the lowest cost and stimulating new
desires and modes of livelihood. Adding to the political mix, these diver-
gences were crosscut by the shifting parameters of contest and collaboration between state-based institutions and the nonstate actors, whether
northern residents, West African traders, or representatives of European

merchant capital, invested in the creation and restructuring of markets for shea as well as other commodities. Such struggles by and for the state via the market can be attributed to what Fred Cooper and Ann Stoller call "the tensions of empire," a perspective that "puts contradiction at the center of the colonial state's operative mode" (1997: 20). As Cooper and Stoller see it, "colonial regimes were neither monolithic nor omnipotent. Closer inspection reveals competing agendas for using power, competing strategies for maintaining control" (1997: 6), qualities that undergird the "contradictory and indeterminate nature of colonial economies" (1997: 19).

With regard to shea, these "tensions" were a product of more than the divergent concerns of metropolitan entrepreneurs, indigenous economic actors, and the state, or even changing interests within the colonial apparatus itself. They derived as well from the diverse conceptions of markets held by those engaged in commercial reform. These varied and at times contentious ideological frames represent an important feature of what may be described as the mobile cultural terrain of colonialism. Nicholas Thomas, remarking on the cultural dimensions of the colonial project, highlights the close relationship between systems of knowledge and the exercise of power:

> Colonialism is not best understood primarily as a political or economic relationship that is legitimized or justified through ideologies of racism or progress. Rather, colonialism has always, equally importantly and deeply, been a cultural process; its discoveries and trespasses are imagined and energized through signs, metaphors and narratives; even what would seem its purest moments of profit and violence have been mediated and enframed by structures of meaning. Colonial cultures are not simply ideologies that mask, mystify or rationalize forms of oppression that are external to them; they are also expressive and constitutive of colonial relationships themselves. (Thomas 1994: 2)

Despite their uneven character however, in their totality the diverse aims (political and economic), agencies (state-based and private, foreign and indigenous), and aspects (material, social, and ideological) of colonial rule in northern Ghana were nonetheless pervasive in their effects as they worked together to engage and reconfigure the physical landscapes, laboring bodies, and conventions of evaluation and exchange in the Gold Coast's savanna hinterland. Bound up with the assertion of control over persons, things, and space, the contours of shea commercialization during the era of colonial rule came to reflect the position of Ghana's savanna communities within the wider political economy of the nation-state. Consequently, the story of shea is a story of politics—of political struggles, ideologies, and institutions—as much as it is a story of markets, cultural values, and rural social practice.

Making Markets and Territorializing the State in Northern Ghana

Ferguson's exploration of the Gold Coast's savanna hinterland set in train a contentious process of transformation deeply affecting the political and commercial profile of the area that would become northern Ghana. Although focused on the procurement and provisioning of specific material resources, including shea, these dynamics were both an engine and an index of a much wider process of change. Prior to Ferguson's entry, private European trading companies and individual merchants operated in the savanna zone seeking markets for European goods (Hargreaves 1966: 335; Braimah and Goody 1967: 107). In sending Ferguson to the north, the colonial administration hoped to build upon these early strands of commercial development, enlarging the markets for imports and promoting the sale and production of exports. Given the competing interests of other colonial powers in the area—namely Germany and France—along with the prevailing force of numerous indigenous polities, the shape and outcome of this process depended as much on diplomacy as on the cultivation of economic ties. In the course of establishing such connections, the savanna hinterland would be subject to a series of political reorderings requiring an uneasy layering of institutions and relationships.

When Ferguson first went north, much of the eastern portion of the territory he covered was already designated an Anglo-German Neutral Zone (Metcalfe 1964: 433). According to an 1887 agreement, within this area traders from the two countries were, at least in theory, to enjoy equal economic access. Essentially a "free trade zone," the neutral territory included Salaga, the most important marketing center in the region, as well as several other central market towns such as Daboya and Yendi. All were stopping points for caravan trade and important sites for the circulation of indigenous commodities, including locally manufactured cloth and salt as well as shea. The western limits of British influence had also been partially established in the course of an 1889 agreement between the British and the French demarcating the boundary between the Gold Coast and the Ivory Coast. In contrast to the Neutral Zone, the French claimed exclusive rather than shared access to key markets in this area such as Bonduku, a long-established center of the gold, kola, shea, and slave trades at the crossroads of Hausa, Mossi, and Mande caravan traffic (Ferguson 1974: 365).

None of these agreements, however, included indigenous ratification of the terms of European political and economic intervention in the northern savanna.[2] Serving as the impetus for Ferguson's journey in 1892, a concern about such a lack of "interior" influence, combined with the actual insecurity of British interests in the Neutral Zone, precipitated the formulation of an alternative strategy of economic access on the part of the British colonial administration. The goal was to create a massive trade corridor

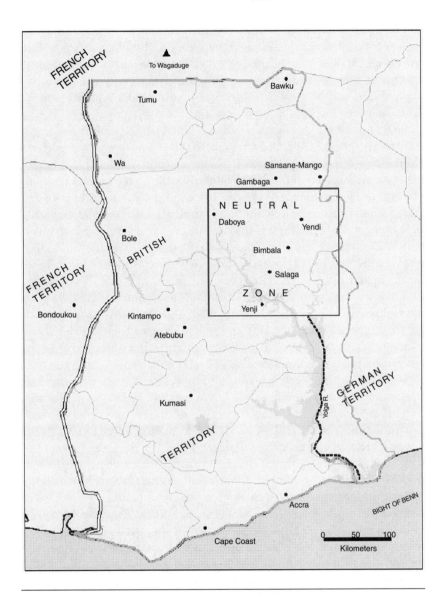

Map 5 The West African Subregion and European Territorial Claims, c. 1898

where Britain was the sole imperial power. Running several hundred miles north from the boundary of the Gold Coast colony into Mossi territory and east through the jurisdiction of the Niger Company, the configuration of such a corridor provided the foundation for new modes of commodity circulation in the savanna zone relying on the linkages between the colonial administration, local polities, and British-backed trading companies. It was to secure the kind of local ties necessary for building such an extensive trade corridor that Ferguson's services in the north were engaged. Combined with a mission of mapping and reconnaissance, Ferguson's main charge was to negotiate "Treaties of Friendship and Freedom of Trade" between the Crown and the leaders of indigenous polities.

Based on this multiple agenda of documentation and diplomacy, Ferguson's forays into the Gold Coast's northern hinterland may be considered a "technology of power" (Thomas 1994) giving form and force to the colonial state. As an agent of the British administration, Ferguson expressed its interests not just in his actions but, of equal import, in his perceptions and evaluations of the region. As the author of the first state-sanctioned surveys of the area, Ferguson was the one who rendered the physical, social, political, and economic landscape of the north knowable and penetrable. Such accounts served as the foundation for a more common knowledge of the north and authorized future action on his part as well as that of others. Thomas comments on this interplay of knowledge and power at the heart of colonial discourses, characterizing them as "efforts that produce scope for surveillance as they describe and identify particular populations and social problems: that create charters for intervention as they express the omniscience of the colonial state" (1994: 41).

Specifically, in chronicling his journey, Ferguson's sights are set on a central object: the unobstructed movement of goods in and out of the savanna zone. This logic informs his reading and recording of nearly all that he encounters, from the waterways, geological formations, and forests, to the strength of rulers and the nature of material culture. He notes the rates and routes of caravan travel, the products of the areas, the European articles that would be acceptable to northern residents, the routes by which trade flows into the northern parts of the colony, the presence of tolls and middlemen, and disputes among chiefs that might disturb trade (Ferguson 1974: 78). Even the presence of Europeans in the area is discussed in terms of their success or failure at trade, the identities of their trading partners, and the sort of items they exchanged (1974: 89). Driven by this framework, the commercial potential of shea, among other indigenous commodities, was researched and remarked upon by Ferguson in great detail (1974: 68, 78).

Despite the singularity of his agenda, by the end of 1895, Ferguson's treaty-making mission began to break down. This occurred as new political imperatives came to the fore, stimulating the colonial regime to increase its power and presence in the north and to pursue increasingly exclusive strategies of rule. Such a political reorientation signaled the renewed importance of direct military intervention among the European powers competing for control of the West African subregion. Termed "effective occupation," the establishment of a military presence emerged at this time as the only means of establishing binding administrative claims. Tied to assertions of exclusive control, these tactics would pave the way for patterns of imperial rule in the northern savanna grounded in notions of territorial sovereignty.[3] In economic terms, this sort of territorialization was marked by a shift from a concern with the cultivation of material flows in and out of the area—that is, the kinds of things that flowed, where, under whose direction—to a concern with the control of particular sites of trade and the conventions of exchange. This was, in short, a move from a preoccupation with the constitution of commodity paths (Appadurai 1986) to the constitution and containment of marketplaces. These shifts would lay the foundation for the later bifurcation of the shea economy into distinctive domestic and export sectors characterized by different values and modes of operation—but not until the competing mandates of the many states vying for control of the region had been laid to rest.

Shaped by the overlapping objectives of forging exclusive and territorially based political control and cultivating market-based patterns of exchange, the strategies of effective occupation pursued by the British colonial administration in the savanna territories north of the Gold Coast revolved around the struggle to control two economic centers: Mossi and Mamprussi. Not only did these two polities and the territories under them encompass the crossroads of a number of indigenous trade routes, they stood, moreover, at the boundary of competing European interests: an Anglo-French interface in the case of Mossi, and an Anglo-French-German interface in the case of Mamprussi. While the British had considered Mossi its ally and trading partner on the basis of prior treaties, by the fall of 1896 these claims were challenged by the realities of French military occupation. A British officer posted in the savanna at the time gave the following report on the extent of French incursions into Mossi territory: "The news from Moshi country. . . . One French expedition consisting of two white officers and 400 soldiers arrived at Wagadugu three months ago . . . burnt the Kings palace, stayed thirty days, withdrawn to Yariga . . . had a flag flying in Waga." (Metcalfe 1964: 493).[4]

Fearing the possible movement of the French south of Mossi as well as the movement from the east of Germans who already occupied the nearby trading center of Sansanne-Mango (in what is today northwest Togo), the British hastened to claim Mamprussi as their own. By the end of December 1896, they had hoisted the British flag, reaffirmed the treaty with the Nayiri (the leader of Mamprussi), and established Gambaga, some twenty-five miles south of Bawku, as their command post for the whole of the Northern Territories and as a launching point for British military dispatches. By October 1897 a commissioner and commandant of native territories of the Gold Coast was selected and stationed at Gambaga, along with a large contingent of soldiers (Metcalfe 1964: 502). In this way the flexible economic alliances encountered and engaged by Ferguson came to be replaced by the permanent and militarized presence of British agents and officials.

The competition for resources and regional dominance among European powers was further complicated by indigenous power struggles, at this time coming from Samory and his army. Samory's forces, operating near the town of Wa at the western edge of the Gold Coast's interests in the savanna (where Ferguson was killed by Samory's forces in 1897), posed a threat to both British and French interests. At the same time, Germany allied itself with Samory's army in the Neutral Zone, deepening British animosity toward both parties. While the French ultimately demobilized Samory's forces in the area, this was not before the British were forced to release their westernmost territorial claims (Metcalfe 1964: 487). With the threat of further incursions resolved, in June of 1898 France and Britain came to an agreement regarding the boundaries of their respective jurisdictions in the Gold Coast colony's northern hinterland.[5] This was followed by an Anglo-German boundary agreement in November 1899.[6] Plans for formal recognition of the northern savanna as a protectorate of the Gold Coast colony got under way in 1900 and were made effective in 1902 (Owusu-Ansah and McFarland 1995: 171). These orders did not mandate the annexation of the Northern Territories to the Gold Coast colony but instead deemed them a separate protectorate under military administration (Ladoucer 1979: 40–1).

The designation of the Northern Territories as a protectorate of the Gold Coast colony facilitated the actualization of a complex of economic controls first emerging through the process of effective occupation. Replacing the colonial administration's prior preoccupation with the creation of extensive trade corridors, these new tactics—made possible by the greatly increased presence of the colonial state and its representatives—were much more localized and intensive. As mentioned above, such interventions centered on the management of marketplaces, beginning with the establishment of government stores alongside the administration's headquarters in Gambaga and Wa to supply European goods to caravan traders. Addressing the location and conventions of trade along with the character of consumers and commodities, they rendered markets in the northern savanna the primary site for the assertion of state power and presence and thus very much a colonial construct, despite their indigenous foundation.

Accordingly, as the number of stations in the northern territories grew, commercial management came to play an increasingly important role in political administration. This was apparent in Bawku, where the colonial government established a permanent outpost in 1909. Less than a year later, the town was described as the "largest market in the Protectorate" (Great Britain Colonial Office 1910, p.8, quoted in Roncoli 1994: 125).

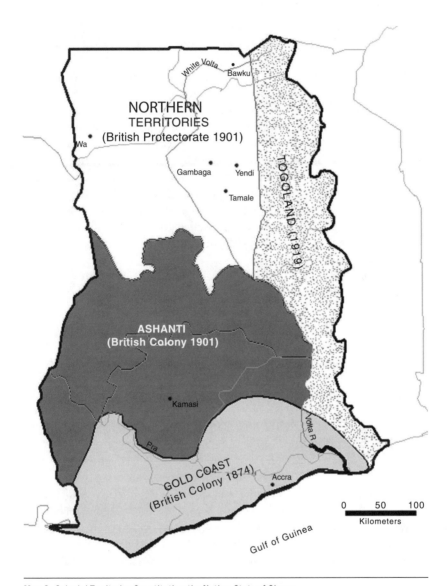

Map 6 Colonial Territories Constituting the Nation-State of Ghana

Here, as in other administrative centers, the sustained and widespread presence of a British officer corps along with native clerks and soldiers at the district and subdistrict levels went hand in hand with the organization of permanent local marketplaces and the institution of highly specific exchange conventions. Prior to colonial incursions, markets in and around Bawku, like other long-established way stations for the merchant caravans

plying the region, already hosted a steady trade in local and regional produce—including grain, livestock, salt, handwoven cotton cloth, and iron
hoes as well as shea butter—in which long-distance traders and local residents took part (Roncoli 1994: 125) As the colonial administration became
more involved in the promotion and regulation of northern markets, these
circuits of exchange were both enlarged and restructured.

Some of the growth can be attributed to the presence of a new class of
consumers, namely colonial officials, who relied on the market for their
own provisioning. Indeed, the local market for shea surged during this period of colonial occupation, as non-African administrators and the Hausa
and Moshi constables alike regularly purchased shea butter, among other
commodities, to use in food preparation. More significant, however, for
the scope and organization of trade as well as the projection and percep-
tion of state authority was colonial officers' regulation of the form and
function of local markets.

Attesting to the administration's concern about the structure of the indigenous economy and revealing the distinct conceptions of economic
order driving colonial practices of economic engagement, colonial records
from northern Ghana abound with observations of market conditions
and the role of colonial officers in their management. Imposing what they
held to be "free-market principles" but what were instead highly specific
tactics for the control of persons and commodities and the generation and
circulation of wealth, expatriate officers operating in the Gold Coast's
Northern Protectorate interfered with the timing, location, parameters,
and personnel of market-based exchange. Fostering the centralizing capacities of markets, colonial officials facilitated the growth of major marketplaces[7] and discouraged the emergence and survival of smaller satellite
markets.[8]

In Bawku, designated a commercial center, the colonial government invested in commercial infrastructure such as market stalls and store blocks,
stimulating the movement of both European imports and local and regional produce in and out of the town (Watherston 1908a: 192). In other
communities, markets were denied improvement or ordered closed
despite the fact that in some cases they were larger and longer-lived commercial venues than Bawku (Roncoli 1994: 128). Further discouraging
commercial activity beyond the realm of administrative mandate, community leaders were fined for permitting trade in markets designated closed.
In contrast, in Bawku—a target of administrative investment and monitoring—the market was expanded spatially and temporally to accommodate nighttime trade and the needs of full-time professional traders.[9]

In the markets of Bawku District, as in other economic centers, colonial officers, under the guise of promoting fair trade, closely monitored
commercial conduct in order to establish and enforce who could right-

fully participate in and profit from trading opportunities. Playing on distinctions between insiders and outsiders—the latter frequently blamed for upsetting the balance of the "natural economy"—colonial officials employed exclusionary tactics to designate lawful versus unlawful modes of market behavior. In the process, Bawku's markets were promoted as "localized" institutions tied to specific populations and places, while the linkages they provided to other persons and sites were curtailed. This is evident in a case heard in the district court, where wives of constables (otherwise known as "native police") were charged by the administration with wrongfully purchasing food for transit trade before it reached the local market.[10]

In another case, Hausa, Moshi, and Dagomba traders were accused of purchasing foodstuffs directly from households to retail in the market at an enhanced price, a practice leading one officer to suggest that a market "exclusively for the natives of the district" be established along with the imposition of taxes on "all alien peddlers and hawkers."[11] In yet another instance of colonial market control, constables were instructed to obstruct cross-border trade and contain the influx of residents from neighboring French territories in order to facilitate the supply of goods to local markets at "at fair market rates," and officers even went so far as to establish "fair market prices" for the goods traded.[12] In this manner, northern markets served as a key site for the designation and monitoring of political subjects by the agents of the colonial state, establishing a foundation for increasing state regulation of the shea economy.

Further demonstrating the political entailments of market controls, colonial officials' restructuring of northern commerce also involved the introduction of new forms of currency. As Hart aptly points out, "there are two sides to a coin" (1986: 646), since money serves as an abstracted and thereby universalizing measure of value (Hart 1982a: 40) at the same time as it stands for authority of the state and "emphasizes the role of law and government intervention" (Hart 1986: 646). Indeed, in northern Ghana the monitoring of currency use within the market was a key way in which the colonial state made its power both public and binding. Upon its initial introduction, the circulation of British currency in the north was confined to markets and stations under the close watch of colonial officers (Bening 1973a: 14), and even when it was circulated more broadly, officers made currency use and abuse the grounds for discipline of savanna traders and residents alike. According to Roncoli:

> Initial reactions to the new currency puzzled British colonial officers, who considered money to be an essential element of civilization and were greatly distressed to find that the new coins were more often used to make jewelry or embroider women's clothing than to exchange things in the market. (Roncoli 1994: 126)

In Bawku District, where the Kusasi and Busansi traders tried to avoid using the British West Africa coinage (probably because the limited denominations tended to enhance the price of local produce), officers worked hard to impose their own economic logic.[13] Several noted in their reports that "efforts were made to explain that the money was 100 per cent tender in British West Africa,"[14] and "as the market happened to be in progress efforts were made to explain its uses and advantages over the cowry, with the result that some of the leaf clad vendors expressed their understanding."[15] Others officers were not so sanguine about northern traders' capacity for economic reform, using the persistence of cowry currencies as proof of their inferiority and need for both overrule and reeducation. Expressing this point of view, the district commissioner of Bawku remarked in his 1913 diary:

> I am convinced that the majority of the people, anyway those connected with buying and selling local produce at the various markets, and these for the most part consist of women, do not realize the value of silver coins, even that of a 3d. piece. Their intellect has not at present been sufficiently developed to grasp the value of more than twenty or thirty cowries (Adm. 56.1.468, Sept. 30, 1913). (Roncoli 1994: 126)

Even traders already using the new currency were the target of administrative admonitions. Merchants were fined and imprisoned if they did not abide by administrative standards. Traders were often punished for profiting from currency conversions, as in one case when a Bawku market trader, Mama Moshi, was sentenced "to fourteen days imprisonment, hard labor, for deducting 16 per cent in changing silver into nickel coins".[16]

These examples convey the critical role played by market controls and trading conventions in the process of state-building. This was not, as many have assumed, because markets were necessarily a source of substantial revenue for the colonial administration—an assertion for which the evidence is equivocal. To whit, while market fees were beginning to be collected during this era, caravan tolls, a much more substantial source of revenue, were being abolished. More decisively, in terms of the expression and actualization of state power, colonial restructuring of northern markets was integral to the instantiation of a new political subjectivity in the northern savanna. Such a political subjectivity was built upon the distinction between insiders and outsiders along with the territorialization of state control in terms of where trade could and could not take place and who could and could not enter arenas of exchange so designated. Going hand in hand with the process of territorialization, as the economic range of each market in terms of commodities, customers, and geographic reach came to be specified, was a dynamic that can be described as "localization," a tactic central to the process of building a nation out of discrete and comparable jurisdictions (Anderson 1991; Bening 1999). Finally, by regulating the conventions of exchange, colonial agents forged a foundation for both monitoring individual persons and orchestrating their incorporation into a much wider body politic that included the Gold Coast colony and the neighboring possessions of British West Africa.

World Markets, Private Capital, and National Vision

By the end of first decade of British occupation, with the system of district administration firmly in place and market controls well enforced and elaborated, colonial economic policy in Northern Ghana changed once again, further affecting the character and expression of state authority in the north and with it the market potential of shea. Tied not to the management of domestic markets as much as to the expansion of external ones, these shifts in economic policy and practice centered on the development of foreign markets for indigenous commodities. Fulfilling the vision articulated by Ferguson on his first expedition north nearly twenty years earlier, these commodities included shea nuts and shea butter. Yet, encompassing economic relationships and arenas of economic life previously beyond the reach of the colonial administration, the realization of this economic agenda extended the realm of state power.

This process was by no means smooth or uncontested. Because it involved close collaboration with actors and institutions outside the state as well as coordination among many different sectors of the colonial regime, this strategy of market development worked initially to diffuse rather than deepen state authority. As a corrective, this would lead some years later to the heightened assertion of state power to the exclusion of other interests. In its earliest instantiations, however, export market development in the northern savanna—in which shea occupied a central place—depended heavily on the joint efforts of private, primarily British, mercantile interests and the colonial government. Within this rubric, private companies did not enter the shea market on their own accord but operated at the behest of the state. Despite such collaboration, the means and ends of both parties were neither constant nor well coordinated, resulting in a rather unstable agenda of commercial reform. This unevenness was complicated further by lack of consensus within the colonial state regarding the significance of resources from the Northern Territories to metropolitan markets and the Gold Coast colony overall and the means of realizing their value. In political terms, the promotion of shea export provided the foundation for new forms of state engagement of northern economies and residents at the same time as it inserted them into new contests between the state and private capital and among state-based institutions and actors.

Upon the introduction of the colonial platform of export development, government agents appealed directly to European commercial interests to establish operations in the Northern Territories. In his 1908 address on "Trade Possibilities in the Northern Territories of the Gold Coast," delivered to the Liverpool Chamber of Commerce, the chief commissioner for the Northern Territories, A. E. Watherston, discussed the gains to be made from commerce in the north, stressing the wide range of forest products, from timber and beeswax to silk cocoons and shea, along with the possibility of cotton and tobacco farming amenable to European-sponsored production and trade (1908a: 192–3). Responding to these commercial opportunities, by the 1910s export markets, albeit limited ones, for commodities from the Northern Territories were gradually emerging. At this juncture, although private commercial interests played an instrumental role in market development, they relied heavily on the state to provide and facilitate commercial opportunities.

Shea was the target of extensive promotional efforts. Colonial agencies touted the possibilities for shea consumption abroad and its potential value to European industry and markets. Research played a prominent role in colonial export promotion campaigns, and numerous studies on shea were carried out by colonial agencies. A large number were publicized in the *Bulletin of the Imperial Institute*,[17] which was both a scientific journal full of detailed measurements, chemical analysis, technology assessments, and botanical terminology, and a marketing handbook devoted to all possible exports from the colonies. As early as 1912, an article examined and compared shea nuts from the Gold Coast, northern Nigeria, and the Sudan (Imperial Institute 1912a: 281–92). Later, experiments were carried out with the aim of devising new uses for shea,[18] including, among other things, the incorporation of the residue from oil extraction in animal feed and the employment of shea leaves for fermentation in gin production, and the results were once again published in the *Bulletin*.[19]

While the information contained in colonial trade publications like that of the Imperial Institute helped to provoke an interest in African exports, the details of commerce were left to be worked out by private firms with the aid of colonial officials on the ground. The Liverpool-based African Association Limited, with branches in the Canary Islands, throughout the Gold Coast, and Southern Nigeria, was one company involved in such a partnership. The African Association functioned as both a broker and a market developer. In the first instance, it linked metropolitan demands and tropical suppliers, soliciting particular commodities at set prices from African sources. Several products from Northern Ghana—"'guinea grains' (a form of millet), kola nuts, beeswax, goat skins and cow hides," as well as shea[20]—were procured for European clients in this manner.

To accomplish this, the African Association mobilized the resources of the colonial regime, appealing to high-ranking colonial officers, including the chief commissioner of the Northern Territories, for market data and the relay of information to its Kumasi and Liverpool offices.[21] Securing samples and arranging for their transport south, the officers functioned like northern-based company agents, making it unnecessary for actual company representatives to visit the supply zones. In fulfilling such a role, these administrators served to mediate the relationship between metropolitan firms and the local commercial institutions. The provincial commissioner of Tamale, for example, in July 1913 engaged the chief of a nearby village—his local liaison and not necessarily a leading or experienced shea trader—to supply him with the shea nuts desired by the African Association's Kumasi branch. The nuts were then sent south via carriers in the employ of the Northern Territories administration to Ejura and by government transport to Kumasi.[22]

Despite many accommodations on the part of individual officers within the colonial government, shea export trials were found to be a financial loss due to high transport charges from the north. Selling for a price of ten pounds sterling per ton in Liverpool in 1914, shea nuts were sold by the African Association for a loss of two to three pounds sterling on each ton.[23] This sort of market failure was both conceptual and logistic in origin. Although shea was a staple good in the West African savanna, where nuts were gathered from the bush and processed at home at no cost or cheaply purchased in local markets, outside the savanna zone—whether the Sahel, coast, or forest—shea was a luxury item, fetching a considerably higher price in the markets of Kumasi than in the savanna in the teens and twenties. European exporters—and their counterparts in the colonial administration—in contrast saw shea as an industrial raw material with mass-market potential that should be sold on the world market at a low price to those engaged in manufacture, like most other tropical exports at the time.

The disjuncture between shea's status as a luxury good within West African circuits of long-distance trade and the industry-oriented ideals of value pursued by European merchants was heightened, moreover, by the uneven role of the colonial state in export promotion. Without a doubt, government personnel and institutions were intensely involved in market development. Yet this support was poorly coordinated both internally and internationally. The state's efforts to foster export markets existed on a very broad scale—in terms of research—and a very detailed one—in terms of the action of officials in the north—but overlooked mesolevel linkages, namely, the institution of a transport system necessary for the movement of goods at a scale and cost compatible with European demand for cheap tropical commodities. Even with these limitations, however, export trials and inquiries from private firms prevailed, intensifying apace with Europe's industrial growth and the burgeoning market for low-priced and versatile raw materials from the tropics (Hopkins 1973; Shenton 1986).

Responding to these shortcomings and opportunities, in the 1920s colonial economic policy was revamped again, combining an agenda of infrastructure improvement with the large-scale promotion of exports from both the northern and southern sectors of the Gold Coast. Yet as the colonial project expanded in scope and scale, intensifying the need for coordination and collaboration, the divergence of state and private interests as well as interests within the state became more pronounced. By this time, colonial objectives in the Northern Protectorate were overwhelmingly outward in orientation, tying the region to the colony as a whole and, in turn, to metropolitan markets. Having more to do with the changing political climate of the protectorate than changing market conditions abroad, this reorientation was initiated with the appointment of F. G. Guggisberg as governor of the Gold Coast colony in 1919.[24] In the service of building a nation out of the diverse territories of the Gold Coast, the program of economic reform promoted by Guggisberg was premised on the idea of consolidation—an initiative that combined the coordination of resource flows with the concentration of political controls.

Guided by these objectives, Guggisberg's economic agenda was multifaceted and multilocal. Guggisberg's plan focused on export promotion and diversification in all regions of the Gold Coast—from the colony to Ashanti and the Northern Territories—and the expansion and improvement of transport facilities—from roads and rails to waterways and harbors—in order to get goods to market cheaply and efficiently (Kay 1972: 42). Within this framework, the Northern Territories were considered a source of substantial though as yet untapped value in their own right rather than marginal to or dependent upon the colony and Ashanti. From Guggisberg's point of view, it was the north, through the production and export of crops such as shea, which held the promise of balancing out and rescuing the economy of the south after the bust of Ghana's cocoa boom in the aftermath of World War I, if only it could be "opened up." The governor's annual address of 1921-to-1922 well illustrates this "nation-wide" market model:

> Rice, copra, sisal and sugar are all articles of produce which the government is now encouraging, but when all is said and done, none of them is likely to turn into huge items of export. We must not neglect them—indeed we must encourage both them and any small item of export in any possible way. But what we want is something that will rival cocoa—something that will place us more firmly than ever at the top of the crown colony produce ladder. Now honorable members, I have been accused of being a faddist about the northern territories. I plead guilty to the accusation, but if I am a faddist, I am a faddist backed by reason . . . I repeat now what I said last month . . . that the whole future of the

Gold Coast is bound up with the development of the ground nut and shea butter industries of the Northern territories. As for the shea-nut we should be in an unrivalled position . . . with means of transportation—with a deep-water harbor at Takoradi and a railway from the neighborhood of Tamale—we will assure the safety of the gold coast trade. We shall have four large baskets of articles greatly in demand—cocoa and palm oil from the south—ground-nuts and shea butter from the north—together with seven little baskets of rice, copra, sisal, corn, sugar, coffee and tobacco—little baskets . . . but good. . . . And with the safety of our trade assured comes assurance of our revenue—the sinews of war for our campaign of education and progress. (Kay 1972: 51–2)

Hence in Guggisberg's eyes the economy of the Gold Coast as a whole promised improvement if all three regions were thought of in common terms of export potential, and if the movement of goods were parallel (cocoa and palm, shea nuts and groundnuts), coordinated (big and little baskets), and contiguous (sharing the same pathways of export). Yet in the case of the northern savanna, the premise of consolidation driving Guggisberg's inclusive rhetoric did not always match the realities of policy implementation. As is evident with regard to shea, while export initiatives intensified, so did competition between the colonial state and private firms. As both groups struggled to assert control over shea exports, their involvement in the northern economy grew apace, increasing the presence of foreign agents and the engagement of indigenous actors and economic institutions as new patterns of shea processing and procurement were introduced. Ultimately, the power and interests of the colonial state came to prevail, limiting private firms from further investment in the export sector and enabling the colonial government to build its own set of economic controls upon an edifice previously established by private capital.

The growing tension between state actors and private merchants during the 1920s may be attributed to the increased strength and shifting orientation of European firms in northern Ghana. Compared to the previous decade, by this time there was a large number of European companies involved in shea export.[25] Some, like the African Products Development Corporation, were tied to much larger conglomerates, in this case the Niger Company. The African and Eastern Trade Company was likewise affiliated with Lever Brothers.[26] Others, such as the Accra firm of W. Barthalomew and Co., their letterhead reading "Motor Engineers and Produce Merchants," were somewhat smaller and more locally based. In contrast to the few firms that had previously dabbled in shea export, most of the new entrants into the shea market desired to export nuts or butter on a relatively large scale, seeking trial shipments of nuts from 200 to 1000 tons. They were characterized, moreover, by an industrial rather than mercantile orientation, indicating the entry of shea and shea trading firms into Europe's rapidly growing manufacturing sector.[27]

Signaling their generally competitive stance, several private firms sought to apply technological innovations to the processing of shea even prior to export. MacIlwaine Patents Syndicate, for one, proposed a process for pressing and baling shea nuts prior to transshipment in order to reduce bulk and lower transport costs.[28] These sorts of mechanical innovations are indicative of private companies' continued efforts to remake shea physically and conceptually into a tropical commodity ideally suited to the European market: low in cost, portable, ever manipulable, and effectively equivalent to other tropical oil seeds. This was clearly a different sort of commercial value from that represented by shea within the West African economy, whether as a staple of the savanna economy appreciated for its own unique and diverse qualities or as a luxury good within long-distance trading circuits and regional markets.

Such a proactive approach to market opportunities on the part of private firms was equally apparent in their relationship to the colonial state. Rather than allowing the state to define the parameters of commerce as before, state institutions and agents were enlisted to fulfill a game plan the companies had already devised. Most firms, for example, asked the administration to defray a percentage of their transport costs. One, Millers Ltd., after it had already established a purchasing system, requested the administration's support in convincing local people of the fairness of the company's price for shea.[29] The same company also arranged a partnership between a Kumasi transport firm and the government Motor Transport Department to haul government stores to and shea nuts from Salaga, bypassing the input of local officials.[30]

The intensification of private firms' involvement in the export sector—and the challenge this presented to colonial control—was also evident in their increased presence in the Northern Territories. A large number of firms commissioned agents, some based abroad, others working out of Kumasi or Accra, to check out the shea nut market "on the spot" during brief visits or long-term postings in northern supply zones.[31] Rather than confining themselves to only the better-known markets, these private company agents explored a wide range of sources for shea, along with new ways to access them.

As they sought to exploit the economic space of the north, transportation became a clear priority of private investors. Walkden and Company, proposing to "open up buying stations in various centers," inquired if "there are any good roads tapping the various districts suitable for motor transportation?"[32] And the African Products Development Corporation even suggested building motor roads themselves in order to access nuts.[33] Indeed, the growing tendency for private companies to put their personnel and installations literally "on-site" helped to assert their interests and control. This is strikingly evident in the African Products Development Corporation's proposal to establish a shea butter processing plant in the Northern Territories. Along with the establishment of a plant "somewhere in the vicinity of Yeji or Salaga" to meet the needs of Messrs de Bruyn, the "big [Belgian] margarine makers," the company sought to arrange "with certain prominent chiefs" exclusive rights of access to nuts from prime supply areas.[34]

Despite the colonial administration's professed interest in export development, investors' efforts to establish private export processing and procurement zones were blocked by top colonial officials due to the threat they presented to the state's interest in commercial control. Rather than laying the foundation for long-term investment, firms were granted only temporary rights to purchase and process shea with strict conditionalities.[35] Representing the rising rift between the imperial state and private European enterprise, colonial administrators' opposition to the commercial aspirations of private firms involved in shea commercialization had several bases. Most significantly, colonial agents were concerned that whoever took initial responsibility for export development would ultimately reap the greatest benefit. According to this logic, the ease of deferring responsibility to private firms early on would eventually result in the state's loss of resources and control over their allocation in the long run. These sentiments were made explicit in the remarks of the Gold Coast director of agriculture to the British secretary of state in reference to the privatization of a similar commercial endeavor a few years later: "Where the risks of failure are so great and the benefits resulting from success so general to the whole Colony, it seems to me that, not only is the government justified in accepting the responsibility, but the matter should not be left to private enterprise" (Kay 1972: 226).

In addition to the competing interests surrounding access to material resources in the north, the question of ties to indigenous institutions and leaders also stood between the colonial government and private firms. By establishing their own contacts in savanna communities, the private companies were felt to threaten a crucial source of administrative power, potentially undermining colonial agents' ability to command cooperation from local rulers and communities in other endeavors.

Landscapes on Value and the Labors of Rule

At the same time as private firms were attempting to intensify their stake in the export of northern commodities, state agencies were laying the groundwork for a new series of interventions into the savanna economy also focused on the exploitation and export of shea. As the colonial administration worked to gain control over the dynamics of export promotion in the Northern Territories, its agents, procedures, and ideals entered into realms of rural economic life from which they had heretofore been absent, leading to a multiplicity of projects and policies centering on the assessment, stimulation, and realization of shea's export potential. Much more than simply controlling the circulation of shea, colonial directives involved remodeling the shea economy *in toto*, and included, for the first time, efforts to restructure shea production.

This economic project, like that which preceded it, was inherently political in nature, extending the reach of the state into new arenas of life, introducing new values, and inciting contestation from within and without. The tactics of intervention employed and political outcomes achieved were rather different in character from what came before, however. Imposing a totalizing conceptual grid upon its economic subjects, they rendered state presence in the Northern Territories all the more pervasive and fueled the ascendance of the Political Office over and above other sectors of the colonial government at the same time as they undermined the opportunities for private capital in market development.

An essential feature of this new rubric of economic intervention was empirical research on shea carried out within the colonial territory rather than abroad. This included research by numerous sectors of the colonial bureaucracy, from regional and district-level political officers and members of the Forestry and Agricultural Departments in the Northern Territories to the colony's chief agricultural officer at the main research station of Aburi outside of Accra. Some studies, documentary in nature, centered on evaluating the prevalence of nut and butter supplies and identifying the conditions and methods of cultivation and processing, generating the highest yields. Others, more innovative, experimented with new modes of cultivation, processing, and use, and focused on incentives to intensify commercially oriented nut and butter production. They incited as much dissent as cooperation, and the result was a proliferation of expert opinions and objectives.

These research agendas relied on modes of classification and measurement that may be characterized as "intellectual technologies"—subtle yet pervasive conceptual grids integral to the assertion of state power (Miller and Rose 1990). Encompassing various procedures—written, numeric, and schematic—of documentation, computation, and evaluation that rendered material conditions "into a knowable, calculable and administrable object" where they could be "debated and diagnosed" (1990: 5–7), these symbolic logics represented a form of political ordering in that their "institutions, procedures, analyses and reflections allowed the exercise of power over populations" (Thomas 1994: 42)—in this case, the residents of the Northern Territories.

Fostering distinctive forms of political order and furthering the power of the state, the classification schemes upon which colonial programs of research and commercial development depended and served to reproduce were thoroughly bound up with ideas of objectification, treating value as eminently concrete and calculable. The programs of rule built upon these shared notions of value, however, were not easily applied to the social or material reality they claimed to represent. This is attributable only in part to local resistance or the resilience of alternative sources of economic motivation and conceptions of worth. Exemplifying the manifold "tensions of empire" underlying what is typically considered to be the common project of colonial rules and rulers (Cooper and Stoller 1997: 20), the difficulty of instituting economic programs premised on such ideas of objectification is equally attributable to dissonance within the colonial state itself, as different sectors of the colonial regime used this framework to promote distinctive goals.

Guided by a common vision of value and productivity, despite the disparate ends to which it would eventually be applied, documentation of shea economy and ecology began in earnest in 1920. At this time the conservator of forests requested the chief commissioner of the Northern Territories to involve officials from all the districts in the north in a comprehensive survey of shea. The survey was to document the quantity of butter produced in each district; the yield of a given quantity of nuts; the fraction of available nuts collected and reasons why nuts were left uncollected; and the existence of attempts at plantation-style cultivation. Responses to the conservator's inquiries were brief and generally impressionistic, reporting wide-ranging numerical differences in nut and butter yields. There were, however, several observations held in common by Northern Territory officials: shea grew wild everywhere; there were large and untapped nut supplies; trees tended to experience uneven yields, going through cycles of two good years and one bad; and shea butter was produced for local use with the surplus being traded in other communities.[36] With the simple goal of gaining access to the wild tree stocks, the conservator of forests recommended in his assessment of these findings that adequate shea supplies for export could best be obtained by building roads to otherwise hard-to- reach shea forests.[37]

The next year a more rigorous research plan would supplant these initial haphazard accounts, and an alternative commercial vision would override the conservator's proposal, but not before controversy over assessments, interests, and funds erupted between the Political Office and the Department of Agriculture. In 1921, under orders of the governor, shea research was established as the purview of the Department of Agriculture. At this time, a single officer was dispatched to the north to inspect shea supplies and market conditions and to act as the liaison between the government and private companies still operating in the area.[38] After a brief tour in the vicinity of Salaga, Tamale and Yendi, the officer concluded that northern shea supplies were much lower than previously reported and suggested that earlier assessments by political officers were based on confusion between shea and a similar-looking tree of a different species.[39] He recommended, finally, that shea promotion efforts should be curtailed,[40] leading the Department of Agriculture to drop funding for further shea research.[41]

Struggling to reclaim one of the pillars of his authority in the north, the chief commissioner of the Northern Territories staunchly opposed the rulings of his counterparts in the Agricultural Department. Asserting the rightfulness of the political officer's mission in the north, the commissioner wrote defensively to the head office of the Agriculture Department at Aburi: "I do not suppose there is a single political officer in the Northern Territories who does not know a shea butter tree when he sees it and if he does not he must be decidedly wanting in intelligence." He went on to argue that the recommendations of the agricultural officer were entirely illegitimate as they went against the orders and interests of the Gold Coast governor.[42]

Although this clash may seem trivial, it was actually quite telling, as it encoded multiple levels of dissonance that were to resurface in the course of negotiating export promotion policies. More than indicating the likely disparity between the governor's aspirations and actual conditions on the ground, the exchange between the chief commissioner of the Northern Territories and the Department of Agriculture brought to light the competing purview of agricultural versus political officers, along with the different understandings of commercial potential to which they subscribed. While officers in the Forestry, Agriculture, and Political departments were all interested in maximizing the amount of shea available on the market and surveying the physical landscape to calculate this potential, each group employed different criteria to evaluate shea's commercial promise.

Familiar with the character of woody species and the highly diversified character of plant ensembles in the bush (whether virgin forest or overgrown fallow), foresters saw few obstacles to tapping this dispersed resource base that could not be solved simply by "getting there," as mentioned above. Agricultural officers, on the other hand, oriented to a model of intensive cultivation in the tropics based on spatially concentrated monocropping at odds with the reality of a wild woody species like shea, were noticeably distressed by what appeared to be the sparse and unreliable distribution of shea. Shea could conform to the standards of the agricultural officers under only one set of circumstances: plantation-based production. With this vision in mind, by 1922, agricultural officers in the north turned their attention to the establishment of a shea reserve in Yendi, forsaking the productive potential of already existing tree stands.

While sharing forestry and agricultural officers' concern with maximization, political officers held a different understanding of how to realize that value. Rather than the control of particular places, as in the case of forestry, or the concentration of resources, as in the case of agriculture, for political officers this centered on the control of persons—a perspective reflecting the department's broader mandate of defining and managing proper political subjects. Preoccupied with the application and availability of labor, the agenda of political officers in the Northern Territories sought to further distinctively capitalist notions of value and productivity. In the course of their research, not only was the physical landscape rendered a site of empirical observation and measurement, but so, too, was the human landscape, since human labor was held to be a discrete force shaping the commercial potential of shea.[43] Objectified in this way, both the physical environment and people's work were considered manipulable in a manner that would maximize their inherent worth. Such a labor-centered perspective, first articulated within the Political Office, would gradually infiltrate the policies and outlook of both the Forestry and Agricultural departments.

As a first step in applying a labor-centered approach to the realization of commercial value, in 1922 political officers in the Northern Territories carried out an extensive research program detailing shea cover and yield in each district. They aimed to locate the highest-yielding trees and areas and to identify the reasons for their productivity. They also sought to document the most productive methods of nut picking and shea butter preparation. Political officers were instructed to collect botanical specimens of leaves, flowers, and fruit as well as butter samples, along with detailed records of their source and history. Foremost, officers in the north were charged with carrying out a special governor's directive that "[e]ach DC from time to time while traveling will mark off a temporary 10 acre plot for survey in order to find areas in districts with highest tree density."[44] To obtain this knowledge, it was necessary for political officers themselves to apply their own labor to the landscape of the north, requiring them to come to know the economic terrain of shea through the very same logic they would use to represent and control it. For district officers and their staff in the Northern Territories, this was a form of labor thoroughly bound up with measurement and calculation, with identifying sources of material and quantifiable value and the processes responsible for them. Through the logic of labor, then, the landscape of northern Ghana became both knowable and known to these representatives of the colonial regime and hence an object of engagement.

Like their forebear Ferguson, political officers became deeply immersed in the physical environment of the Northern Territories in their quest to comprehend and realize the commercial potential of its resources. However, the administrative expedition on which they embarked was fundamentally different from the one that had occupied the agents of colonial rule some thirty years earlier. Whereas Ferguson focused on motion and the realization of value through the movement of commodities from one place to another, political officers in the north were concerned with the notation and creation of value in place, treating commercial value as inherent to the immediate landscape, not external to it. Central to this endeavor was an extensive mapping project intended to locate and count the stands of shea trees in each district, collect and measure the yields of selective plots, and measure tree growth. With the counting of shea trees operating as a "locus" of knowledge (i.e., of knowing about the local/e), political officers became engaged in a multifaceted, wide-ranging, and ongoing interaction with the territories under their jurisdiction.

A. G. Cardinall (1920, 1927), a lawyer turned district commissioner and amateur ethnographer, remarked on the all-consuming character of this tracking project, of which he was part: "I venture to state that no white man has ever covered so much of the bush as I have. By which I mean that the country lying off the paths and roads is more familiar to me than to any other."[45] Cardinall was not alone; between 1922 and 1924 reports on shea were compiled by political officers throughout the entire Northern Territories, from Eastern and Western Gonja,[46] Bole,[47] Dagomba,[48] Kratchi,[49] Southern Province,[50] North and South Mamprussi,[51] Kusasi,[52] Zuarungu,[53] Navrongo,[54] Lawra-Tumu,[55] and Wa,[56] as well as the Mandated Area of Togoland.[57]

Officers from all districts counted shea trees and assessed yields on an average of forty-six 1- to 10-acre plots *each*, with individual district observations ranging from a high of 161 plots in Western Gonja[58] to a low of fourteen plots in North Mamprussi.[59] Sometimes the plots were marked out within a few miles of the district headquarters; more often, however, they were established throughout the district, in territories familiar and unfamiliar, cultivated and not, during a commissioner's patrols.[60] In the course of a 450-mile journey, one officer stopped ninety-five times to count shea trees—once every five miles.[61] Not only were trees counted, but each 10-acre plot was measured, its edges marked on boundary trees, and location logged and mapped—forms of calculation and situation that in the colonial mentality stood for order and knowledge.

Drawing on ideas similar to those of Miller and Rose (1990) regarding the way scientific knowledge both disguises and propels the symbolic logics of domination, McClintock remarks on the role of maps as technologies of power employed in the creation and exploitation of empire:

> The colonial map vividly embodies the contradictions of colonial discourse. Map-making became the servant of colonial plunder, for the knowledge constituted by the map both preceded and legitimized the conquest of territory. The map is a technology of knowledge that professes to capture the truth

about a place in pure, scientific form, operating under the guise of scientific exactitude and promising to retrieve and reproduce nature exactly as it is. As such, it is also a technology of possession, promising that those with the capacity to make such perfect representations must also have the right of territorial control. . . . The map is a liminal thing, associated with thresholds and marginal zones, burdened with dangerous powers. As an exemplary icon of imperial "truth," the map, like the compass and the mirror is what Hulme calls a "magic technology," a potent fetish helping colonials negotiate the perils of margins and thresholds in a world of terrifying ambiguities. (McClintock 1995: 27–8)

In the case of shea, McClintock is correct to point out the function of maps as a tool for the imposition of foreign values and visions, and indeed, the contradictory nature of colonial science (or any science for that matter), couching subjective interests in supposedly objective representations. Surely the mapping exercise undertaken by colonial officers in Northern Ghana imposed an alien numerical and topographical order on a landscape with its own logic, dually mapping foreign values onto a series of sites and at the same time mapping those sites into this preconceived framework. Such maps, by rendering the terms of shea's representation equivalent to the intended terms of its exploitation, effectively naturalized both. The cartographic exploits of each district office resulted in the visualization of the entire northern region in terms of the past, present, and future existence of shea, much like the commodity maps of encyclopedias and geography textbooks which still decorate the back covers of the Ghana Education Service notebooks. The configuration of other features of the environment—from physical characteristics to social ones such as population density, agriculture, and markets—were framed in terms of their relation to shea. In their detail and comprehensiveness, these images, in which shea was the central value, served as an overview of the whole of the north and were considered both meaningful and satisfactory to the governor, the colonial secretary, the chief commissioner of the Northern Territories and even the director of Agriculture.

Despite the many preconceptions driving it, the colonial administration's mapmaking exercise did not simply or singularly impose foreign values on the physical and social landscape of northern Ghana. As much as it rendered the landscape in terms familiar to colonial rulers, it also provided the means for colonial agents to forge an awareness of indigenous ecology and economic practice in the Northern Territories. In this manner, colonial mapping, as a form of ideological domination, depended on the acknowledgment and the recasting of the point of view and material realities of those it sought to control (Scott 1985). Caught in this exercise of colonial cartography, several officers noted distinctive patterns of tree growth and density in relation to the contours of land, the proximity of river beds, and the prevalence of soil types.[62] Preoccupied with the potential and application of labor, many more noted the relationship between human cultivation and habitation and shea tree density, size, and health. Observing farmers' practice of leaving shea trees standing in the fields—the older trees preserved and the healthiest of the seedlings protected—a number of political officers began to read the landscape in terms of the history of human agricultural practice through the state of shea trees, identifying new agricultural plots, recent fallows, and long-forgotten farms deep in the bush.[63]

The melding of an imposed optic with a new awareness of local conditions and practices was also evident in the second part of the documentation project: the creation and monitoring of experimental shea plots in each district. The purpose of this exercise was to calculate nut yields and the effect of particular silvacultural practices, especially burning, on yields and tree growth. Indeed, these measurements were subject to exhaustive computation—an exercise reflecting imperialism's valorization of quantitative rationality—as is clear in the report from the northwestern district of Lawra:

> Seventy 10 acre plots have been counted in different localities in the district. The 700 acres on which shea has been counted give the following statistics: 36241 shea trees (of whatever size) totaling an average over 700 acres of approx. 51 per acre. The greatest number of trees in any ten acre plot was 2200 and the least number was 10. 33 plots in the Tumu section show 19067 trees or approx. 58 trees/acre. 35 plots of 10 acres counted in the Lawra section give 17174 trees, approximately 46 per acre. There are estimated to be 1483456 acres in the District which grow shea trees. Statistics taken on 100 trees in the ten different localities over 100 miles of the country in 1924 showed that only 35 per cent were bearing fruit . . . some yields of trees weighed this year in which 941 lbs. per tree was the greatest yield and 7 lbs. the least, it has been approximated over the district 25 lbs. per tree which gives the total annual yield per annum for the district 397,189,625 lbs. of shea kernels.[64] (Adm 56.1.275: 19.7.24)

In the course of managing the experimental plots and arriving at these elaborately derived figures, political officers directly engaged members of surrounding communities. These encounters, much like the mapmaking exercise, initiated an enlargement of colonial models of and guidelines for managing the shea economy rather than their reformulation. On the Yendi reservation, one plot was "accidentally" burned by workmen in December (when local fields were usually burned), earlier than the agricultural officer planned. With that plot providing the best yield, recommendations were made to incorporate burning into protocols regarding commercial management. Cardinall, a meticulous observer of his surroundings, was confident that burning did no harm to the shea trees and worked to convince the Agricultural Department of this:

> It is beyond doubt that if the bush were not burnt the women with whom the collection of the nuts lies would not enter the bush. Not only would it would be almost impossible to pick up the windfalls or mature droppings but at the same time the danger of snakes would be too great. I have had many conversations on this point and all have agreed. The very fact that every year fires occur and every year the women collect the harvest from the same tree is sufficient evidence to disprove the theory of damage caused by fires.[65] (Adm 56.1.275: 11.8.24)

There was also a more concerted and deliberate emulation of local labor on the experimental plots. After observing and obtaining interview data on local collection methods, the officers copied the indigenous procedure of only collecting nuts from the ground rather than picking them from the shea trees.[66] Also in replication of the practices of local women, instead of gathering all of the nuts from one tree at a time, colonial officers made frequent sweeps of the entire plot.[67]

Colonial officials' growing knowledge about indigenous methods of shea production and procurement by no means inspired an ethic of preservation and instead was used to configure a very different commercial agenda from that pursued locally. This new initiative, while it advocated the replication of a number of established practices, did so on such a tremendous scale and in such an altered context that they took on entirely unprecedented significance. Articulating this program was a 1924 report, "The Shea Butter Industry of the Northern Territories of the Gold Coast," issued by the superintendent of Agriculture and Forestry. Premised on the idea of maximization, it endeavored to incite every able-bodied female, by which was meant "all women and girls over the age of six," to collect every possible nut from every tree, working every day for the ninety-day shea fruiting season.[68] Execution of this program promised a market of nine million pounds sterling in Liverpool.[69]

Colonial export promotion schemes also sought to combine longstanding modes of shea production and procurement in new ways, further rendering the familiar a vehicle of transformation. Though premised on observed facts, the permutations on which they were based made them highly speculative. It was surmised, for example, that people would readily camp out in remote "bush" areas to collect shea nuts just as they camped out on their fields during the height of the farming season.[70] Similarly, although shea was considered a woman's crop, once its commercial value increased, colonial officials speculated that men, since they already demonstrated an interest in wage labor and the marketing of other goods, would enter into the business of shea procurement and trade.[71] Likely based on the experience of the cocoa boom in Asante, colonial officials in the Northern Territories assumed that market forces would inspire large-scale population movements. As one department head put it: "The amount of over 53,000 tons could be increased by a migration of the population to the productive area, which would probably be a natural consequence of the growth of the industry."[72] In conjunction with the production and procurement of shea nuts, the colonial logic of *mise en valeur* or "putting into value" was extended to encompass the shea trade, similarly harnessing established commercial forms to the development of new commercial trajectories. Because there was already a regional market for butter, colonial officials expected that an expanded nut market geared to export could be incorporated into this commercial path,[73] and it was suggested that salt canoes from Addah, accustomed as they were to carrying butter, could easily accommodate the nut trade.[74]

In addition to building on already established forms, colonial administrators devised new mechanisms of distribution that they thought would best facilitate the realization of shea's export potential. In 1923 the superintendent of agriculture in the north set out to establish an independent marketing system geared to the purchase of nuts for export. Traveling throughout the Yendi, Tamale, and Salaga area, he met with local leaders "and as many followers as could be summoned"[75] to inform them of the colonial government's export marketing plans for both shea nuts and butter for the coming season. Similarly, the Gold Coast director of Agriculture proposed the establishment of shea trading centers within easy reach of local carriage as export markets.[76] Various district commissioners attempted to enlist local chiefs to convince their constituents to send nuts to select markets for sale to Europeans (Kay 1972: 73).[77] Even the governor of the Gold Coast became involved in mapping out the details of shea market reform, recommending that a nut purchasing scheme be centralized at Yendi (Kay 1972: 219). In 1928, one district commissioner proposed an elaborate purchasing scheme relying on male waged-labor gangs hired to collect the nuts and oversee their preparation for sale abroad—a laborious process of boiling, cracking, and drying. This was to be accompanied by the outfitting of nut processing centers with permanent installations of equipment for boiling and storage.[78]

These directives, posing labor intensification as the foundation of commercial growth, assumed this notion of value to be universal, or at least potentially so. Projecting this standard on residents of the north, one district official suggested "[t]he native of the north is an extremely industrious person who, notwithstanding the cheap and plentiful crops he raises has plenty of time hanging heavily on his hands which he would only be too willing to fill in undertaking any work which would make it worthwhile."[79]

Indeed, for colonial administrators, the need for labor could be satisfied by engaging what they took to be people's "natural" consumer mentality. Articulating this taken-for-granted point of view, in his annual address of 1923-to-1924, governor Guggisberg discussed the demonstration effects of wealth, asserting that a penchant to consume would spur export market growth. As he saw it, in the north, "trade is eagerly awaited by over 500,000 inhabitants whose desire for manufactured articles is daily whetted by laborers returning from the south" (Kay 1972: 203).

The colonial administration's concern with labor and the possibilities of labor intensification was equally apparent in its treatment of shea butter processing, which, like shea nut procurement and trade, was rendered an object of administrative scrutiny. Costing approximately fourteen pounds sterling per ton in Tamale and fetching thirty-two in Liverpool, butter exports promised a much greater potential for profit than nuts, which often sold for a loss on the European market due to the high cost of transport (Kay 1972: 219, 223, 226). Throughout the 1920s, district-level political officers along with representatives of the Agriculture Department collected extensive information on native methods of shea butter extraction. The evaluation of their findings once again reflected a widespread preoccupation with the calculation and maximization of yields.

With butter production, rather than harnessing the labor power of northern residents to fulfill its commercial goals, the colonial administration tapped into a different means of producing value and a different constellation of political controls. Substituting mechanized sources of labor for manual ones, colonial officials sought to replace indigenous methods of butter extraction, thought to be inefficient as they yielded only 25 percent of the nuts' fat content, with industrial processing techniques promising to double butter yields.[80] Building upon the ruins but perhaps not the lessons of prior market reforms, in the late 1920s, plans were made to establish a small butter processing plant in Tamale on the premises of the defunct Tamale Cotton Gin, making use of the leftover but still working engine (Kay 1972: 224). Relying on processing technologies premised on ideals of efficiency and uniformity in the stead of the idiosyncratic techniques and outcomes of manual extraction, this agenda would accelerate the transformation of shea into an industrial raw material even before it reached the European market.

To accomplish this end, the colonial administration did not act as a wholly independent agent, as it relied on resources derived from private firms—the states' former partners in commercial development. In light of the sharp restrictions imposed on private enterprises involved in the shea market a few years earlier, this dynamic may be construed as a move to bring private capital back into the business of shea export. However, even in this new phase of economic restructuring, the terms of private-sector involvement remained highly contained, with the state mandating the terms of private firms' assistance rather than simply permitting their participation. Not only were specific firms asked to share the technology they had developed, but they were also expected to purchase refined butter from state-run processing plants (Kay 1972: 221, 227). Indeed, the reinstatement of private participation in the shea butter market was construed according to a narrow array of opportunities and interests driven by the state. Just as indigenous participation in the shea export economy was reduced to a singular set of interventions, private companies, although no longer excluded, were similarly reduced to an adjunct of the colonial administration. Not only did this severely reduce the play of efficiency and competition as arbiters of market growth and development, but it also created a new realm for the assertion of state control in northern commercial life.

Despite these elaborate agendas and the extensive programs of research on which they were based, the colonial government's market development schemes met with substantial difficulty when it came to implementation. To begin with, there was little local precedent regarding sales of large quantities of nuts, let alone transporting them to distant markets. Accordingly, people living off the main roads resisted head-loading nuts to newly established buying centers.[81] There was also great regional disparity in nut prices, reflecting differences in yields in particular areas and the quantity of nuts purchased, all conditions making it difficult for the administration to come up with reliable calculations of expenses.[82] Similarly, because the preparation and trade of shea nuts was considered women's work, male laborers could not be enticed to engage in it, as the administration had hoped.[83] Given the additional hard work of boiling, cracking, and drying nuts, not to mention the collection of firewood for heating the water entailed in preparing surplus nuts for sale, even women resisted the administration's expectations of labor intensification.[84] Hence government buyers had little choice but to purchase unprocessed nuts at prices and in quantities set by the suppliers.

The development of the export market for shea was further hindered by the government's lack of commitment to infrastructure development specifically with respect to transport. Despite the centrality of a northern railway line within Guggisberg's development agenda, by the late 1920s, with the Depression taking its toll on the colonial economy, the government's enthusiasm and funding for constructing a northern railway were on the wane. Under these circumstances: "The matter was discussed for the last time in the spring of 1930 and the Executive Council agreed unanimously that the project is too speculative to justify undertaking at a time when considerable difficulty is being experienced in balancing revenue and expenditure" (Ladoucer 1979: 46).

For all these reasons, colonial export promotion initiatives were in economic terms far from successful, doing little to expand the export-oriented production and trade and much to undermine it. As Devries (1976: 32) points out with regard to commercial growth in early modern Europe, "The problem to be overcome was of course not simply logistical—transport and distribution; it was also technical and political—to increase the peasant surplus and to legitimize new relationships between the peasants and their superiors." This fact did not escape colonial officials in the northern territories. Colonial administrators were well aware of the political entailments and political opportunities of commercial reform—so much so that their political investments overwhelmed their economic objectives. Yet, while the state's efforts of market promotion were an economic failure, their political implications were both systematic and significant.

Providing a means for state agents to come to know the social and physical terrain of the north and in turn, extend and deepen their presence there, the colonial regime's export agenda put into place the institutional foundations of state power. While this did not increase the contribution of the north to the larger Gold Coast economy, as Guggisberg had envisioned, it did intensify the web of colonial intervention in the north, in keeping with his program of consolidation. Moreover, by asserting a singular and exclusive framework for export promotion, the state's program of control, despite its own failure in material terms, undermined both the development and the success of other modes of intervention. In this manner, state power operated in a negative sense, preventing the rise of alternative forms of social and resource control. Given these consequences of the state's export agenda, deepening the claims and presence of the state in the northern territory, explanations of export market stagnation in the north based on notions of state neglect do not bear out (cf. Sutton 1983). On the contrary, the nondevelopment of the shea export market during this period of colonial rule may be attributed to the intensity of state intervention, not its absence, and in turn to the ascendance—intentional or not—of political imperatives over economic ones.

This is not to say however, that state intervention in the shea economy was without economic effect. Even though limited resources were channeled into the commercial institutions organized by the state, the exactions of the colonial regime with regard to shea contributed to a far-reaching process of economic restructuring in the north. For one, the colonial administration's attempt to assert control over shea export, dependent as it was on new patterns of production, procurement, and trade, resulted in the bifurcation of the shea economy into effectively discrete domestic and export sectors with only limited overlap. Rather than a single market that could be tapped for the purposes of export or domestic use, colonial policy worked to cultivate a separate export sector dependent on distinctive supply lines, personnel, pricing, and purchasing arrangements. However, contrary to the desires of colonial officials, the changing economic landscape of the Northern Territories which they had worked to create spurred the development of the domestic shea market, rather than the export sector. To understand this growth of the domestic shea market—and not just its differentiation from the export trade—it is necessary to take into account a broad set of economic shifts, not all directly related to shea, occurring in the north beginning in the late 1920s.

Relocating the North, Domesticating Shea

Even as colonial officials continued to intensify their involvement in the shea market in the name of export promotion and a platform of economic consolidation that aimed to put the Northern Territories on equal standing with other sectors of the Gold Coast, by the late 1920s and early 1930s an alternative agenda of economic development and integration was gradually taking shape. Marking a turning point in the political and economic standing of the savanna zone, this program of reform would resituate the north—as both a territory and set of commercial potentials—within the economic and political space of the Gold Coast. Rather than serving as a source of value parallel to that generated within the Gold Coast colony and Asanti, as Guggisberg had hoped for, within this emerging rubric the Northern Territories were rendered subsidiary to other parts of the colony and the colonial administration more generally.

Resource flows from the northern savanna were diverted from prior and potential engagement with overseas markets and reoriented to serve the economic needs of other parts of the colony by providing food and labor to the growing markets in the southern and central regions of the Gold Coast. Responsible for the emergence of these new commercial trajectories was the changing place of the state in the northern economy. Highly ambivalent, the state at this juncture both obligated northern residents to provide financial support to the colonial administration to a much greater degree than before and withdrew the sort of concerted investments it had formerly made, effectively denying the region resources or recognition commensurate with state exactions. By rendering the north a critical source of material aid, this agenda of economic reform intensified the incorporation of the Northern Territories into the Gold Coast at the same time as it marginalized the region within the economic and political profile of the colony as a whole.

By inciting new conditions and patterns of subsistence, these reforms did the most to intensify shea commercialization in the Northern Territories. But instead of their engaging foreign demand for shea, the growth of the shea market was nearly entirely domestic in orientation, as northern residents sought new and greater sources of income to satisfy the exactions of the colonial state along with their own need to participate in the region's growing markets. In this way, colonial policy, though largely unintentionally, did more to stimulate the regional shea economy than the export market despite the long history of concerted intervention by the colonial state in the name of export promotion. Indeed, by the early 1930s the colonial government's export promotion agenda initiated by Ferguson and built during the first three decades of northern occupation was effectively dissolved. Rather than seeking markets for northern commodities overseas, the administration now focused on meeting internal needs and tapping production and distribution systems already in place.

Even shea, for years touted by the Colonial Office and local administrators because of its export potential, was revalued and noted for its worth on the regional market. Indicating a rather abrupt about-face on the part of the colonial administration, policies of commercial promotion for shea—to the extent that they continued to exist—now centered on the valorization of manual rather than mechanical processes of oil extraction, along with southern consumers.[85] Suddenly enthusiastic about shea's potential to generate revenue as a regional commodity despite the long history of administrative denial and subversion of the domestic shea trade, one northern administrator asserted, "I think our Native Administration might work up a local export trade to the colony."[86]

Serving as the foundation of these reforms, by 1932 a system of indirect rule relying on native administration was instituted in the Northern Territories. Within this framework, expatriate officers were to establish and coordinate the contours of a political administration incorporating indigenous institutions and representatives. Molding those institutions and offices so that they conformed to imperial ideals, native administration and indirect rule were strategies for cultivating political order and asserting imperial interests "on the cheap." Enabling colonial authorities to cut down on the cost of administration and mandate internal revenue generation, these policies formed the foundation of what Berry calls "hegemony on a shoe-string" (1993a: 22). Given a worldwide trade slump during the years of the Great Depression and the overall economic downturn of the interwar period which precipitated a fall in demand and prices for cocoa and other tropical commodities on which the colonial administration relied for the generation of public and private incomes, such a politics of parsimony made economic sense for the colonial state.

Going hand and hand with the suspension of external financing was the Native Treasuries Ordinance. A central component of indirect rule, this ordinance mandated local financing of the colonial administration. Providing the means for self-support, it included several forms of local revenue generation, ranging from market tolls, fines, and licensing fees to taxes assessed on an individual and household basis (Bourret 1960: 97; Hailey 1952: 586). Prior to the imposition of the Native Treasuries Ordinance, residents of the Northern Territories were already firmly involved in the circulation and commoditization of goods, money, and even labor and held internally driven incentives for market participation. Yet the colonial administration's policies of direct taxation and accompanying forms of revenue generation increased northerners' involvement in the market and heightened the place of the market as an arena for the working out of state-society relations, however indirect.

To begin with, the necessity of northern revenue generation, combined with the limited resources invested by the state to facilitate this effort, spawned new patterns of northern participation in southern markets. One powerful vector of linkage was the demand for agricultural foodstuffs—namely groundnuts—from the north within the rapidly expanding markets of Asante and the colony. Catering to southern demand, throughout the 1930s, forties, and into the fifties, the groundnut trade, and with it groundnut production, from the Northern Territories exploded (White 1956: 120).[87] Previously cultivated for domestic consumption and only secondarily for trade, groundnuts had long been part of the northern economy (Roncoli 1994: 131). Yet until the 1930s their circulation was largely local, despite the efforts of Hausa merchants and their families to extract groundnut oil and sell both oil and nuts on a regional basis. Indeed, in the 1920s, groundnuts and groundnut oil were more expensive and harder to find than shea in the markets of northern Ghana.[88]

While northern-grown groundnuts did move into southern markets prior to the 1930s, the scale of this trade was rather small for what was to become a staple good. In 1927, for example, the estimated amount of groundnuts moving from the north—Navrongo to Yeji—to Kumasi was recorded to be 4000 tons. The regional trade in shea butter, considered a luxury commodity in the south compared to the use of groundnuts as an ordinary foodstuff and cooking oil, equaled 1050 tons, an equivalent of about 5000 tons of shea nuts, and was thus considerably larger in scale than the regional groundnut trade (Kay 1972: 164). By the mid-1930s, however, market-oriented groundnut farming was widespread and served as a major strategy of revenue generation in many sections of the north. In the area around Bawku District, groundnut production rose from 200 bags in 1933 to 9,378 bags in 1936 (Roncoli 1994: 132). Sonya and Meyer Fortes (1936: 244), who worked among the Tallensi fifty miles to the west of Bawku, remarked on the rapid expansion of commercial groundnut cultivation around this time: "almost every man and boy able to wield a hoe and most adult women have their own groundnut fields . . . the yields of which were typically sold." Likewise, in the nearby Kusasi District, the district commissioner in 1938 reported: "Nearly every farmer in Northern Kusasi now seems to try and find a corner for groundnuts" (Roncoli 1994: 133) and attributed "the spurt of house building and quantity of cloth and petty merchandise sold" to money earned from groundnut sales (Roncoli 1994: 135).

The expansion of the groundnut trade had varied implications for the character of northern economic life. As indicated by the widespread and rapid adoption of groundnut farming by men, women, and youth, obtaining adequate factors of production was not difficult, as groundnut farmers built upon existing economic relations and potentials to access the requisite land, labor, and time. Even female farmers, often disadvantaged in the face of new economic opportunities (Boserup 1970), had little trouble entering the market as they borrowed land from cognatic kin and drew on the labor of junior males (Fortes and Fortes 1936: 244). Because it was largely restricted to land unsuitable for other crops, groundnut cultivation did not undermine prevailing conventions of land allocation or use (1936). However, the production of a commodity as widely tradable and valued as groundnuts did alter northerners' relation to the market. Most of all, the opportunity to sell groundnuts provided northern residents with the cash necessary to purchase foodstuffs—especially staple grains—during times of want (Fortes and Fortes 1936: 245–6; Roncoli 1994: 136). Already beset by shortage and unpredictable yields due to microclimatic variation along with the vagaries of agricultural decision-making, staple-grain production in the northern savanna would be further compromised by other emerging vectors of north-south engagement, making participation in agricultural markets all the more important for meeting basic needs.

Given the limited investment of the colonial state or metropolitan enterprises in new patterns of income generation in the north at this time, simply complying with the exactions directly and indirectly imposed by the colonial government on northern residents—let alone engaging in material accumulation—necessitated for many the pursuit of alternatives modes of livelihood in the south, where opportunities were available. Hence, alongside the groundnut boom and for the same reasons, Northern Ghana experienced a substantial labor exodus to the south during the 1930s. Responding to the growing need for labor in the colony and Ashanti, northern migrants were involved in cocoa farming, the cultivation of food crops, and urban labor markets, both formal and informal (Hart 1982a). By the mid-1930s, even with the contractions of the depression still in the air, northern labor migrants stood at 6 percent of the total population of the Northern Territories (Fortes 1936: 37).[89] Considering that migrants were largely able-bodied males, the figure jumps to nearly 25 percent.[90]

Labor migration had significant implications for the organization of the northern economy, as it precipitated northerners' increasing dependence on trade and markets. This was to have a substantial effect on the domestic shea economy. With 10 percent to 20 percent of male members and increasing numbers of female members away, northern households experienced a loss of labor for staple food cultivation.[91] Responding to the ensuing labor shortage, in the 1940s northern chiefs "complained that no laborers remained to farm the land and opposed labor migration to southern farms" (Sutton 1983: 480). Plange (1979: 671) suggests that this labor drain incited shifts in the gender and generational division of labor, stating "a common sight in Northern Ghana from the 1920s onwards was a woman or man well advanced in years working laboriously on the farm or women and children herding cattle. Thus, gradually, communities were depopulated, leading to diminishing returns in production." In the process, women were becoming increasingly responsible for household food provisioning and reliant on the market to do so. Women's growing involvement in groundnut cultivation (Fortes 1936: 244), where male labor was not crucial, served as one way they accomplished this end.

Petty trade was another route pursued by women to satisfy new material imperatives. As Fortes noted as early as 1936, women's trading activities—including the sale of both shea nuts and shea butter—were of fundamental importance to the domestic economy in northeastern Ghana: "Every woman adds to the food supply of her primary family" (1936: 242). He continued: "[A] woman sells some groundnuts, dried vegetables, shea nuts, shea butter or some dawa dawa seed balls (kpalug) to buy grain. In this way does the market help to eke out the domestic supply of grain. A woman's market purchases go to feed her family (1936: 246)." In Bawku by the mid-1930s, women's involvement in small-scale trading was widespread. One district officer noted in his diary: "There is such a lot of food selling by night during the dry season that we have started a night food market in the new iron-roofed stalls and it is very popular. The pennies are tumbling in because most of the women who sell food at night are different from the day sellers."[92]

In Bawku District, the oldest living generation of shea butter-makers and traders—women seventy and eighty years of age in the mid-1990s—recall entering the butter market at this time in response to rising urban demand coupled with a growing need for cash. Although most of these women resided in rural villages when they first entered the shea market, their commercial endeavors invariably targeted Bawku town. There they found, as one woman described it, "workers and people with money, as well as strangers, and those who would buy for resale." Among the market's attractions, another recalled, was the likelihood that "anytime you went to market, you could sell all of your butter for cash, even on a non-market day." Until then, market-oriented production had been the purview of immigrant Yarse women, the wives of Yarse professional weavers living at the edges of the district. For women native to the area, commercial production of shea signaled a departure from earlier economic priorities centered on butter production for home use and only occasional butter sales.

One longtime shea butter-maker, a woman well advanced in age and the wife of the former chief of the village of Kolpeleg, an area rich in shea trees about five miles from Bawku town, explained that when first married, she and the other women in the household would pick nuts from the household farm, processing a large batch of butter that could be saved to prepare food through the year. Other women stored the nuts until the start of the rainy season in order to make butter for the preparation of food for work parties engaged in cooperative farming. From time to time they might sell a small amount of the butter they produced. By the mid-1930s, however, she recounted, production for the market was gradually becoming a primary goal rather than an afterthought of consumption-oriented processing, resulting in the increasing frequency and scale of butter manufacture. With butter production emerging as the mainstay of female livelihood in the chief's compound and the wider community, it soon came to be recognized as what she described as *tenga tolon* ("the trade of the place") and a source of personal and local identification.

While butter sales sometimes took place in the village markets, more often they were directed to the larger markets in the area. Inspired by the rising urban demand, women from outlying areas, like those from the area around Garu in the southern reaches of Bawku District, found a strong enough market for their butter in Bawku to make the forty-mile three-day journey to the market and back worthwhile. Along with other butter producers, they sat under a kapok tree in the very spot where butter-makers in 1995 were still located in Bawku market. One senior butter-maker from a village a few miles beyond Bawku who also traded her butter in the town's market recalled that "the army ladies, the wives of the army men, bought the butter . . . Mr. Saam, a white man, brought the army people." Rural markets were not entirely left out of these commercial developments. Butter-makers traveled widely from smaller and more remote trading centers in order to buy and bulk shea nuts in quantities large enough to sustain their commercial endeavors. Also controlled by women, the growth of the shea nut market at this time is another indication of the way shifts in colonial policy both directly and indirectly spurred the growth and reorientation of the domestic shea economy, contributing to the commercialization of rural and especially female livelihoods.

Conclusion: Shea, the Colonial State, and Commodity Rule in Northern Ghana

This chapter has aimed to convey the thoroughly dynamic and highly politicized character of northern Ghana's shea economy. It argues that despite the long history of shea commercialization and the long-standing presence of shea within commercial circuits cutting across the West African subregion, the shape of the shea economy, even during the first decades of colonial rule, was neither static nor uniform. Although shea was—and remains—deeply embedded in savanna ecology and domestic economy, the contours of shea commercialization are equally and profoundly shaped by external actors, institutions, and imperatives. Since the early part of the colonial era, the shea economy has been affected by world market trends, the designs of foreign enterprise, and the shifting parameters of state-based governance as much as by the currents of savanna commerce and rural modes of subsistence. As a primary site for the entry of external interests into Ghana's savanna economy, shea commercialization stands as a bellwether of the scope and character of connection between rural resources and livelihoods in the savanna zone and wider political economies, be they private or public, national or global in nature. Representing more than economic imperatives alone, the commercial forms emerging from these intersections provided a stage for the articulation of political contests regarding strategies of rule and the cultural bases of their imposition and legitimacy. In this manner, the shea market in northern Ghana has operated as grounds of struggle not just over resources but, equally important, over the processes and parameters of statecraft—from the means and scope of territorial control to the cultivation and monitoring of political subjects and the constitution and operation of bureaucratic administration.

The dynamism of the shea economy is clearly evident in the multiplicity of commercial roles played by shea over the span of just a few decades. Beginning with the early years of colonial rule in the last decades of the nineteenth century through the mid-twentieth century, shea was inserted into multiple frameworks of value characterized by varied concepts of worth and exchangeability, modes of circulation, and notions of utility. At the turn of the century, shea was touted by Ferguson as an indigenous commodity of general value that could easily find a place in overseas markets. A decade later it was reconceived as an industrial raw material and subject to mechanized refinishing making it appropriate for further use in the manufacturing cycle. By the 1920s, the value of shea was being reworked once again, as its commercial potential was now considered to hinge on the totality of labor with which it was endowed. This ideal was soon displaced by another that overlooked issues of use and fabrication altogether. By the early 1930s the value of shea within the colonial economy would derive from its exchangeability alone, based on the capacity to generate value on the market commensurate with any other good.

Successively imposed, each of these rubrics of valuation invoked a specific range of circulation. Ferguson, for one, aimed to promote the outward and unobstructed flow of resources. Once the Northern Protectorate was established, this initial ideal was replaced by a more localized orientation that sought to keep persons and goods in place, restricting their mobility. The renewed interest in export that followed reiterated Ferguson's expansive vision yet endowed it with greater structure and specificity. Circulating in channels parallel to those carved out by other resources from the Gold Coast, especially cocoa, shea was to flow to European industry and provide a basis for the entry of European industry into colonial territory. According to this framework, however, not all shea was considered appropriate for these sorts of external linkages, and export was restricted to only those shea supplies that met with specified criteria of production, processing, and evacuation. This agenda severed the shea market in two, resulting in an export sector distinct from the domestic shea economy. In the 1930s this external focus would be replaced by an internal one, as colonial officials directly and indirectly promoted the continued and intensified circulation of shea within local and regional markets and withdrew support for export initiatives.

Bound up with the constitution of state power in the Northern Territories, the Gold Coast colony, and the British West African empire more generally, each of these frameworks of commercialization was thoroughly political in its motives and implications. In addition to the control of revenue and resources, integral to this process of state-making were the circumscription of territory, the cultivation of political subjects, and the extension and regularization of a distinct set of bureaucratic orders. Though short-lived, the commodity flows envisioned by Ferguson and fostered through the trade pacts of the 1890s were a first step in incorporating the northern savanna zone into the expanse of the British colonial empire through the establishment of permanent trade ties. The orchestration of trade and markets in the north during the early years of the twentieth century would provide a foundation for the achievement of exclusive and territorially based control by the colonial administration and the monitoring of the movements and livelihoods of northern residents by colonial agents.

During the teens and twenties, the subsequent reopening of the export market, accompanied by the participation of private firms, enabled the colonial administration to tap into new sources of capital and expand the scope of its influence, domestically and abroad. At the same time, Guggisberg's promotion of shea export as part of a larger policy of consolidation worked to reposition the Northern Territories within the political space of the Gold Coast as a whole, both integrating the north with the other parts of the colony and demonstrating its distinctive character. Moreover, the intensified involvement of state agents in the documentation, monitoring, and restructuring of shea processing and procurement at this time increased state presence and bearing in rural communities. Not only did this sort of penetration make the state more visible on the local level as it made the local more visible to the state by sanctioning certain forms of economic activity as opposed to others, but it also established the terms of inclusion and exclusion in national economic life and provided the grounds for the emergence and enforcement of a range of political and economic distinctions. Centered on issues of labor, these distinctions found expression in the characterization of northerners as lazy or diligent, ignorant or educable, worthy of state support or marginal to the nation-building process.

With the introduction of Indirect Rule in the early 1930s, the colonial state's engagement of the resources, residents, and space of the Northern Territories was once again recast. Yet, despite the withdrawal of direct state support, given the already existing foundation of state engagement in the northern economy via trade and market controls, the expression of state authority within the Northern Territories was not substantially reduced. By the time policies of indirect rule were pursued by the colonial administration in the Northern Territories, state agents and institutions—operating largely through the control and constitution of markets—were already well established. With mechanisms for the control of persons, resources, and territory already in place, indirect rule, contrary to assumptions (cf. Sutton 1983), was more about the terms of incorporation of the north into the emerging nation-state rather than its exclusion from it. Indirect rule signaled not the neglect of the north by the colonial administration but a deliberate and enduring strategy of underdevelopment in which the market would continue to serve as the primary means of creating and engaging political subjects in the northern territories, much as it had since the days of Ferguson's explorations.

As links to export markets were severed, a new set of market-based relationships between the north and the other territories of the Gold Coast was cultivated. Dependent on the flow of labor and foodstuffs as well as revenue into the markets of the south, these relationships rendered the Northern Territories a subordinate yet integral component of the wider colonial economy. Through the extension of the market in this manner, the north became further incorporated into an emergent national space and further ensconced in its hierarchical order. The increasingly protonational orientation of the political economy of the Northern Territories was accompanied by a parallel process of redomestication, as new types of connections to the Gold Coast economy *in toto* and new expectations on the part of the colonial administration stimulated new forms of local market participation geared to revenue generation. For many in the northern savanna, especially rural women, this included participation in the trade of staple foods, among them shea. Here, the market served as a site for confronting and negotiating the changing face of state power rather than any sort of refuge from it.

What this means is that given the colonial state's a history of exercising power through the market, the apparent "longevity" of shea commercialization in northern Ghana needs to be recognized as a function of historically specific relationships with state agents and processes of state-based rule rather than a sign of reversion to any sort of natural economy or precolonial order. This is evident in the varied commercial profiles of shea within the West African economy. If the shea economy of the pre- and early colonial periods was characterized, on the one hand, by long-distance trading networks in which shea was a semiluxury and, on the other, by a subsistence-oriented economy in which shea was produced on the household level largely for home consumption rather than sale, once colonial policies were firmly entrenched, shea came increasingly to occupy a different commercial path as a local staple produced by rural women specifically for sale in savanna markets. Rooted in particular political arrangements and historical conditions, it is this commercial form that has come to dominate and characterize the domestic shea economy in northern Ghana.

CHAPTER 3

Market Reform and Economic Citizenship in Northern Ghana

Promoting and Politicizing Shea
in the Wake of Liberalization

As the colonial era drew to a close and the economy of the savanna zone was reduced to an adjunct of the south in the area that would soon become the modern nation-state of Ghana, shea's significance to the government agenda faded rapidly. Consisting almost entirely of the sale of shea nuts rather than butter, shea export, like that of a host of other commodities—from cocoa to pineapples—was placed under the exclusive purview of the state marketing board, first known as the West African Produce Control Board and later as the Cocoa Marketing Board (Meredith 1988: 295). For all but a brief period in the 1950s, shea would remain in its domain through the early 1990s.

Going hand in hand with the state's rather indifferent monopoly over the shea export market—and leaving the market for butter entirely out of the range of regulation—the domestic market for shea nuts was subject to limited and inconstant state oversight reflecting the varied philosophies of the succession of regimes that ruled the country in the aftermath of independence. Indicative of this inconstancy in the 1950s, toward the end of the colonial period the domestic shea nut trade was opened to private purchasing agents (Anyane 1963: 158), but in the 1960s, during Nkrumah's administration, this changed with the appointment of a parastatal as the sole domestic buyer. After just five years, however, in 1966 a multibuyer system was reinstated. In the early 1970s, under Prime Minister Busia, the state reasserted its control over the domestic shea market only to face the return of private buyers with the rise of Acheampong regime in the latter part of the decade (Agrovets 1991: 18).

Despite these haphazard policy directives, during this period Ghanaian shea exports gradually expanded. This was largely an outcome of the initiatives of a small number of private buyers, such as Kassardjian Enterprises, a Lebanese family firm that began buying shea nuts in Ghana in the 1950s and continued to do so in various capacities depending on the state regulations of the day. At this time, shea's status as a world-market commodity remained largely hidden, as it was incorporated into a myriad of processed foods and manufactured staples, from margarine and soap to animal feed (Fold 2000: 98; www.hort.purdue.edu). In the 1960s, the demand for shea on the world market, although still largely industrial in orientation, experienced a bump due to the growing recognition of its value as a cocoa butter substitute to be used in chocolate processing. Yet even with this new source of international demand, the Ghanaian government was little concerned with promoting shea's export potential and only minimally involved in the domestic market or export market. In the 1980s, this would all change.

In the eighties, after languishing for decades as a commodity of minor significance to the national government and its coffers, shea reemerged as an object of state interest. Not only was shea reinstated as a site of state intervention in the northern economy, but it also found itself a target of negotiation between the national government and international financial institutions. Born out of such a convergence, all of this subjected the rural shea economy—specifically the shea nut trade—to substantial restructuring. Although coincident, state interests in shea and those of international actors were characterized by different and in some cases contradictory aims and inspirations. While the state sought to reaffirm and deepen its control of the domestic market, international financial institutions pushed for the rapid and thoroughgoing privatization of all aspects of the shea economy, from domestic purchasing to export sales. Highlighting the ascendance of state imperatives in the face of international intervention along with the fragile social contracts involved in their realization, this chapter explores the intersection of these two agendas.

The chapter makes clear the uneasy compromise between national governments, supranational institutions, and societal interests lurking behind the restructuring of markets for tropical commodities like shea. Foremost, the course of shea market reform in the 1980s calls into question the assumption that the conditionalities of international financial institutions are nonnegotiable even in a country held to be a model student of liberalization such as Ghana (Pearce 1992), as Callaghy (1990) has shown in other settings. Yet in Ghana, the national government's assertion of control over the market reform process, while it did subvert the interests of international actors, was not to restore old forms of order. The mandates of market reform introduced by international financial institutions and adopted in a time of crises by a regime already in the throes of transformation were selectively used and reworked to manage political imperatives in new ways. Indeed, in Ghana, as Staudt (1995: 236) suggests more generally, the implementation of neoliberal reform was driven by domestic political concerns much more than any singular economic logic.

This is not to say that the market reforms promoted by international financial bodies were of little significance to the government's agenda. Rather, they were implemented in highly strategic and selective ways. In northern Ghana during the 1980s, with the restructuring of shea economy, commoditization—the very organizing principle of neoliberal economic reform—emerged as an important arbiter of citizenship and served as a foundation for the renewal of state power, not its diminution. The etiology of such a dynamic and its implications for rural economic life will become apparent below.

Shea Market Reform and Economic Citizenship in Northern Ghana

As many have noted, the 1980s were a time of political transition and suspense in Ghana (Chazan 1991; Herbst 1993; Rothchild 1991). After four coups in a fifteen-year period punctuated by less than two years of democratic rule, the government had come to provide little opportunity or accountability for the bulk of Ghana's citizens and instead subjected the nation's populace to progressive instability and disenfranchisement. In 1981 J. J. Rawlings assumed power for a second time through a military-led putsch. Espousing an agenda of populist reform, Rawlings and his supporters in the Provisional National Defense Council (PNDC) styled themselves a revolutionary front. Promising to undo the excesses of its predecessors, the regime sought to inspire popular participation by creating a wide-ranging infrastructure for citizen activism. There were Workers' Defense Committees fostering worker participation in the management of state offices and enterprises, People's Defense Committees drawing nonelites into community affairs, a national Mobilization Program increasing the rural labor supply, as well as People's Militias and public tribunals (Chazan 1991). These institutions, the PNDC promised, were to provide a foundation for a "people's democracy" (Mikell 1991: 89)—a "people's revolution" in Rawlings' words (1982: 66)—appealing to working classes throughout the country, and rural dwellers in particular, who were identified as the most politically alienated of Ghana's citizenry (Nugent 1995: 138).

Going hand in hand with the prolonged dissolution of representative government and contributing to the atmosphere of insecurity, by the early 1980s after two decades of exorbitant state expenditures and failed attempts at economic development, Ghana was in the throes of economic crisis aggravated by drought and the poor conditions of international finance (Pellow 1986; Tabatabai 1988). As exactions and expenditures providing few public returns came to dominate national economic policy during this extended phase of economic decline, so too did participation in parallel economies evading official regulation. According to World Bank estimates, transactions in Ghana's parallel market mushroomed from one quarter of gross domestic product (GDP) in 1972 to one third in 1982 and continued to grow steadily throughout the decade (Nugent 1991: 74). They involved illicit trade in agricultural produce—including cocoa, Ghana's major source of export revenue—and consumer goods otherwise subject to price controls (Azarya and Chazan 1987) as well as the diversion of land and labor to the production of foodstuffs that could be directly consumed or traded without being taxed (Rimmer 1992: 157). All of these activities left the state with little revenue, economic control, or clout (Pearce 1992: 14–15), a predicament that Rawlings's government strove to correct (Chazan 1991: 28).

Faced with these woes, the economic platform of the PNDC sought both to rebuild the capacity and legitimacy of state monopolies and to recapture market-based trade (Hutchful 1989: 101–2). Highly visible and frequently marked by considerable force, these reforms were more than simply an attempt to reclaim the material benefits of commercial control; they were a demonstration of the renewed power of the state over the Ghanaian citizenry. As a consequence, during the early years of Rawlings's rule, the market would emerge as a primary battleground between society and the state and thus central to the negotiation and in many cases the imposition of a new social contract between rulers and the ruled. Reinforced by the violent legacy of the market interventions of Rawlings's first regime in 1979, when soldiers confiscated trading stocks and destroyed marketplaces across the country (Clark 1989; Robertson 1983), in the early 1980s the PNDC agenda of market reform centered both on rooting out commercial activities in flagrant violation of state regulation (Nugent 1995: 79) and reordering even those long-standing trading practices that posed little direct challenge to state authority. Sometimes marked by violence and sometimes not, according to Clark and Manuh (1991: 225): "J.J. Rawlings made a determined attempt to adjust the terms of trade through strict price controls of both imports and local foodstuffs during 1979 and the years 1981–84. Trading in the market was outlawed for many imports and manufactures and new marketing channels were organized."

Reeling from years of political and economic disenfranchisement (Ladoucer 1979), not to mention the recent removal of Hilla Liman, a native son, from the presidential post, the north was not left out of this exercise in nation-building *qua* market restructuring. Given the intensity of smuggling activities in the area due to the proximity of international borders (Azarya and Chazan 1987), cracking down on *kalabule* (the black market) was a key dimension of market reforms in the northern savanna (Nugent 1991: 77). Yet, taking what was perhaps a more proactive stance than that pursued in other parts of the country, in the north the Rawlings government made a concerted effort to promote what it considered to be legitimate commerce—that is, trade controlled by the state—rather than just to undermine existing commercial practices. The restructuring and reinvigoration of the shea export market was central to this economic agenda. Like Guggisberg's 1920s campaign to make shea a major export and source of revenue, giving the north a central place in the Gold Coast economy, Rawlings' program marked a decisive effort to reintegrate the northern economy and populace into the national whole. In this way the shea market once again emerged as central to the redefinition of economic citizenship in the north, if citizenship is taken to stand for the parameters of participation in and recognition by the nation-state (Shafir 1998).

As is evident in a speech Rawlings delivered in the administrative center of Bolgatanga in northeast Ghana, the government well recognized the fragile loyalty of the north's largely rural constituency and the challenge this posed to both the Ghanaian nation and state:

> People of the Upper East Region, I understand that there was once a time when you would jokingly call this region lower Upper Volta, and that when you were going to travel to Kumasi or even just as far as Tamale, you would talk of "going to Ghana." This is an indication of how you felt isolated from the rest of the country—not just physically but remotely from the mainstream of what was happening nationally. (Nugent 1995: 206)

In striving to overcome this legacy of alienation, the reinvigoration of the shea export market was an important way the Rawlings regime attempted to rebuild a northern constituency and bring the region back into the fold of the national economy and state-based controls. To these ends, less than a year after assuming the position of head of state, Rawlings traveled throughout the north, informing residents of his plan to revitalize the shea nut industry (1982: 67):

> It is clear that the that the contribution which the farmers and people of this area can make to the economic war is to improve the production of sheanuts [*sic*] and make systematic efforts to turn it into a major commercial crop like

3.1 Cement Statue of J. J. Rawlings, c. 1990. A local artist erected this polychrome effigy on the trunk road from the regional capital Bolgatanga to Bawku, a reminder of the rare presence of the head of state in Upper East Region.

cocoa. In that way we shall be taking steps to end our economic dependence and improve our standard of living and material culture. (Rawlings 1982: 70)

Rawlings called for the expansion of the shea market at all levels. In the realm of production, he proposed the creation of shea plantations and the intensification of collection efforts, "even if it means asking every school child to gather a certain quantity of fruit each day for sale" (1982: 69). In terms of marketing, a new payment system was introduced with the aim of encouraging the state-licensed purchasing agents to sell shea nuts to the Produce Buying Company (PBC), a subsidiary of the Cocoa Marketing Board, the parastatal with exclusive control over the shea export trade (1982: 54).

International Financial Agendas, Economic Recovery, and Shea

Soon after Rawlings's pronouncements regarding the shea trade and the revival of government presence and institutions in the north, Ghana found itself confronting a wholly different paradigm of economic reform emanating from the international community. Encompassing the national economy *in toto*, the economic program proposed by these foreign bodies signaled an abrupt if not radical change in the country's economic goals and strategies (Herbst 1993; Hutchful 1989). Specifically, in 1983, with little independent means to overcome the inherited economic crisis, the government of Ghana accepted a massive loan package from the International Monetary Fund (IMF) and the World Bank, tremendously powerful international financial institutions (IFIs) and embarked upon a comprehensive structural adjustment program as a condition for its receipt (Rothchild 1991: 7). In contrast to the Rawlings/PNDC platform of self-reliance, economic equity, and state economic oversight, this agenda, termed the Economic Recovery Program (ERP), was thoroughly market-oriented as it aimed to induce economic stability and growth by tapping market forces both at home and abroad. Hinging on promotion of private enterprise and privatization of state-owned firms, devaluation of the cedi, exchange rate liberalization, and rehabilitation of the export sector by way of export diversification (Pearce 1992: 16), the ERP was attuned much more to the "bottom line" than to the social and political concerns infusing Rawlings's earlier policies and rhetoric (Mikell 1991: 89).

According to the stalwarts of international finance, the sale of state-owned firms would relieve the state of inefficient expenditures and generate much-needed revenue. Likewise, expansion of the private sector and reduction of state-subsidized enterprises would promote more competitive firms and therefore better prices and better products for consumers (World Bank 1981). Along the same lines, export diversification would enable Ghana both to enlarge and to stabilize its foreign exchange earnings by reducing its long-standing dependence on a narrow range of goods—especially cocoa—for which world market prices were highly unstable (Herbst 1993: 130; Nugent 1995: 131). The shea economy was an obvious target of these initiatives. Considered a nontraditional export despite the actual longevity of shea export activities, shea, among other commodities—from fresh fruit and vegetables to handicrafts—was made a candidate for export diversification (USAID 1994: 14, 16). As a result, the structure of shea purchasing and sales became a target of reform. With the shea export trade dominated by the PBC, shea marketing was slated for privatization.

Although the shea economy was substantially altered during the first phase of Ghana's economic recovery over the course of the 1980s, the nature of this restructuring conformed little to IFI's neoliberal agenda and instead contributed to the ascendance of state-based institutions and interests. By the time the agenda of neoliberalism was put into play in Ghana, shea was already enmeshed in an alternative trajectory of transformation which was much more national than international in orientation. Contrary to the logic of market-based reform, rather than reducing state involvement in the shea economy, during the 1980s state control of shea marketing—both purchases and sales—was intensified and the activities of private firms and entrepreneurs was curtailed. Further diverging from the IFI focus on institutional streamlining and specialization—yet very much in keeping with Rawlings's state-centered and populist inclinations—the numbers of persons participating in the shea trade increased while the terms of their engagement were increasingly restricted by state mandates.

Exemplifying the near-reversal of IFI directives with respect to shea, in 1984, less than a year after the adoption of the structural adjustment initiative, the Rawlings regime eliminated all vestiges of private commerce from the shea export market. Dismantling a purchasing system that had relied on state-licensed private buying agents, an arrangement in place on and off since 1954, the PNDC government ceded complete control of both domestic purchasing and shea export to the Cocoa Marketing Board and the PBC. This was a direct contravention of IFI expectations. Further enlarging the mandate of the PBC with respect to shea, the government ordered the formation of highly structured agricultural cooperatives known as shea nut farmer societies (SNFSs) in northern Ghana. These cooperatives were recognized as the sole legitimate suppliers to the state-run marketing board.

Certainly the contradiction between this sort of anti-free-trade mentality and the supposed promarket orientation of structural adjustment and the ERP was not confined to shea. But in other cases, such as the legalization of private foreign-exchange transactions or the "regularization" of galamsey (small-scale mining) (Anyemedu 1991: 213), it was resolved not long after the government committed itself to the World Bank/IMF conditionalities. However, the state's stringent and increasing regulation of the shea trade during the 1980s and into the early 1990s rendered the shea economy an irrefutable "pocket" of state-orchestrated market closure and control in an era where Ghana was otherwise touted as a champion of market reform (Rothchild 1991).

Indeed, the sharp divergence between the directives of international financial bodies—a leading edge of globalization—and the actual course of shea market reform in Ghana makes evident the ambiguous relationship between global institutions and the state. Not only does the success of global initiatives depend on the cooperation of states (in this case, as the main implementers of IFI programs) (Sassen 1996; 2000), but states also manipulate global processes for their own ends even as they rely on global resources and the successful implementation of global mandates for their very survival. As a consequence, in the course of market and financial restructuring, political concerns may override strictly economic imperatives—a situation that is all the more complicated in new regimes like that of the PNDC, struggling to manage diverse constituencies and agendas.

State-Society Relations and the Social Dimensions of Shea Market Restructuring

Caught between the contradictory impulses of a fragile regime and the pressures of international financial bodies, by 1984 the shea economy—specifically the buying and selling of shea nuts for export—was in the throes of transformation. The reorganization of the shea nut market, centering on the formation and operation of SNFSs in all corners of Ghana's northern sector, had substantial bearing on social relations within northern communities as well as the relationship between northern communities and the state. Garnering the participation of all segments of northern society—male, female, youth, farmer, trader, chief—and seeking to access shea supplies from all corners of the northern economy—farm, bush, rural markets, urban trading centers—the PBC's promotion of SNFSs extended both the reach of the state and the shea export market.

This popularizing impulse, however, replicated and in many cases intensified the hierarchies infusing northern communities. At the same time, enlarging the net of state patronage and building upon models of political participation already in place, these tactics of mobilization did little to challenge the underlying basis of state authority, reinforcing the low status and dependence of northern residents.

State Authority and Shea Nut Farmer Society Membership

The PBC was the ultimate arbiter of the terms of both the shea nut trade and participation in the shea nut farmers societies. Nuts were to be collected from farms and bush or purchased from rural and urban suppliers by SNFS members and sold only to the PBC at a fixed price. No nuts were travel across district boundaries unless authorized by the PBC, and it was illegal to store more than ten bags of nuts unless they were earmarked for sale to the PBC. Even when PBC agents were not present, shea traders risked being reported to the local Committee for the Defense of the Revolution (CDR), the party cell established by the Rawling's government to maintain law and order. Abiding by PBC directives, members of individual SNFSs were to coordinate their activities, storing nuts in common warehouses and working together to weigh and bag nuts when PBC personnel came to pick up their stocks. Society members were promised cash advances early in the season to help finance nut purchases and a commission for every bag of nuts they sold to the PBC. As a further incentive to obey PBC guidelines, members were given the opportunity to purchase otherwise scarce and costly consumer items and agricultural inputs, such as cloth, cooking pots, boots, and cutlasses, at discount prices.

Hence not only did the new frameworks of exchange instituted by the PBC alter shea suppliers' opportunity structure, but PBC policy also changed the commodity status of shea nuts more generally. As the demand for shea nuts grew along with the financing available for their purchase, shea nuts became more of a cash crop worthy of investment rather than a source of residual value of interest only to the rural poor. Yet at the same time as shea nuts became a more attractive candidate for exchange, they were subject to a battery of restrictions emanating from the state—from price, timing, and point of sale to the identity of buyer and supplier—attenuating their free circulation. Made commensurate in this way with other goods for which access and availability were limited due to government-imposed import regulations, shea nuts came to be marked as a state-controlled commodity. As a result, the specific conditions of their circulation at any one time or place served as an indicator of the range of state power or lack thereof.

The SNFSs established by the PBC certainly stimulated an increase in northern residents' participation in the export economy. The question of SNFS membership and equity, however, is beset by a fundamental tension. This is because the very term "farmer" is a misnomer, inappropriate to shea. Shea nuts, which grow wild, are not "farmed" in the sense of cultivation. Deliberate or not, this misattribution, by creating an imaginary category of "shea farmer" to which no one actually belonged, served as a trope enabling the PBC to set and regulate the terms of participation in the export market. As a result, with neither a history of organization nor a clear-cut membership, the character of the SNFSs was open to invention.

Acting upon this license, once the state had ordered the withdrawal of private purchasing agents from the export trade in the early 1980s, PBC representatives traveled to the major areas of shea supply in northern Ghana to establish the farmer societies. Cultivating the hierarchical potentials of rural society, the organizational strategies of the PBC both engaged preexisting cleavages and brought new forms of differentiation into the

3.2 Cocoa Board burlap sack used by the Produce Buying Company and Shea Nut Farmer Societies to store and transport shea nuts. (Photo by Daniel Smith).

shea market. PBC representatives worked through elites, informing chiefs, other community leaders, and well-established traders about the new marketing arrangements and requesting their help in the organization of local shea suppliers.

Reinforcing the reach of the state as well as local power differences, it was not uncommon for CDR members to accompany PBC agents and participate in the organization of the farmer societies. Further accentuating status distinctions, SNFSs, according to PBC guidelines, were to have two levels of participation: one for "rank-and-file" members and the other for an elected seven-member executive committee of each society. Abiding by these parameters, the formation of SNFSs institutionalized the divide between village dweller and town dweller, shea collectors and shea traders, and elites and nonelites. Not only did this endow such economic distinctions with the added power of state sanction, but for those on the upper end it also offered new forms of state-based privilege.

Enforced by the state in this way, the creation and operation of SNFSs worked to undermine the long-standing domination of the shea economy by the rural women who gather shea nuts from trees growing wild in the bush or left standing on family farms and who have long been the backbone of the shea economy. Rather than pushing them out of business, though, the PBC's efforts at market restructuring centering on the formation of SNFSs did much to increase their participation in export marketing. The PBC actively encouraged rural nut collectors to join the SNFSs. In the village of Songo, for example, only people with farms of their own and hence access to substantial nut supplies were invited to join the farmer societies and provided with loans and ID cards authorizing them to sell nuts to PBC agents. Even when rural suppliers did not belong to an SNFS, those who were members would go to rural households to purchase nuts or secure the commitment of potential suppliers. Rural nut collectors would also bring their stocks to the larger market towns to sell to SNFS members. This strategy of inclusion, however, opened up new possibilities for collaboration and competition between rural people, especially females long familiar with shea work and both men and women new to the shea business.

Differentiation and Alliance among Shea Suppliers

Despite the expanded scope of nut collectors' participation in the shea trade, the SNFS provided only limited opportunity for leadership or gain and instead exposed rural collectors to new forms of risk and dependence. When their nut stores spoiled or were deemed unacceptable to PBC inspectors, they were denied their livelihood. Likewise, when rural suppliers invested additional capital in purchasing shea and PBC payments were delayed, they were left with little cash to spare for other endeavors, including emergency expenditures. The very timetable of PBC export purchasing, combined with the seasonality of shea and the larger agricultural cycle, posed some hard economic choices for less-prosperous rural suppliers. With the SNFS system in place, those individuals who collected shea found a new and ready outlet for their supplies relatively early in the season, a period when the availability of local capital and resources was especially meager. However, by selling all of their shea supplies to the PBC early in the season, as required, they gave up the opportunity to store them until prices rose.

The ambivalent position of rural suppliers in the farmer societies was further complicated by PBC's recruitment of traders, many of whom lacked prior experience with shea, to participate in export marketing. Nut collectors and traders played different roles in the farmers societies. As might be expected, the inclusion of rural shea suppliers in the societies generally depended on location, with village-based organizations containing more collectors, and town-based societies containing more traders. This rural collector/urban trader divide was in part a reflection of PBC policy. One informant reported that the PBC actively discouraged farmers societies in urban communities from recruiting members who were collectors rather than traders in order to take advantage of urban traders' money and connections and thereby maximize supplies. Shea collectors and traders also expressed different goals and economic mentalities, making for uneasy coexistence in a single society. In Bugri, a village with a growing market and entrepreneurial class, a shea nut farmer society that initially included both collectors and traders split into two groups after a few years due to the initiatives of the trader members. With collectors draining advances and commissions—and hence investment capital—away from traders, the latter had little interest in staying together.

Even within those societies that remained intact, traders and collectors played different roles, with the former financing and bulking nut purchases and the latter supplying nuts. In the town of Pusiga, a former SNFS member explained that traders used their own capital to finance nut purchases through collectors. Traders working in this way served as buyers for specific communities, linking rural pickers who had little experience bulking nuts and marketing beyond the local community to PBC buying schemes. A number of entrepreneurs who had formerly served as licensed buying agents in the 1970s and early 1980s prior to market restructuring and were initially left out of PBC's project of local mobilization eventually found a niche as farmer society financiers, using their wealth and knowledge of the market to advance money to particular SNFSs in order to purchase large quantities of nuts. Although these arrangements expanded rural collectors' economic opportunities, they nevertheless turned collectors into traders' agents, denying them full recognition or the commissions they deserved from the PBC.

Distinctions between traders and collectors were heightened as well by the PBC's tendency to groom traders for executive positions within the farmer societies despite the official policy of all society members voting for the executive council. In Garu, an agricultural marketing center located in an area rich in shea trees, although rural collectors made up the bulk of SNFS membership, the executives were all prosperous traders. Primarily women, these individuals had gained wealth and recognition through a variety of endeavors such as large-scale trade in the marketplace, ownership of private enterprises such as restaurants and transport, and the investment of earnings from salaried work. Already well known in the community, most had been contacted by PBC representatives to organize shea societies and were hence considered the obvious choice for leadership posts. The appointment of such businesspeople as executives, with the privilege of receiving PBC advances and distributing PBC funds, did little to make their relationship with collectors more equitable. Status differences between members and executives were all the more accentuated by the PBC strategy of recruiting what Ghanaians call "moneyed people" as society leaders. In addition to having access to capital, many were local politicians and professionals—chiefs, regents, district assembly members, head teachers, health post directors, agricultural officers—already connected to the state and considered "opinion leaders" at home.

Further consolidating their economic and political privilege, SNFS executives were granted membership in the national Cocoa, Coffee and Shea Nut Farmers Association (CCSNFA). Serving as a forum where executives from different areas could discuss members' concerns and as a platform from which to interact with policy-makers in the Cocoa Marketing Board, in a region where few associations had national standing the CCSNFA provided the opportunity for northern elites to gain status and recognition on an extralocal level. Accordingly, society executives, especially those elected as the district and regional representatives of the CCSNFA, took great pride in their appointments, garnering respect from both SNFS members and the wider community. This was so despite the minority status—both in terms of numbers and the value of the commodity they represented—of SNFS executives in the wider association.

Negotiating the Terms of Economic Citizenship: The Gender and Class Dynamics of Shea Nut Farmer Societies

By promoting the involvement of categories of people with little or no previous experience in the shea economy, such as "newcomer" traders, the PBC farmer society system dramatically altered the class and gender dynamics of the shea economy. The inclusion of newcomers broadened the spectrum of participants in the shea trade, subjecting experienced nut collectors and traders to a double and rather contradictory dynamic. At the same time as they were brought into the export economy, they also faced the risk of being pushed down in the supply chain. Indeed, the overall financial situation of the SNFS system, with members needing capital to buy cheap nuts early in the season and the PBC unable to assure adequate advances, enhanced socioeconomic differentiation between members of individual societies. Only wealthy society members could afford to buy nuts without prefinancing. Poorer society members who were unable to pick nuts instead relied on credit. Not only was this both costly and risky given the low prices offered by Cocoa Marketing Board and the frequent delay in paying for produce, but it also contributed to their economic dependence by leading them to appeal to society executives for loans.

The class bias of the PBC's purchasing scheme was paralleled by its gender bias. Providing new economic opportunities for men while taking them away from women, the PBC system altered gender relations within the shea economy. Replaying a widely occurring dynamic of valorization of female roles and resources in the course of export promotion (Etienne 1980), many of the traders joining the SNFSs were men attracted to new economic opportunities and the connection to the state that membership afforded. Not simply a matter of choice, the growing interest of men in shea nuts, traditionally a woman's crop, was facilitated by the recruitment strategies of PBC representatives and official representations of the shea economy. Reiterating the sentiments of colonial administrators of the 1920s, Rawlings, in a speech on the shea industry in the early 1980s, encouraged "every interested person to get involved in gathering shea nuts" (1982: 68) due to the fact that women, "with all the responsibilities they shoulder as housewives have very little time at their disposal to gather any appreciable quantities of nuts" (1982: 67).

Similarly validating male participation in the shea economy, an *Educational Guide for Sheanut Farmers* (n.d.), published in the 1980s by the Cocoa Marketing Board for the PBC to promote the new purchasing system, contains as many illustrations of men collecting and processing nuts as it does of women, despite the fact that men had virtually no experience with this work. And it is a man who is depicted delivering nuts to the PBC clerk and receiving his check from the state. It is unclear whether the creators of this pamphlet were simply misinformed about the gender division of labor in the areas of shea supply or making a deliberate attempt to add men to the ranks of shea nut traders and "farmers" in order to increase the scale of the export economy and perhaps even reduce rural male underemployment in the north. What is evident, however, is that the PBC program for stepping up shea exports through a rural mobilization scheme was modeled after the cocoa economy, the cultivation and trade of which was an equally appropriate and common vocation for men and women (Mikell 1986: 81). With the tools and techniques illustrated in the *Educational*

3.3 Former members of a rural shea nut farmer society recalling the abuses of the PBC purchasing scheme.

Guide, from baskets and drying racks to people's postures, being much more common in cocoa-growing regions than in the north, this sort of southern bias runs throughout the program of shea market reform. Imposing a singular national vision of economic citizenship centered on production for the state by both southerner and northerner, male and female, such an image of economic order failed to recognize—and thus worked to unseat—northern women's long-standing control of the shea economy.

Male participation in the shea economy did not mean that men took over roles formerly held by women; rather, new forms of dependence and dominance emerged as men gained access to women's knowledge and control over their services. Because shea nuts are traditionally considered a women's crop, with women responsible for procurement, distribution, and processing, women are the repositories of specialized knowledge and skill related to shea. Discerning good from bad nuts requires assessing their age and origin, water and oil content, and the presence of mold and infestation through a careful examination of the physical properties of the nut, including color, smell, taste, hardness, and even the sound of the nuts when rubbed together. Hence, male newcomers to the shea market depended on women to educate them about the criteria and practices of this sort of qualitative assessment. Men also relied on women to take care of nut purchasing and funded their close female relatives—wives, sisters, cousins, and so on—to travel to villages and markets to buy for them. They also relied on female shea bulkers serving village and town markets who had a long history of trading shea. Even in farmers societies with both male and female members, it was usually the women who would take care of sorting and bagging nuts when PBC personnel came to inspect and collect the produce. Burdened by this responsibility, a woman who was an active member of a large SNFS in Garu complained that she miscarried a pregnancy because of the physical exertion of weighing and packing nuts for collection by the PBC for other members of her group.

The rising demand for nuts and men's increased participation in the shea trade also altered the enforcement of gendered entitlements regarding shea nut collection. Women held customary rights in the nuts they picked on their husbands' farms, although these nuts were technically men's property. The idea was that while women could dispose of the nuts in any way they chose, the family would ultimately benefit from a woman's decision to make butter for family consumption or to trade the nuts in order to purchase foodstuffs for the household. However, as nuts gained value outside the domestic economy, in a few cases men enforced their claims, taking a share of the nuts picked by their wives and only occasionally reimbursing them. In Songo, for example, husbands would ask their wives to pick nuts for them from the family farm, allowing the women to keep one third of their cache, reserving the remaining two thirds to sell to the PBC. Similarly, in Basiyunde, the former chair of the village's shea nut society described how the wives of male society members would pick nuts from the bush and farm and be paid a share of the money they received from the PBC.

Hence, many rural women experienced a sort of "displacement by staying in place," as the field of opportunity expanded and they helped men and other newcomers gain skills and resources necessary for entry into the shea market. This is a vivid example of the way market-reform policies incite gendered struggles over resources in which the state is deeply implicated, a dynamic both confirming and complicating Staudt's observation that "[t]hose women who work at the periphery of state control have traditionally had to cope more with the vagaries of the market than with patronage. But increasingly, political machinery ensnarls them as well" (1995: 229). Yet as the value of shea to the state and more privileged political actors increased in the aftermath of market restructuring, women became much less likely to access political favor via shea.

This is not to suggest that the revamping of the shea export economy was entirely negative for women. Certainly there were women—mostly established and successful middle-class or medium-sized traders—who used access to new opportunities afforded by the new purchasing scheme to expand their enterprises. While some incorporated shea into the repertoire of goods they already traded, others became more specialized in shea, closing up shop for other commodities and trading exclusively in shea during the height of the season. Typically occupying executive positions within the shea nut farmer societies, these women were also able to gain status on a par with men who held comparable posts within their own or other farmer societies. Exemplifying such cross-gender parity among rural elites, in Bugri, the leading members of the community's farmer society were male and female. In Songo as well, a number of women were society executives, including the wife of the district assemblyman, who was himself an executive. In Garu, the large majority of executives were female.

Given all the evidence, however, it is reasonable to claim that the new system provided more new economic opportunities for men while it took away opportunities from and increased the obligations placed upon less-prosperous rural women. Such incursions of men into an economic domain that was traditionally feminine did not go unnoticed or uncontested by northern women. In 1986, just a few years after the establishment of the new export regime, representatives of women from the three regions making up Ghana's northern sector petitioned the government to make the shea economy the exclusive preserve of women. According to the magazine *West Africa*:

> The resolution pointed out that the COCOBOD, the main buyer of the commodity, had given huge sums of money to agents who operate in a manner which did not favor women, who are the real producers. . . . The resolution observed that it is only the women who know the peculiar problems pertaining to the industry. ("Ghana: women" 1986: 321)

Not only did this encounter give voice to women's specific grievances but it also signaled the emergence of shea as a legitimate platform for northern political participation and recognition. Even though their specific requests remained unfulfilled, northern women's public voicing of such pleas did at some level indicate their internalization of the terms of membership in the nation-state earlier articulated by Rawlings. Seeking to reclaim the reciprocities between state and citizen first established by him, northern women's protests may be considered a first step in the actualization of Rawlings's agenda of constituency-building and political subject-formation, despite the criticisms of state practice they encoded.

The Decline and Survival of Shea Nut Farmer Societies

Although the PBC offered new economic opportunities for many, involvement in and enthusiasm for its shea purchasing scheme declined the longer the shea nut farmer societies were in place. While former SNFS members recalled the two to three years of PBC's initial success, beyond that they expressed frustration and disappointment, first with PBC policies and second with the PBC's failure to live up to its promises. Almost all former SNFS members complained of the low prices offered by the Cocoa Marketing Board and the difficulty of making a profit due to the company's unreliable payment and pickup schedule. The remarks of Mary Anaba, the chairwoman of a shea farmer society in Garu composed predominantly of rural women, point to a host of grievances shared by many who participated in the PBC program:

> When PBC didn't pick up as promised, people had to store nuts for a long time. This made it difficult for those who purchased nuts on credit since they couldn't pay their debts and would have to request a loan from the group leader. When the PBC finally arrived for the nuts, it would still take a long time to cash their checks. The women did not have a storage shed and were forced to keep the nuts in the yard. If the rain spoiled the nuts, the PBC would not purchase them and the women would lose. This was very problematic for the leader. The PBC promised to pay a commission, but the women never received it. The PBC also promised to provide cloth for the women, but they never brought it.

The members of the Garu women's group were not alone in their complaints. In almost every farmer society surveyed, nut financing and the access to ancillary economic opportunities were the ultimate arbiters of compliance and noncompliance with the PBC. Contentions over prefinancing arose soon after the PBC farmer society scheme was put in place. In the initial years of operation, large preseason advances had been ceded to the farmers societies. Not long after, the PBC found itself confronting a situation of widespread loan default. While some societies repaid the balance of their loans the following year, others remained in debt, making the PBC wary of investing too much money in prefinancing. This did not deter SNFS members from requesting advance funding and using it as a prerequisite for their participation in the PBC program. Reflecting the different mentalities and capacities of different SNFS, those societies dominated by traders, savvy about managing money and accustomed to working as middle people with outside funding, were especially adamant in their requests for prefinancing. Payment of commissions was also a source of tension between society members and the PBC. Although commissions had been paid by the PBC to shea suppliers in the mid-1980s, by the latter part of the decade they had been withdrawn, leaving the expectations of SNFS members unfulfilled.

Echoing the concerns of the Garu women, SNFS members across Bawku East cited the PBC's failure to provide promised consumer items as a reason for the curtailment of their operations. Informed about the opportunity to purchase highly desirable consumer goods such as wax print cloth, kerosene lanterns, boots, and cutlasses on credit and at discounted rates when the SNFSs were first organized, many former society members considered this "consumption opportunity" a highlight of the PBC system. In some areas the goods such as never delivered at all, causing great disappointment. In others, they were sold to SNFS members at the same price as they commanded on the market. In the words of a former society executive, "CMB fooled us each year, saying it would be different and promising radios and mats that never arrived." Of little surprise, years later, perks produced for exclusive distribution to farmer society members could be found in rural households and markets after being sold out by PBC representatives.

Even more basic, numerous society members complained about PBC's lack of provision of the burlap sacs used for measuring and storing shea nuts in bulk, making it necessary for them to use their own. Society members likewise often had little choice but to cover the cost of nut transport. An elderly Busanga lady, for example, recounted her three years of participation in the PBC marketing scheme, vividly recalling her efforts to transport nuts from Pusiga to the PBC storage shed in Bawku at her own expense. Such expenditures, minor as they may seem, combined with the low prices offered for shea nuts by the PBC, robbed society members of financial benefit. As a prosperous trader and former SNFS member from Garu explained, "If the CMB came back, I wouldn't work for them again.

3.4 A disabled tractor, formerly used for the excavation of shea nuts, parked outside a rural depot built by the Produce Buying Company in the 1980s. (Photo by Daniel Smith).

You would work hard for them and then have to buy aspirin from your own profit!"

Despite all of these failings, the PBC continued to command the compliance of a number of SNFSs and their membership. For society executives especially, the potential for political influence and involvement gained by working with the PBC made up for the threat of financial loss. Demonstrating the overlap of local and supralocal political contests, even within the same community executives vied among themselves for ascendance, as farmer societies competed with another to deliver the greatest volume of nuts to the PBC. Long after the eventual dissolution of the farmer society system, executives recalled with pride their appointments as society leaders. They proudly recounted their opportunities to attend regional and national level meetings of the CCSNFA and to serve as representatives on a par with those from other parts of Ghana.

While executives clearly had more to gain, both financially and politically, from participation in the PBC's shea marketing scheme, they were supported by ordinary society members. With few other options for participation in national-level economic institutions and initiatives, society members made extraordinary investments of time, energy, and income to purchase, store, and transport nut stocks in pursuit of the promise of PBC recognition and influence over policy. Investing in political access in this manner, although in a different manner from the protesting women described above, these society members and executives selectively embraced the new criteria of economic citizenship devised by the Rawlings regime notwithstanding the uneven returns and narrow terms of participation they offered.

Conclusion

Despite the extensive intervention of international financial institutions in the Ghanaian economy and the concomitant pressure to conform to the conditionalities of market reform, during the 1980s the shea economy was buffered from the direct effects of IMF and World Bank directives. Rather than surrender to international imperatives and reduce its hold on the shea market, the state at this time asserted greater control over the shea nut market, even as it relinquished its hold on other sectors of the national economy. The renewed attention of the state to shea after years of relative indifference was an outcome of a number of different dynamics. Most important was the attempt by the Rawlings administration to recapture a northern constituency and reorient the northern economy in the wake of decades of progressive disenfranchisement and disengagement. The Rawlings government likewise sought to protect the Cocoa Marketing Board—which oversaw shea export and was a major source of income and national and international clout due to its control of Ghana's cocoa trade—from the incursions of international institutions and policy prescriptions. Heightening its control over shea nuts and doing little to reduce the depth of its oversight of the cocoa market, the PBC's orchestration of the shea farmer societies nevertheless appeased donor pressure for export diversification.

At the same time as shea nuts were made an adjunct to the circulation of Ghanaian cocoa on the world market, Ghana's cocoa economy was posted as a model for the economic *cum* civic duty of northern shea producers. Although neither platform was an economic success, in terms of political significance they did increase northerner's participation in state-based institutions and provided a foundation for the reincorporation of northern residents into the national whole. These inclusions had both desired and unexpected consequences, shaping the terms of discussion among northern residents about expectations and obligations in relation to the state and, for some shea suppliers—especially society executives—holding out the promise of new avenues of political influence and access within national political bodies.

In addition to instigating a repatterning of state-society relations, policies of shea market restructuring during the 1980s also inspired new relationships among different social groups, accentuating class- and gender-based inequalities. Even as the formation of SNFSs fostered new forms of collaboration among urban traders and rural residents, wealthy and poor, male and female, these same relationships heightened economic distinctions. Most of all, they contributed to the dependence of poorer rural women on their more elite counterparts in shea societies along with the expropriation of female labor power, knowledge, skill. In short, the emergence and operation of the PBC's SNFSs both challenged international mandates and reinforced the commodity-centric value system of neoliberalism, as it fostered the ascendance of state authority and new terms of economic citizenship in northern Ghana. Such a return of the state to the north via the shea market brought increasing value to the work of rural women at the same time as it threatened their control of a market which they had previously dominated.

CHAPTER **4**

Chocolate Wars
and Cosmetic Contests
Shea as a New Global Commodity

Closely tracking the formulation and implementation of global commercial initiatives, this chapter investigates the processes surrounding the repositioning of shea on the world market over the course of the 1990s and the early years of the 2000s. At this time, shea, after many decades as an unnamed ingredient in the manufacture of mass-market confections, began to occupy a new economic niche as a luxury cosmetic noted for its purity and restorative capacities. Focusing on the sometimes divergent, sometimes complementary character of the ensemble of forces contributing to shea's movement from "mass" to "class" commodity, the chapter makes evident the inherently unstable nature of new forms of tropical commoditization. At the same time, it draws attention to the myriad ways in which state power is reconstituted and not always reduced even as markets grow in size and prominence—a process that brings order to the shea market and contributes to its contingency.

Specifically, the shifting face of the shea economy makes it clear that the battle between state and societal interests over the contours of the national economy is played out on the global stage and involves global entities and actors as much as a national ones. Under these circumstances, not only do global bodies rely on state actors and infrastructure and hold a vested interest in their preservation, but state institutions, far from being undermined by global initiatives, actively engage global directives to shore up their own authority, resource base, and political support. As the case of shea makes evident, this does not lead to the reproduction of state institutions and authority structures *status quo ante*. Instead, a more dynamic process of restructuring is induced, mutually enjoining states and global coalitions and altering the objectives and capacities of both. Indeed, if Raikes and Gibbon are correct in their assessment that globalization is precipitating new and extreme forms of deregulation[1] within African economies (2000: 53), the case of shea does well to suggest the significance of considering the ways in which such deregulation opens up new spaces for the state—whether within or beyond the terrain of the nation—even as it closes others. As they see it: "The issue is not simply one of marginalization, but of a more complex process of redefinition of economic role whereby some of Africa's established links with the global economy are strengthened, others are weakened or disappear, and others are restructured" (2000: 53). In Ghana, by the 1990s, these sorts of global repositionings were well under way.

Cocoa and Shea at Home and Abroad

At the beginning of the 1990s, the government of Ghana, still under the leadership of J. J. Rawlings, faced yet another crossroads. Forced to confront the contractions of the late 1980s (Kraus 1991: 134–5) and the fiscal shocks of the early 1990s (World Bank n.d.a), along with the pressures of holding democratic elections for the first time after ten years of military rule (Nugent 1995), the government sought to recapture the trajectory of economic growth that the country had experienced during much of the previous decade (Rothchild 1991: 3; "Missing Ingredient," 1992). Even as it struggled to repay past loans, the Rawlings regime turned once again to the IMF and World Bank in order to garner additional aid. At this juncture, there was little choice but to deepen the commitment to the conditionalities of international lenders despite their unshaken view that the expansion of markets—both domestic and foreign—was the fundamental means and ends of economic development.

It was of no surprise that in Ghana cocoa—the country's major source of foreign exchange—was the centerpiece of the International Financial Institution (IFI) platform, with an emphasis on privatization of the industry at home and stabilization of prices abroad. Under renewed pressure to liberalize the cocoa sector, which was still under state control as it had been since the colonial period, the government embarked upon a path of deregulation affecting the Cocoa Marketing Board's ever-ramifying economic edifice (World Bank n.d.a). This restructuring of the Cocoa Board, though widespread, was highly selective and had a greater direct impact on the shea economy than on cocoa itself. The Produce Buying Company (PBC), the state-owned subsidiary of the Cocoa Board in charge of shea market-ing, was targeted for top-to-bottom restructuring. As a part of this, in 1992 the PBC's domestic purchasing plan, centered on the shea nut farmer soci-eties, was officially dissolved. Further undermining the deep and exclusive involvement of the state that had characterized the shea economy during the 1980s, the majority of PBC personnel involved in shea marketing lost their jobs, and the agency lost most of its funding. All price regulations and buying restrictions were removed from the shea market, and private for-mal-sector enterprises were officially invited to participate in both domes-tic purchasing and export.

Cocoa marketing, in contrast, was subject to only limited reform, affect-ing domestic purchasing but not export sales, as private buyers were allowed to enter the domestic market and the Cocoa Board retained its monopoly on external marketing ("Ghana: economic," 2001: 27; World Bank n.d.b). Here was a situation, paralleling the 1980s, where the mandates of international lenders were unevenly enforced and the Rawlings regime sought to protect and pursue its own political and economic imperatives, simultaneously sub-verting IFI directives and manipulating them to its own ends. In this case, privatization of shea via the dismantling of the PBC system served as an olive branch of sorts, demonstrating the Cocoa Board's ostensible commit-ment to liberalization while protecting the cocoa sector.

The linkage of cocoa and shea in the face of international initiatives was not restricted to the IFI-led project of privatization. At the same time as shea's place within the Ghanaian economy was being reframed due to IFI mandates, shea's position on the world market was being redefined by a number of supranational bodies concerned about the status of the world market for cocoa and cocoa products—especially chocolate. Reflecting wider currents of political and economic restructuring occurring within the indus-trialized nations of the North Atlantic, these global realignments were tied to a range of changes in the structure of demand for shea on the world market, from pricing and corporate purchasing patterns to consumption trends, re-finement techniques, and international regulation of standards of use and quality. Born of distinct and at times disparate initiatives, they did little to stabilize an already fragile market.

While the shea economy did experience considerable growth over the course of the 1990s, it was highly uneven, as Figures 2 and 3 illustrate. Ex-port volumes reached a peak in both dollar value and tonnage in 1998 and 1999, sustaining a takeoff that began in 1996. However, by 2000 and 2001 export prices and volumes had fallen dramatically, retreating to 1994 and 1995 levels. The dynamic character of the shea market cannot be attrib-uted to the workings of supranational entities and interests alone, whether corporate, consumer, or multilateral in nature. Of critical signifi-

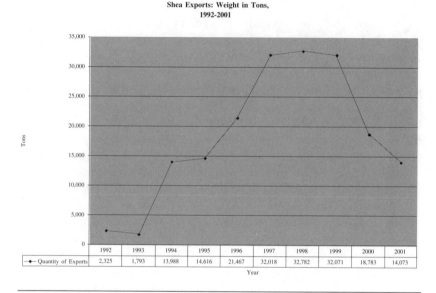

Shea Exports: Weight in Tons, 1992-2001

	1992	1993	1994	1995	1996	1997	1998	1999	2000	2001
Quantity of Exports	2,325	1,793	13,988	14,616	21,467	32,018	32,782	32,071	18,783	14,073

Year

Fig. 2 Shea Export: Weight in Tons, 1992–2001

cance to the uneasy process of shea market reform were the initiatives and interests of individual nation-states—both the tropical states where shea and cocoa are sourced and the industrial ones where they are refined and consumed.

In the case of Ghana, the entanglement of the government in the global shea economy at this juncture was at odds with the mandate of market promotion and diversification promulgated by the World Bank. In a process facilitated by the governments of a host of other African nations and at the same time driven by domestic motives, the Ghanaian state used the global arena to limit the shea market and to promote its own standing and interests at home. At the crux of this dynamic once again lay Ghanaian cocoa. As the growth of shea exports threatened to usurp even a small share of Ghana's cocoa trade, powerful coalitions within the government of Ghana, together with their allies in neighboring cocoa-producing nations, asserted their interests on global stage to oppose the expansion of the shea economy and instead promote cocoa export, reproducing the imbalance of power between the country's northern and the southern sectors. In this way, the reduction of the state's direct involvement in the shea market in order to free it—in keeping with the mandates of the World Bank and IMF—worked to the opposite effect. Rather, the performance and potential of the shea economy remained highly, albeit indirectly, controlled and constrained by the continued involvement of the state in the cocoa sector.

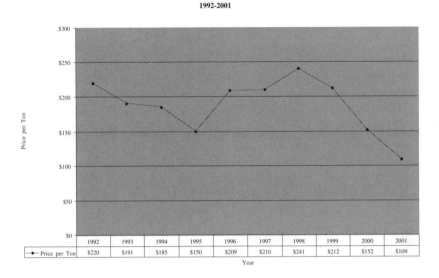

Fig. 3 Shea Export: Price per Ton, 1992–2001

In short, though the shea market floundered during the era of PBC domination in the 1980s because of too much intervention, during the second phase of market reform initiated in the 1990s it continued to struggle because of behind-the-scenes regulation endorsed by the state through the chambers of the world market. In the process, state institutions tied to the cocoa economy claimed a new mandate, buffering cocoa from new threats and allowing the government to preserve its hold on revenue while asserting its accountability to cocoa producers.

Chocolate-Making Standards and the European Union

Despite the recent attention given to shea within the cosmetics industry and its high visibility in the health and beauty market, standards of chocolate production remain the single most important influence on the demand for shea on the world market. Accordingly, interventions by the government of Ghana within the global economy regarding shea export have focused on the specification of these standards. Although most consumers are little aware of the exact contents of a chocolate bar other than cocoa, sugar, and perhaps milk, within advanced industrial economies shea's primary use is in chocolate processing. This is because shea is a popular cocoa butter substitute (CBS). With the incorporation of shea, chocolate products are easier and cheaper to manufacture than from cocoa liquor and cocoa butter alone (Lipp and Anklam 1998). In addition to shea, a number of other tropical oilseeds may be used as CBSs in this manner. They include palm oil (*Elaeis guineensi, Elaeis olifera*), sourced in Malaysia, Indonesia, and West Africa, as well as illipe nuts (*Shorea species*), commonly known as "Borneo tallow," also from Malaysia, and secondarily, sal nuts (*Shorea robusta*) and kokum gurgi (*Garcinia indica*) from India, and mango kernel oil (*Mangifera indica*) ("Are Cocoa Butter," 2002; "Directive 2000/36/EC," 2000). Among potential substitutes shea is the most popular and the closest to cocoa butter in composition ("Do Cocoa Butter," 2002; "Foodstuffs: MEPS," 1996).

A key source of attraction of CBSs such as shea for chocolate producers is the fact that they are cheaper than cocoa butter. This concern with price accounts for both the popularity of substitutes and the volatility in demand for them. As more and more tropical nations produce cocoa for export, the world market has become glutted with cocoa stocks, lowering the price for both cocoa butter and cocoa liquor, the main components of chocolate (Kassardjian 2002). This in turn reduces the price that chocolate producers are willing to pay for substitutes like shea.

Price aside, there are a host of other reasons cocoa butter substitutes are attractive to chocolate manufacturers. Not only is the expense of chocolate production reduced, but also chocolate products made with shea are more durable and versatile than those without. They have less potential to develop the whitish discoloration known as bloom and exhibit greater hardness and gloss along with what's called "snap" in the chocolate industry—the ability to break evenly without crumbling. CBSs, moreover, can be refined to make them suitable for specific uses and can help to neutralize differences in cocoa bean and butter quality, producing a chocolate with a more reliable and uniform taste and consistency (Fold 2000: 101–2). For all these reasons, chocolate products made with shea and other substitutes are well suited to mass marketing and manufacture. Popular with large-scale chocolate processors, they are suitable for wide distribution and the exploitation of new market niches.

Having a substantial bearing on the market for CBSs, international standards of chocolate production vary widely. In the United States, CBSs are not allowed in chocolate, although milk fat is a common additive, similarly reducing cost and in some cases, quality.[2] In Europe, shea has been used for several decades as a cocoa butter substitute in an array of countries accounting for almost three quarters of the world chocolate market ("Trade: chocolate" 1997). Figure 4 illustrates the primarily European destination of shea exports from Ghana, indicating the popularity of shea among European chocolate manufacturers.

In the early 1990s, with great implications for world-market demand for shea, the use of CBSs within the European chocolate industry and the

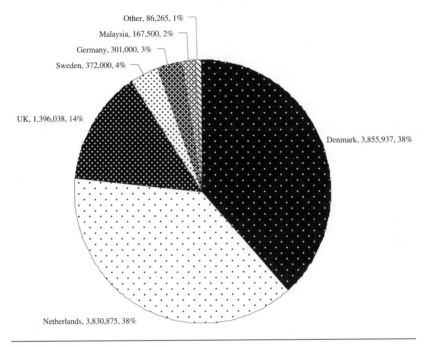

Fig. 4 Destination of Shea Exports, 1998

global confections sector emerged as a topic of substantial debate. Involving chocolate manufacturing nations as well as cocoa-producing countries, this debate centered on the establishment of legal standards of allowance for cocoa butter substitutes such as shea in chocolate production for all members of the European Union, a ruling with major implications for the conventions of chocolate manufacturing worldwide.

Although the standards of European chocolate processing had been codified in the 1970s by the European Economic Community (EEC) via the European Commission 1973 Chocolate Directive (74/241/EEC), the growing membership of the European Union (EU) and the concomitant drive to harmonize commercial policy and codes in the early 1990s brought renewed attention to this matter. In the 1990s concern revolved around questions of maximum CBS allowance, whether and how to protect individual country variation in chocolate standards, chocolate labeling and nomenclature, and the specification of substances deemed acceptable as CBSs. These questions had previously been resolved by deferring to the national chocolate-making traditions of new members of the

EEC. For example, Britain, Ireland, and Denmark were granted a derogation allowed the use of up to 5 percent CBS when they joined the EEC in 1973 ("Chocolate: COPAL" 1993). Similarly, when Portugal joined in 1986 the derogation was extended ("Chocolate commission" 1995). However, in the mid-1990s what has been referred to as the "European Chocolate War" (Fold 2000: 93) began to flare with the proposed accession to the EU of Sweden, Austria, and Finland. In all of these countries the use of CBS is widespread, ranging from 5 percent in Sweden and Austria to a high of 10 percent in Finland ("Cocoa/chocolate producer" 1995). As the EU expanded to incorporate these nations and at the same time sought to further integrate the economies of its members by revising the 1973 directive and extending the 5 percent CBS allowance to all ("Chocolate: COPAL" 1993), a prolonged and contentious negotiation process ensued.

As this debate unfolded, two different positions emerged regarding the proposed chocolate standards, each backed by distinctive and in some cases competing national interests. Eight states, consisting of the six original EU members (Belgium, Germany, France, Italy, Luxembourg, and the Netherlands) plus Greece and Spain, supported a "purist" position. This bloc, representing 71 percent of the EU's population, advocated low and in some cases zero allowances of CBS in European chocolate, annulling earlier exceptions ("Foodstuffs:" Ivory Coast 1997). With the enlargement of the EU in 1995, however, a second and equally powerful bloc emerged, asserting an alternative point of view in favor of CBS usage. Consisting of those nations who already held the right to use CBS, the states endorsing the pro-CBS position manufactured over 70 percent of the European Union's chocolate and controlled a major share of the world chocolate market ("Trade: chocolate" 1997).[3]

African Consortia and the Battle for Chocolate

Operating through international consortia, African cocoa-producing countries were quick to claim a stake in this argument.[4] At a time when international cocoa prices were experiencing instability and decline and world cocoa stocks continued to rise ("Cocoa: CPA" 1994; "Commodity Price Index" 1999a), cocoa-producing nations expressed deep concern that the expanded use of CBSs would further destabilize an already weakened cocoa sector. For Africa's leading cocoa producers, Côte d'Ivoire and Ghana, this was an especially serious issue. Not only did the EU consume 40 percent of world cocoa, 85 percent to 90 percent of which came from West Africa (Sarno 1998; "Trade: chocolate" 1997), but European standards typically serve as the reference for the Codex Alimentarius, a code defining international foodstuff standards administered by the World

Health Organization (WHO) and the Food and Agriculture Organization (FAO) of the United Nations ("Cocoa/chocolate" 1996). Hence a change in European law was seen as a threat to chocolate standards and cocoa markets worldwide. This included the fear that lowered costs of chocolate production would renew competition with "the EU's giant chocolate producers [to] bring the United States to align with EU standards, resulting in a fall of exports to the US as well" ("Trade: EU" 1997).[5]

For Ghana this was a matter of great import. The world's leading producer of cocoa from the early part of the century until the late 1970s ("Ghana is one" 1998; "Cocoa agreement" 1979: 69; "Ghana: economic structure" 1996: 10), in the 1990s Ghana competed with Indonesia and Brazil for the number two slot after its first-ranking neighbor, Côte d'Ivoire ("World cocoa" 2002). Nevertheless, cocoa remained the country's economic mainstay and its prime foreign-exchange earner ("Ghana is one" 1998; "Missing ingredient" 1992), accounting for 30 percent to 40 percent of export revenue annually ("Prospects: Ghana" 2000; "Cargill invests" 1999) and contributing to the livelihoods of a substantial share of the population.[6] Yet with world market prices fluctuating from year to year and domestic and world production unpredictable, it was also a highly volatile commodity ("Commodity Price Index" 1999c; "Ghana backs" 2000). With the national economy already reeling from the aftershocks of neoliberal reform, throughout the 1990s Ghana's government was especially cautious about any international action that might threaten the cocoa economy. Comments by the presidential advisor on cocoa in Ghana represent the seriousness of the government's stance on the use of CBSs such as shea:

> around 6 million of Ghana's 16.5 million people directly or indirectly depend on cocoa. . . . Enough cocoa is available for the manufacture of chocolate and other cocoa products and I do not see the necessity for introducing substitutes . . . the policy would spell doom for the cocoa industry, given the fact that current producer prices of cocoa is so low and unrewarding for the producer. (*Public Ledger* 1995)

This was not just a matter of sustaining the livelihoods of cocoa growers. Equally if not more important was the support the state itself derived from the cocoa market. Despite the pressures of liberalization, in the 1990s Ghana's Cocoa Marketing Board, along with a parallel institution in Côte d'Ivoire, were among very few parastatals in sub-Saharan Africa that had survived more than a decade of market reform. Prices continued to be set centrally, input subsidies were still in operation, and the government maintained its export monopoly (Raikes and Gibbon 2000: 73). Indeed, even as Côte d'Ivoire opened its market in 1999 (Commodity Price Index

2000; "Ghana: economic" 2001: 27), in Ghana as late as 2002 only domestic cocoa purchasing and a small share of exports had been turned over to private firms. Cocoa remains and has long been a lifeline for the Ghanaian state, which earns considerably more on the world market for the cocoa it sells than paid to farmers for what they grow (Beckman 1981; Mikell 1989; Swift 1998b: 12).

Working in tandem with representatives of other cocoa-producing states, the government of Ghana was able to influence EU chocolate standards, giving voice to clear-cut national interests regarding the prospects of the international cocoa market. Leading this effort was the Cocoa Producers Alliance, or COPAL, a multinational consortium of cocoa-producing nations in which African nations maintain a strong presence. COPAL's membership includes Côte d'Ivoire, Brazil, Ghana, Malaysia, Cameroon, Ecuador, Gabon, Mexico, Nigeria, the Dominican Republic, São Tomé and Príncipe, Togo, and Trinidad and Tobago ("Cocoa producers" 1993).[7] Formed in 1962, COPAL is concerned with monitoring international trade policy and prices for cocoa along with the cocoa stocks and production targets for each of its members ("Chocolate: COPAL" 1993). More of a watchdog and advocacy group than an effective cartel, COPAL's influence has waxed and waned over the years due to the shifting capacities and commitments of its members (Krasner 1974). However, in the 1990s, the organization—making the debate over CBSs the centerpiece of its platform—was focused and well coordinated in its efforts ("1999 target" 1998).

As it sought to influence the standards of European chocolate production and, in turn, world-market demand for shea, COPAL inserted itself into debates already in play within the EU. Indicating the variegated yet fluid nature of a global economic order containing within it multiple national agendas and economic bodies, COPAL, with the aim of curbing the usage of CBSs, forged a series of unlikely alliances. Cutting across political boundaries—both ideological and territorial—these coalitions were themselves inherently global even as they furthered distinctive national platforms. Organizing and attending international forums, issuing statements, sponsoring research, and mobilizing popular awareness of the "chocolate war" both at home and abroad, COPAL aggressively pursued its pro-cocoa, anti–CBS/shea platform. In doing so, the alliance worked with business groups, consumer advocates, state governments, political parties, development activists, and other supranational organizations. Hence for Ghana's state apparatus, rather than being overwhelmed by global forces, the global battle over chocolate emerged as a platform for the pursuit and promotion of its own concerns. Taking advantage of the vast yet disintegrated character of chocolate interests worldwide, Ghana's government representatives worked to forge new global blocs and exploit the fissures already existing within established global entities.

International Chocolate Blocs and European Union Contradictions

Attesting to the diverse and often conflicting agendas of supranational *cum* global organizations, COPAL pursued a number of avenues within the EU to work against the proposed European Chocolate Directive. Early on in the negotiation process, COPAL brought to the attention of the EU its earlier statement of commitment to cocoa-producing nations—a commitment COPAL interpreted as nullifying the new EU provisions supporting the use of CBS. COPAL referred specifically to the 1993 International Cocoa Agreement, Article 33, which, as COPAL saw it, bound the EU to take all practical measures to increase cocoa consumption ("Chocolate: COPAL" 1993) and prohibit materials of noncocoa origin from being used in place of cocoa in a manner that could mislead consumers ("Chocolate: draft" 1995).

COPAL members also worked to point out other contradictions between existing EU accords and the new chocolate standards. In doing so, COPAL sought the support of the wider Africa, Caribbean, and Pacific Rim Conference known as the ACP. Endorsing the interests of COPAL and its member states, the ACP used its relationship with the EU to publicize the adverse implications of the EU directive for cocoa producers, repeating COPAL's call to disqualify all use of CBS in chocolate ("Cocoa/chocolate" 1996; "Cocoa/chocolate producer" 1995). In 1995, the ACP-EU Joint Assembly issued figures projecting a 200,000-ton drop in cocoa bean exports ("EU/ACP" 1995), accounting for 8 percent of global production in 1996 ("Chocolate: yet" 1996). Lowering cocoa prices at the same time ("Foodstuffs-MEPs" 1996), this would amount to revenue losses of ECU 350–400 million a year ("EU/ACP" 1995). Such an assessment was corroborated by the International Cocoa Organization (ICCO), a trade association made up of cocoa and chocolate producers, which speculated that the proposed chocolate ruling could reduce African producers' revenues by 12 percent to 24 percent (Sarno 1998; "Trade: chocolate" 1997).

Continuing to press the cocoa issue, late in 1996, the ACP-EU Joint Assembly adopted a resolution stating that the EU proposal "contravenes both the spirit and letter of the Fourth Lome Convention goal of promoting ACP exports" and asking the European Parliament to reject the amendment ("Foodstuffs" 1996). Even when EU was made aware of these contradictions, a common position was hard to come by. As late as 1998, taking up the issue of the Chocolate Directive once again, the European Parliament voiced its concern about cocoa-producing countries while the

European Commission rejected the need for further study ("Chocolate directive" 1998), with both the Parliament and the Commission being powerful bodies within the EU.

Development Agendas

A second constellation of interests in the pro-cocoa camp in which COPAL found and provided support was tied to a broadly defined development community. The thrust of its argument centered on notions of sustainability and ecological balance. This platform sought to preserve both the natural qualities of chocolate and the rights of those considered to be closest to nature—in their view the cocoa producers. Members of this ad hoc coalition ranged from Green Party representatives, international nongovernmental organizations involved in sustainable development, and fair-trade lobbying groups. Together these associations provided a tacit endorsement of state economic controls and state-propelled exclusions within cocoa-producing nations.

As a case in point, Oxfam, along with the Liaison Committee of NGOs, pressured the EU Development Council to acknowledge the negative implications of increased use of CBS for cocoa producers ("Chocolate: yet" 1996; "Chocolate directive" 1998). Likewise, the European Fair Trade Association (EFTA), an alliance of eleven European organizations, voiced its support for both cocoa producers and chocolate consumers. Articulating an anticorporate platform, it sought to protect these groups from what they saw as the inherent greed and duplicity of big business, a perspective evident in its remarks that: "The chocolate industry will make chocolate using the new cheaper substitutes while charging the consumer the same price as before. For the fat industry, it will mean a whole new market for their products," (Sarno 1998).

COPAL also came together with distinctly political bodies within the EU that sought to protect chocolate from adulteration. Here the most vocal public body endorsing pro-cocoa position was the Green Party ("Foodstuffs: MEPS" 1996). Working through the European Parliament rapporteur, a Green from Belgium, the party pushed to minimize the use of CBSs and for explicit labeling requirements for products that did contain them. Like that of the fair-trade advocates, this position was held to favor the interests of both consumers and cocoa producers ("Foodstuffs: MEPS" 1996; "Foodstuffs: MEPS" 1997). Such a perspective was evident in the statement of the European Parliamentarian leading the battle for the reconsideration of the proposed chocolate directive. As he saw it, "The parliament's Environment Committee was cowardly in confronting the interests of chocolate multinationals" ("Trade: EU" 1997).

Expressing values in line with the Green's pronature stance, COPAL members moreover sought to prohibit the use in chocolate of fats that have been synthesized or refined using "enzymatic" processes. According to a report commissioned by Côte d'Ivoire for producer countries belonging to the International Cocoa Organization, the use of synthetics "could pave the way to all sorts of abuses, such as the introduction of genetically modified fats, the health effects of which are not clearly understood" ("Foodstuffs: Ivory" 1997). For those supporting the Green position in the European Parliament, the employment of enzymatic processes threatened to further "reduce market access for natural tropical products" ("Chocolate directive," 1998).

This endorsement of tropical raw materials for use in chocolate production by the Greens was by no means to be confused with the endorsement of shea as a chocolate additive. The European Parliament rapporteur explicitly rallied against the use of shea in the name of sustainability and small business despite its tropical origins and natural qualities. Speaking of shea-producing countries, including Mali and Burkina Faso, which derive 20 percent of their export revenue from shea nuts, he asserted:

> These countries cannot afford the large-scale investment involved in waiting 15–20 years for the trees to bear fruit after they have been planted. Moreover, there is no guarantee that the chocolate industry will use shea butter, as palm oil sells for a third of the price of shea. At the same time, the cocoa pressing industry and small scale producers would be under threat as they would find themselves at a competitive disadvantage vis a vis the big companies. ("Foodstuffs: MEPS" 1996)

Chocolate Culture

The government of Ghana, via its membership in COPAL, intervened in the global chocolate market in other ways to shape world-market demand for shea. At the same time as COPAL was working with organizations outside the state apparatus that were decidedly anticorporate and attuned to the status of African cocoa producers, COPAL representatives also worked hand in hand with corporate interests and state bodies to call for the restriction of CBS within the chocolate industry. Central to this initiative was once again the notion of purity. Conceived not in the essentialist terms underlying the nature-oriented value system espoused by Oxfam, Green Party members, and fair-trade advocates, the sense of purity promoted by these interests had much more of a cultural foundation. It derived less from a concern with the purity of tropical raw materials than a concern about the purity of products fabricated from them. From this vantage point, rather than cocoa farmers the producers at issue were chocolate-makers. Supporting this agenda, the Ivorian minister at the helm of

COPAL, acting on behalf of African, Latin-American, and Asian cocoa producers, embarked on a European tour at the height of the CBS debates expressly to promote "pure cocoa" chocolate ("Producers continue" 1995). Targeting the corporate sector, he sought meetings with industrialists in Spain, Italy, Germany, and Belgium—all countries that did not support the EU's permissive stance regarding the use of CBS, as well as representatives of the Association of the Chocolate, Biscuit, and Confectionary Industries of the EC (CAOBISCO) ("Producers continue" 1995).

Such a concern about processes of chocolate production extended to another sector of the chocolate market in which chocolate-making is regarded as more of a craft than an industry (Terrio 1996). Here the members of COPAL found an ally among small-scale artisanal chocolate makers ("Chocolate: yet" 1996) who also opposed expanded use of CBS as it would only intensify the price and product competition from large-scale manufactures and further distort the standards of chocolate quality. In those countries where the artisanal chocolate sector remains vital and chocolate quality is considered a definitive feature of national heritage, chocolate-makers received the support of the state in the effort to limit CBS. This was boldly evident in the remarks of the Dutch delegate to the International Cocoa and Chocolate Organization convention, who espoused fervent support for the "zero" option; that is, "Zero percent of vegetable oils in chocolate for all European countries, even the new comers to the EU" ("Cocoa: ICCO" 1995; "Cocoa/chocolate" 1995).

Likewise, delegations to the EU from France, Belgium, and the Netherlands, all countries with a history of high-quality chocolate production, rejected the use of cocoa butter substitutes. Demanding careful monitoring of chocolate production and labeling ("FEDIOL" n.d.; "Directive 2000/ 36/EC" 2000: 7), they went so far as to suggest that "pure cocoa butter chocolate be called 'real chocolate' and the less-pure version drop the name chocolate altogether" ("Chocolate: yet" 1996). The Belgian government, in light of the EU agenda of harmonizing CBS standards, went so far as to promote the products of chocolate manufacturers who use no CBS, by issuing a special quality label through the state-sponsored Traditional and Quality Chocolate Association ("Cocoa: Belgium" 2000).

Outcomes

After close to a decade of debate, in June 2000 the EU's new chocolate directive ("Directive 2000/36/EC" 2000) was finally approved. It contained the following regulations:

> The addition of certain vegetable fats other than cocoa butter to chocolate products up to a maximum of 5% should be permitted in all member states;

those vegetable fats should be cocoa butter equivalents and therefore be defined according to technical and scientific criteria. (L 197/19)

Chocolate products which contain vegetable fats other than cocoa butter may be marketed in all of the Member States, provided that their labeling, as provided for in Article 3, is supplemented by a conspicuous and legible statement: "contains vegetable fats in addition to cocoa butter." (L 197/20)

The addition of animal fats and their preparations not deriving solely from milk shall be prohibited. (L 197/24)

The following vegetable fats, obtained from the plants listed below, may be used: Illipe, Palm-Oil, Sal, Shea, Kokum gurgi, Mango Kernal. (L 197/25)

("Directive 2000/36/EC" 2000)

Although the new directive did not meet all of COPAL's demands, by operating within global networks, cocoa interests within the Ghanaian state were able to further and protect their interests in a number of ways. While the use of CBS was not eradicated, it was contained, and limits were imposed across the EU, with potential effects further a field. In addition, individual EU members were prevented from maintaining or instituting standards greater than the 5 percent allowance. They were also barred from using non–tropical oils or synthetics produced with the aid of enzymatic processes. Similarly, the involvement of COPAL in deliberations over the chocolate directive delayed both the formulation and implementation of new standards, preserving at least for a period of time the received standards of cocoa marketing and chocolate-making.

Yet all the while and without much intention, the COPAL platform overlapped with national and private interests, including both business and consumer groups, to spawn a new type of chocolate market not entirely under the singular control of even a powerful global entity such as the EU. This was the remaking of the high-quality chocolate market. Central to its emergence was the very notion of purity used by COPAL and anti-CBS chocolate-producing nations and firms both within and outside the EU to argue against CBS. This new market niche opened up new areas of demand for chocolate which specifically prohibited the use of CBS and at the same time renewed consumer attention to custom-made yet industrially processed chocolate products, creating a new and revitalized high-end chocolate sector.

Hence at the same time mass markets for chocolate permitting the use of CBS were growing in Eastern Europe, the former Soviet States, and Asia (Sanik 1996), by the late 1990s, a different range of chocolate products were finding their way onto the market. Though distinguished from the truly artisinal and most expensive brands of chocolate on the market, these were relatively costly chocolates made from organic cocoa beans, heirloom

4.1 Label from a high-quality chocolate product made with natural ingredients and promoting socially conscious consumption. (Courtesy of Endangered Species Chocolate Company).

cocoa varieties, and selective cocoa blends. These products were sold by small companies—many of them new—in the United States and Europe, sometimes with African partnership or profit-sharing (Gadsby 2002: 67, 70; Swift 1998d: 30).

Whether more established chocolate-makers such as Valrhona and Michel Cluizel, or newcomers with names like Echocolates, Green and Black's, Endangered Species, and Tropical Source, these companies highlighted the handcrafted quality of their product and the raw materials used to make them, drawing attention to the "rustic" and "ancient" character of their beans, the "eco-friendly" manufacturing process and their promotion of social causes, from fair-trade and fair-labor practices to the protection of endangered species (see, e.g., dagobachocolate.com, chocolove.com). These companies account for a growing share of chocolate sales, according to industry experts, and expectations for this market are exceedingly high, with profits rising 60 percent to 70 percent per year (Vreeland 2000: 51).

Naturalizing Consumption and the Repositioning of Shea

During the 1990s—the same period when the use of shea as a cocoa butter substitute was being challenging by COPAL members with the support of a wide range of interest groups—shea, and specifically shea butter, moved into its new market niche in the health and beauty industry and began to appear in a wide range of products related to self-presentation and restoration. Despite the apparent difference of product type—cosmetic versus confection—the development of this new market niche for shea butter was driven by the very same ideals regarding nature, purity, and renewal that had been voiced by backers of the anti-shea movement in the chocolate industry and proponents of new high-grade chocolates without shea. In short, shea butter represented the very same values to the cosmetics, beauty, and health sector that the new chocolate presented to the confection industry. While the consumption of high-end chocolate made possible the realization of all sorts of internalized bodily pleasures along with a host of social and environmental objectives, shea butter fostered the realization of similar capacities through its application on the exterior of the body.

Raising questions about the direction and character of global market linkages, shea's movement into this commercial niche differs from other trajectories of tropical commoditization connecting luxury commodities to mass markets. Tropical exports, initially rare and restricted, tend to follow a course of "massification" as they become increasingly affordable and accessible. This path of commercial transformation is well illustrated by the case of sugar, brilliantly described by Mintz (1985) in his classic *Sweetness and Power*. From an expensive and highly restricted item consumed primarily by elites, sugar was gradually transformed into a mass-market item as the possibilities of industrial production fell into place, creating new sorts of products and consumers. Although sugar continued to serve as a source of leisure and pleasure, in the course of its popularization it became an affordable and commonly used item.

Shea, however, initially an industrial commodity and only recently an object of elite consumption, in many ways reverses this typical trend. Shea has more in common with the sort of commercial enclaving described by Roseberry (1996) for coffee, yet it stands apart from this commercial trend too in a number of significant ways. In contrast to sugar's commercial devolution, the market for shea, like coffee—once a generic commodity consumed with little concern or reflection—is becoming increasingly variegated (Talbot 1994). Characterized by specialty brands, products, and preparations, coffee consumption is now a marker of social status distinction and requires a considerable investment of time, money, and knowledge among a subset of consumers whom others strive to emulate (Roseberry 1996). Although shea, similar to coffee, has moved from a mass commodity to a high-class one, in contrast to coffee, shea was not a recognized consumer item with which people were already familiar prior to this shift. Likewise, its consumption still remains relatively restricted.

Shea butter's newfound commercial identity as a luxury item finds a better match not in the classic tropical commodities whose history it otherwise shares but in a different range of tropical products that are apparent new-comers to the global market and characterized by growing popularity and an expanding range of circulation. Most evident in the fresh fruit, vegetable, and botanical sector (Goodman and Watts 1997; Little and Dolan 2000; McMichael 1994), this is a new stream of high-value tropical commodities (Jaffee and Morton 1995) that includes an array of nontimber forest products and indigenous species like shea, such as essential oils, medicinal plants, and wild nuts and seeds to be used for cooking, curing, or other forms of self-care (Carr et al. 2000: 134). Here elite markets, focused on an overlapping range of products, merge with and encompass smaller and better-established alternative markets for natural goods and ethnic products at the same time as they bring new commodities into them.

Symbolic of an emerging consumer consciousness (Bonnano et al. 1994; Gereffi and Korzeniewicz 1994), these goods answer to the growing demands of cosmopolitan consumers devoted to "taste" as both a sensual experience and a specific form of knowledge about their own bodies and lifestyles as well as other people and places. Although these items are nowhere as widely consumed as the old luxuries like sugar or new ones like designer coffee, this trend has brought goods formerly considered exotic and out of reach in terms of their price, origins, or the cultural knowledge required to consume them (Cook 1994) into the realm of everyday consumption for a growing number of upper- and, increasingly, middle-class consumers.

While these goods are largely considered new to the mainstream market, shea alerts us to consider the place—or at least the potential—of tropical "crossovers" like itself within this commercial path. Despite shea's long-established presence on the world market as a low-cost industrial input, because it has largely been hidden from view (unlike coffee and sugar, which were always consumer items) shea is well suited to assume a new and very different commercial identity on the world market as consumer item in its own right. Hence, if sugar and coffee represent two different moments in the history of tropical commercialization, one of popularization and the other of segmentation, shea speaks to another moment of change taking place at the end of the twentieth century. Here a class of tropical commodities considered obscure or unknown enter into a space opened up but not satisfied by these other streams and come to populate an increasingly selective mass market. In all of these cases, old tropical commodities and long-exploited tropical landscapes are being reassessed for new consumer potentials.

Yet it is not just shea's proven exportability or its hidden past that makes it an attractive candidate for this emerging global luxury market. The popularity of shea butter is linked to another critical shift in postindustrial lifestyles and consumption habits: this is the pursuit of respite from the alienations of capitalist mass production. Above all, the repositioning of shea butter on the global market—and with it a wide array of other seemingly "new" tropical products—is tied to the urge to get back to nature and grasp what Simon Schama has called "a healing wilderness" capable of "curing the ailments of industrialized society" (quoted in Tannen 1994: 98). Indeed, products with shea represent a leading edge in a burgeoning natural-cosmetics market valued at $2.5 billion by the late 1990s (Brown 1998). This trend is tied to not just the growth of the elite market but the "naturalization" or "greening" of it.

One reason why the beauty market is experiencing a surge of development (Wilck 1997) is that this new class of goods fills out the vast middle space of a sector that in the past consisted primarily of basic and interchangeable products and brands and a very expensive specialty sector. Incorporated into high- and mid-priced products geared to health and beauty and reflecting worldliness, self-awareness, and good taste, shea is well suited to this shift in consumption standards. And this is where the "purity" of products made with shea butter is fundamental to their popularity. From the apparent purity of raw materials and production processes to the purity of their application and the intentions of those who market them, the consumption of shea products is seen as an alternative to the mores and mechanics of late capitalism, even as the availability and desire for them is entirely a product of it (Chalfin 1998).

This perspective is evident in the imagery surrounding shea products. Across a wide range of goods and manufacturers, shea butter is marketed as an artisanal item both rare and newly discovered by cosmopolitan consumers. Accentuating shea's natural origins, goods made from shea butter are portrayed as carefully processed with a minimum of industrial interventions or chemical inputs. Packaged in "homespun" materials—brown paper wrappers, raffia, unadorned pharmacy bottles—they are presented to the consuming public as extraordinarily pure with a minimal imprint of manufacture. Rather than being synthetic, the cosmetic, body, and beauty products made from shea—soaps, lotions, balms, shaving creams, sunscreens, skin and hair moisturizers, baby ointments, massage oils—are touted as plant-based and all natural, and labeled "100 percent pure," "hand-processed," and "chemical-free" time and time again ("Ébène" 2002; "African Shea Butter Company" 2002; Gain 1996; "Natural shea," n.d.; "African Shea Butter" 1997). Distinguishing it from the superficial outcomes of industrial manufacture, shea butter is identified as "authentic" ("TC Naturals," 1994) and presented as a product of deep-seated knowledge. Labels on shea butter products describe it as "Africa's age-old answer, used by African healers for Centuries" ("TC Naturals" 1994; "Natural moisturizers," 1998; "Catalogue," n.d.a). Invested in such ideals, one company named its line of shea butter products La Source ("La Source," 2002).

What labor these products do contain, it is suggested, derives from that which is itself close to nature. Here imagery of rural African women looms large. Labels and advertising material, drawing on idyllic notions of pre-capitalist labor forms, tell us that African women process shea by hand. According to these sources, African women apply their labor power directly to the bounties of the earth using simple instruments of stone and wood, unmediated by technological advances or social controls that might alienate the producer from her efforts ("Catalogue," n.d.c). Similarly posed as an alternative to the depersonalizing tendencies of capitalist production routines, shea butter is presented as "active," retaining its natural energies, rather than being "denatured" in the process of extraction ("Shea butter or Karite," 1997; "Power of nature," 1998). Contrasted with the destructive and expansive character of industrial capitalism, shea's production is touted as sustainable and renewable, posing no threat to persons or the environment ("Product alert," 1995). Once again countering the supposedly dehumanizing character of capitalism, the shea tree, its products, and their producers are commonly identified as sacred ("100% pure shea," 1997). Conveying this ideal, L'Occitane's catalog contains a picture of women wearing waist clothes and head wraps pounding nuts in a large wooden mortar, with a caption reading "Mesmerizing and bewitching, it is only these women who are able to extract shea's ancestral secrets" ("Soap label" n.d.).

Not only are the women who process shea considered to a have a moral purity due to their material poverty, but those who manufacture and sell shea products are also portrayed as driven by moral purpose rather than pure profit motive. The Body Shop purchases shea butter through its "Community Trade" initiative, which aims to "contribute to the eradication of poverty and inequality worldwide" ("Catalogue" n.d.b)—part of the company founder's ethical business philosophy as laid out in her autobiography, aptly titled *Body and Soul* (Roddick 1991; Frankel 1998). Many others tout their investment in shea as part of a development agenda aimed at boosting household incomes and food and economic security ("Uganda shea" 2001; "Marketing news: Body" 2001).

Consumption itself is seen to be driven by equally untainted motives. Having nothing to do with the usual artifice of the cosmetics industry, shea products "nourish and protect" ("Natural shea," n.d.), "heal and cure" ("Shea butter; Karite," 2002), tapping into consumers most basic needs. Not only physical, these needs are presented as cultural—as in TC Natural's "Take Pride in Your Roots" campaign—as well as spiritual, thereby exemplifying a wider trend of blending enlightenment with self-care

4.3 Ethnographically styled marketing material accompanying shea products from L'Occitane. (Courtesy of L'Occitane).

(Green 1999: B7). These commentaries on the character of shea production are widespread and appear well credentialed, making use of field photos, quasi-ethnographic reports, and other forms of personal or apparently scientific reportage.

Contributing to the aura of shea as an antidote to the ills of corporate capitalism and the alienation and anonymity wrought by mass production and mass consumption, cosmetics made with shea were first and continue to be marketed by firms outside the corporate mainstream. This trend was initiated by The Body Shop, originally a family-owned business run out of a garage and eventually expanding to over a thousand outlets (Davidson

4.4 Advertisement for products with shea from TC Naturals. (Courtesy of the Stephan Company).

1996; Kochan 1997; Roddick 1994). The Body Shop cultivated an image of alternative corporatism—consumer friendly, honest about ingredients and driven by a "do-good" motive. This sort of business style has continued to define the cosmetics sector for shea. Shea butter is sold by hundreds of small firms who package and reformulate the butter under their own labels, purporting to by-pass the depersonalizing tendencies of mass-production and mass-marketing. Combining shea with other natural ingredients, they promote the ideal of a custom-made product catering to specific rather than generic customer needs and artisinal rather than corporate commitments ("Provence Santé" n.d.).

Even truly large firms involved in the sale of shea have cultivated this sort of "small is beautiful" image. The Origins line, with a wide range of shea products, is branded by Estée Lauder, one of the world's biggest cosmetics firm. For a long time however, Origins products were not retailed with other Lauder products but were instead restricted to small stand-alone shops on street corners and in shopping malls. Presenting themselves as alternatives to the mass market, Web sites and catalogs contain testimonials, contact information, and a virtual encyclopedia of information regarding the nature and origins of shea ("African Shea Butter Company" 2002), as well as origin stories of company founders recounting their personal "discovery of shea" ("Shea butter; Karite" 2002).

These possibilities of product and firm type—all natural, small in scale, and specialized in orientation and preparation—are nevertheless predicated on an overall process of corporate concentration. At the same time as shea butter is moving into hundreds of new products and businesses, the shea market is controlled by a small number of European and Asian refineries. Indeed, the imagery of shea as an alternative to late-capitalist industrialization and depersonalization obscures the fundamental dependence of the shea industry on these very economic forms. And it here that shea's place in the beauty market intersects once again with the chocolate market. This is because the three firms that dominate the market for African shea nuts are the very firms who dominate the market in the production and sale of cocoa butter substitutes. Technologically advanced, they consist of the Swedish firm Karlshamns ("Shea butter family" 2002), the Danish firm Aarhus Olie ("Vegetable fats" 2002), and Loders Croklaan (see www.croklaan.com), formerly part of Unilever and now Malaysian-owned (Bekure et al. 1997; Fold 2000: 99). With a small number of international buyers and an uncertain demand schedule tied to the highly volatile chocolate market (Kassardjian 2002), shea prices are notoriously low. As Fold (2000: 98) explains:

> Industrial processors have been unwilling to increase prices. . . . Prices have rarely been competitive compared to prices (and labour inputs) of other cash

> crops and to the domestic use value of shea nuts. . . . The existence of some
> kind of monopsonistic agreement between the major CBE (cocoa butter
> equivalent) manufacturers (a maximum purchasing price) cannot be pre-
> cluded, though; evidence points to the temporary existence of such an agree-
> ment in Burkina Faso.

Indeed, further reducing prices and competition, these firms are moving deeper into the shea economy. Aarhus, for one, has a permanent office in Ghana's capital, Accra, where it arranges purchases of shea directly from private buying companies, increasing its involvement in and influence over the export market.

The domination of shea export market by just a few firms has a series of effects shaping the development of both the confections industry and the cosmetics market. First, contrary to the imagery stressing the African sourcing of shea butter, in actuality a very small minority of shea products circulating in cosmopolitan markets are prepared from African-made shea butter. Rather, the bulk of shea products are industrially manufactured in Europe, Asia, and North America from shea nuts purchased in Africa and refined abroad. Indeed, even the small amount of butter that comes from Africa is industrially refined outside the continent before being incorpo- rated into consumer goods.[8] Second, the low purchase price of shea nuts enables the firms to keep the price of the cocoa butter substitutes they pro- duce relatively low compared to the price of cocoa butter in order to main- tain its attractiveness to chocolate makers. At the same time, the low price paid for unrefined nuts allows the firms to invest in the development and application of new refinement techniques to expand the number and uses of the cocoa butter substitutes they offer and still keep them affordable. This enables them to use the cocoa butter substitute fabrication process as a key arena for adding value to their products.[9]

Not only do these arrangements help to insure the continued relevance of cocoa butter substitutes like shea in the confections industry, but they also open up a space for shea in the cosmetics sector. This is because the same strategies of research and development regarding shea processing and refinement for chocolate production have proved relevant to cosmet- ics makers. According to representatives from the leading firms, the use of shea in cosmetic preparations is fundamentally tied to the process of re- finement, and without that refinement, use of shea in cosmetics on a par with consumer standards would be impossible (Balle 2002; Bekure et al. 1997: 16; "Sheabutter extraction" 1997).

Karlshamns, among others, aggressively promotes the use of refined butters in cosmetics. As the company puts it: "Formulators in the cosmet- ics industry are constantly facing the challenge to come up with new for- mulations with improved functionalities. . . . Therefore, Karlshamns has put together a range of shea butter derived products to be used in the formulation works. The shea butter family will help formulators come up with new, elegant formulations in an efficient way" ("Shea butter family" 2002). Trying to enlarge the demand for shea in cosmetics, Karshamns in this regard offers a wide range of shea butter preparations for cosmetic manufacturers—from liquid to solid, enriched to water soluble—a variety that begins to parallel the "tailor-made" quality of shea butter substitutes formulated for the confections industry.

No doubt some refinement processes are considered more desirable—notably those that do not use chemical solvents—because of the higher-quality butter they yield and consequently are more costly, yet prices for refined butter even at this higher grade still remain relatively low. Equally, as the shea market opens up, quality has become both less and more of a concern for consumers. Just as high-grade shea butter products are touted to those who are most knowledgeable, there is a wide array of new and highly processed preparations that contain only trace amounts of shea and little resemble the "pure" product (Kassardjian 2002; "Palmer's" 2002; "Beautyguide; skin" 2000).

This pattern of corporate concentration providing raw materials at a low price and offering technologically sophisticated refinement has fostered the emergence of a market where barriers to entry are relatively low, enabling the participation of a tremendous number of firms at many levels. There are myriad firms of a range of sizes involved in the retail of shea products. Generally invisible to consumers, there is also a large number of small firms involved in the sale to cosmetic manufactures and retailers of shea in a wide range of stages of refinement and preparation—an arrangement indicating a long and highly variegated supply chain for cosmetics containing shea (Bekure et al. 1997; "Hair care" 1999; Oyewole 1997). Indeed, even as small firms begin to bypass large buyers and attempt to purchase directly from African markets ("Uganda shea" 2001), they benefit from the low prices already established by the larger multinationals that dominate the market—both in Africa and offshore. These possibilities for participation by small firms in the shea market are further extended by the fact that consumers are already willing to pay more for natural cosmetics and body preparations such as shea, once again enlarging the opportunity for and profitability of entry into the production and sale of shea within cosmopolitan markets.

Conclusion

Highlighting the many factors contributing to shea's shifting commercial identity, this chapter has tried to draw attention to the spaces of convergence and disparity in the making of a new global market for shea. It has been by mapping out the contours of this global economic and political field that the multiple determinants of shea's transposition from chocolate additive to health and beauty aid were made evident. Rather than seeing shea's positions in the confection market and in the cosmetics market as diametrically opposed, this chapter makes apparent the very interdependence of these commercial trajectories. It has become clear that despite the differences in product visibility and type and the vehemence with which chocolate and cocoa producers have endorsed pro- or anti-shea positions, the actual development of these market has gone hand in hand, spurred by similar values and processes and growing simultaneously.

The market for shea has expanded not against the chocolate market but very much with it. Responding to the potential of new mass markets in parts of the world where consumer buying power was in the past limited or restricted to a narrow sector of brands and commodities—such as Eastern Europe, the former Soviet states, parts of Asia, and even Africa—the growing use of shea within less expensive and novelty chocolate formulations is unstoppable. As we have seen, at the same time as the mass chocolate market is growing, the chocolate market is invested in another trajectory of development endorsed by the same voices and values that argue against the use of shea as a cocoa butter substitute—this is the emergence of a new specialty chocolate sector. This market niche is oriented around notions of purity and the preservation of natural quality—from the unadulterated taste of pure cocoa to the sustenance of organic, heirloom, and regionally specific bean varietals and the foregrounding of ties between consumers and producers. The consumption of such products thus engages a consumer sensibility built around not just the sense of pleasure or status but wider systems of knowledge and belief regarding health, the environment, and the global economy. Tied to a broader set of trends where mass goods become restricted (reversing the trajectory Mintz (1985) describes for sugar) and the mass market becomes crowded with an array of products capable of marking class specific aspirations and identities (see Roseberry (1996) on coffee) these are the very foundations upon which the popularity of shea within the cosmetics sector rests.

The link between the confection and cosmetics sector does not end here. Despite the apparent renouncement of capitalist values they both represent in the eyes of consumers, the new move toward a naturalized luxury niche occurring in the confection and cosmetics markets is predicated on similar shifts in the structure of corporate capital. The emergence of both these markets depends on corporate consolidation, as the concentration of raw material purchasing and refinement creates a place for smaller firms.[10] Corporate consolidation lower prices, enlarges demand, and streamlines supply lines. This creates openings for smaller companies not only at the point of sourcing but even more later on in the supply chain. Indeed, the very processes and technological innovations (whether new modes of communication, refinement techniques, or marketing strategies) driving the movement of corporate capital into new places and product niches are also contributing to the repositioning of shea as a luxury item. It is clear here that the incorporation and indeed celebration of shea within the cosmetic sector is in no way an antidote to or escape from late-industrial capitalism—as many of those who market and consume shea cosmetics would have it—but entirely a product of it.

Pointing to its persistent and continued incorporation into mass-marketed confections even as it moves into the cosmetics sector is not to debunk shea's status as a "new" global commodity. The point, rather, is to locate its newness in its duality, in the fact that it appears in what seem to be two very different markets. That shea's current status in the beauty industry masks or obscures its past at the same time as it is predicated on it is one aspect of what makes it new. Shea's status as a new commodity is intimately tied to this process of economic "multiplication"—the capacity to operate in several different markets carrying several seemingly disparate but highly interconnected identities. In this way, the circulation of shea out of Africa and back again into cheap chocolate and fancy cosmetics and medicinals is very much an instance of what Pred and Watts (1992: xiv) identify as capitalism's "ability repeatedly to reinvent itself in the face of overinvestment and overcapacity crises[;] its remarkable ability to self-mutate has not only resulted in uneven development and a multiplicity of capitalisms, but precipitated a multiplicity of experienced modernities."

This is all part and parcel of the remaking of shea's global trajectory along with its commercial identity. Shea does not move from here to there—from fallow fields and forest tracks of the savanna zone to shopping malls and specialty shops, medicine chests, and vanities—in any linear form. Although shea's geographic transposition might follow such a direct course, the factors and forces that make this course possible are much more diffuse and highly globalized. Not only is demand for shea globalized—occurring in millions of spaces around the world—but the possibility of shea circulation is created by myriad global forms. These include the alliances among COPAL members, ACP, and the International Cocoa Organization, links between COPAL and select EU bodies and representatives, multinational corporations, deterritorialized ideals of cosmopolitan lifestyles and identities, information networks, the movement of travelers and businesspeople to and from Africa, to name a few—all engaged in a constant process of negotiation. What makes this different from the globalization driving commercialization in the past is not simply the stretch of their reach or the rapidity of their communication, but their multiplicity and diversity, creating a vast yet unstable network through which commodities, interests, and power relations are conducted.

Although it is evident that state bodies have not directed shea's transposition from chocolate additive to luxury good, they have no doubt been involved in it as one among several sets of interests and actors. Indeed, as the battle over chocolate standards unfolds, all sorts of global organizations—international, supranational, and transnational—as well as national ones interface with bodies representing African states to pursue common goals. In this way, state interests have become incorporated into global initiatives rather than subsumed by them. Equally, in the course of these negotiations, state agendas have gained recognition on the international stage, legitimating and furthering distinctive state projects. Rather than posing this as a question about the triumph of state versus global interests, it seems more productive to consider the place of the state in the forging and unfolding of particular global processes. In the case of the "chocolate wars," the ultimate outcome was different from that envisioned by either EU or COPAL members. This is because the process of deliberation and application for the EU Chocolate Directive was swept up in a much wider constellation of forces related to consumption and corporate capital that could have been neither foreseen nor driven by any single body involved. As Roseberry (1996: 773) urges us to appreciate, the forces of globalization "do not act in concert, that there is no single controlling interest (despite obvious power relations)."

While this network might appear coordinated and efficient from the vantage point of those in whose favor it operates, it does not always operate as such. The sort of convergences that make these shifts possible within the space of late-industrial economies and lifestyles, where shea is consumed in the form of low-cost snacks or high-priced body lotions and curatives, are neither smooth nor taken for granted in the late-agricultural spaces of the tropics where shea grows. If globalization may be experienced in the powerful states of the North Atlantic as natural and coordinated, for African nations it is a much bumpier and uneven process. What follows is a consideration of the sorts of volatility and instability that accompany this trajectory of economic transformation in the rural economies of the West African savanna where shea continues to be sourced for both newer and older global markets.

CHAPTER 5

Remaking Markets and Shape-Shifting States

Privatizing Shea in Northern Ghana

At the same time as demand for shea on the world market was taking a new course, the conditions of supply and sourcing for shea—specifically shea nuts—in Ghana were being altered for many of the same reasons. On the face of it, as mentioned in Chapter 4, these shifts were instigated by the conditionalities of the IMF and World Bank, on whom Ghana relied for massive loans. Promoting a wide-ranging program of liberalization, these institutions pushed for a massive privatization effort on the part of the Ghanaian state. As a result, in 1992 private formal-sector firms were invited to enter the shea market and authorized to purchase nuts from the domestic market and sell them abroad. The state-run Produce Buying Company (PBC), in turn, was expected to withdraw from the market and instead oversee and insure the fair operation of private firms.

This chapter looks closely at the complex process of domestic economic restructuring accompanying the privatization of Ghana's shea economy and the shifting conditions of global demand during the 1990s. Beginning with a discussion of the ways in which the state both withdrew from and was reimplicated in the export market, it considers the strategies employed by private firms to engage rural communities and supply lines. This is followed by the examination of rural traders' responses to the demand for shea emanating from private buyers and their impact on the character and control of rural markets for shea.

Even with the potential growth in demand for West African shea promised by its increasing popularity in the cosmetics sector and the overall expansion of the market for inexpensive chocolate, the private companies moving into Ghana's shea economy faced a host of difficulties as they sought to tap the new opportunities afforded by liberalization. These obstacles were both of external origin—stemming from the particular conditions of the world market for shea—and internally based—emerging out of the specific features of Ghana's political economy and the structural characteristics of the firms themselves. External determinations made demand for shea unstable and endowed Ghana-based exporters with little power to determine market conditions in relation to the small number of northern European firms importing nuts for industrial refinement and manufacture. The unsteady nature of consumer taste—especially the potential for luxury consumption trends to fade away or devolve—contributed to the insecurity of the nut market, as did the threat shea faced from other tropical oilseeds in the manufacture of cocoa butter substitutes. This was heightened by a general worldwide trend toward the overproduction of cocoa, lowering cocoa prices and the demand for substitutes. Shea nut exporters, further, received little help in promoting their wares to foreign buyers. Rather, as we have seen, shea was the object of negative publicity abroad emanating from representatives of the Ghanaian government, wider African coalitions, and transcontinental organizations.

Within Ghana, private buyers faced a different set of challenges once they entered the export market. These challenges revolved around the uncertain place of the state in the shea market—an uncertainty emanating from within the state itself and from private companies' and rural shea nut suppliers' own indecision about the proper and necessary role of the state in the market. This was compounded by the conflicting status of the state in the development policies advocated by international financial institutions versus the actual development practices endorsed by them.

All of these challenges were situated within an even more basic problematic of amassing substantial supplies of a wild resource in a wide catchment area where rural suppliers maintained the option of circulating shea within the regional market rather than selling to exporters. No doubt the very existence of a strong regional market for shea nuts was a boon for private buyers, providing them with a ready-made source of nuts. Yet, as was evident even in early part of the colonial era, private buyers had to work hard to obtain the appropriate knowledge and contacts to enter these markers and maintain access to them, as rural nut suppliers still held the option of catering to the domestic market rather than the export sector.

From the outset, this meant that private firms could not easily or automatically engage the supposed opportunities of privatization. The strength of these barriers to participation is well attested to by the fact that few of the firms that registered with the state to participate in the export trade

5.1 Johnson Farms employees at Tamale office with shea stocks purchased for export.

ever purchased nuts at all and fewer still survived the vagaries of the state, the global market, or the rural economy. While twenty-five firms and individuals received shea export licenses for the 1992-to-1993 season, only seven were active in the shea market. This cohort included companies of a range of sizes and origins. Outside of Unilever, an early participant in privatization and an early dropout, none was particularly large or of international repute. Among these companies, which what might be classified as small multinationals—very similar to what Raikes and Gibbon (2000: 77) describe as "second or third-rank players" in their discussion of multinational corporations involved in African export crop agriculture—were Kassardjian, a firm owned by a Lebanese family with a parent company in London and long history of business ties in Ghana; Agrotrade, a Dutch-owned firm involved largely in agricultural import and export; and Olam, a highly diversified firm of Indian origin that was based in Singapore. They were joined by a small number of Ghana-based businesses. These were Johnson Farms, a firm strongly oriented to the savanna economy through its investments in long-distance commercial transit between Ghana and Niger and the establishment of cashew plantations in Ghana's northern sector; Sabary, a small company based in southern Ghana that sought to tap into the nontraditional export sector; and AA Dimbala, a private business based in Tamale, the capital of Ghana's Northern Region. Also based in Ghana, another firm, Farmers Service Company of the Upper Regions (FASCOM), was nominally part of this group. Born of a government-based development initiative from the 1970s and still receiving state support, this firm straddled the boundary between public and private, as will be discussed below. By 1996, Sabary and Unilever had dropped out of the export market, and by the end of the decade, only three companies—Kassardjian, Olam (both multinationals), and FASCOM—remained active.

That no private Ghanaian firms remained involved—or at least, profitably so—in the shea market half a dozen years into the reform process is not entirely surprising. Among other things, the performance of private Ghanaian firms engaged in the shea trade was limited by the Ghanaian banking system. Across sub-Saharan Africa, financial and operational difficulties have been identified as a widespread obstacle to the success of private firms. A 1989 World Bank reports cites liquidity problems resulting from the credit constraints of the national banking systems as a key obstacle to the development of the export sector, despite other facilitating factors of the structural adjustment program (Younger 1989: 145). Economists studying the export sector in Ghana during the early years of structural adjustment noticed similar limitations imposed by Ghanaian banks. Anyemedu (1991) notes that "the credit squeeze which has been part of the macro-economic policies of ERP, has hit very hard the small scale export sector, and exporters of semi-processed products . . . have not been able to fulfill export orders because of their inability to obtain the necessary working capital to produce the requisite volume of output" (1991: 219). Jaffe (1994; Jaffe and Morton 1995), writing about "High Value Food Markets" elsewhere in sub-Saharan Africa, identifies the weak development of formal financial markets as the most pressing obstacles to market growth and development. No doubt, the same inadequacies adversely affected Ghanaian firms struggling to enter and remain in the market for products such as shea.

The handful of firms that were able to claim a stake in the shea trade in the absence of adequate financial services still had to cope with the uncertain character of the world market for shea, the only partial withdrawal of the state from the domestic market and the unpredictable nature of rural supply lines. Grappling with these obstacles, the companies who remained active in the shea market had little choice but to employ a wide range of unorthodox strategies in order to secure a share of nut supplies. A combination of aspects of state-based or state-styled regulation, formal-sector business practice, and informal marketing systems resulted in a multiplicity of loosely institutionalized economic forms. Little conforming to neoliberal ideals regarding private sector structure or performance, such a process of economic improvisation affected equally rural trade patterns and the character of state intervention in the shea market.

Shea Export, 1992–2001

Year	Exporter	Quantity (Tons)	Dollar Value
1992	Agrotrade	1,575	$330,750
	Johnson Farms	494	$125,970
	Thama Container & Trading	256	$55,130
	Total (3 exporters)	**2,325**	**$511,850**
1993	Kassardjian	1,000	$176,905
	Agrotrade	575	$120,750
	Johnson Farms	218	$44,749
	Total (3 exporters)	**1,793**	**$342,404**
1994	Kassardjian	10,697	$2,072,810
	AA Dimbala Farms	1,416	$226,551
	Sabary Enterprise	1,145	$171,750
	Farmers Service Co. (FASCOM)	500	$85,100
	Johnson Farms	230	$36,000
	Total (5 exporters)	**13,988**	**$2,592,211**
1995	**Total (6 exporters)**	**14,616**	**$2,193,314**
1996	**Total (3 exporters)**	**21,467**	**$4,484,600**
1997	Kassardjian	17,415	$3,655,500
	Olam	5,012	$1,052,084
	Farmers Service Co. (FASCOM)	3,408	$715,350
	Unregistered exporters	2,897	$608,000
	Johnson Farms	2,738	$574,746
	AA Dimbala Farms	548	$115,098
	Total (6 exporters)	**32,018**	**$6,720,778**
1998	**Total (6 exporters)**	**32,782**	**$7,892,079**
1999	**Total (4 exporters)**	**32,071**	**$6,806,549**
2000	**Total (3 exporters)**	**18,783**	**$2,864,151**
2001	**Total (3 exporters)**	**14,073**	**$1,532,877**

Source: Federation of Ghana Exporters, the *Export News;* Maxwell Osei Kusi, Export Development Officer, Ghana Export Promotion Council; A2/Export Forms.

Fig. 5 Shea Exporters and Export Values, 1992–2001.

Three observations regarding the combined effects of neoliberal reform and global economic restructuring on Ghana's shea economy emerge from the exploration of these dynamics. First is the thoroughgoing ambivalence of the privatization process. This ambivalence derives from the state's hesitancy to let go of the market, whether as detractor or benefactor, as well as the desire of those in the market to retain or reproduce state authority. Sec-

5.2 Local Unilever agents discussing the shea market at Econs's store in Bawku.

ond and related is that processes of privatization incite new trajectories of hybridization within African economies. Built tenuously upon preexisting economic and political forms—from parastatals and rural cooperatives to family firms and multinational capital— and responding to the conditionalities of international donors and the simultaneously tight and tenuous conditions of international demand, such hybrid entities of shea market privatization are far from stable or predictable. They are what Moore describes as "part structures being built and torn down . . . a complex mix of order, anti-order and non-order . . . and contingencies of form" (1987: 730). The third point to be made from these examples is the necessity of viewing so-called local institutions—such as the rural marketplaces found in the "out of the way" areas of northern Ghana's savanna zone—in thoroughly dynamic and open-ended terms. As apparent during the colonial period, the boundaries and mores of these markets are highly fluid and thoroughly dependent on global and national processes as well as more proximate ones.

The State Loses and Reclaims Its Place in the Shea Market

For the private firms purchasing shea for export, a substantial source of uncertainty about their own position and possibilities in the shea market stemmed from the highly ambiguous and unstable role of the PBC—the state agency previously controlling the export market—in the privatization process. Although the mandate of privatization was paired with official dissolution of the state export monopoly, the PBC played the role not so much of the proverbial "dying swan" but of a "dying chameleon." In the midst of its dismantling, the PBC assumed new roles and goals in the shea economy, eventually moving back into the shea trade. For private buyers, the implications of the PBC's return to the shea market were somewhat murky. On the one hand, PBC's presence occluded private firms' capacity to develop rural supply lines, especially the cultivation of ties to influential community members who could garner wider cooperation. On the other hand, however, by remaining in the market, the PBC provided support to private buyers, although selectively so.

Moving Out and Moving Back

When the privatization of the shea market was announced during the 1991-to-1992 season, PBC's purchasing activities were already slowing down due to layoffs, low prices, and the growing dissatisfaction of suppliers in shea nut farmers societies (SNFSs). Effectively demobilizing the agency's operations, in the wake of liberalization a further 80 percent of PBC personnel were "retrenched" and the agency was denied both the capital to buy shea nuts and attendant authority to set prices. With limited capacity or opportunity, rather than buying nuts, the PBC preoccupied itself with issuing purchasing and export licenses to the private firms vying to enter the newly opened shea market. Thus displaced, the PBC purchased no nuts at all and began to sell off its depots and equipment while retaining its role as market overseer. The company remained responsible for informing SNFS leaders about the entry of private firms into the shea market, supervising the licensing of private buyers, and inspecting shea nuts purchased by private firms prior to export, for which it collected a modicum of fees.

Despite the dramatic contractions PBC faced during the first two seasons of privatization, by the following year the PBC mandate was being reassessed and the agency was deemed eligible to return to the shea market as a shea nut purchaser and exporter if it conformed to a new operating plan. The PBC had to abide by the same standards as private firms; to reenter the shea market it was required to prove itself profitable, self-financing, and sustainable without subsidy. Guided by these expectations, late in the 1993-to-1994 season the PBC sought once again to buy shea nuts. Aiming to recoup its former place in the shea trade, the PBC used a purchasing plan that in many ways resembled the one it had employed during the mid- and late 1980s prior to privatization. The company continued to rely on SNFSs for nut supplies and only slightly modified its mode of operation. PBC regional managers, shoring up their commitments to shea suppliers, appealed to a select group of farmer society leaders to serve as PBC agents and promised them a per-bag commission. Granted greater independence than in the past, the PBC agents were also allowed to chose their own subagents and make their own purchasing and transport arrangements. Regardless of these adjustments, however, due to poor timing and the low prices offered—two thirds of those paid by the private buyers—the PBC was able to purchase only a very small proportion of the total volume of shea nuts exported.

Notwithstanding the poor returns of the previous year, PBC returned to the shea market once again for the 1994-to-1995 season. This time the selection of agents was even more deliberate, coming down to just a handful of individuals in each of the three regions of northern Ghana. According to the PBC manager for Upper East Region—one of a small number of people still in PBC employ—only the leaders of the most successful farmers societies were recruited, and of them, as he put it, only persons with a reputation for loyalty and honesty, a record of active membership in the Cocoa, Coffee and Shea Nut Farmers Association (the executive association of the SNFSs), and the status of "opinion leader" in the community. Designated agents received preseason visits from PBC officials who explained the new buying plan and sought their cooperation. This strategy also showed poor results. Some of the selected agents refused to participate due to the low prices offered by PBC. Others agreed to participate only if purchasing funds were advanced. And even when the funds were advanced, they were received late in the season when shea prices were already high, limiting agents' capacity to buy nuts.

From Competitor to Partner

PBC efforts to recapture the shea market finally showed some signs of success when the company allied itself with another remnant of the state-controlled buying plan. This was the regional council of the Coffee, Cocoa and Shea Nut Farmers Association (CCSNFA). Although these two groups had previously occupied opposite ends of the bargaining table, with CCSNFA voicing the farmer societies desire for better terms of trade and PBC officials representing the interests and financial limitations of the state, the new alliance was beneficial to both.[1] Indeed, when CCSNFA leaders from northern Ghana were first informed of the PBC plan to withdraw from the shea market, the organization emerged as one of the staunchest defenders of the company. Invoking the same terms of economic citizenship previously promulgated by the state, the CCSNFA sent a petition to the Cocoa Marketing Board (CMB) pointing out the political liabilities of such a move. Now the CCSNFA argued that a PBC pullout would be interpreted as the government's abandonment of the north, endangering both the northern economy and northern political support.

Coming to the aid of the PBC during the 1994-to-1995 season, CCSNFA executives provided the PBC with much-needed assistance through the CCSNFA chief farmer for the Upper East Region and his secretary. The chief farmer contacted his most loyal followers, enjoining them to cooperate with PBC requests for shea nuts. Having maintained close ties with former farmer society leaders in order to shore up their own political status even as formal participation in the societies broke down, CCSNFA executives were able to call on their allies in these otherwise defunct associations. The logistical support of the CCSNFA was equally crucial to PBC operations. CCSNFA leaders spread the word of PBC's reentry into the shea market. The chief farmer's pick-up truck, previously awarded to him by the CMB, was used to transport nuts from rural suppliers to the PBC depot, as the PBC's own vehicles were in disrepair. The renewed presence of the PBC in the shea market with the farmers association's aid gave CCSNFA executives a temporary *raison d'etre*, helping them legitimize the association's continued existence after most SNFSs had dissolved due to inactivity. With this arrangement in place, the PBC garnered a fair amount of compliance despite the low prices it offered. More than a source of revenue, working with the PBC was perceived as an attractive source of patronage by former society executives. This was so much the case that shea nut traders who were not selected to assist the PBC complained of disregard and advocated to be appointed as PBC agents in the future.

The PBC's forging of new relations with CCSNFA members had the unintended effect of stimulating new forms of mobilization among rural suppliers, along with attempts to assert control over the export market. Struggling to sustain itself as its constituency collapsed, the CCSNFA sought to regulate local market arrangements as the PBC had done in the past. According to this plan, all export company agents would be required to register with CCSNFA before purchasing nuts. The agents would then be introduced to association representatives who would coordinate shea nut purchases in a given community. At the end of the season, a commission would be paid by the companies to the association, which would be distributed to the supply areas for improvements in the community at large.

If this plan of market regulation were to succeed, just as the PBC controlled the farmers societies in the 1980s, the CCSNFA would have authority over local-level marketing arrangements, limiting the free movement of private companies and individual suppliers in the shea market. These controls would in turn allow CCSNFA members to rebuild their power base and economic standing. Although by the late 1990s this plan remained unrealized, its very articulation and widespread endorsement among CCSNFA members is indicative of the stake that residents of the north retained in economic forms organized around state presence. In envisioning market governance in terms earlier devised by the state, the farmers association found this still a resonant mode of controlling resources and projecting authority. In sum, by maintaining and cultivating ties to rural political elites, the PBC sought to recapture its former authority. This tactic in turn made it difficult for private firms to forge new links to influential rural residents and at the same time provided rural opinion leaders with new aspirations regarding their own potential to influence and engage the export market, presenting a further obstacle to private company entry.

Recapturing State Authority

Even as the PBC sought to usurp an economic role that was—at least in theory—the purview private firms, the private companies were equivocal about the role of the PBC and the state more generally in the export market, sometimes seeking their presence and participation and on other occasions, rejecting them. The PBC, by the same token, in addition to working with members of the SNFS executive council, built ties to the private firms now dominating the shea sector, holding out attractions to some

private buyers and upsetting others. The PBC had little choice but to cultivate alliances with private firms. Having lost its position as the exclusive
Ghanaian supplier to markets abroad, the PBC lacked the financial and
managerial capacity to sell shea nuts directly to importers on the world
market. Hence, pressed not only to procure nuts but to find a buyer for its
own goods, the PBC pursued association with those private companies
that did have the capacity to export.

The contradictory nature of the PBC's dual role as an overseer of the
market and a competitor in it is evident in the following scenario, in which
PBC executives chose to grant a domestic purchase and export license *ex
post facto* to a well-endowed private firm that was new to the market and
promised to buy the PBC's stock of nuts. An anathema to the other private
buyers in the shea market, the company had first entered the Ghanaian
market during the 1994 season, taking the liberty of operating for most of
the season without the required license. The company, moreover, was accused of recruiting the employees of established firms and shattering market equilibrium by offering exorbitant prices for shea nuts and buying
them in huge quantities, causing competitors to fear that it was attempting
to shut them out of the market. Although PBC executives claimed no conflict of interest between the PBC's "private-like" side and its role as market
overseer, by selectively carrying out its monitoring functions and determining which companies entered the market and on what terms, PBC carried out its regulatory role in its own interests. Selectively doling out
benefits to private firms in this way, the PBC altered market structure as it
advanced its own position in the market.

Even if they failed to benefit from the PBC's exclusions and voiced re-
sentment about them, the private firms were reluctant to dismiss the PBC
from the market altogether. In fact, the private companies worked hard to
emulate and reinstate aspects of PBC authority over the shea nut market.
Paralleling the CCSNFA's attempts to control internal marketing arrangements by emulating the PBC's domestic trade regulations, the leading private export companies worked to form a Licensed Buyers Association
modeled after strategies of export market regulation earlier exercised by
the PBC and effectively created an export cartel; all private firms purchasing shea nuts in Ghana would be required to join this association. According to this plan, the association would establish top prices to be paid for
shea nuts on the domestic market during different periods of the shea season. It would also establish a fixed export price for each of the different
grades of nuts from Ghana. As the proponents of this arrangement explained, through the creation of an export pool and facilitating of shipping
discounts for bulked nuts, all shea exporters in Ghana could enjoy equal
access to the world market.

Although this program of export control ostensibly promoted and protected market equity, it was created, like the CCSNFA plan to control domestic shea trade, with particular interests in mind. Authored by firms with a history of operation in Ghana (whether related to shea or to other economic endeavors), the licensed buyer scheme sought to manage the entry of new firms into the shea market and most of all to prevent market takeover by better-funded multinationals. The founding members of the Licensed Buyers' Association were furthermore part of an entrepreneurial elite well connected to the CMB. Hence the association's pleas and the board's responsiveness to them renewed an older brand of "crony capitalism" (Ravenhill 1993: 35) in which private-sector elites exact state-based patronage in return for political support, thus preserving established interests even as the boundaries and functions of both state and market are reworked. Indeed, Barad (1994: 186) points to a similar dynamic in the Togolese economy, where the private and often foreign-based firms replacing state-owned enterprises exacted the same market protections from the state as those held by their state-based predecessor. With the reinstatement of the terms of state control, if not their institutional form, for these firms, as in Ghana, the mantle of regulatory oversight and with it, economic privilege, was hard to drop and natural to reproduce.

Another State Enterprise Replicates PBC's Form and Function

There were other, more dramatic ways in which the state rebuilt its influence over the shea market while appearing to uphold a commitment to liberalization. Here, the revival of state control within the shea market depended neither on the PBC nor on private export firms alone. Indicating the contradictory interests of states as well as international bodies, this aspect of state-rebuilding was fostered by the very international financial institutions that promoted privatization and state withdrawal from the market in the first place. This occurred when a different state-based agency, known as Farmers Service Company of the Upper Regions (FASCOM), moved into the shea market as the functions of the PBC were being farmed out to private companies. The involvement of FASCOM in the shea nut market resurrected the very state-based privileges that were being undone by the IMF's and World Bank's privatization drive, but on a smaller scale and in a more clandestine manner. A remnant of the integrated rural development programs instituted in much of Ghana (Chambas 1980), FASCOM was established in 1978 to provide agricultural inputs at low cost to farmers in Ghana's Upper Regions, two of the most economically depressed areas of the country and a major supply zone for shea nuts. FASCOM is considered a parastatal, in which the majority of shares are held by the government of Ghana and the rest by the Bank of Ghana, Ghana Commercial Bank, and the members of local-level FASCOM cooperatives.

Well established throughout Ghana's Upper East and Upper West Regions, FASCOM was easily prepared to move into the shea nut market once the PBC system was officially dismantled. In addition to receiving large supplies of agricultural inputs and building materials at low prices for resale due to the waiver of tax and licensing restrictions, FASCOM has privileged access to office space, storage sheds, vehicles, and tractors—all of which could be used for its shea purchasing operations. Extending the assets already held by the company, some of the materials that were formerly used by the PBC for shea buying found their way to FASCOM. Indeed, at the FASCOM Upper East headquarters in Bolgatanga, employees could be seen painting over the Cocoa Marketing Board logo on dozens of tarps that had previously been employed by the PBC for shea nut storage. More important to FASCOM's success in the shea export trade than these physical resources gleaned from privileged ties to the state was the support provided to FASCOM by TechnoServe, a U.S.-based NGO operating under the auspices of the U.S. Agency for International Development (USAID).

Through TechnoServe FASCOM was assured of bank credit, debt cancellation, and the assistance of Ghanaian embassies abroad in finding external markets for shea. TechnoServe also helped FASCOM gain access to shea supplies by mobilizing rural cooperatives and providing them with loans and managerial assistance. Exemplifying the contradictory tendencies of efforts at market reform, the United States—a key player in the development and imposition of the World Bank's neoliberal agenda geared to the promotion of private enterprise, competitive markets, and the diminution of state-based economic privilege—was using its development arm to foster and enlarge the place of the Ghanaian state in the shea market. This was all the more paradoxical given TechnoServe's apparent commitment to market-based economic development. TechnoServe, staffed primarily by MBAs and with a logo reading "Business Solutions to Rural Poverty" (2002), has long seen itself as a leader in what it describes as "market-driven" and "business-oriented approaches to generating economic growth" ("Strategy and services" 2002). The support provided to FASCOM, though it facilitated rural economic opportunity as it helped to move Ghanaian shea nuts onto the world market, also played a key role, whether intentionally or not, in bringing the Ghanaian state back into the shea market.

With the aid of USAID and its subcontractor TechnoServe, FASCOM began to buy shea nuts during the 1993-to-1994 season. Because it was perceived as a government organization commanding substantial resources and had a large network of employees like the PBC, FASCOM easily solicited the services of established traders who had earlier participated in the shea farmer societies. Indeed, although nut suppliers understood PBC and FASCOM to be separate organizations, both were consistently referred to by rural shea nut traders as "the government." Guided by TechnoServe, FASCOM also engaged in outreach activities, organizing less-well-off rural women into supply cooperatives, similar to the PBC. As did the PBC in its early era of success, FASCOM offered cash advances to nut suppliers and, with its many vehicles, was easily able to provide assistance in transporting nuts for storage in its several warehouses.

Although FASCOM did not offer prizes to shea suppliers as the old PBC did, it offered a range of economic benefits and bonuses. Facilitated by FASCOM's ties to the state, these enticements could hardly be matched by its competitors in the private sector. Rather than accepting a cash payment for nuts, FASCOM's largest nut suppliers had the option of bartering nuts for discounted goods sold by FASCOM in its service centers. These commodities, especially the building materials stocked by FASCOM and purchased through the state tax- and duty-free, were otherwise expensive and difficult to get in the remote towns and villages of the north. Furthering the economic benefits accrued from working with FASCOM, many nut suppliers would resell these materials at market rates.

In addition, shea nut suppliers who established a good reputation with FASCOM would be awarded the opportunity to work as FASCOM agents, selling goods from its service centers on commission in small towns and villages. These agents, moreover, could be advanced short-term loans for their own needs. Even the rural women who were organized into supply groups received selective benefits from working with FASCOM that private firms did not easily provide, including easy access to credit to purchase nuts early in the season when prices were low, storage facilities, and banking advice.

Although all of these purchasing arrangements enhanced the economic opportunities available to nut suppliers, by giving FASCOM a stake in a growing market and providing the organization with a new source of revenue and a new purpose, they helped the state regain some part of its former position and privilege in the shea market. Even in 2002, after a decade of privatization and the eventual withdrawal of the PBC from the shea trade, FASCOM has maintained an enduring presence on the shea market as one of the country's few suppliers of nuts for export.

Private Companies and State Models

Enmeshed in a sort of love-hate relationship with the system of state control that preceded privatization and the forms of state influence that remained in play once it was in place, private companies could hardly reject the well-formed specter of the state that continued to pervade the shea economy. During the 1990s, despite the overarching agenda of liberalization, private export companies across the board activated PBC-style purchasing strategies and relationships in order to gain access to nut supplies. Nearly 50 percent of private company personnel were former PBC/CMB employees, and these individuals brought their connections to specific traders, leaders, communities, and transporters—extremely valuable forms of social capital—to their new line of work. Agrotrade, one of the leading private buyers of shea nuts, was founded by a former PBC executive. All of the company's regional managers had many years of experience in the shea business, working for either the PBC or the CMB. These managers in turn hired many of their former employees when setting up local operations. Likewise, in another private firm, the regional manager was the former chair of a large SNFS. When he was hired to oversee the company's operations in Upper East, he chose to employ several individuals who were former PBC purchasing clerks. In each case, familiarity with the PBC farmer society system provided a ready-made operational template.

During the 1994-to-1995 season, Agrotrade's purchasing strategy was modeled after that of the PBC—and was perceived as such by local-level suppliers. As one community leader told a company spokesman: "You are coming to replace the dead societies." Following the path of the PBC, company representatives targeted rural communities with a strong record of SNFS activity and sought pledges of nuts by reactivating farmer society patterns of operation and structures of authority. Past society leaders were asked to organize their members and seek financing from local "big-men" and "big-women" who had played this role under the PBC. When company representatives visited Zongowire in Bawku West, they bypassed the chief and instead worked through the vice-chairman of the local SNFS. Consolidating elite privilege and state authority in Kusanaba, another village in Bawku West, the district assemblyman, also a former farmer society member, was asked to organize a shea supply group and oversee the financing and storage of nut purchases. When he remarked to the company representative: "This is the same system as the PBC," the company representative replied: "Yes, it is."

The private company also emulated the PBC's policy of awarding top producers with attractive consumer goods such as wax print cloth, kerosene lanterns, and Wellington boots. So tied were they to the operational models of the PBC and their own former identities as state agents that company employees practically misrepresented their mission as state-directed. When a village chief responded to their requests by saying "shea nuts are a government commodity and we must take government instructions," they were loath to correct him. In short, while the PBC was allowing

5.3 Agrotrade agents in Bawku West inspecting shea trees and stocks.

5.4 Agrotrade trucks and employees on a purchasing expedition.

the farmer society system to "die a natural death," as one of the PBC's regional managers put it, private firms were trying hard to bring the aura of these associations back to life.

Private companies' attempts to replicate PBC policy and structure were not always successful. The rather uncritical adoption of PBC ways brought both the good and the bad, and corruption characteristic of the PBC's bureaucratic jungle found its way into the new operations. Halfway through the 1994-to-1995 season, one of the PBC veterans, a regional manager for Agrotrade, was forced into retirement after underpaying suppliers and pocketing the difference between the company's price and his own. The company also faced the same cash-supply problems as the PBC had, making it difficult to pay suppliers on time and causing it to lose access to nut stores. Private firms' employment of PBC strategies was further hampered by the resistance of local suppliers. In many communities, companies were forced to contend with the "school of hard knocks" education gained by former SNFS members who had suffered under the PBC. Remembering well the pitfalls of the PBC plan, these individuals did not easily acquiesce to its reinvention. Holding their ground in the face of private company requests, they negotiated for up-front cash payments, storage supplies, and the purchase of nuts at several times and different prices throughout the season.

Those few companies that continued to operate on the local level were forced to become more exclusive in their commitments in order to secure a share of the market. Strengthening their claims on nut suppliers, these firms homed in on a small number of communities and raised the stakes of their investments. One private company, Johnson Farms, for example, rather than repeat the usual promises of postseason prizes to top suppliers, pledged to build a health clinic for the entire community at the end of the shea season. Even though the company director was a native son, it was necessary for him to strike such a high-stakes bargain to win the exclusive support of community members and keep competitors out. Pushed into the role, the company, more than simply a benefactor, assumed the mantle of development agent, a service typically performed by or in tandem with the state.

Along similar lines, Olam, operating in Ghana for the first time, secured local-level supplies by paying inhabitants of remote rural areas in desired and hard-to-get commodities such as cloth, clocks, and bicycles. This arrangement was attractive to rural shea suppliers because it saved them a trip to market and provided a ready investment for their earnings. By substituting commodities for the government-issued currency, Olam posed itself in effect as a mediating body poised between the national economy and the local one. At the same time, by fostering commitments to the company alone, Olam cultivated the same sort of exclusive loyalties that were previously devoted to—or at least demanded by—the PBC. As private companies like Olam put more resources into designated rural communities, mimicking the territorial controls of the state, they became more protective of their domains, warning other companies to keep out of their economic space. Although these tactics allowed companies to increase their access to specified supply zones, the security of this control was nevertheless tenuous, as it depended on their ability to make good on extravagant promises over the long term.

Private companies experienced other challenges to their employment of PBC-derived operating strategies. Although they pursued a buying plan modeled after a state-based organization, it was still necessary to contend with the agents of the state who actually held and enforced state power on the local level. Unlike the old PBC, which took advantage of its national mandate and the weakness of district-level governments in the 1980s, in the 1990s private firms could not easily override the demands and authority of current district assembly members (DAs). Sometimes working through the DAs enabled the export companies to gain the compliance of the wider community. This was true in Kusanaba, for example, where the DA was a former SNFS executive and had an interest in and the capital necessary to restart the shea export trade. Other assembly members, while attracted to new sources of wealth, were more skeptical of export company motives and their promises of both personal and local profit. These officials threatened to hold up the company's purchase of nuts from households and markets in their area if they did not work through them and pay local tariffs. They also demanded prefinancing for the village-level suppliers, most of whom were too poor to supply large-enough quantities of nuts without a cash advance.

Yet despite the acrimonious nature of the initial encounters between some DAs and company representatives, the assembly members were subsequently advised by the Ministry of Trade and Tourism to court the interests of private company personnel. Both replicating the state's old role in the shea market and repositioning the state in relation to private firms new to the market, the Ministry of Trade and Tourism promised to help assembly members make these connections as it instructed them to organize PBC-modeled shea supply societies that could amass large-enough quantities of nuts to entice exporters.

Penetrating the Regional Market

In response to the growing expectations and demands they faced in the course of operating within rural communities, private firms had little choice but to rework their purchasing plans. Limiting their presence and liability in the market, firms turned away from the farmer society model and instead selected regionally based "chief" agents to purchase shea nuts for them. The agents, free to choose their own suppliers and set commission rates, were issued funds to buy a designated number of bags of shea nuts for which they were solely responsible. These agents were not in a company's direct employ but they continually served as partners in transactions and operated as chief suppliers in a given area, receiving bonuses for loyalty and reliability. Instead of cultivating community- and household-level commitments, agents were encouraged to buy in town and village markets, giving them greater flexibility and helping them to avoid the accountability problems generated by prolonged contracts.

Although rural markets provided a ready-made source of nuts, and private buyers controlled substantial capital, gaining and sustaining access to those markets was not always easy. Catering to the regional nut trade and the needs of local butter processors, rural markets were also highly competitive, as many parties—butter-makers, specialized traders, investors, bulkers, and retailers—sought to buy and sell nuts. Rural markets were also characterized by idiosyncratic transactional norms, sometimes making it difficult for private buyers to navigate the nuances of trade in different locales. In other cases, private buyers were at first able easily to gain access to markets, but their own behavior incited the construction of new sorts of transactional barriers, rendering the supply lines they sought to tap less rather than more accessible over time. These intrusions also had uneven implications for the nut traders supplying private firms. While rural traders were generally enthusiastic about engaging new economic opportunities and market conditions, company incursions destabilized nut prices and supply lines, upsetting traders' relationships with one another and with the butter-makers who typically purchased nuts from them.

What resulted was an uneasy absorption of private-company buyers into rural markets, with no singular or stable set of outcomes. Sometimes private buyers conformed to the standards of rural trading systems; on other occasions, these standards were reworked in response to private-company incursions. In some markets, traders were receptive to newcomers, and in others, they were more resistant. In all of these encounters, however, a gradual recasting of the boundaries between rural markets and private firms ensued as private buyers persistently sought to blur or undo boundaries, and traders, for the most part, sought to assert or codify them as they tried to cope with the dual demands of export buyers and rural butter-makers.

Tracing these developments, the remainder of this chapter discusses the interactions of private company representatives and nut traders within three markets in Bawku District, beginning with Bawku Central Market, and moving to two rural markets, Songo and Worianga. In Bawku District, as elsewhere in northern Ghana and West Africa more generally (Fold 2000: 97), the regional shea nut trade is largely the purview of women.[2] As professional merchants, these traders bulk the nuts collected by other women from shea trees located on farms or in forests and sell them in large lots to butter-makers or investors who purchase nuts to store and resell. A core group of such traders make their base in Bawku's Central Market, where they cater to the needs of butter-makers with limited or no access to nuts on their own or nearby land. These traders regularly visit a handful of rural markets located in the more heavily forested southern reaches of the district where shea trees grow in abundance, Songo among them, to buy directly from nut collectors. Nuts may also be purchased in larger rural trading centers with their own merchant class, such as Worianga, embedded in its own ring of satellite markets distinct from that of Bawku town.

Bargaining and Bifurcation in Bawku

Bawku Central Market, the district's largest market, is tremendously crowded and busy. Nut collectors occasionally sell their wares in Bawku, but they occupy a small portion of the nut market. Rather, Bawku is home to large-scale nut traders who bulk and retail the nuts they purchase in rural markets. This core group of professional shea traders works out of a

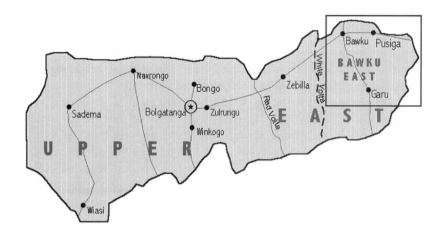

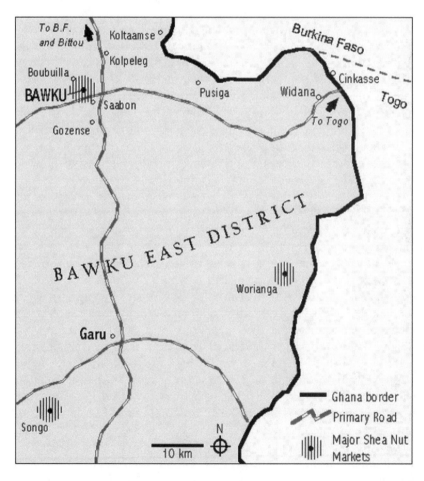

Map 7 Shea Nut Market Locations in Bawku East District

10-by-20-foot shed devoted to the nut trade, crowded with 65-kilo bags of nuts, 20-liter basins full of nuts, and various measuring bowls and bordered by rows of women selling foodstuffs and sundries. Although clusters of nut traders can be found elsewhere in the market, this is the only place in the whole of the market where nuts can be found for sale year-round. The traders involved in the nut trade full-time are loosely organized. Although not elected as such, there is a leader, or shea nut *magazia* (Hausa for "market queen"), Madame Halima, a surly and independent woman in her sixties. If a problem arises, by virtue of her seniority it is Halima's responsibility to solve it. Otherwise, coordination and cooperation among the group of traders as a whole is generally limited.

Despite the lack of formal organization in the group, traders nevertheless work closely with each other and in support of each other's endeavors. This is evidenced, however, outside the market rather than in it, as the social lives of most of these women are closely intertwined through kin and residential ties. These affiliations create a base of common knowledge and assistance, providing a foundation to their market-based interactions. Almost all of Bawku's professional bulker-retailers (nine out of eleven) live in the same neighborhood. Five of the women, Mariama, Naab-pal, Nyabpoa, Shetu, and Zeinabu, live in the same household. Another, Mbil, lives next door. Bonola lives in a related household about 200 yards east, and Fati lives about a quarter of a mile away. Sala, Fati's junior sister, is also a shea nut trader; she resides a short way up the road. The only two women who are not tied by residential or kin ties are Halima, the leader, and another trader new to the shea nut business.

During a single season, beginning in late August and ending in early November, export company agents visited Bawku market close to ten times. When the company agents first arrived in the market, some traders were wary about selling to them. This may have stemmed from the common association and, at times, confusion of company buying agents with the state-based PBC representatives of yore. Mariama, for example, commented: "It is reported that those people are buying for the government to weigh." Halima too initially refused to sell to the private firm, although she had nuts available. She claimed that the price the company offered to pay was too low for the nuts she had in store, arguing that she had a reputation with butter-makers for selling high-quality well-cooked nuts which she would not compromise. Others were more complacent. Sala agreed to sell nuts to the private firm even though she complained about the low purchase price, providing only 500 cedi profit per bag. Sala and her friends rationalized that if they did not sell, others would, causing them to lose out. Even one of the market storekeepers, who had worked with the PBC but had suspended his participation in the shea trade since the breakdown of

5.5 Madame Hadiza, the Bawku shea nut *magazia*.

the SFNSs, used the arrival of private company agents to get back into the shea market. Curious to engage whatever economic benefits cooperation with private buyers might bring, he commissioned the itinerant nut traders sitting near his store to buy several bags of nuts for him to resell to the company.

Overcoming their initial ambivalence, over the course of a few weeks Halima and her cohorts began collectively to assert power over the terms of transaction with the company representatives. This was a hard-won process; the collective potentials of the Bawku traders were first made apparent during company representatives' second visit to Bawku. At this time, the company agents sought to arrange purchase of fifty bags of nuts for 9,000 cedi per bag, the same price they had paid to the Bawku traders on a previous buying trip a few weeks earlier. Unhappy with this arrangement, the nut sellers pleaded for 9,500 cedi per bag, to no avail, and warned the representatives of a 500-cedi-per-bag price hike the next time they came to market. When the company representatives returned the next market day to pick up the nuts, the bulker-retailers initiated a significant shift in tactics. With Halima as spokesperson, they bargained with the company as a group, demanding 9,500 cedi per bag. Embroiled in several hours of negotiation, the nut sellers eventually dropped the price to 9,200 cedi per bag, yet were ultimately rebuffed and forced to sell at 9,000 cedi, as company representatives successfully argued that the traders had agreed to the lower price at the time of the visit the day before. Despite Halima's failure to secure higher prices that day, the seriousness of traders' pleas and the coordination of their interests were made evident to the company agents, shaping the terms of future transactions. When the company returned the next week, they had no choice but to pay 9,500 cedi per bag. Coming back two weeks later, they agreed to another price hike of 300 cedi, bringing the price per bag to 9,800 cedi, and 10,000 cedi the following week.

Just as the Bawku nut traders learned to assert their interests collectively in terms of price, they also used their expertise in the shea market to manipulate the quality and measurement of nuts sold. When selling wholesale, nut traders usually sell by the bag. This is a somewhat tricky endeavor in the absence of a scale. Though bags are a standard size designed to hold 65 kilos of nuts, a bag's exact weight and volume are hard to estimate. Not only do bags stretch in the course of use, but nuts also shrink as they dry out, rendering a bag that appears to be packed full during the rainy season to be of substandard volume several months later. Accordingly, buying by the bag is often a source of acrimony between buyers and sellers. Private company representatives, in contrast, buying nuts in large lots and with limited personnel and equipment, were not inclined either to measure out the volume of each bag bowl by bowl or to weigh them—as was the practice of their predecessors in the PBC. Observing company representatives' lack of interest in measurement, local nut traders soon realized that they could reduce the standard volume of the bags they sold to the private companies without being detected. Removing three to four bowls of nuts out of a bag holding thirty-six bowls became standard practice; as Sala put it: "They won't mind or even know, since everyone does it."

As with the dissimulation of nut measures, nut traders covertly manipulated the quality of nuts sold to the private firm, once again enabling them to establish favorable terms of trade with little notice or need for outright negotiation. Shea nuts are available in a range of grades stemming not so much from the conditions of their growth but from how they are processed and stored after picking. Nut grades depend on whether nuts are well dried or wet and whether they have been boiled prior to shelling. Butter-makers and professional nut traders consider dried and boiled nuts to be of the highest quality. Company representatives, Bawku traders learned, were indifferent to nut quality, and did not inspect the nuts in the market before purchasing nor before sending them to the company headquarters. Nut traders consequently made a special effort to purchase the cheaper, uncooked nuts to sell to the private firms. Because butter-makers had no desire for the uncooked nuts and knew better than to buy them, this tactic helped, at least in part, protect the butter market. At the same time it allowed the nut traders to develop a new and profitable economic niche, effectively bifurcating the market to the overall disadvantage of private buyers.

Given their ability to forge favorable terms of trade with respect to price, measure, and quality, a large majority of local nut traders sold nuts to the private firm. Ranging from two to six bags per trader, most sold modest to middle-sized lots of nuts to the company agents on each of their half-dozen buying trips. A small number of nut traders declined to sell to the firm altogether. Fati, just getting back into the nut business after the birth of her third child and struggling to amass enough nuts to supply her butter-maker customers, was one trader who chose not to participate in export-oriented trade. But there were other traders who sold relatively large lots of ten to fifteen bags of nuts each time company representatives came to market.

As private companies began to buy larger lots of nuts however, it became impossible to supply them with only the lower-quality uncooked nuts, a situation that diverted nut supplies from butter-makers to the private companies. Not only did this limit butter-makers' access to nuts, compromising traders' relationships with their usual customers, but it also exposed traders to the vicissitudes of a rather unreliable market. The private firms, it soon became evident, despite their promises to return to Bawku on a given market day to pick up nuts and pay for their goods, were largely unpredictable,

sometimes arriving a week or two behind schedule. After buying nuts especially for the company or withholding them from their usual customers,
traders complained about tying up funds for what was proving to be an uncertain customer base. Others withheld their nuts from butter-makers one
week, only to sell them the reserved nuts the next. While this was an easy
way out for the nut traders, it frustrated the usual pace of exchange, pro-
longing reimbursement and the possibility of reinvestment.

Private-company accountability was problematic in other ways. Because the company's system of ordering, paying for, and picking up nuts
was irregular, it was difficult for both agents and traders to keep track of
their accounts. Although the company generally managed to avoid misun-
derstandings regarding payments, this was not entirely possible. Throughout the whole of the shea season, one woman complained vigorously about
the money owed to her by the company, claiming she sold two bags to the
agents but never received payment—a story corroborated by one of the
agents.

Companies also proved unreliable in terms of their bargaining strategies. Despite the hard work of Halima and her cohorts in pursuing their
desired price and the company's begrudging acceptance of even an incremental price hike, when the company was offered large lots of nuts from
individual traders, it easily agreed to purchase them at higher prices.
Hence, despite Bawku traders' efforts to establish a place for company representatives in the shea market by offering them what might be considered
a market of their own—albeit a somewhat inferior one—the loyalties and
material conditions upon which it depended were rather fragile. In short,
although Bawku nut traders' organizational capacity and superior knowledge of the shea trade offered them some protection as well as new opportunities in the face of private buyers, they were only partially successful in
securing this new sort of economic boundary.

Opening Markets and Competing for Control in Songo

In addition to visiting Bawku Central Market, representatives of private
firms also visited rural markets in Bawku East District in search of shea
supplies. With their own truck, a driver, and two assistants, the company
representatives were instructed by their regional director to tour the major
supply markets in the area, both to buy nuts and to assess future supplies.
In late August 1994, private buyers attended the market in the village of
Songo. Located in a less-populated area of Bawku District, Songo market is
rather small. However, due the relatively rich agriculture of the area, Songo
is a popular trading center for the bulking of agricultural produce and is
attended by traders from throughout Bawku District, including Bawku
town itself. Here private firms were able to purchase shea nuts without

being subjected to the sort of boundaries and manipulations they experienced in Bawku.

Remote enough not to be overcrowded, Songo market's popularity was relied on by residents of the area for their livelihood, and they were hesitant to restrict it in any way. With local traders so dependent on outside buyers, company representatives were able to purchase goods directly from rural nut collectors and local-level bulkers without any problem. In fact, operating with little concern about the exact weight or quality of nuts—as in Bawku market—the company buyers offered a better deal to rural nut collectors than did the regionally based nut traders from Bawku and Garu who also attended the market. As a result, private buyers experienced very limited local resistance to their presence in the market. The only local challenged they faced was when the Songo district assemblyman noticed the strangers and their trucks, loaded with bags of nuts, at the edge of the market and asked them to identify themselves and their mission. Although the assemblyman was perturbed by what he took to be the intrusion of company agents—mostly because they did not seek his support or promise any benefit to him—he could do little to encumber their already accomplished transactions.

Likewise, the Bawku-based nut traders who arrived in the market after the company representatives had started buying could do little to inhibit the firm's activity despite their concern about the competition it posed. As outsiders in the market, albeit familiar, the Bawku traders had few means to challenge the changing market conditions brought about by the presence of private firms. This was problematic for the Bawku women in a number of ways. First, by buying huge lots in one day in small rural markets where nuts were usually put up for sale over the course of the season due to the staggered pace of the shea harvest and rural savings and investment patterns, company representatives reduced the supply of nuts available. The company's superior access to supplies was further facilitated by the agents' control of their own means of transport. Not only did this enable them to arrive in the market before the Bawku women, who relied on the market trucks, but it also allowed them to access nuts stored in homes far from the market that the Bawku traders could not get to, further diminishing the supplies available to the Bawku buyers.

The presence of the private firms also brought about significant price increases. On one market day in Songo, the price of nuts per bowl jumped more than 10 percent, raising the price of a bag from 6,800 to 7,700 cedi, making it difficult for Bawku traders to maintain their profit margin. Private buyers, in addition, drew bulking agents away from Bawku traders, further frustrating their efforts to buy nuts.

Hence Songo, due to its remote location and the limited economic opportunities available to its residents, oddly enough, operated as a relatively

5.6 Sala, a Bawku-based nut bulker, at work in Songo market.

"open" market where local traders held no advantage over private firms. Instead, private firms, due to their superior endowments in terms of capital, transport, and timeliness, were able to garner a strong position in the market. Not only did this threaten the livelihoods of Bawku nut traders, but perhaps more significantly, the possibility of export buyers raiding rural supply centers early in the nut season severely reduced the nut supplies available to rural butter-makers, both undermining the redistributive potentials of rural-to-urban trade and the value-creating potential of rural industry.

Resistant Engagement and Relocalization in Worianga

In addition to their incursions into Bawku Central Market and remote rural hamlets such as Songo, private-company purchasing agents also sought nuts in the rural trading center of Worianga, which is located in the southeast part of the district less than a mile away from the Togo border and is known for its substantial shea supplies. A popular source of nuts for local investors with funds to spare from the lucrative trade in livestock and un-regulated cross-border transactions in the area, Worianga is an extremely competitive market. It was in Worianga that the most significant and direct confrontation between private firms and rural shea traders occurred.

Reversing the scenario in Bawku, Worianga nut traders initially accommodated private buyers, only gradually mobilizing themselves against the private-company representatives operating there. And in contrast to Songo, despite its similar rural locale, access to the market in Worianga was difficult for private buyers to maintain. In addition, in Worianga, unlike Songo, like-minded rural traders and local politicians were able to forge and protect a common cause. Indeed, compared to the price and quality controls imposed by Bawku traders, in Worianga private companies ultimately had to face a situation of full-fledged market closure forged by traders and politicians.

In Worianga, purchasing nuts directly from nut collectors is nearly impossible for insiders and outsiders alike and requires the hire of bulking agents. For private-company representatives with little knowledge of district geography and infrastructure, the challenges of market access in Worianga were compounded by their ignorance of the town's exact location and the transport route to reach it. To overcome these obstacles, the company appealed to Mary Anaba, a leading Garu shea investor, to serve as their agent and guide in Worianga. Mary was well known throughout the district and had a long history of buying large quantities of nuts to sell to the PBC. Recalling the profits and status gained while working for the PBC and lured by expectations of a generous trading commission and the potential for a long-term contract, Mary did not hesitate to comply with the company's request for assistance.

Harnessing Mary's knowledge and connections, the company was able to gain entree into Worianga market without any problem. Mary's role as escort served as an effective cover, legitimizing the company's presence in the market through the simple fact of her visibility and the practical assistance she provided. Mary was also instrumental in convincing Marizua, a Garu bulking agent with trading experience and reputation in Worianga, to accompany her to the market in the company truck. Not wanting to disappoint Mary, her patron in many trading endeavors, Marizua agreed to participate in the excursion though she had no opportunity to establish the terms of her involvement with the company agents.

Despite Mary's support and Marizua's cooperation, the company's operations in Worianga were fraught from the start, fomenting tensions among local traders as well as between traders and private-firm employees. As soon as they gained a foothold in the market through Mary's introduction, private-company agents, out of ignorance and blatant disregard of local standards, flouted market conventions. Although these practices were met with individualized protest, the highly competitive nature of the market and its intricate division of labor initially made it difficult for local actors to recognize and redress their collective interests vis-à-vis the company.

One of the first mistakes made by company agents was the importation of loading "boys" hired in Bawku town to work in Worianga. With its own team of able and experienced loaders, Worianga market was already well equipped in this regard—a point that the many young men vying for loading work angrily impressed upon company agents. Arguing strenuously and upholding private-company commerce for nearly half an hour, the Worianga loaders had little success with the company representative other than convincing them to hire a few extra hands for to carry sacks and load trucks. Once this dispute was resolved, private-company representatives initiated negotiations with local bulking agents. Contacting three male bulkers positioned at the market's edge, the company agents proposed a purchasing plan based on advance payment to bulkers for a designated number of bags. Though this arrangement was in no way unusual, it did have uncertain repercussions for other traders. Taking on a maximum order of twenty bags each, these bulking agents abandoned already negotiated contracts in favor of company work. This resulted in an explosive altercation between the male bulkers and a nut trader from Bawku who had prepaid the agents for her order, only to be spurned for the "Johnny-come-lately" company. Though her money was returned, allowing her to seek out a new agent to help secure nut supplies, the Bawku trader, loudly haranguing the bulkers for several minutes, injected an air of tension into the negotiation of purchasing arrangements and drew attention to the intrusive presence of the private company.

This discomfort was reiterated by Marizua. She was prepaid to purchase nuts by the company, but her efforts were frustrated by the below-market price of 7,100 cedi per bag offered. Only by painstakingly roaming the market and cleverly combining lots could she amass bags at this rate, let alone achieve any profit for herself. With no mention of a commission from the company, she was disheartened by her limited purchasing power and profit potential under the company scheme. Mary, on the other hand, with no obligation to purchase nuts for the company, was nowhere to be found. Once she had introduced the company people to the appropriate bulkers, she took advantage of her unexpected visit to Worianga to socialize and purchase supplies for the small restaurant she ran in Garu. Mary's independent preoccupations left Marizua without anyone to advocate for a higher advance price or a guaranteed commission, accentuating tensions between the two women.

As a result of low buying prices and incentives, by the end of the market day the company had amassed only twenty-seven bags of nuts, considerably less than half of its eighty-bag quota. Nine were purchased from producer-retailers by one of the male bulkers; another nine were purchased from producer-retailers by Marizua. The remainder was purchased by the company agents themselves from local investors with large stocks of nuts.

With such poor results, the company agents faced a series of dilemmas. Expected to return to Bolgatanga that evening and lacking the authority to commit to returning to Worianga in the near future, company agents had to go about the delicate task of collecting unspent funds from poorly remunerated bulkers. Although this might seem a straightforward task, it was complicated by the resistance of certain bulking agents. For more than an hour one bulker, with no apparent motive other than duplicity and slight financial gain, refused and confused the company representative's pleas for the return of funds. His protests were based on an irrational account of payments and expenditures that left him a few thousand cedis ahead. Unclear about whether the bulker's calculations were in jest or not and wanting to secure their funds without a physical confrontation, the company agents endured the bulker's charade, patiently negotiating for the return of their funds. Whatever the true foundation of the bulker's beliefs and behavior, it is reasonable to interpret them as an effective challenge to company procedure. They operated as an after-the-fact resistance paralleling Marizua's earlier and more straightforward complaints about the company's low purchase price and inequitable buying arrangements.

Once their capital was secured, company representatives had a more serious problem to resolve: how to buy a substantial stock of nuts before the market closed. Desperate to find nuts for sale, the company agents decided to raise their buying price from 7,100 to 8,000 cedi per bag, moving from a below-market price to an above-market figure. Once this news was made public, the wife of the town's *imam* volunteered to sell fifteen bags of nuts she was storing at home. Agreeing to this deal, much to the chagrin of Marizua who could have easily purchased nuts in the market at the higher price, the company agents and loading boys entered the yard of the imam's house to help the old woman repack her nuts. When this transaction was nearly finished, an old man from a nearby house notified the buyers that his wives had ten bags of nuts for sale at the price of 8,000 cedi each. Relieved to find additional supplies at this late hour, the agents moved to the second house to purchase the wives' stocks.

Though accompanying the company representatives to both houses, Mary's participation in the transactions was generally quiet and subdued. Only in the second house did she take a more vocal and forceful role. In the process of rebagging the women's nuts, it became apparent to Mary that the bags were grossly underweight. Bringing this concern to the attention of company representatives, she advised them to demand a standard weight. The family members in turn argued that the bags were full when purchased, explaining that the volume fell in the course of storage due to settling and shrinkage. Betraying the family's assertions, however, were several other quite fully packed bags remaining in the storeroom that they refused to sell. Despite threats to abandon the sale unless additional nuts were added to the lot, the company agents' demands were rebuffed. With their desperation apparent to all involved, the agents had little choice but to purchase the bags and settle for substandard volumes.

With fifty-two bags of nuts loaded in their vehicle at eight o'clock in the evening, the company representatives finally left Worianga, ten hours after their arrival, to begin the four-hour journey back to Bolgatanga. Dropping Mary and Marizua off at Garu, they give Mary a 1,500 cedi bonus for her help and Marizua 500 cedi. Appalled by the paltry remuneration for their many hours of hard work and patience, especially on the part of Marizua, the two women swore never to assist the company again. Marizua accused the company of misrepresenting its purchasing system. With a buying price established by the company virtually by decree, she assumed that her lack of input would at least be rewarded with a per-bag commission at the end of the day, as is the standard local practice. If not, she argued, she would have tacked on the fee before agreeing to the company's purchase price.

When the company representatives returned to Garu on the way to Worianga the next week, the two women made good on their threats. Mary refused to help them, claiming she was busy. She explained the logic of her noncooperation in terms of the company's breach of a commonsense contract: "you help someone in order to gain; you don't help someone for free." According to Mary, although she might assist the company's regional

5.7 Private Company agents bagging nuts in Worianga.

director in Bolgatanga, she did not trust the agents, given their inexperience and apparent disrespect for her work. Marizua, whom the company agents encountered when they returned on their own to Worianga, orchestrated a more dramatic withdrawal of assistance to the company. Not only did she refuse to work with them, having made her own case known to the other traders in the market, she incited a collective process of noncompliance, rendering the company incapable of purchasing any nuts at all in the Worianga market.

Soon after this incident, the company confronted a similar set of obstacles in Garu. They were the result of the concerted effort of bulking agents who chose to work with local customers, including Bawku nut traders, before responding to company requests. This diffidence on the part of local traders was supported by the town's chief. Learning of company's interests and habits from the chiefs and district assemblymen of the nearby Songo and Worianga, the Garu chief asserted that by entering the town market without seeking his permission, the company representatives had breached local market etiquette. Given the chief's usually limited involvement in the regulation of trade and the general openness of Garu as a transit market, it is likely that the chief's pleas were motivated by self-interest rather than concern for local nut traders. Nevertheless, they helped to ratify and enforce local traders' defiance of private-company requests.

In sum, despite the highly competitive nature of Worianga market, private-company agents were able to negotiate a point of entry by harnessing the assistance and reputation of a nut trader who was well known throughout the region. Yet, even with this inside track, they were hard-pressed to navigate the prevailing norms of transaction, eventually alienating the very traders on whom they relied to secure supplies. Though individual traders did not hesitate to express their displeasure with the company's purchasing methods, the coordination of their disquiet into a concerted resistance took somewhat longer to establish, given the competitive and decentralized organization of Worianga market. However, once mobilized, the collective actions of both Worianga and Garu traders—along with the support of local political leaders—not only set the terms of market participation but barred private buyers from the market altogether, reasserting the boundaries of the rural nut market in both practical and geographic terms.

Discussion

Given the overall openness of Bawku East District's periodic marketing system, in all three markets—Songo, Bawku, and Worianga—the direct intervention of private-company agents was fairly easily accomplished, at least in its initial phases. Once in the market, however, private-company representatives faced a complex stream of resistance and accommodation tempered by the specifics of the market context, trader positions, and transaction types. All of these factors were shaped by the capacity of local nut traders to forge and enforce strategies of collective action. Despite the more common atomization of trading relationships in the domestic nut trade, such collective norms played a decisive role in reforming the export trade and partially preserving the domestic nut market.

In Bawku's Central Market, a core group of nut traders had substantial (but not complete) influence over the terms of private-company operations. In this generally open market, nut traders' expression of their authority became possible as they gradually began to coordinate their sales practices and interactions with private-company representatives. Effectively bifurcating the shea market into domestic and export sectors, Bawku traders were able to maintain a degree of control over the parameters of the nut trade and their own place within it as well as partially to protect the nut supplies for rural butter-makers.

Perhaps even more dramatically than Bawku, Worianga proved a context where local traders were able to redefine company directives through collective action. However, this came at the cost of considerable tension between local traders and the eventual rejection of new economic opportunities supplying export agents. Compared to Bawku, in terms of transactional norms, Worianga was fundamentally a much more "closed" trading system. A highly competitive market, attractive to local and more far-flung entrepreneurs, Worianga market was characterized by many fine gradations in trading roles and etiquette. Mobilizing the social capital necessary to penetrate this complex trading system, private buyers were able to gain entrée into the market without much difficulty. Yet after they had transgressed transactional norms again and again, private buyers were soon shut out of the market, as traders in a range of market positions sought to coordinate their sales tactics and maintain a share of the domestic market. They found support for their efforts among local politicians, themselves striving to reinstitute the benefits they had derived during the days of PBC control of the shea trade. Orchestrating what can be seen as a "relocalization" of the shea trade, both groups, alone and in tandem, advocated for greater control over the new export market or else pushed for its demise through the insulation of the domestic nut trade.

In contrast to both Bawku and Worianga, in Songo market export agents encountered and maintained free access to the nut market. Despite the joint interests of Bawku traders and the district assembly representatives in curbing private-company activity, they posed little influence on the terms of private-company participation without the endorsement of this effort by rural nut collectors. Rather, the very remoteness of the market and nut collectors' desires to engage any economic opportunity presented to them made Songo a particularly "open" market, offering little protection of nut supplies for rural butter-makers. Hence compared to the compromise tactics of Bawku traders or the eventual exclusions of Worianga market, Songo represented a case where private buyers, bypassing the authority of local leaders and large-scale traders, were received well and operated with ease.

Conclusion

The dynamics of shea market reform occurring in Ghana during the 1990s on all fronts confound orthodox expectations regarding the path and possibilities of liberalization within new states and largely agrarian economies. With regard to presumptions about the ease of state diminution and withdrawal from economic life, the efficiencies of private-sector promotion, and the responsiveness of rural entrepreneurs to new opportunities, the case of shea market liberalization shows a different set of processes at work in each case. Rather than disappearing, the state was in many respects revitalized, and the private sector underwent a process of monopolization on the one hand and informalization on the other. Rural entrepreneurs were equally varied in their engagement of the reform process and the new economic actors and ways of acting and accumulating wealth it presented, at once opening up some markets, closing others, and creating new ones.

Given its legacy in Ghana, the persistent quest of the state to remain in the shea market comes as no surprise. With its political and economic authority built upon a rather monolithic extractive apparatus—as has been demonstrated in many African settings—the remains of the state are sure to loom large even as economies are liberalized. Even in the case of a new, neoliberal regime, the conditions of shea export are in keeping with a widespread trend of state survival in the face of market reform. Indeed, throughout Africa state-owned enterprises like the Cocoa Marketing Board and its subsidiary, the PBC, are singled out as prime arenas for the preservation of state authority. Grosh and Mukandala (1994: 248), for example, state that "public enterprises will be around to stay on a large scale in Africa and that the debate should center on the specifics of what they do and how they do it." This point of view is endorsed by scholars working in a number of countries (Barad 1994a; Steffen 1994; Van de Walle 1994a; Wilson 1994).

To some, this sort of state persistence in the face of reform and resultant process of partial or "false" privatization can be explained by the problem of state capacity. Clapp (1997: 4), in her study of structural adjustment and agriculture in Guinea, asserts that "the state's weak capacity hindered implementation of the reform program," a point that suggests the fundamentally contradictory position of the state in the reform process. Namely, the successful implementation of market reforms requires strong states, but strong states are unlikely to undo themselves. Here the inherently political character of the market reform process becomes apparent (Staudt 1995: 236). Indeed, even Herbst (1993), despite his characterization of Ghana's structural adjustment program as an economic about-face, alludes to the political entailments of privatization. He remarks, "[p]rivatization is not the central issue in determining the future borders of the state in Ghana or elsewhere because privatization per se is not grounded in a basic view of what the state should or should not do" (1993: 95). Berry likewise points to the mutual determination of commerce and control:

> no market system functions in a political vacuum; no environment for perfect competition ever survived for long, if at all. A competitive environment is a hazardous one; competition not only drives down prices and profits but impels people to try to protect themselves from its vicissitudes. Competition breeds market controls as well as lower costs, and even competitive markets seldom remain competitive indefinitely. The choice facing African governments is often not one of selecting between controlled and competitive prices, but one of choosing to regulate prices themselves or letting other factors take control. Berry 1986: 74)

What stands out in the close reading of shea market reform in Ghana is the uneven and many-layered process of forging and securing such patterns of market intervention. No doubt the force of the Cocoa Marketing Board over the Ghanaian economy is extreme (Raikes and Gibbon 2000; "Currency trends" 2000a; "Prospects: Ghana" 2000), but even the board operates in partial, fragmented, and conflicting ways. While one part of the CMB promotes shea privatization at home and undermines it abroad, another—specifically, the PBC—subverts it at home as its agents struggle to hold on to a piece of the market. These political maneuvers are not confined to the space of the state or even the state's mobilization of constituencies and resources in the public realm. What seems remarkable in the case of shea is the way supposedly private entities strive to reinstate state authority and modes of market access and control in the face of state diminution and withdrawal. Here is a situation of markets holding onto and, in some situations, emulating states. This is a different sort of process from the classic picture of states claiming a stake in the market as described by Bates (1981). Instead, we see a much more multifaceted picture of institutional reproduction, as the structures and strategies of state-owned firms are remade by a variety of interest groups both within and outside the state.

Taken together with the tendency of institutions like the CCSNFA, spawned by the PBC in the course of its reign, to rewrite state-derived policy into the new economic script, or the parastatal FASCOM to move into the shea market with the backing of international financial interests, the problematic character of what Little and Watts (1994: 15) call "the fallacy of the simple public-private dichotomy" for comprehending both the processes and outcomes of economic liberalization is all too clear. Rather, what is emerging is a set of hybrid forms—the "part structures being built and torn down" to which Moore (1987: 730) refers. In these operations, states and markets are thoroughly interwoven and interdependent, giving rise to new sources and systems of resource access and control and at the same time making space for the resurfacing of established interests, but via new channels.

This hybridization process is by no means restricted to those actors or entities anchored in the state or the formal sector. It is equally forged by members of rural society involved in the shea trade, whether shea nut collectors, larger-scale shea nut bulkers, or rural opinion leaders of both official and unofficial standing. Without a doubt, rural entrepreneurs shape the parameters of private-sector participation in the shea market—how to bag, buy, bargain, contract, and reward. In turn, they are spurred to pursue their own process of market restructuring, enlivening otherwise dormant commodity associations, creating new commodity categories, restricting channels of market access, and even calling for state intervention in the market. As difficult as it is to track these forms, it is more difficult to know how to classify them. Does the entry of private firms into Bawku, Songo, and Worianga, for example, indicate the rationalization of the local or the informalization of the private, or both, or perhaps neither? More compelling than questions of classification, however, are the implications of such restructuring for rural patterns of resource access and control. Taken together, they represent a compilation of various processes of opening and closure, with different implications for livelihoods, power relations, and forms of accountability and entitlement in rural life.

Consequently, the contours of rural economic life are also undergoing a process of reframing. In some cases, as in Bawku and Worianga, a process of boundary construction is under way, as rural traders increasing restrict the terms of access to particular commodities, suppliers, and trading venues. But even as private companies are pushed out of certain market relationships, they come to pervade others, often in a less overt but potentially more problematic way. With restricted access to larger markets like Bawku and Worianga, private representatives may gravitate to smaller ones with few barriers to entry, like Songo. This allows the deeper and more direct influence of export firms over the terms of rural commercial life. Similarly, private firms may revert to a tactic of building local monopolies, setting up shop as the exclusive buyer in particular communities. Although they may not hold any formal political means of enforcement, by offering nearly exclusive access to valuable resources—desirable commodities, communitywide investment, or simply access to cash—they can certainly uphold their interests. Moving in another direction, private companies may also, as we have seen, become more dependent on local entrepreneurs working as purchasing agents. Already, the distancing of export companies from village market and community-level suppliers has led to the reemergence of tier of upper-level traders specializing in shea as a cash commodity and contributing to the growing stratification within rural markets and communities. Though not identified as such, they may more easily and insidiously impose the demands and expectations of private buyers on rural economies even in those ostensibly closed spaces like Worianga. This is all part of a process through which privatization brings with it new forms of regulation, though not in a way envisioned by the promoters of neoliberal reform programs.

Indeed, this sort of blending or recombination of liberalization and regulation emerging in the context of structural adjustment and so-called economic recovery in Ghana is what accounts for the notable shift in the relationship of the state to the rural economy. Rather than the complete demise of state-based influence and controls, the state is assuming a much more decentralized and muted place in the market. With regard to the shea economy, during the 1990s much of this influence was channeled through what remained of the PBC. Not only did the PBC continue to administrate shea export, but it also catered to the interests of more able private firms through personal ties and the support of the decisions of private-company executive organizations. Similarly, the PBC firmed up its alliances with organs of civil society, such as the CCSNFA. State influences resurfaced as well in local-level institutions such as the district assembly, which national-level organizations—whether the PBC or the Ministry of Trade and Tourism—attempted to co-opt. This influence was also apparent in parastatals such as FASCOM and nongovernmental organizations awarded contracts by the World Bank. Most of all, it was powerfully though quietly evident in what the state chose not to do, that is, not to privatize cocoa marketing and not to promote shea abroad. All of these rather veiled assertions of state control and interest may well support Lal and Myint's assertion that "the dirigiste state, in order to reassert control, must liberalize . . . hence, deregulation is not the 'rolling back' of the state but an essential step in its reemergence" (quoted in Collier 1993: 94), without conforming to their rather standardized predictions. Rather, in Ghana at the turn of the millennium, state authority—like private-company operations—is not being streamlined in the name of efficiency and transparency. Instead it is both consolidating, in the case of the Cocoa Board and the cocoa economy more generally, and going underground, making it much harder to identify, influence, or unseat. This is very much a process of liberalization carried out side-by-side with regulation, not in its stead.

CHAPTER **6**

Capital and Cooperation

Rural Women and Market Restructuring

Access to Resources: From Nuts to Butter; From Labor to Capital

Returning to the butter-making communities examined in Chapter 1, this chapter probes the changing social and material conditions of butter production resulting from the restructuring of the export market for shea nuts. While the export of Ghanaian shea butter remained negligible as privatization took hold, butter-makers in northern Ghana still bore the burdens of export promotion because of the new conditions of nut trade it inspired. Despite nut traders' efforts to protect domestic nut supplies from the incursions of exporters, women engaged in commercial butter processing competed with private buyers and state officials. Shea nuts—previously available in abundance and on casual terms of credit—became expensive and scarce. These new terms of trade dramatically heightened the capital requirements of indigenous butter production, with profound effects on the organization of butter processing and the prospects and parameters of income generation for savanna women.

As discussed in Chapter 1, prior to the privatization of the shea nut market in the 1990s, access to labor was the primary determinant of a woman's ability to enter the shea butter market. Commercially minded butter-makers considered the shea business to have a nearly unfettered potential limited only by the availability of labor, lack of which could be overcome by extending the scope of labor exchange. Because of the changes in market conditions brought about by the privatization of the nut trade, labor exchanges, whether embedded in the household or the cooperative networks of Nyoor Yinii, were no longer the key to sustaining—let alone

225

expanding—commercial butter production. Instead, in the course of privatization, access to nuts emerged as the critical determinant of a woman's capacity to participate in commercial butter-making. This meant that butter processors had not only to maintain their access to labor but also to obtain the capital necessary to purchase nuts and ascertain where, when, and from whom nuts were available in times of scarcity. With limited access to credit and a shortage of both nuts and capital, many Bawku butter-makers had little choice but to curtail production, making less butter, less often. In some cases butter-making was suspended altogether, as among a number of older women who wistfully described themselves as "sitting down, as if we did not want to work."

Indeed, as the export market grew and state agencies and private firms sought out shea nuts, butter-makers in and around Bawku complained again and again about the attenuation of credit and the lack of capital available to purchase nuts. It was not unusual for nut prices to rise 5 percent a week over the span of several months. Equally detrimental to enterprise reproduction, on some days no nuts could be found in Bawku market at all. Mariama, the head of the Boubuilla butter-makers, explained that there was not enough money to buy nuts. Not only were nuts expensive, she said, but butter-makers were unable to purchase them on credit. Rather than providing credit, many nut traders in Bawku market implemented a down-payment system, allowing butter processors to reserve nuts by paying a deposit early in the market day, with the price to be paid in full by the end of the day. This arrangement still made it difficult for butter processors to continue to sell butter on credit, forcing them to delay processing until all their debts were collected. Even on those occasions when nuts were available on credit, the repayment period was severely reduced and did not allow butter-makers enough time to process and sell the butter from the nuts they purchased.

Azara, a Saabon woman, aptly summed up in this situation: "This year, no one wants to wait for debts to be repaid." Attesting to the unusually competitive conditions of the nut market, Teopoaka, a butter-maker in Gozense, likewise complained that Bawku nut traders refused to bargain over the price, as was normal. The possibility of accumulating wealth or enterprise expansion was undermined because butter-makers who had the assets to purchase nuts and stay in the market could earn only enough to buy a modicum of soup ingredients for their families and plow the rest of their earnings into the cost of replacing the same quantity of nuts they had purchased previously. Indeed, even the most enterprising and industrious butter-makers found themselves operating at a loss in the face of extraordinarily steep nut prices.

Butter-makers were not alone in contending with these sorts of economic shifts in the wake of market liberalization. Based on research in southern Ghana, Clark and Manuh (1991) identify a similar process of economic decline befalling female traders in the face of structural adjustment. Clark and Manuh (1991: 230–2) argue that neoliberal policies of market reform reduce the availability of working capital, much to the detriment of female commercial livelihoods, at the same time as the capital requirements of work increase. For rural women engaged in shea butter production, already the poorest of the poor, coping with such a capital and credit squeeze is particularly problematic. In northeast Ghana, average per capita annual incomes are extremely low, standing at $133 in 1999 (Ghana Statistical Service 2000a: 102) and placing 97 percent of the population below the national poverty line.[1]

Here, as in many other parts of the country and the continent, rural women bear a disproportionate burden of impoverishment and are especially cash-poor. Males, with nearly three times the levels of literacy and school enrollment of females, enjoy greater access to waged work (2000a: 10, 12). Meanwhile, women are saddled with the greater share of nonwaged work, such as collecting water and wood, cooking, and caring for children (2000a: 39), in addition to laboring on the plots of other household members without equal access to agricultural opportunity and assistance. Even as both men and women struggle to support a family in times of hardship, it is the women who are ultimately responsible for cash expenses related to feeding, clothing, and the well-being of their offspring, requiring a substantial investment of time and resources (Tripp 1981: 21; Whitehead 1995: 49). Hence new expectations to generate capital are especially onerous for rural women already operating at the margins of the economy and facing heavy obligations in the context of limited opportunity.

This chapter looks closely at rural women's responses to the new capital requirements of butter-making and the way in which they interface with the conventions of cooperation—especially cooperative labor mobilization—at the heart of commercial butter processing. The story of the Bawku butter-makers suggests that although the heightened importance of capital forced the majority of them to curtail butter production and a number to drop out entirely, cooperative endeavors remained essential to the sustenance of commercial butter processing. Not only were collaborative work patterns maintained in the face of the new capital requirements, but whenever possible they were reworked to enable butter-makers to garner new resources. Indeed, cooperation was integral to the host of diversification strategies pursued by butter-makers in their efforts to maintain their place in the butter market.

Building on the book's opening chapter, these findings present a further challenge to the thesis that commercial intensification undermines collective behavior. At the same time, the material presented here reminds us that cooperation should not be considered an indicator of socioeconomic equivalence. Rather, rural butter-makers in northeast Ghana exhibit an array of socioeconomic distinctions that were intensified in the face of new capital requirements and only partially tempered by potentials of cooperation or the possibilities of diversification.

Butter Production and Reproduction

In Bawku District, butter-makers pursued a range of economic strategies to cope with the changing conditions of shea nut supply. While some strategies enabled women to secure their standing in the butter market, others were relatively minimal in their returns, allowing women simply to gain access to the necessary inputs for butter production but providing little profit or guarantee of their future availability. In the face of an increasingly competitive economic environment, all of these strategies entailed the engagement of diverse economic activities and the pursuit of resources both within and outside the market. Taken together, these dynamics make it clear that while shea butter-makers are effectively guaranteed access to labor through household-based ties and Nyoor Yinii networks, gaining access to capital is much more problematic. Hence, despite butter-makers' hard work and resourcefulness, the strategies they employ in the pursuit of capital, important as they are to enterprise survival, are equally an arbiter of socioeconomic differentiation.

Continuous Production

Even without the added pressure of nut scarcity and rapidly rise prices, women involved in commercial butter production try hard to protect the meager capital they invest in their enterprises. Given the heavy workload necessary to meet basic needs and their tremendous responsibilities to others, this is not an easy task. The best way for shea butter processors to ensure access to capital is to produce butter for sale year-round, never leaving the market. The goal here is not solely to service customers reliably and thereby maintain a share of demand but, more important, to keep one's capital caught in a flow of expenditure, debt, repayment, and reinvestment. When a woman goes to market to sell shea butter, her first priority is to buy foodstuffs for her family and to cover her business expenses, which include paying for shea nuts, grinding fees, transport, and market tariffs. Because these expenditures are considered women's working capital, this cycle of investment has its own rhythm and is largely shielded from the demands of others.

At certain times of the year, however, threats to divert or disperse the concentrated capital needed for shea butter production may be strong. This is true throughout the rainy season, lasting from June through October. During this period households face both food shortages and limited access to cash, rendering butter processors' capital especially vulnerable to familial expenses. The rainy season is also the period when the demand for agricultural labor peaks, making it difficult for women to find the time or energy to process shea in addition to their responsibilities on family and individual farms. Only more urbanized women or women from wealthier households whose husbands have no farms at all or enough capital to hire agricultural labor are spared these infringements on their cash, time, and labor.

Due to these many obstacles, nearly half of the butter-makers surveyed in Bawku East typically curtail or stop their processing activities during the rainy season. Those who do continue to process have to navigate the labor demands of the more senior members of the household (usually men) and their own labor obligations within the wider community, as well as the labor requirements of independent agricultural production, in order to secure the requisite time and labor power for butter-making. Women meet these challenges by reworking their production schedule to fit into the interstices of the agricultural timetable. They make butter at dawn before going to the farm and late at night after returning home and preparing the evening meal. In Gozense, Barkisu, for one, pounded her nuts long after dark by the light of a lantern and carried them to the grinding mill early in the morning. Although daughters with adequate strength for butter-making might be at home during the day, it is considered unwise to leave them to the task without adequate supervision, as the fresh nuts of the rainy season require extra skill for good-quality butter extraction.

Butter-makers who cannot process year-round pursue other ways to remain in the shea market continuously and preserve their working capital. One way they do this is through a strategy of "substitution." In this case, butter processors from Bawku will purchase already-made butter in bulk from specific rural markets where it is relatively cheap due to the abundance of shea trees and ready availability of nuts, buying from rural producers as much as they might make in a fortnight or month. Pursuing such a strategy, Maimuna from Boubuilla typically traveled to Garu every week or two to purchase butter for herself and for a number of other women in her neighborhood who gave her money to purchase for them. With a bit of free time on her hands after "begging" some other women to help her finish weeding her groundnut plot, she had enough flexibility to make this several-hour excursion. Other butter-makers with less time to spare and/or lacking the truck-fare could also buy butter in the Bawku market from wholesalers who purchased butter in the marketing center of Gushegu in Ghana's northern region to sell to traders in Niger and Burkina. Rather than selling their new stock directly, Bawku butter-makers melt it and reapportion it into the same clay pots in which they sell homemade butter.

In addition to aiding with pricing, this tactic masks the fact that the seller did not make the butter herself. With butter from different towns and regions considered to be of different qualities, this sort of impression

6.1 An old woman retailing ready-made butter.

management is important for maintaining customer loyalty. Butter substitution does more than simply allow butter processors to save time and energy during the busy rainy season. Because ready-made butter, especially that from the Northern Region's Gushegu market, is occasionally available on credit, purchasing it allows women to avoid some of the capital requirements of home-based butter processing. Even though the profits from butter resale are about half of that earned from selling one's own butter, the opportunity to obtain butter on credit is especially important for processors who lack the cash necessary to purchase nuts, as it enables them to stay in the market until they have the time and money to process on their own.

Complementary Economic Activities

Butter-makers also rely on alternative sources of income for the capital they needed to buy nuts and otherwise sustain their enterprises. Although this sometimes requires the diversion of resources away from butter-making and into other enterprises, it enables women to reproduce and even fortify their position in the shea market with the income they have earned elsewhere. Agriculture, in the form of cash-cropping, is a primary source of capital for investment in shea processing. For a large majority of shea processors, agriculture and butter-making are closely linked in the yearly work cycle, with work priorities and resources moving from one to the other. While women are required to contribute labor to family farms, many control their own agricultural production on cash-cropping plots that they independently oversee. Butter-makers typically use the earnings from these farms to invest in shea. There are, however, substantial differences in the way women do this, in terms of the capital they amass, how and when they invest it, and the conditions of access to land and agricultural labor they confront. These differences reflect the range of economic situations in which butter-makers find themselves and create for themselves. For example, women may be allocated land by their husbands or male kin; they may borrow land for a nominal fee in cash or kind; or they may hire land for cash rent. When women do not have access to land of their own, they may participate in cash-cropping by working for relatives in return for a share of the produce or by selling their labor for a wage.

The flow of resources between shea and agriculture is often reciprocal. The capital generated through the butter trade could be invested in agricultural production through hiring labor or renting land. Profits from farming are then invested in shea. Almost invariably, when there is agricultural surplus to be sold, butter-makers invest their profits in nut purchases. Again, women manage in different ways the articulation of shea butter production and cash-cropping as a way to gain access to capital for nuts. Some women sell farm produce early in the season in order to buy fresh nuts for immediate use or to store; others store farm produce to sell when the price goes up during the dry season and then buy shea the following rainy season. The choice has to do with the capital on hand as well as women's reading of the relative price curves for the different commodities. Selling farm produce early or late may well be an indication of relative socioeconomic status, with those who sell early being cash-poor and those selling late having a cushion of assets to carry them through the next several months.

In Bawku, women who engage in cash-cropping typically cultivate either groundnuts or rice (Roncoli 1994). In Gozense, where agricultural land is relatively plentiful, most women have rice farms. In one butter-making household, the landlord allowed two women of the household to divide one of his fields among themselves for rice cultivation. When they harvest the rice, the women explained, they remove a portion of the rice for next year's seed and divide the rest into two shares, one for feeding and the other to use toward the purchase of shea. Likewise, two cowives from Saabon who each had a small rice farm pooled their money from rice sales to buy nuts for shea production. Although they were unable to buy large quantities of nuts, they were able to amass just enough to restart their enterprise once the rainy season was over. Azara Musa in Saabon also had a rice farm on land bequeathed to her by her late husband before his death. So busy was she with shea processing that she hired three women for a by-day wage to help her cultivate the plot. In another case, Maimanatu, also from Saabon, did not have a rice farm of her own but was able to help her sons on their rice fields. In compensation for her labors, Maimunatu received a share of the harvest, which she sold to support her shea business. Rather than rice, women in Boubuilla cultivate groundnuts to raise cash for shea. To conserve capital, like their cohorts elsewhere, they rely on the assistance of other women under the rubric of Nyoor Yinii for help with weeding and harvesting.

Farming, however, is not without risk or adverse effect on shea production. In the words of Maimuna, a prodigious butter-maker in Boubuilla, "If you don't farm well, where are you going to get the money to make butter?" Women often complained about the poor yield of their cash-cropping plots and the expense of cultivation. Mariama, the leader of the Boubuilla group, described the land that she and her cowife rented as *zalim*, a word meaning "zero" or "naked" in Kusaal. In Saabon, Ramatu similarly described her extensive investment of capital to pay day laborers in a farm that yielded only enough groundnuts to replace the seed she had already planted. Worse still, she had to sell the entire harvest from her rice farm, meager as it was, to cover the cost of transporting the groundnuts from the farm to her house. In another Saabon household, even when farming showed some profit, the extra capital earned from selling crops was used for child care, leaving women without the necessary funds to buy nuts. Several Saabon women who lacked plots of their own participated in cash-cropping by selling their by-day labor. While these efforts helped them earn enough money to buy soup ingredients for the household, it did not allow the women to accumulate the cash necessary to purchase nuts for shea processing.

Savings, Investment, and Self-Financing

The saving and investment of profits from shea and any other income-generating activities in which they might engage is another strategy typically employed by shea butter-makers to amass the capital necessary to purchase nuts. Some commercial butter-makers do their best to purchase nuts with whatever capital they have on hand each time they go to the market to sell butter or collect their debts. Barkisu, for one, the leader of the Gozense group, buys shea nuts each market day with any amount of cash she has available. Like her cohorts, she might purchase as little as a single bowl of nuts (less than 2 kilos-worth), which she stores for future butter-making. As women in one household explained, it is critical to invest one's earnings in nuts as soon as funds are available, since cash on hand, in any amount, will easily be spent. In the words of Atini: "If someone comes around selling foodstuffs, or the children want something, you will spend the money." So concerned are Gozense butter-makers about threats to their capital that a number of them make a special trip to Asikiri, a village a few miles away that has its market on the day immediately following Bawku market, just to buy nuts, rather than wait two more days when Bawku market reconvenes.

Having enough capital to invest regularly in nuts is not easily accomplished, given the many demands placed on rural women's earnings. As mentioned above, in addition to catering to their own needs, women are responsible for their children and to other household members. With the exception of the staple grain provided by the male household head, women must at the very least, feed the domestic group. This is no small task. Women meet the food needs of the household by cultivating vegetables in small kitchen gardens near their homesteads or on the boundaries of family farms. They collect wild foods in the bush (fruits, mushrooms, flower buds, tree leaves) and reserve a portion of the cash crops they have cultivated for the feeding of the family. A large percentage of food needs, however, is met by purchasing foodstuffs in the market. In northern Ghana, rural women are likely to purchase a significant portion of the ingredients used in preparing the nightly meal. If nothing else, butter-makers use the money they have available from their enterprises to purchase soup ingredients, *zeed* in Kusaal, for their households. Basic food purchases, consisting of okra, leafy greens, tomato, beans, bouillon, dried fish, pepper, peanut, or melon seed paste and at times millet, sorghum, and maize (staple grains of the savanna diet), are made before other expenses are met. Once minimum food requirements are satisfied, many additional needs remain. Devoted to their children, rural women use their meager incomes to purchase medicine and pay health care fees for their offspring as well as purchase shoes and clothing for them.

Women's primary expenditures also include contributions of money to a local banking system called *susu*. *Susu* or *esusu* (a derivative from the Yoruba language) is a term used throughout West Africa for widely popular rotating-credit societies (Bortei-Doku and Aryeetey 1995: 79). For butter-makers in Bawku, *susu* is more than simply a savings system. Every three to six days, in keeping with the three-day local marketing cycle, commercial butter processors will make a small contribution to a *susu* fund. Ranging from as little as 100 cedi (about 10 cents in 1995) to as much as 1,000 cedi (about a dollar)—"whatever you can afford," as Mariama, the Boubuilla Nyoor Yinii group leader, described it—contributions are paid to a specific *susu* banker. Usually a young man in his twenties or thirties, the *susu* collector will visit butter-makers in the market or occasionally at home. Contributions are recorded in the collector's notebook and may be liquidated at any time. Lacking certification, these transactions are thoroughly informal even though they are highly trusted. Women fear little that the collector, often a distant relative and well known to them, will run away with their money.

Butter-makers regard *susu* contributions as an economic priority. *Susu* money may be put aside before the purchase of soup ingredients, and women often stay in the market after dark and the shopping day is over just to wait until the *susu* collector comes around. Because it allows them to accumulate capital, many women use *susu* to make large and long-term investments. *Susu* may well help women accrue adequate funds to purchase shea nuts in bulk; yet as one of many economic concerns, this is rarely guaranteed. Rejecting the opportunity to invest their entire savings in shea, Boubuilla women typically use their *susu* funds for commodities such as cloth or cooking pots. Requiring about three months of steady contributions, these purchases may be made directly through the *susu* collector. Sometimes *susu* savings are earmarked for a specific occasion, such as buying cloth to wear to a family wedding or to prepare for the birth of child. Otherwise, a woman's *susu* account may be regarded as a "rainy-day" fund.

Ramatu, an older shea butter processor in Gozense, for example, explained "anytime I am short of money I can collect *susu*." When conserved, however, *susu* savings can allow women to amass enough money—or some portion of it—to buy nuts to restart their butter business at the end of the rainy season. Awin, the vice-chair of the Gozense butter-making group, re-marked that if she collected her *susu* fund and there was no "problem" for which she needed it, she would use it to buy nuts. Fati, a middle-aged Gozense woman with a large and reliable butter-making enterprise, did her best to dedicate her *susu* account to the purchase of shea nuts. So did Hadiza and Zelisha, cowives from Saabon. While Zelisha purchased only one bag of shea nuts with her *susu* funds, spending the rest of her savings on hospital and funeral expenses for her mother, Hadiza was able to pur-chase three.

Group savings funds are a more reliable source of capital for the pur-chase of shea nuts than the individualized savings of *susu*. One such exam-ple is the Gozense butter-makers who organized themselves into a formal association, the Gozense Kwatuodim, with a banked savings account. When they confronted the increasing need for cash and declining availability of credit to purchase shea nuts, it became apparent that the group's money-saving activities were actually more critical for enterprise reproduction than the labor pooling that had motivated the association's establishment in the first place. The Gozense women's fund, because it was the property of the group, was protected from the individualized incursions that plagued less secure saving systems such as *susu*. Moreover, the fund was deposited in the local branch of the Ghana Cooperative Bank, and any withdrawal re-quired the presence of the group leader and vice-chair as well as the group secretary. The fund was not solely for the purchase of nuts, nor was it as consistently maintained as *susu*. As mentioned in an earlier chapter, the group used its first several months of contributions to purchase T-shirts and clothes. Contributions were also suspended from time to time. In one case, in the name of equity, all contributions were stopped for several weeks when a single member could not pay because a child was in hospital. On another occasion, group members contributed to the purchase of food-stuffs for the secretary's wedding rather than the group fund. Nevertheless, despite these occasional diversions, the group as a whole was able to main-tain a substantial amount of wealth to invest in shea nuts for its members.

There was a very small number of shea processors whose investment op-tions were not confined to the drop-by-drop savings of *susu* or group funds that only accumulate but never generate wealth. These women were en-gaged in more profitable economic endeavors than the average butter-maker, and had enough wealth to make larger and more lucrative investments in goods that accrued and did not just conserve value. One woman who fell into this category was Maimuna Issaka, a resident of Saabon. Maimuna was in her late thirties and the most senior wife of her husband, who worked for Bawku's District Council. In addition to process-ing butter with Asom, an elderly butter-maker from her husband's extended family who lived a few steps away, and occasionally her with cowives, Maimuna was a successful farmer. With the help of "by-day" and plowing services labor paid for by her husband, in addition to the unpaid assistance of other women in the neighborhood, Maimuna cultivated rice and groundnuts on a large plot provided by her father. Seeking investments that would, in her words, "hold the money, rather than waste it," Maimuna stored the produce from her farm and, with the help of her husband, purchased other agricultural commodities at harvest time. Several months later, at the end of the dry season, when food was both scarce and expensive but shea nuts were cheap, Maimuna sold her stocks. As a sign of her relative prosperity, during the 1994-to-1995 season, despite the relative scarcity and expense of shea nuts, Maimuna was able to purchase and store seventeen bags of nuts.

Bypassing the Market: Extramarket Relationships and Nut Access
Loans from Kin

Because butter-makers were battling both a poor farming season and an inflated shea market characterized by scarcity, high prices, and attenuation of credit options, as the 1994-to-1995 season progressed, agricultural incomes and savings were unable to support commercial butter processing. Butter-makers had little choice but to pursue a host of other measures to maintain commercial production. Compared to the tactics of enterprise reproduction described above, these strategies were not self-sustaining, generative of wealth, nor readily available. Typically located outside the market, they relied on new forms of financial dependence, as butter-makers cultivated new relationships or new aspects of old ones in order to access nut supplies. In this way, they both deepened the potentials of existing social ties and networks and contributed to the development of new sorts of alliances between butter-makers and those with whom their ties were otherwise fairly restricted. With few alternatives, these tactics were mobilized not only by economically disadvantaged women with limited assets but by the majority of women engaged in shea butter production, whatever their economic status.

To begin with, the adverse conditions of the shea nut market heightened shea processors' reliance on loans from kin in order to finance nut purchases. Loans were in cash and kind and made available by family members, usually members of a woman's immediate family and household, such as her husband and sons, or her natal household. Because women are generally uncomfortable about requesting such financial assistance, butter-makers tended to go through a third party to relay their needs. Even if not approached directly, a husband might note that his wife was idle in the house without her usual work and offer her some financial assistance. These economic transfers indicate that despite the usual separation of male and female budgets, husbands and wives were not necessarily cut off from each other's economic worlds and structured their separate economies in a manner that was mutually beneficial (cf. Saul 1989: 180). Whether this is an example of spousal altruism or simply represents the strategic investment of one spouse in the endeavors of the other is unclear. It is nevertheless an indicator of spousal interdependence.

As with the loan received by Saabon's Maimuna Issaku from her husband to purchase and store foodstuffs, according to several Boubuilla women, prior to the 1994-to-1995 season it was not unusual for a husband to purchase a large quantity of shea nuts early in the season to store and sell on credit to his wives. Although the price of nuts would be only minimally discounted, the nuts would be readily available to women of the household on favorable terms of credit, with some husbands not expecting payment until the opening of the next season, when the men would need the money for seed. However, just as women faced cash shortages due to poor harvests and rising nut prices, men faced similar economic conditions during the mid-1990s and were unlikely to store nuts as usual. Women complained about their husbands' failure to purchase shea nuts and their own consequent reliance on more limited intrahousehold loans. These loans were more likely to be in cash and of a lesser value than the full amount a husband had invested in nuts in the past. These loans, only enough to supplement the capital a woman already had and at best covering the cost of nuts for the year's first batch of shea butter, were more likely to help a woman get started at the beginning of the dry season than sustain her throughout.

Given the adverse conditions of the nut market, women also attempted to underwrite their shea enterprises through the mobilization of a range of kin ties, requesting in-kind loans of shea nuts from relatives beyond their immediate household. In Boubuilla, Maimuna was able to buy three bags of shea nuts from her mother on credit. Ramatu, the young wife from Saabon, complained that the poor yield of her groundnut farm left her without money to buy nuts; she sought a loan from her "junior mother" (her mother-in-law's sister) for the first time to help finance her enterprise. Similarly, with a dozen and a half bags of nuts in storage, the strong economic standing of Maimuna Issaku in Saabon made her prone to relatives' and neighbors' requests at the same time as it protected her personal butter-making enterprise from the vicissitudes of the market. Because Maimuna was not a professional shea nut trader and stored nuts for use rather than for profit from resale, her transfers of nuts were considered loans (*peng*, to loan or borrow in Kusaal) rather than credit and thus less formal. While the terms of these exchanges were more casual than credit, they were also more restricted in scope. Despite the many pleas she received for aid, Maimuna shared nuts almost exclusively with her husband's senior mother, Asom (whose economic support was otherwise limited), and a few in-laws living nearby.

Credit

Facing a shortage of self-generated capital and the restriction of loans, butter-makers still struggled to buy shea nuts on credit, even if that meant looking outside the market for shea supplies. Women were desperate for credit. They willingly paid more for nuts on credit than the cash price and delayed entry into butter production until late in the season, when nuts were finally available on credit. Butter processors spent considerable time and effort searching for potential sources of nuts and cultivating relationships with potential suppliers who might sell nuts on credit. While nuts were occasionally available on credit from professional nut traders, the seasonality of credit rarely meshed with butter-makers' broader economic strategies and options. Nuts became available for credit very early and very late in the agricultural cycle, two periods when people were least likely to engage in butter production.

Early in the season, most butter-makers were converting their assets and diversifying their efforts towards agricultural production. Thus, only the more prosperous butter-makers, who were able to keep several occupational fires burning at the same time and could continue to produce butter while farming, were able to take advantage of these credit options. These women often had greater access to the assistance of others for both farm work and shea production or husbands who could afford "by-day" labor for the family farms, thereby reducing their work obligations. At the end of the season, when shea nuts were again available for credit, some women were indeed rescued from dropping out of butter production. However, many women had already left the butter business months earlier due to declining profits and lack of credit. Most of the butter-makers who remained in the market by this time were generally more financially secure to begin with, and although they might prefer credit, they could get by without it.

With the chances of obtaining nuts on credit from Bawku market's professional nut traders being slim, butter-makers, in addition to obtaining nuts through those with whom they shared primary ties of kinship and coresidence, cultivated good relations with other people outside Bawku market who were a potential source of nuts. In this capacity, more prosperous rural residents, both male and female, who invested in shea nuts became increasingly important to the success of commercial butter production. Such rural investors, willing to tap their caches of nuts and buying nuts in quantities ranging from just a few bags to one or two dozen, along with other agricultural commodities to store and resell, typically provided better terms of trade than market-based professional nut sellers. Most important, they were more likely to sell nuts on credit for prices that were no higher than the market's cash price. For these traders, selling nuts to butter-makers from one's home or storeroom for a relatively low price was worth saving the transaction cost of bringing the nuts to market and the uncertainties of resale and reliance on middle people.

Although investors' nuts were usually not available until the height of the season, when prices peaked, they were a crucial source of supply, because this was the time when nuts were least available in the market. Investors' nuts might also be available at other times of the year in cases when they were forced by an economic emergency to sell their assets. Hence scouting out investors and keeping in contact with them might prove to be a source of nuts earlier in the season.

In Boubuilla especially, quite a few butter-makers were able to benefit from their ties to those who bought and stored nuts. Not long after the end of the harvest season, Ramata was able to buy shea nuts on credit from a man living in Bugri, a village about ten miles away. She had purchased nuts from him in the past, and while he did not buy any nuts during the 1994-to-1995 season, his wife did. Although the price of nuts had not yet peaked, the woman had asked her husband to sell one bag of nuts to Ramata because she had recently given birth and needed money to buy things for herself and the infant. A few months later several other Boubuilla women were able to obtain nuts from a number of other investors.

By the height of the dry season, as nuts became scarce and prices climbed, investors and butter-makers sought each other out. Boubuilla women renewed contact with suppliers they had worked with in the past, and investors sent messages to butter-makers in the home and the market indicating they were ready to sell their stocks. One man, for instance, instructed the Boubuilla processors to come to his home a few miles away to collect ten bags of shea nuts that he wished to sell. The nuts were purchased on credit, allowing the women ten to fifteen days to pay their debts. On another occasion, nut investors from a village on the outskirts of Bawku came to the market to tell the Boubuilla women that they were ready to sell their nuts on credit.

As the Boubuilla women's dependence on nuts purchased from investors outside the bounds of Bawku market grew, new economic roles and relationships began to emerge among butter-makers. This was because as the scope and importance of extramarket nut purchases increased, more and more effort was needed to oversee and coordinate nut sales between suppliers and butter processors. Such a role became the purview of a forceful and well-respected Boubuilla woman named Asana, who was already

6.2 Asana (center) leads Boubuilla women in work and song as they use wooden paddles to seal the mud floor of a home's interior courtyard.

widely known because of her skill coordinating the activities of the community's Nyoor Yinii dance and work groups. Reducing her own butter-making activities, Asana served as the primary contact for both nut buyers and suppliers, informing butter-makers about nuts for sale and leading negotiations about prices and terms of credit. Going hand in hand with Asana's newfound role as an informal nut broker for the Boubuilla butter-makers was the increasing coordination of nut purchases among butter-makers themselves. Because investors typically sold nuts in large lots, new forms of cooperation became essential, whether pooling funds for nut purchases and transport, or group decisions about acceptable prices and terms of trade.

In addition to rural investors, another set of individuals involved in the nut trade and operating outside Bawku market proper became an increasingly important source of nuts for commercially oriented butter processors. This was a group of salaried women—mostly nurses and teachers as well as rural agricultural extension agents—who chose to invest a portion of their earnings in shea, each storing from one dozen to as many as four or five dozen bags each. Shea, cheaper than groundnuts or grain, was an appropriate investment target for the professional women. They could afford to buy a few bags every week during the first few months of the shea season, and their investments would be protected from family food needs, unlike other agricultural commodities. Nuts could also be sold at the height of the dry season, when the depressed economy forced down the prices of the consumer items—from cloth and electric fans to televisions and motorcycles—the professional women desired.

Some of these salaried workers *cum* traders, especially those who traveled between town and village for their work, were particularly well placed to profit from the shea trade. In several cases, nurses who worked with rural health teams and Ministry of Agriculture employees who surveyed rural markets and advised farmers were able to buy nuts directly from those who gathered them and transport them home to Bawku for free in their employers' vehicles. What's more, as the price of shea nuts rose dramatically over the course of a single season, they became an increasingly lucrative investment, no longer regarded as an affordable rural commodity that only maintained value but a source of substantial gain.

Realizing that these salaried women controlled significant stocks of otherwise hard-to-find nuts that they would otherwise sell to professional traders in the market, particularly savvy shea butter processors began to cultivate ties to them. From Boubuilla, Maimuna took the time to visit one of the women, Ruth, a teacher, who lived near Maimuna's natal home, to learn about her stocks and intentions to sell. The salaried women, in turn, became familiar to butter-makers and professional nut traders alike as they frequently stopped in Bawku market to inquire about nut prices and demand and even to initiate purchasing arrangements. For example, Dorothy, a nurse, came to market and made it known that several salaried women living in a middle-class suburb on the outskirts of town had dozens of bags stored, trying to entice the butter-makers to come directly to her to purchase them.

Competition, Pricing, and Customer Relations

Even as the price of shea nuts rose and the need for cash increased, butter-makers found it difficult to charge more for the butter they produced. As often as processors warned customers of price rises, the customers refused to pay more. Thus, processors rather than consumers were forced to absorb the rising cost of shea nuts. Zeinabu, a butter-maker living on the edge of Saabon, made this clear: "If the price of nuts is high I won't get much profit since the customers will force me to keep my prices low." Azara, another Saabon woman, reiterated that if she raised the price of butter, her customers would refuse to pay.

One major barrier to raising the price of shea butter had to do with the price of other edible oils available in the local market. In addition to shea butter, groundnut oil processed from locally grown groundnuts, along with factory-pressed vegetable oils from Ghana and abroad, and relatively small quantities of palm nut and palm kernel oils were sold in Bawku market. Shea butter, because of its low price, familiar taste, and ease of use in the preparation of soups and snack foods, was considered the oil of choice in most rural households and among those who prepared food for sale. However, if butter prices rose too high, processors could find themselves competing with those who sold groundnut oil. Not only was groundnut oil (*sumaa-kpam*) typically more costly than shea, but it was also considered a higher-status oil due to its lighter texture and taste and association with more urban and middle-class lifestyles, especially that of the Hausa, who controlled its production and trade. As Barkisu, the Gozense group leader, put it: "Even though the price of nuts is rising, with groundnut oil now in abundance, we can't raise the price of shea butter if we want to keep our market."

Bawku butter-makers also found themselves in competition with butter-makers from other areas of the north who sold their wares in Bawku market. Because the town was a regional trade and transit center due to its location just a few miles from the borders of Togo and Burkina Faso, it was easy for traders from other parts of the north to find transport to Bawku each market day. Likewise, merchants from Bawku could purchase butter elsewhere and bring it back for resale. As a result, shea butter and butter-makers of diverse origins could be found in the town's market. Some traders sold butter from the Northern Region market of Gushegu, over a hundred miles to the south. Others brought butter from the area known as "Hilltop," made up of the towns of Gambaga, Nalerigu, and Nakpanduri, about thirty miles south. Yet others brought butter from Walewale, seventy miles to the southwest.

Butter from each area could be distinguished by its size, shape and consistency: Gushegu butter was especially thick and was sold from tremendous calabashes one to two feet in diameter, Hilltop butter was sold in balls, and Walewale butter was sold in lozenge-shaped portions. Bawku butter, sold in clay pots in a range of sizes, was considered to be of particularly high quality because of careful processing and lack of need to adulterate the butter to harden it for transport and storage. Yet even with the added expense of transport, due to the greater abundance of trees and wider availability of nuts—and thus their cheaper price—in the more southern and less populated parts of the savanna where the other butter originated, these butter-makers were able to compete with Bawku butter processors on their own turf, once again keeping butter prices low.

Because their local residence gave them a regular presence in the market and greater familiarity with local shoppers and cooked-food sellers, Bawku butter-makers were able to manage the competitive conditions of the butter trade through the provision of credit to their customers. Despite the constraints this placed on the availability of capital for nut purchases, as Awin, the Gozense vice-chair explained: "In order to keep customers, we sell our butter on credit." Whether buying butter from Gozense, Boubuilla, or Saabon women, customers expected to buy butter on credit and did so on generous terms, with as many as nine days (three market cycles) to pay their debts. With butter-makers spending about half their time in the market trying to collect their debts rather than selling butter, not only did these expectations make it difficult for them to amass enough cash to reinvest regularly in nuts for production and process when nuts could no longer be had on credit, but customers were also especially prickly about paying more for butter. Sometimes, selling at a loss, butter-makers often delayed raising their prices. Before doing so, they would be sure to inform their regular customers at least a week in advance. And even when they finally raised prices, they succumbed to the pleas of their regular buyers, selling at higher prices only to newcomers.

Falling out of the Market

Due to the scarcity and high price of shea nuts resulting from the privatization and promotion of shea export by the Ghanaian government in the face of international financial mandates and new sorts of international demand, at least half of the butter-makers in each of the three communities studied scaled back production over the course of the 1994-to-1995 season. Not only did some women curtail their processing efforts in the face of new market conditions, but some dropped out of the shea business entirely. In Gozense, 50 percent of the butter-makers for whom information was gathered regarding the scale and frequency of production over a ten-month period reduced their processing activities. Similarly, 50 percent of the Boubuilla women lowered both the volume of butter produced and the rate of production. Of these women, half suspended production altogether, with one half purchasing butter to resell and the other half leaving the butter business. Exemplifying a more serious decline, in Saabon, nearly 60 percent of the butter-makers surveyed reduced their processing efforts during the 1994-to-1995 season. Half of these women suspended production entirely; only one in four remained in the butter business by retailing ready-made butter, while the rest withdrew completely.

Reflecting the differential endowments of individual butter-makers and the varied economic base of their communities, the contraction of commercial butter production took several different forms. For the large majority of butter-makers, it was nearly impossible to expand their enterprises because the rising cost of nuts would consume their profit from the previous week. Women described how all the earnings from shea production, after subtracting the cost of soup ingredients, were plowed

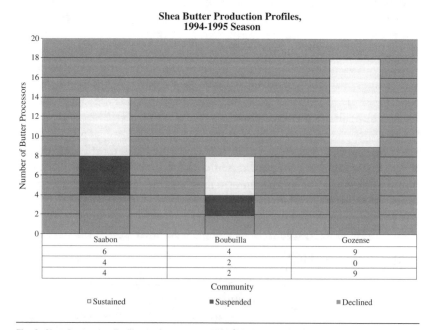

Shea Butter Production Profiles, 1994-1995 Season

Community	Saabon	Boubuilla	Gozense
Sustained	6	4	9
Suspended	4	2	0
Declined	4	2	9

□ Sustained   ■ Suspended   ■ Declined

Fig. 6 Shea Production Profiles by Community, 1994–1995

back in the business to resupply nuts. Others complained that once they had bought their nuts, they realized they had run out of money for soup ingredients. Most of the women who stayed in the market did so through a downward spiral of declining production and returns.

What emerges is a picture of a small number of well-off butter-makers with enough capital to weather the price hikes and nut shortages and consistently produce large quantities of butter, processing a 65-kilo bag of nuts every three days. Here we find Gozense's Barkisu (via continuous production), Boubuilla's Maimuna (via substitution), and Saabon's Maimuna Issaku (via agricultural investment). Behind them is another group that also managed to maintain regular participation in the market by producing smaller quantities of butter with less frequency, processing half a bag of nuts every three to six days. A third group of butter-makers also struggled to stay in the market but their productive efforts were more erratic. For these women access to nuts or financing was neither steady nor guaranteed, leading to a gradual drop in production and sometimes to dropping out. They processed butter every nine or twelve days, compared to the usual three- and six-day schedule, and used only ten or fifteen bowls of nuts rather than the usual eighteen that filled half a 65 kilo bag. Finally, there was another group whose lack of access to credit and capital at the beginning of the season prevented them from sustaining commercial shea processing. While intending to manufacture their own butter at some point during the year, they were reduced to retailing ready-made butter throughout or dropping out of the butter trade.

On both an individual and a community level, the reasons for butter-makers' survival in or withdrawal from the shea butter market varied widely. Not only did individual butter-makers have different trajectories of success or failure, but so did the different butter-making communities. This suggests that there is significant socioeconomic variation among rural women, even in same industry and same locale—a point argued by Ardener (1978) many years ago but eclipsed by a focus on the wider conditions of female subordination to male privilege (cf. Stichter and Parpart 1988). This variation is attributable to the complexity of the economic landscape and the diverse histories of the communities within it as well as the role of individual initiative and decision-making, in other words, both structural and individual variation. The pillars of structure and agency however do not fully capture the dynamics of the shea industry for women in northeast Ghana. At the same time, there is a third term that is equally integral to shaping the character and potential of rural livelihoods. Clearly evident in the case of shea processing, this is the contour of group initiative and cooperation, as demonstrated in the varied fates of Saabon, Gozense, and Boubilla butter-makers.

Saabon

Saabon women's vulnerability to the vagaries of privatization and export promotion is attributable to demographic factors of butter-makers' ages and community locations. Of the three communities studied, Saabon, located closest to the center of Bawku town, was the most urban. While this allowed easy access to the market and other urban amenities that facilitated butter production and trade, such as electric-powered grinding mills to crush nuts and water taps within or near to homes, Saabon's urban location made it difficult for its female residents easily to engage in agricultural opportunity. Farmland, when it was granted, was typically located several miles away in the home village of Zagabo, making it hard to access and consistently cultivate. Thus for most Saabon women, farms provided only a limited source of capital to invest in shea.

The community's location also made trade—be it in manufactures or agricultural commodities—a more lucrative source of income than butter production for many women in the community. This limited butter-makers' access to the labor of their cowives and made the pooling of capital to purchase nuts less likely. These disabilities were heightened by the relatively advanced age of the female butter-making population and the fact that conditions of forced relocation nearly a decade earlier had left them without many of the material investments typically held by rural women. Lack of the usual array of cooking pots, cloth, sleeping mats, and more, limited Saabon women's wealth and increased their expenditures. Although hard-working, a large number of Saabon women had limited capacity due to age and related infirmity to trek the several miles to outlying farms and exert the energy necessary for sowing, weeding, and harvesting. Their advanced age at the same time rendered them increasingly dependent on the labor and assistance of younger women in the community, many of whom eschewed the rigors of shea butter production in favor of petty trade. And with their own husbands aged or deceased, access to other forms of familial support for these women was similarly restricted. Hence elderly women like Moropoa found themselves forced out of the butter business and reduced to carrying basins of water to sell to others, an activity that generated a small fraction of the profits possible with butter production.

Although cooperative endeavors did help to assuage these liabilities in Saabon, they were rather circumscribed in scope. More of an extension of household assistance than extended networks in their own right, they were regularly pursued by only a small portion of women. Bridging generational and class divides, Maimuna Issaka extended loans of nuts to her next-door neighbors and relatives, Asom, an elderly woman, and Ramatu, a sister-in-law, and received labor in return. Likewise, in the Sumaila household, the elderly women who resided there—their husbands long dead—were joined regularly for shea processing by married daughters and former cowives who now resided in households where income-generating activities other than butter-making were the norm. Pooling labor and capital and even sharing profits or the purchases made with them, women working in this setting were able to sustain their butter-making enterprise over the course of the year, despite the adverse market conditions they faced. Other than these two instances, however, the scope and frequency of cooperative work patterns was small and irregular, taking the form of sales partnerships—as when a butter-maker consistently contracted with a former butter-making partner to retail butter for her—rather than productive endeavors.

Hence in Saabon, while certain forms of cooperation were preserved and a spirit of mutual aid was maintained, what obtained was more a pattern of specialization rather than diversification. Although Saabon women continued to work with each other, they pursued different and often hierarchical roles rather than reciprocal relations. At the same time, for most women, even if they were involved in a range of economic pursuits, it was difficult to move resources from one pursuit to another as no single one was particularly profitable. In Saabon, then, the potentials of labor exchange embedded in women's networks could compensate little for their limited access to capital.

Boubuilla

With the capacity to diversify their activities both within and outside shea production and to enlarge and innovate their cooperative pursuits, Boubuilla butter-makers, compared to Saabon women, were better able to manage the changing conditions of the shea economy. Indeed, for Boubuilla women, diversification and cooperation were closely related, with one accommodating the other. Given their periurban location just a few kilometers from Bawku town and near the bush paths leading into Burkina Faso, a wide array of markets was available to Boubuilla butter-makers. Carrying their butter to a range of markets in this border zone, they were able to seek an alternative to the competitive conditions of Bawku market and thus guarantee the sale of their wares. Making the trek to Bittou—despite its distance of about fifteen miles—allowed butter-makers to sell for cash rather than credit and to be paid in CFA francs (the currency or Ghana's francophone neighbors) at higher prices than in Bawku. These women's wide-ranging travel to markets outside Bawku town made the trade in an array of agricultural commodities, both purchased and homegrown, an easy supplement to shea butter production and sale, further sustaining their livelihoods.

Such diversification in terms of sales venues and strategies was facilitated by the large size and common location of collective processing activities in Boubuilla. Itself an innovation based on the experience of several women in palm processing in central Ghana, this allowed women to make butter on a varied and flexible schedule geared to a wide range of markets. Although not as cohesive a group as the Gozense butter-makers, Boubuilla women's productive arrangements allowed them to cope easily with contingency.

Boubuilla women were also able to tap into the market for ready-made butter, enabling them to sustain their role in the shea market when their labors were otherwise invested in agriculture and when the entry costs of butter production were otherwise prohibitive. The success of this strategy was once again built on cooperation, as individual women were dispatched to southern supply centers to make purchases for several others. Boubuilla women also devised new cooperative strategies to help them manage the vicissitudes of the nut market as they coordinated their efforts to purchase nuts from investors outside Bawku market. These fluid patterns of cooperation among Boubuilla women accommodated their agricultural pursuits, whether family farming or cash-cropping. Although there was certainly differentiation among Boubuilla women, it was somewhat muted by the varied forms and crosscutting networks of cooperation in which they engaged, allowing them to occupy different positions of leadership and dependence in each.

Gozense

Compared to butter-makers in both Boubuilla and Saabon, Gozense women were best equipped to manage the burdens of privatization and export market growth. Gozense is furthest from Bawku town and the most rural of the three communities studied, and so, unlike Saabon women, Gozense women could much more easily engage in agricultural endeavors, complementing their work as shea processors. Other than agriculture, their opportunities to diversify outside the shea trade were limited. However, they did pursue alternatives within the shea economy. Unlike the Saabon women who could only purchase nuts in Bawku market or were saddled with the high cost of transport when searching for nuts elsewhere, the rural location of Gozense allowed butter-makers access to relatively cheap sources of shea nuts from small village markets close to home such as Asikiri. Even though Gozense butter-makers had limited capital to spare, the proximity of Asikiri enabled them regularly to purchase small quantities of nuts that they could gradually accumulate for later use. They also made sure that they consistently invested in *susu* savings. Similarly diversifying within the scope of butter-making, Gozense women responded to commercial pressures by changing the orientation of their cooperative activities. An indication of the importance of group savings, Gozense women benefited above all from their well-coordinated efforts as a group, especially their capacity to pool funds to invest in bulk purchases of shea nuts. Providing access to nuts when supplies were otherwise expensive and difficult to find, this collective savings fund helped to stabilize their processing endeavors.

The overall cohesive ethos of the Gozense women's group, moreover, helped to support butter-making activities during an otherwise difficult season. Although this did not prevent or ameliorate economic differentiation in the community, it did temper it. This occurred as better-off buttermakers, like Barkisu, Awin, and Ramatu, continued to process nuts on a regular basis. As they commanded the assistance of neighbors and cowives who had reduced their own processing activities due to poor market conditions, this caused some women to give more aid than they were getting. However, the steady pace of processing within the community and their continued access to the assistance of others may well have helped these more marginal producers stay in the market. Indeed, it was typical in Gozense for women to continue to process even small quantities of nuts on a reduced though regular basis when women in other communities were more likely to drop out.

Conclusion

Interfacing with the global market through the conditions of the nut trade rather than the butter trade itself, rural butter processors still felt the pinch of export-market growth and privatization, however indirectly. They found themselves in competition with private buyers, a situation resulting in higher prices for shea nuts, nut scarcity, and poor terms of credit. All of this heightened the capital requirements of shea processing, paralleling the outcomes of neoliberal reform for women's income-generating endeavors elsewhere in Ghana and on the African continent more generally. Based on extensive research in southern Ghana, Clark and Manuh make an observation that is entirely accurate in the case of Bawku's shea butter-makers: "the capital squeeze forced many middle-level traders to withdraw into less profitable operations, widening the gap between rich and poor and closing off avenues of upward mobility" (1991: 228–9). "This gulf is further enlarged as many low-capital traders are forced to drop out of the market while only the more highly capitalized traders can survive" (1991: 226).

Such a capital squeeze is highly problematic for rural shea processors like those in Bawku. In an area plagued by persistent rural poverty, accessing capital is particularly difficult for rural women. Not only are their in-

come-earning opportunities limited, but women also face tremendous demands and responsibilities to contribute to the well-being of their offspring and to the household and self-support more generally. Within shea
processing as well as outside it, rural women in northern Ghana cope with
the need for and scarcity of capital through strategies of economic diversification as they try to glean and shift resources from one endeavor to another. This situation is well in keeping with Guyer's and Idowu's (1991:
258) observation that "women's welfare appears to be enhanced, above all
to be less vulnerable to permanent marginality and to rapid and devastat-
ing fluctuation, in rural economies characterized by diversity." Certainly,
among shea producers diversification has proved important to maintaining a place in the shea market. Indeed, shea producers sought new sources
of income to help sustain their enterprises. Nonetheless, women's capacities to master the changing conditions of commercial butter production
were not entirely successful, challenging economic and enterprise reproduction. Even as they sought to diversify, over half the butter-makers studied were forced to curtail their processing activities, with many women
dropping out of the market, a process that contributes to their impoverishment and stratification.

In accounting for the relative failure and success of different women as
they confront the new conditions of the shea market, what seems more important than diversification alone is the sort of diversification in which
they engage. Indeed, in all three communities studied, diversification is evident, yet it has varying effects on women's management of the capital requirements of commercial shea processing and the possibilities of
enterprise survival. In Saabon, for example, diversification provided little
economic security or possibility of accumulation. In the other communities, diversification was more fruitful. This seems to stem from a number of
dynamics. A key factor is the economic standing of the women involved. As
Guyer and Idowu (1991: 258) readily point out, socioeconomic differentiation shapes the possibilities for diversification in both production and
market relations, significantly constraining the welfare level and future
prospects of rural women, especially those in the lower strata. Indeed, as
we have seen among Bawku butter-makers, better-off women tended to divert and reproduce capital from shea production in income-generating activities such as agriculture, where they had access to family or low-cost
land and a modicum of labor services from other household members, as
well as investments in foodstuffs, shea nuts, or ready-made shea butter.

However, there are other aspects of diversification that need to be considered as well; this is the relationship of diversification to cooperation. In
both Boubuilla and Gozense, women have had greater success in coping
with the adverse conditions of the butter economy by innovating and di-

versifying their cooperative capacities and pursuits. This includes new forms of cooperative butter production and cooperative nut purchasing in Boubuilla and new forms of collective savings and investment in Gozense. In both cases, women pursued cooperative activities outside direct labor exchange and provided support for each other's activities outside the shea trade. While such cooperative activities do not counteract the heightened tendency toward stratification that comes with increased capital requirements, they do at least buffer shea producers from their intensification. This is in contrast to Saabon, where limited cooperation, bordering in some cases on patronage and what appears to be more of a process of resource dispersion than diversification, is found together with greater socioeconomic differentiation and a diminished capacity to manage new market conditions. Here, once again, for a rural industry like shea butter processing, collective endeavors—now as much about accessing and generating capital as concentrating labor—remain key to rural women's management of both commercial opportunity and adversity.

Reconstructing Tropical Commodity Regimes

Cosmopolitan Consumption, Postcolonial States,
Multinational Capital, and Rural Livelihoods
at the Turn of the Millennium

This book has sought to unpack the complex interdeterminations of global markets, postcolonial states, and rural economies in order to account for the outstanding character of shea as both a new breed of global commodity and an enduring feature of the West African commercial landscape, procured, processed, and sold for consumption within the regional economy. Tracing the circulation of shea within and between the households and markets of rural West Africa and the shopping malls and shipping lanes that make up the global economy makes it clear that the movement of tropical products into cosmopolitan economies depends on a multiplicity of forces emanating from states, international bodies, rural social institutions, metropolitan class fractions, multinational capital, nongovernmental organizations, trade associations, supranational blocs, and more. Although they intertwine and overlap, these forces neither are produced in concert nor do they operate in such a manner. Instead, each contains its own contradictions and developmental trajectories. This renders the rise and reproduction of new commodity streams unpredictable, despite the clear-cut forces of change they unleash.

As we have seen in West Africa, rural communities are crosscut by gender, class, kinship, and political distinctions. For cosmopolitan consumers, taste, status markers, and buying power all shift rapidly. States, too, are beset by

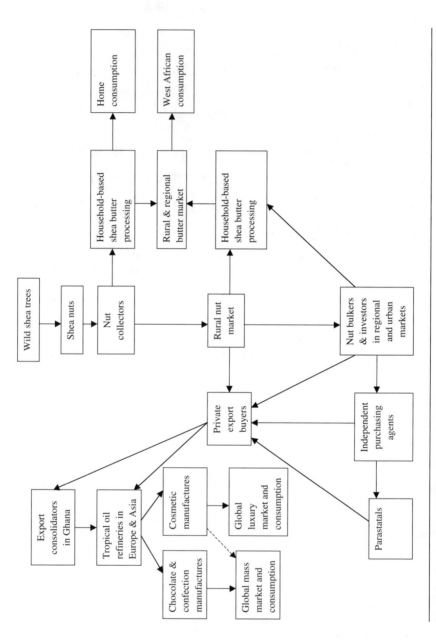

Fig. 7 The Development of the Shea Commodity Chain

difference as politicians and bureaucrats pursue alternative mandates and seek to manage diverse constituencies within a climate of economic and political instability. Multinational configurations, whether public, private, or a mix of the two, from the EU, ACP, and COPAL to fair-trade advocates, Green Party activists, and nongovernmental development organizations, likewise express divergent interests. The same is true of corporate capital, which is constantly on the lookout for new markets in which to buy and sell goods and for new modes of profit-making and self-presentation.

Global Markets, Consumers, and Commodities

Such a diversity of institutions and agendas shaping shea's global circulation affirms Hardt's and Negri's compelling observation that the globalization process is neither transcendent nor ruled by a singular rationale (2000: 1). Like the microtactics of rule underlying the fragile authority of colonial empire-building (Cooper and Stoller 1997), the manifold determinants of shea commercialization exemplify the multiple and dynamic form of late capitalism. More matrix than system, this is a configuration of forces—totalizing and differentiated, coincident and contradictory. In seeking a middle ground between approaches to global economic change that posit a singular logic-governed order and those that ascribe to it only disorder and indiscipline, this study has sought to identify the multiple points of integration and overlap that structure the shea market without attributing to them a false sense of permanence or common governance. The study equally aims to dispel the assumption that new forms of tropical commoditization replace and overwhelm those of the past, obviating older commercial pathways and organizational principles.

What, then, are these points of coherence, how do they build upon and rework preexisting commercial patterns, and, not least of all, how do they engage the problematic of globalization? Spanning continents and hemispheres, the tropical commodity regime in which shea is embedded is geographically global like countless other commercial circuits for tropical goods in the past and the present (Wolf 1982). Yet this global geography plays out in a host of new and striking ways. One such global innovation relates to the consumption of shea, whether as an unnamed ingredient of mass-marketed chocolate or a much-touted luxury item. Unlike older forms of tropical commoditization, shea consumption is not concentrated in the North Atlantic, nor is its tropical source restricted only to a role in production. As we have seen, as an indigenous and domestically processed commodity, shea is widely consumed throughout West Africa. This is paired with the expansive range of circulation and consumption of shea products—in diverse preparations and degrees of refinement—around the world, moving far beyond Africa and back to it.

Shea is an ingredient of low- and mid-priced chocolate the world over, from England and Switzerland to East Asia and the former Soviet states. Produced primarily in highly industrial states of the global north, cosmetics and other items for self-care containing shea are likewise globally consumed, whether in Paris, Dubai, São Paolo, Tokyo, Toronto, Accra, Abidjan, and Johannesburg. Indeed, many of those who consume shea as part of a project of status marking are themselves global in their own geography and self-awareness. Their cosmopolitan outlook is often attuned to elite lifestyles around the world and to some degree cognizant of the conditions surrounding the sourcing of shea.

A similar combined concern with geographic and status positioning is found among many of the companies that sell, promote, and formulate products made with shea. These firms, whether small or large, seek to establish, enlarge, or at the very least imagine their connection to the rural economies where shea is sourced. This is part of the allure of the products they market. These new ways of conceptualizing and experiencing the spatial dimensions of social connection and difference demonstrate how the expansive trajectory of globalization, despite the wider dynamic of space-time compression and deterritorialization which it engenders and on which it thrives (Appadurai 1996), works at the same time to create a new sense of place or at least a new recognition of spaces considered remote or somehow left behind. As we know, shea's profile as a luxury good is thoroughly bound up with an acknowledgment—whether entirely accurate or not—of its African origins.

This may well be considered both a variation and refutation of the commercial outlook expressed by metropolitan consumers at the beginning of the twentieth century, when shea, along with a host of other tropical products, was gaining currency as a world-market commodity. During this earlier era of mass-market formation, product refinement was tied up with the erasure of a commodity's tropical origins, as the global circulation of tropical products was part of a wider civilizing mission in both the colony and the metropole (McClintock 1995). From this perspective, not only would tropical commodity producers be brought into the modern world through the logic of the market, but those who consumed tropically sourced products would also gain status as a new type of economic citizen with generic rather than particularistic working-class identities (Mintz 1985). In contrast, at the end of the millennium, consumers seek to uncover and elaborate upon the origins of tropical commodities. This is a selective process of "un"-refinement, where only certain "natural" characteristics are endowed with importance. The space of origin is enmeshed once again in a civilizing project. In this case, however, it is not the target of a reform but its agent, as the economic life of the tropical other is considered to provide access to forms of knowledge and truth transcending national and cultural difference.

Along with the sense of a differentiated though linked global space that accompanies the promotion of new sorts of tropical goods, commodities such as shea are also global in the "simultaneities" they actualize. As shea spreads in both its mass and class manifestations, there is a convergence of lifestyles. In addition to low-priced chocolate confections, even the luxury cosmetics in which shea is a prime ingredient are being emulated by manufacturers who serve a mass market. As shea moves quickly along the market chain, though once highly restricted, it becomes increasingly popular, affordable, and readily available.

Despite the parallel process of luxury demotion this emergent process of shea popularization suggests, it does not appear to be driven by the type of generic class aspirations that accompanied the spread of sugar consumption among the working class in the late nineteenth century, as discussed by Mintz (1985). It seems to have more in common with the trends Roseberry (1996) describes for late-twentieth-century coffee consumption, where the coffee market has gained new popularity in the course of being divided into distinctive niches representing different lifestyles and preferences. In the case of coffee, as formally exclusive consumption habits become more accessible (i.e., cappuccino at the convenience store; flavored syrups mimicked by flavored creamers), their variation remains a source of value. Likewise, in the growing market for shea, popularization is more about equalizing access to marks of distinction rather than erasing a sense of difference.

The simultaneous proliferation (chocolate to cosmetic) and convergence (restricted to popular) of consumer positions within the shea market find a parallel in the corporate forms accompanying these commercial trajectories. Despite the appearance of a seemingly new breed of small-scale and specialized global businesses—like the myriad companies involved in making and marketing natural cosmetics with shea—they are nonetheless dependent upon processes of corporate concentration. In the case of shea, the domination of shea import and export as well as refinement by just a few large firms keeps prices down and innovation high, providing a possibility for the entry of smaller businesses at many stages of shea fabrication and retail because of the affordability of shea. Here again, corporate consolidation and market segmentation are paired rather than alternative economic processes. Though driven by different aims and business philosophies (specialty versus common products; personalized versus corporate procurement), these diverse commercial streams work together to enlarge the market for shea. They are both competitive and complementary, and even as consumers move from one to another—from the Body Shop Body Butters selling for $5 per ounce to the Jergens shea lotion selling for $.25 per ounce and back again—as their needs, knowledge, and buying power shift, and business leaders in each sector decry each other's practices, taken together these trends heighten consumer awareness of and access to shea products.

The Dispersion of State Power:
De- and Renationalizing the Shea Market

What is the role of the state in this process of corporate growth and diversification and the apparently personalized transpositions from one mode of shea consumption to another? Contrary to the idea that states are necessarily undermined by the globalization process and the ascendance of private capital accompanying it, the case of shea reveals states to be players—although perhaps not the leading ones—in the manifold struggles to determine the course and garner the spoils of the global economy. No longer the unequivocal mediators standing between tropical economies and metropolitan markets, states now operate in a wider and more differentiated field—both within the nation and beyond. While this may well undermine old modes and guarantees of authority, it also engenders new possibilities for articulating political interests and asserting power. As we have seen, in the negotiation of chocolate-processing standards, Ghana, along with several other West African nations, claimed a stake in a series of global debates involving COPAL, the ICCO, the ACP, and the EU, enhancing its international profile and utilizing an international agenda to reinforce regional hierarchies and further sectional interests on the domestic front.

Equally, state engagement of the policies and processes of economic liberalization put forth by international financial institutions—despite their obligatory character—gave the government of Ghana a new source of international legitimacy and new resources to wield at home. This sort of globalization of state imperatives, with government bodies asserting their interests via trans- and supranational associations and campaigns, and supra- and multinational institutions bearing upon domestic policy, signals what Sassen calls "denationalization," in which national policy is formed by state organs outside national territory and external interests operate within national boundaries to shape state policy (2002: 2). Yet, in the case of shea, "denationalization" is attached to a commensurate process of "renationalization," as external debates and nonnational interventions fuel and are fueled by national power struggles. As we have seen, the policies and processes of economic liberalization in which the rise of new global commodity regimes is enmeshed have wide-ranging implications for the reproduction and remaking of state structures at home. Rather than privatization initiatives imposed by international financial institutions undoing state authority in Ghana, throughout the nearly twenty-year history of structural adjustment the state has used liberalization to enforce its own mandate, protecting and mobilizing resources both political and economic. This was evident in the 1980s, when the Rawlings government, under the guise of export diversification, used the institution of shea nut farmers societies as a way to instantiate a rural constituency and reestablish state presence in the northern savanna zone.

Even in the 1990s, when privatization directives were more strictly imposed, they remained selectively enforced by the government. Specifically, the privatization of shea rather than cocoa enabled the consolidation of power within Ghana's Cocoa Marketing Board and secured the state's hold on the cocoa sector. And despite the ostensible privatization of the shea market, the state still retained a strong presence in and influence over it, however indirect. In this regard, state involvement in shea, instead of being concentrated in a single set of institutions and agendas, was increasingly decentralized, surfacing in a range of institutions and initiatives. Making the state's place in the market more difficult to specify without entirely undermining its effectiveness, in the 1990s the regulatory capacities of the state were continually brought back to life by state agents, international organizations, private-company representatives, and rural residents alike and transformed by them. This sort of state breakdown, then, signals a dispersion of state power, not its disappearance.

Here the dynamics of colonial rule draw attention to the profound importance of such decentralized and embedded forms of political control at moments of state-building in the early part of the twentieth century as well as at the century's close. As evident in myriad forms of administrative intervention pursued by colonial agents, imperial rule in northern Ghana was born of a plethora of seemingly minute administrative measures which eventually began to penetrate the whole of northern economic life. Working out the relationship between rulers and ruled through the cultivation and monitoring of commercial norms surrounding shea in the Northern Territories, the colonial state gradually imposed new political and economic hierarchies. Indicative of an important link between the administrative reforms of the past and the market reforms of the present, during the early colonial period when the use of such tactics was at its height and in the current era of globalization when they are resurfacing, the sovereignty of the state is only weakly institutionalized. Drawing attention to the similarities between what Cooper and Stoller (1997) call, with respect to colonialism, the "tensions of empire," and the tensions of globalization well into the postcolonial era, these may well signal parallel instances of indirect rule.

As the tropical commodity regime surrounding shea and the more general conditions of Ghanaian political economy intersect with the forces of globalization, the state is resurrected in numerous ways, propelled by state institutions and personnel with a variety of distinct capacities and agendas. In the face of the reforms of the 1990s, they include the movement of FASCOM into the shea market at the behest of the development initiatives of TechnoServe and USAID; the attempts of petty officials within the PBC to maintain their political stature and privileged access to resources; the desire of shea nut farmer society executives to preserve ties to national-level political organizations; and the attempts of new sorts of political actors, such as district assembly members, to oversee the shea economy. These moves to reconstitute state authority were pursued as much by actors within the state apparatus as by those located outside of it, namely the representatives of the private firms purchasing shea nuts for export.

This mode of state production similarly replicates the close association, uneasy as it may have been, between the British administration and private capital during the colonial period. In the 1990s, private companies, whether consolidating rural supply lines through the promise of patronage and regional monopolization or securing access to export markets through preferential licensing and pricing agreements, sought to reproduce the strategies and protections of the state as much as state actors sought to guide private participation in the shea market. Intertwined in this manner, states and private firms pursue a parallel course in the new shea economy, seeking to fuse their aims and patterns of operation. But where, over the course of colonial rule, the division between state and private entities and initiatives grew as administrative power took hold, at the end of the twentieth century we see the reverse tendency in play where state and private capital are more and more fused. Signaling the emergence of a "postdevelopmental state" (Ong 1999:21), this recent phase of economic reform is marked by the ascendance of private models in which the state is increasingly selective and profit-oriented in its investments and private firms come to stand in for the state in their provision (or at least promise) of public goods and the exclusivity of their access to resources.

Not only do private firms replicate state operations, but also, like the state, they are subject to an array of pushes and pulls, making them a key point of intersection melding and mediating wider processes of change and contestation. Accounting for the distinctive character of new tropical commodity regimes, the operations of private firms, among other things, reflect the convergence of a number of global processes. In addition to IFI directives opening up West African shea supplies to private buyers and new consumption patterns enlarging demand for West African shea nuts, the capacity of private firms to connect the two successfully is tied to their multinational standing. One sign of the attrition of domestic ventures in Ghana is that the three companies remaining active in the shea market after a decade of privatization are all multinational in scope. In first place is Kassardjian, a family-owned, Lebanese firm based in London; second is Olam, an Indian chemical firm headquartered in Malaysia, and far behind in third place is FASCOM, supported by bilateral development aid via USAID and TechnoServe, a not-for-profit, international, nongovernmental organization. The diverse constitution of these businesses defies assumptions about the character of multinational capital operating in tropical contexts as necessarily large, private, North American, Northern European, industrially based, and profit-driven.

The increasing involvement of such unorthodox or underrecognized multinationals in African tropical commodity regimes in the wake of liberalization is by no means restricted to Ghana's shea economy and has been identified for other commodities in other parts of the continent (Raikes and Gibbon 2000: 77). These idiosyncratic commercial forms recall the private concerns active in the shea economy during the first few decades of colonial involvement in the economy of Ghana's northern savanna. While in the past serving as a precursor to the emergence of large transnational corporations that eventually overwhelmed them, today they operate in tandem with corporate giants, raising new questions about their form as well as their function. Specifically in the Ghanaian case, what stands out about these commercial configurations is the place they hold in a seemingly new global division of labor. The significance of this process becomes apparent if we compare it with two other trends that appear to be characteristic of the globalization of African export crops. In an overview of this topic, Raikes and Gibbon identify two sorts of restructuring at work in Africa in the face of liberalization (2000: 72–7). One is a renewed reliance on smallholder production, as exporters limit their investment in local markets via contracting arrangements and the like. The other is the increasing consolidation of export regimes as individual and typically multinational firms take over more and more aspects of the export process, from commodity production and transportation to processing and importation. The organization of shea export stands between these two extremes.

While large multinational firms are increasingly involved in different aspects of the export economy, there seems to be a clear and deliberate separation between their operations and those of the smaller private firms involved in domestic nut purchasing. As we have seen, large-scale buyers and refiners of tropical oilseeds such as Aarhus Olie and Karlshamns seek to buy West African shea nuts at low cost directly from exporters. However, they themselves are not interested in nut procurement. Even Aarhus, after establishing an office in Ghana's capital, Accra, has shied away from purchasing nuts from markets and traders in the savanna zone. Rather, it relies on the smaller private firms to undertake this job and shoulder its attendant risks. This may well signal the emergence of a new sort of contracting arrangement in which large multinationals indirectly control domestic markets not by asserting power over rural producers through the specification of production routines, crop yields, and prices, as in conventional contracting arrangements (Little and Watts 1994), but by asserting power over other sorts of multinationals through the specification of the quality, quantity, and price of nuts they procure on the domestic front. As Aarhus routinizes its operations in Ghana, possibly to be joined by other refiners, this relationship is likely to emerge as an increasingly significant link in the shea supply chain, open to challenge and negotiation and revealing much about the interplay of forces that make up the shea economy. Once again, this is a global order that thrives on heterogeneity, not encompassment.

In addition to coping with the structure and demands of global capital and state entanglement in shea export, private firms in the domestic market must also navigate the diverse conditions and potentials of the rural markets and communities where they seek to purchase nuts. Subject to mechanisms of both exclusion and inclusion, private firms' access to rural supply lines is uneven and unsteady. While they may be kept out of the market in some instances, such as in Worianga and Garu, and held at bay in others, as in Bawku, they may still gain easy access to rural supply lines, as in markets such as Songo, where rural traders are thoroughly receptive to the new opportunities offered by private buyers. Private firms may also find a space for themselves as the new patrons of rural communities, promised a reliable supply of shea nuts in return for ongoing investment. But whether rural traders accept or reject their advances, traders have only limited control over the market in which they operate, contained from above by more powerful multinationals and below by the well-established alternatives offered to rural nut suppliers and traders by the indigenous shea economy.

Explaining the Endurance of the Domestic Shea Economy

Just as much as the shea export economy is shaped by the character of corporate capital, consumer trends, and international financial arrangements and mediated by the state and private firms, it is even more profoundly determined by the character of the domestic shea economy and shea's status as an indigenous commodity. Defying the widespread imagery of shea as somehow removed from the market that is promulgated by companies promoting shea's status as a new breed of cosmopolitan luxury, it is by now evident that the circulation of shea on the world market depends not on the commercialization of economic forms that heretofore were noncommercialized but on the enlargement of vast and long-standing commercial circuits. From the start, shea's attraction to metropolitan markets and merchants and their agents, Ferguson included, derived from its already well-established commercial value and identity. As we have seen, shea was in circulation throughout the entire West African subregion prior to colonial contact.

Throughout the century spanned by this book, beginning in the early years of colonial rule and moving into the early years of the twenty-first century, shea's status as an indigenous commodity had contradictory implications for its movement into the world market. On the one hand, the fact that shea was already produced for sale and widely consumed in West Africa simplified its movement into new commercial realms, as the shea market needed only to be reoriented rather than built from the ground up. On the other hand, the long-standing market for shea within West Africa, characterized by high demand and well-developed trade networks, served as an obstacle to export.

For rural shea nut traders and butter processors, the regional shea economy, time and time again, whether during the colonial era, under the rule of Rawlings, or in the face of neoliberal reform, proved an alternative to direct engagement of the external markets. Nevertheless, for savanna residents or those involved in export promotion, state agents and private-company representatives alike, these very same features of the indigenous shea economy have allowed for considerable flexibility regarding the terms of export market engagement. Side by side with the breakdown, failure, or fading away of earlier programs of export, the indigenous economy remained a reliable source of nuts and hence ready to engage or be engaged by subsequent initiatives. Likewise, for rural residents—specifically, rural women—the indigenous economy served as a steady source of support even as they sought temporary or long-term involvement in the export market. This potential for limited investment and temporary commitment provided by the strong domestic economy has no doubt contributed to the constantly changing character of the export market but it may also underlie that market's overall endurance. Indeed, as we have seen, at the turn of the twenty-first century the long-standing character of the domestic shea market does much to account for the renewed interest in shea products globally, both as a marker of meaning and a source of material value.

Despite the obvious functionality of shea's status as an indigenous commodity to the export market, it is still necessary to account for the continued centrality of shea and shea commercialization within the economy of northern Ghana. How has the shea economy remained oriented to domestic provisioning despite the pressures and vagaries of export promotion? On a most basic level, the preservation of the domestic shea economy can be explained by the strength and scope of local demand for shea. Clearly, shea butter, as an edible oil with manifold uses in food preparation, medicine, cosmetics, and craft, has enough local uses to support commercialization without an export sector. Not only is shea multipurpose, but, because it is locally procured and processed for little cost, it is also cheap compared to industrially manufactured or locally grown goods serving the same functions, further ensuring its continued consumption. The market for shea is also geographically extensive, giving those who buy or sell shea nuts and butter a wide range of market outlets and options and helping to sustain their economic endeavors.

However, even in the face of strong conditions of demand, in order to be sustained, the making and marketing of shea products must be able to resist threats to the raw materials, time, labor, and knowledge that go into them. Let us consider these in turn. As a wild crop, shea nuts can be found dispersed throughout the savanna landscape. Other than the time it takes to gather them, their production requires little human input. Likewise, shea trees, as an indigenous species, are well suited to the savanna environment and hence able to withstand the vicissitudes and extremes of geography and climate, ensuring their availability and viability over time and space. Responsive to rather than threatened by human activity, they thrive at the margins of farm and forest and on fields left fallow.

Nut collection requires little expertise and may be pursued at any scale, facilitating its integration with other work routines. Considered a women's crop, well suited to female work schedules and physical capacities, shea collection has remained the purview of rural women, protecting shea trees and stocks from overexploitation and helping to guarantee their reproduction. Echoing the omnipresent but dispersed character of shea tree cover within the savanna landscape, the conditions of access to shea nuts are largely decentralized. Reflecting more of a horizontal than a vertical marketing structure, nuts may be sought from a range of sources, whether rural or urban markets, collectors, professional traders, or occasional investors, one's own efforts, or the efforts of friends and neighbors. The existence of so many specialized roles and positions in the nut market alone, as a diversification strategy of a sort, means that there are manifold channels of nut access within the producing region, protecting the nut market as a whole from being overwhelmed by external pressures or interventions.

Like the collection and purchasing of shea nuts, the time, labor, and knowledge involved in making shea butter are all gleaned from the margins of other economic activities and built upon already established economic relationships. As we have seen, rural women make time for making shea within the wider stream of domestic work. Pooling their knowledge and physical effort between trips to the farm and market, butter processors work early in the morning and late at night, during heat of the afternoon when other rest, and throughout the dry season. Varied in form and reflecting the exigencies of rural livelihood, the parameters of butter-making are highly flexible and hence can be maintained even as wider economic conditions shift.

This sort of institutionalized flexibility is facilitated above all by the cooperative work routines that surround shea production. Multipurpose in character, women's work groups are firmly grounded in relations of kinship, coresidence, and occupational solidarity. Reflecting the shifting priorities and economic capacities of their members, these groups are marked by great fluidity, allowing butter-makers to adjust their efforts in keeping with the opportunities and demands of farm work, trade, labor migration, and family fortune. As established solidarities, they permit both ongoing and sporadic participation, minimizing the resources—financial and otherwise—necessary for an individual to invest in butter production. Yet of signal importance to continued participation in them is that these cooperative work relations permit and foster individualized financial returns and recognition. Finally, women's involvement in these productive arrangements, which are seen as an exclusively female preserve, is generally secure, serving as a further incentive to their engagement.

Given these attributes, the decentralized and deeply embedded character of the domestic shea economy, with so many bases of resource generation and control, has always presented a rather elusive target for export promotion efforts. Unable to capture to this complex whole, export initiatives, though continuous over time, have been institutionally inconstant, focusing on different aspects of the domestic shea economy but not its entirety. This means that the domestic shea economy has been repeatedly—albeit partially—"domesticated" in new ways and under new circumstances, giving it a highly dynamic form. Colonial-era interventions, as we have seen, had a dramatic effect on the character of the rural shea economy. Although they did not create the type of export market the colonial administration hoped for, the need for cash and the conditions of labor migration that came with colonial rule created new pressures for income generation among rural women, precipitating a shift in shea's status from a good produced for home consumption and/or long-distance trade to one increasingly produced by rural women to serve the local market.

In the 1980s, after several decades of only modest exports, the strong arm of the state returned to the shea trade, having a different effect on the domestic shea economy. Intervening in rural markets and communities as never before, the state worked hard to enforce a new economic mandate, giving rural suppliers little choice but to rework the conventions of trade to accommodate first the export market and then domestic needs. While the state's renewed attention to the export market gave new value to shea within the rural economy, it also created new contests over it, leading rural women's control over shea to be threatened by the incursions of urban traders, male and female alike. Responding to these challenges, rural women soon began to question the promises and capacities of the state and to devise new ways to protect domestic shea stocks and supply lines from state exactions and the pressures of local merchants. In stimulating a new appreciation of shea as a source of value and power within the wider context of the nation-state, this realization—and the strategies of market preservation and capture that went along with it—would linger in the minds and practices of northern shea suppliers as they confronted the next wave of market reform in the 1990s.

At this time rural shea suppliers, coping with the imperatives of privatization, did not reject export initiatives but strenuously sought to set the terms of participation for those seeking to purchase nuts in rural markets and communities even as they tried to maintain a hold on the selective benefits doled out by the state. Building and strengthening community- and occupation-based coalitions, shea suppliers worked together to impose a strict performance code on exporters, whether the private firms seeking exclusive, community-based, purchasing contracts, private-company representatives buying nuts in rural and urban markets, or state agents and institutions seeking to maintain a role in the shea market. While rural suppliers were in many cases able to command compliance, in other cases these self-made market controls caused some private buyers to retreat from the rural market. Spurning such rural conditionalities, these export buyers sought to establish a much less integrated supply system based on loose ties to local merchants and buying agents already involved in rural trade.

In short, if export promotion during the colonial period led inadvertently to the rise of an autonomous domestic market for shea butter and nuts, in the 1980s the state's export agenda worked to infiltrate and transform the rural shea market through the imposition of a strict operational code by means of the PBC and the shea farmer societies. In the 1990s, with privatization and the lingering presence of state institutions and agents, rural shea suppliers in turn sought to reassert control over the domestic shea market not by cutting it off from the export sector but by imposing rules of conduct on those buying nuts for export and reserving a portion of the nut market for domestic trade. Countering attempts by rural traders to demarcate a separate domestic market, exporters sought to maintain a singular shea market in which they could establish an elusive although potentially overwhelming presence. Hence after the process of market separation in the colonial period and the overwhelming interventions of the state during the PBC era, the more recent period of privatization is marked by an effort on the part of nut suppliers to reorder the terms of export without completely rejecting them.

Despite its strength and endurance, not only has the rural shea economy been substantially transformed by the enticements and pressures of export, but those groups and individuals performing different roles within the shea economy are differentially impacted by them This is nowhere more evident than in the contrasting effects of export promotion on nut traders versus butter-makers. In the era of privatization, nut traders have been able to interact directly with exporters and tap into a new market for nuts, gleaning benefit from their relationship to and influence over it. Butter-makers, in contrast, have no direct tie to newcomers in the shea market and gain no new outlets for their wares or new sources of nuts. Rather, export growth undermines butter-makers' access to shea nuts altogether, rendering nuts scarce, expensive, and hard to procure on credit. In such a reduced position, butter-makers are pressed to find not only new sources of nuts but also new sources of the capital necessary to purchase them.

Coping with these new and generally adverse market conditions, in Bawku, butter-makers had little choice but to reorient their production routines. Although deployed in new ways, cooperation remained essential to rural women's capacity to manage the constraints of export growth and the new capital requirements that come along with it, indicating its continued centrality to commercial butter-making. In Gozense, rural women used already established networks of cooperation to accumulate capital to purchase nuts through various savings and investment strategies. In Boubuilla, cooperative networks were used to gain access to ready-made butter as well as nuts for sale outside the marketplace. In Saabon and elsewhere, the ongoing rhythms of cooperative work routines helped butter-makers sustain their enterprises even as production frequencies were otherwise reduced.

While important to their management of changing market conditions, collective strategies alone could not guarantee the reproduction of butter-making enterprises for women in Bawku. Butter-makers had little choice but to mobilize more individualized strategies of resource access, accentuating differences among them, as they sought cash, nuts, and credit from neighbors, kin, and more far-flung associates and their own ancillary economic endeavors. Even as these pursuits allowed some butter-makers to maintain a place in the shea market, not every one was so lucky. Faced with a tight market for nuts and little means to access them in the absence of credit, most butter processors were forced to curtail their efforts, and some to drop out of the butter market altogether, making commercial butter production an increasingly specialized pursuit despite the collective endeavors and mentalities that it reinforced and was founded upon.

What do these processes portend for the future of shea commercialization, especially the viability of butter production for the domestic market? Even though Ghana's export economy is currently organized around the sale of shea nuts, as in Mali and Burkina Faso (Carr et al. 2000; Fold 2000; Harsch 2001) there is a growing number of foreign firms seeking to purchase shea butter directly from butter-makers and a handful of entrepreneurs in Ghana seeking to produce shea butter for sale abroad. With several of these concerns interested in labor-saving technology, this may offer butter-makers new technical skills and commercial opportunity. However, it may also cause them to lose control over the production process as well as their capacity to balance their involvement in shea production with other economic pursuits.

More threatening to the rural shea economy is that as more nuts move into export markets in response to the attractions of value-added processing, the supplies available for the regional market and household-based butter processing are likely to become increasingly scarce and expensive, further restricting rural women's capacity to serve the domestic market. This may well mean that the majority of rural women involved in shea butter production will be contributing labor to the mechanical processing of nuts destined for the world market, a dynamic that will lower the cost of butter on the world market and boost its incorporation into mass-market commodities, causing, in turn, a further rise in prices and a further reduction of access to both nuts and labor within the rural economy. This very same dynamic is likely to render domestic shea processing for the regional and local market an increasingly rarified pursuit, transforming shea from a rural staple into a semiluxury, symbolic of a fading past within the savanna zone itself.

Notes

Introduction

1. Based on the observations of Mungo Park, published in 1799, the name *shea* is originally from the Bambara. *Karite* is the Wolof term, very likely derived from the Fulani *karaje* (Dalziel 1937: 350).
2. By "cosmopolitans" I am a speaking of persons with access to a plethora of widely recognized cultural forms by virtue of their own spatial mobility and/or the mobility of such cultural material by virtue of its own deterritorialization (Appadurai 1996). This is an idea of not so much a homogeneous "global" class but a group of people who can operate within and across multiple cultural realms, synthesizing them in new ways (Hannerz 1987; 1989).

The Setting

1. A long-standing chieftaincy dispute exacerbated by national political rivalries is the source of sporadic violence.

Chapter 1

1. See Bryceson (1995), Guyer and Idowu (1991), and Whitehead (1990: 460) on economic diversification and extraagricultural pursuits among rural women in both East and West Africa.
2. The other economically useful trees that are protected in farming areas are *Parkia filicoides*, commonly known as "locust bean;" *Adansonia digitata*, baobob; and *Parkia clappertoniana*, "dawadawa" (Peiler 1994).
3. Trees of this stature have also been described as "overmature" (i.e., past prime productive stage) (FAO 1981: 20). This may indicate the long-term overexploitation of shea trees as agricultural expansion and demographic pressure limit the type of shifting cultivation that facilitates the regeneration of fallows and the relaxation of tree harvesting efforts.
4. Because shea trees' reproductive cycle is far ahead of that of cultivated species, farmers sometimes run the risk of singeing shea flowers and buds when they burn their fields a few months before planting. Otherwise, the practice of burning fields is symbiotic as it clears ground cover and seedlings that might compete with a mature tree.
5. This position indicates the ritual and historical connection of the living members of a community to a territory and to the ancestors who previously farmed and settled there.

269

6. In such cases of political control of resources procured from community property, it is important to note how the overseer disposes of the produce or payment procured. For example, Cardinall (1920), with respect to the Tallensi, suggests that payment is nominal and is incorporated into sacrifices to "land" and hence ultimately used by the *tendaana*, "the keeper of the land." In contrast, Skinner (1964: 116) and McPhee (1926), drawing on data collected during the colonial era, suggest that the cash payments received by a chief in return for license to gather shea products as well as the actual produce collected as a tax on land use were used by leaders as a source of personal income and a way to procure revenue for their administration.

7. The name of the village of Koltaase in fact refers to the shea trees in the vicinity: *kol*, meaning "river" in Kusaal, and *taamas*, meaning "shea trees."

8. The necessity of girls' labor may well contribute to the extremely low levels of school enrollment for girls in the rural savanna, as indicated in national survey data (Ghana Statistical Service 2000b: 9; Ghana Statistical Service 2000a: 54).

9. In the Kusasi and Mamprussi compound house, each woman has her own sleeping and work areas separated from the rest of the household by a low mud wall. All of the residential units making up the household are enclosed by a higher exterior wall, which may be relocated and rebuilt to make room for the living quarters of a new family member. This architectural record of demographic processes gives each compound a maze-like quality (see Bourdier 1996).

10. Women's identities and social standing are closely tied to the space in which they work and reside. While a house *in toto* (*yin*) is known by the name of the seniormost male, the *yiisoob* or "landlord" living there, the various areas (*zakin*) into which the inner courtyard is divided are known by the name of the woman who works and resides in each (i.e., Amina-*zakin*, Shodiya-*zakin*).

11. Smith (1978) identifies similar cooperative work patterns among Gurunsi in northern Ghana, women residing just west of Bawku District involved in decorative wall painting. He writes: "If the decision has been made to decorate, then the activity will be coordinated but not controlled by the senior woman of each compound section or by the senior woman of the entire compound" (1978: 37); "In addition to the other female compound members, a woman may call upon her husband's brothers' wives and her friends for help. She is responsible for providing both food and drink. Usually the senior woman will present her views and after consulting with the other women will decide on the particular motifs and design to be used" (1978: 40). Like wall painting elsewhere in West Africa (Adams 1993), both the act of working together and the final product serve to display and affirm distinctive female identities, solidarities, and economic roles.

12. In seeking to secure and enlarge their commercial efforts, it was not only shea butter producers who mobilized Nyoor Yinii alliances and tied them to broader bases of support. Just as the Gozense Kwatuodib sought to harness the organizational parameters modeled by the state and NGOs, so too did these organizations engage butter-makers and the economic potentials of Nyoor Yinii with the dual aim of promoting shea processors' commercial prospects as well as their own economic and extraeconomic agendas. This was especially evident in the case of the 31st December Women's Movement, which used Nyoor Yinii as the model for the women's groups it established in the Bawku area. Barely increasing butter-makers' access to labor but helping them save cash and gain credit, 31st December representatives in Garu for example, used their involvement in butter-producing communities to rally political support for their organization and political sponsors as well as to bolster their own political and economic standing by fostering butter-makers' clients dependence.

Chapter 2

1. In Japan, the liberalization of import rules in the late 1990s permitted the sale of products with shea butter. Attesting to shea's status as a truly global and cosmopolitan commodity, the decision to import shea followed strong sales to Japanese tourists visiting Paris ("New cosmetics," 1997).

2. Posing the greatest threat to the pursuit of colonial economic and administrative interests was European failure to acknowledge the might and scope of the Asanti confederacy. Occupying the forest zone between the Gold Coast colony and extending its influence into the

northern savanna (Wilks 1961), the Asanti confederacy had long resisted British occupation and was one among many obstacles to the expansion of British influence throughout the large sweep of territory that now constitutes modern Ghana.

3. Despite its now-widespread expression in the modern nation-state system (Anderson 1991), such an equivalence of polity and place was not at all a "natural" order. As Geertz (1983) points out, different conceptions of sovereignty are tied to distinct ways of using territory.

4. "Captain D. Stewart to F. M. Hodgeson," Gambaga, December 29, 1896.

5. This was the "Convention between Great Britain and France for the delimitation of their respective possessions to the West of the Niger and of their Respective Possessions to the East of that River," signed at Paris June 14, 1898.

6. This was part of the "Conventions between Great Britain and Germany for the settlement of the Samoan and other questions," signed at London November 14, 1899.

7. Adm 57.5.9, 1.25.12.

8. Adm 57.5.4, 6.27.15.

9. Ironically, these regulations caused a temporary commercial decline in Bawku itself. Diminishing the prosperity of outlying markets, they in turn limited the prosperity of the communities that depended on them, forcing many people to curtail their participation in Bawku's central market (Bening 1973a: 12).

10. Adm 57.5.9, 7.21.14.

11. Adm 56.1.126, 1911.

12. Adm 57.5.9, 7.23.14.

13. Adm 56.1.126, 8.22.11.

14. Adm 57.5.4, 2.28.15.

15. Adm 57.5.9, 2.28.15.

16. Adm 57.5.9, 3.30.15.

17. This manner of scientific market research and promotion was also pursued in France and published in journals such as *Bulletin de l'Office Colonial* and *Les Matieres Grasses.*

18. Adm 56.1.152, 2.28.22.

19. Shea was to be featured a number of times in the *BII*: 1930, vol. 28; 1931, vol. 29; 1932, vol. 30; 1933, vol. 35.

20. Adm 56.1.152, 2.27.13.

21. Adm 56.1.152, 8.18.13.

22. Adm.56.1.152, 7.6.14.

23. Adm.56.1.152; 4.4.16.

24. Guggisberg is notable among colonial civil servants as he was the first in the British colonial empire to propose and pursue an integrated developed agenda aimed at both revenue generation and the improvement of material welfare (Robertson 1984:15).

25. Ghana National Archives files contain records of six firms involved in or inquiring about participation in shea export. They are the African Association Limited, which later became the African and Eastern Trade Company; Millers, Limited, London, which appears to have worked as an agent or subcontractor of African and Eastern; HBW Russell and Company, Liverpool; John Walkden and Company, African Merchants, Manchester; MacIlwaine Patents Syndicate, London; W. Barthalomew and Company, Accra; and Raffineries du Congo Belge, Messrs. de Bruyn Limited, Belgium.

26. Adm 56.1.152, 1924.

27. There were two industries for which shea was considered particularly desirable: margarine and soap.

28. Adm. 56.1.152, 12.13.23.

29. Adm 56.1.152, 6.15.26.

30. Op. cit.

31. Adm 56.1.152, 6.30.21, 6.15.26.

32. Adm 56.1.152, 11.16.23.

33. Adm 56.1.152, 9.22.19.

34. Adm 56.1.152, 9.22.19.

35. Adm 56.1.152, 2.4.20.

36. The completed surveys are included in the following files, all contained within Adm 56.1.152: from the Provincial Commissioner, Northwest Province 8.1.20; from the Provin-

cial Commissioner, Southern Province, 30.1.20; from the Provincial Commissioner, Northeast Province, 7.1.20, 27.1.20; from the District Commissioner, Navarro-Zaurungu, 8.1.20; from the Provincial Commissioner, Wa, 8.1.20.

37. Adm 56.1.152, 3.12.20.
38. Adm 56.1.152, 8.22.21.
39. Not long after, it was discovered that this tree, known as "false shea" or the "male shea butter tree" grows only in the Tamale-Salaga area in the southeast quadrant of the Northern Territories (Adm 56.1.152, 7.19.22).
40. Adm 56.1.152, 7.27.21, 8.15.21, 10.18.21.
41. Adm 56.1.152, 10.24.21.
42. Adm 56.1.152, 11.28.21.
43. For a discussion of this implicit theory of value, see Marx (1967): "The two-fold value of the labour embodied in commodities," (1967, "Commodities and Money" in Part 1).
44. Adm 56.1.152, 5.3.22.
45. Adm 56.1.275, 8.11.24.
46. Adm 56.1.158, 3.29.23, 1923.
47. Adm 56.1.158, 8.4.23.
48. Adm 56.1.158, 12.4.22.
49. Adm 56.1.158, 8.9.23.
50. Adm 56.1.158, 112.22, 5.3.22.
51. Adm 56.1.275, 4.19.23, 2.16.24, 8.11.24.
52. Adm 56.1.275, 7.24.24.
53. Adm 56.1.275, 7.11.24.
54. Adm 56.1.275, 4.25.23.
55. Adm 56.1.275, 7.19.24.
56. Adm 56.1.275, 7.19.24.
57. Adm 57.5.4, 4.19.23.
58. Adm 56.1.158, 1923.
59. Adm 56.1.275, 2.16.24.
60. Adm 56.1.275, 4.25.23.
61. Adm 56.1.152, 4.24.23.
62. Adm 56.1.275, 7.19.24, 7.24.24, 8.11.24.
63. Adm 56.1.152, 1923; Adm 56.1.158, 5.3.22; Adm 56.1.275, 5.22.22, 4.19.23, 7.19.24, 8.11.24.
64. Adm 56.1.275, 7.19.24.
65. Adm 56.1.275, 8.11.24.
66. Adm 56.1.275, 8.11.24.
67. Adm 56.1.275, 7.19.24.
68. Adm 56.1.158, 9.28.24.
69. Op. cit.
70. Adm 56.1.275, 7.19.24.
71. Adm 56.1.158, 9.28.24.
72. Adm 56.1.152, 9.28.24.
73. Adm 56.1.158, 3.29.23.
74. Adm 56.1.158, 5.22.22.
75. Adm 56.1.152, 4.24.23.
76. Adm 56.1.152, 11.3.24.
77. Adm 56.1.158, 3.29.23.
78. Adm 56.1.158.
79. Adm 56.1.158, 5.22.22.
80. Adm 56.1.152, 9.28.24.
81. Adm 56.1.152, 4.24.23.
82. Adm 56.1.275, 9.18.26, 11.1.26.
83. Adm 56.1.275, 10.6.28.
84. Op. cit.
85. Adm 2: 4.2.32.
86. Adm 2: 4.2.32.
87. Yams were also a major export to the south at this time (White 1956: 120; Sutton 1989: 653), but their production was restricted to the southern half of the Northern Territories, giving groundnuts a much wider range of sources.

88. See Hogendorn (1978) for comparison with the northern Nigerian groundnut trade.
89. Following a steady rise in migration rates through the 1940s and a more extreme rise in the 1950s, in 1960 an estimated 23 percent of the population (men as well as women—though not in equal proportions) of Ghana's northern sector were counted as migrants (Hart 1971: 23).
90. In areas, such as the northeast, where rates of labor migration were particularly high, this could mean that nearly half of the male population would be away on either a temporary or a permanent basis.
91. In 1931, in the Northern Territories the male-to-female ratio stood at 95 to 100; in 1948 it dropped to 89 to 100, and in 1960 further still, to 75 to 100 (Hilton 1968, quoted in Plange 1979: 671).
92. Tamale Archives, March 10, 1937, *Bawku Subdistrict Informal Diary for the Month of March.*

Chapter 4

1. Raikes and Gibbon characterize deregulation in terms of "the dismantling since 1980 of large parts of the national-state regulatory systems set up after 1945" (2000: 52).
2. This is in accordance with the U.S. Standards of Identity as outlined in CFR21 (Zeigler 2002). In the United States, the only fats permitted in chocolate are cocoa butter and milk fat, which has some but not all of the advantages of cocoa butter substitutes like shea. Although similarly cheaper than cocoa butter, milk fat is not easy to emulsify with cocoa butter in the preparation process, and some chocolate connoisseurs refer to it as "barnyard" chocolate due to its distinctive taste (Brenner 1999).
3. The United Kingdom alone was home to both Mars and Cadbury, among the leading chocolate producers in the world ("Trade: EU" 1997).
4. Mali and Burkina Faso, two of the leading suppliers of shea to the world market, in contrast, endorsed the perspective of those EU members advocating for the use of cocoa butter substitutes in European chocolate. Neither Ghana nor Côte d'Ivoire, which also exported shea, however, sought to represent the interests of the shea producers within their country.
5. As a case in point, following the finalization of the EU directive that laid open the definition of chocolate as an object for debate, at the CODEX meeting in November 2000, "Japan stated that there should be no qualitative or quantitative restrictions to the use of vegetable fats in chocolate" (Chocolate directive" 2001: 10; "A clone" 1997).
6. In the late 1990s, cocoa was estimated to account for 24 percent of labor force, 30 percent of export earnings, and one third of land use in Ghana (Safo 1999: 38).
7. Indonesia, competing with the top world producers—Ghana, Malaysia, and Brazil—for the number two position in the world cocoa market, is noticeably absent from the list of COPAL members.
8. Even The Body Shop, one of the few cosmetics firms that exports shea butter directly from West Africa (in this case Ghana), subjects the butter to an elaborate refining process.
9. If we take the examples of Aarhus and Karlshamns, each offers at least a dozen preparations suitable for CBS.
10. A parallel shift in the world coffee market is described by Roseberry (1996) and Talbot (1994).

Chapter 5

1. Van de Walle (1994a: 164) notes a comparable entrepreneurial zeal among some parastatals in Cameroon, which, like the PBC, engage whatever economic opportunities and alliances are available—even those that go against their official mandate—when threatened with extinction.
2. Indeed, in Ghana women may control a greater share of the shea trade than in elsewhere. Reporting on Burkina Faso, Fold suggests that women are involved in the circulation of shea within local and regional markets (2000: 97), while middlemen sell nuts to foreign customers. In northern Ghana in the mid-1990s, however, rural women continued to sell nuts directly to export firms. This may stem from different developmental trajectories of the shea market and the history of state-controlled marketing systems for staple food dominated by male merchants in Burkina Faso (see Saul 1986).

Chapter 6

1. It is a testament to the material poverty of the area that living standards here are among the lowest in the country, with nearly 90 percent of households using wood as a source of fuel and kerosene as a source of light (Ghana Statistical Service 2000a: 51) in homes that are made from mud and roofed with thatch (2000a: 48), 70 percent of which lack toilet facilities (2000a: 51). A further indicator of the region's poverty is that with the lowest consumption levels in the whole country (2000a: 99), annual expenditure, calculated at $166 per person (2000a: 84), is still higher than income levels.

Bibliography

"100% pure shea butter." (1997) Mistrall online. http://www.mistrall.com/soaps/shea.html.

"1999 food additives directory: Oils/fats." (1999) *Chemical Week* June 9, p. 59.

"1999 target." (1998) *Africa Today,* January 28.

Abu, K. (1992) "Report on Busunu village," manuscript, Ghana: GTZ.

"A Clone is being proposed; it would be false chocolate" (1997) Paper for the European Fair Trade Association and the Network of European World Shops. January. FEDIOL online. http://www.eftafairtrade.org/pdf/STUDY-EN.DOC.

Adams, M. (1993) "Women's art as gender strategy," *African Arts* 26.

"African Shea Butter." (1997) African Sheabutter online. http://www.action2000.com/newpg/Clear-Skin.htm.

"African Shea Butter Company." (2002) African Shea Butter Company online. http://www.hala-lessentials.com.

Agrovets (1991) "Prospects for the development of the sheanut and kolanut industries in Ghana." Ghana: United States Agency for International Development.

Alence, R. (1990–1991) "The 1937–38 Gold Coast cocoa crisis: The political economy of commercial stalemate," *African Economic History* 19: 77–104.

"Alerts and Updates: Ghana." (2000) *Business Africa* October 16–31: 6.

Amin, S. (1974) *Accumulation on a World Scale.* New York: Monthly Review Press.

Anderson, B. (1991) *Imagined Communities: The Origins and Spread of Nationalism.* London: Verso.

Andrews, E. (1997) "Chocolate fight: The dark side of politics." *The Denver Post* October 24.

Anyane, S. L. (1963) *Ghana Agriculture.* Accra: Oxford University Press.

Anyemedu, K. (1991) "Export diversification under the economic recovery program," in D. Rothchild, ed., *Ghana: The Political Economy of Recovery.* Boulder, CO: Lynne Reinner.

Appadurai, A. (1986) "Introduction," in A. Appadurai, ed., *The Social Life of Things.* Cambridge, UK: Cambridge University Press.

———. (1990) "Disjuncture and difference in the global cultural economy." *Public Culture* 2, 1: 1–24.

———. (1996) *Modernity at Large* Minneapolis, MN: University of Minnesota Press.

Apter, D. (1972) *Ghana in Transition.* Princeton, NJ: Princeton University Press.

Ardener, S. (1978) *Defining Females; the Nature of Women in Society.* New York: Wiley.

"Are Cocoa Butter Equivalents (CBEs) cheaper than cocoa butter?" (2002) Loders Croklaan online: Confectionary/Q&A/Chocolate formulations. www.croklaan.com/confectionary/en/content.html?tool_id+2andmenu_id=25.

Arhin, K. (1970) "Aspects of the Asanti northern trade in the nineteenth century." *Africa* 40, 4: 17–37.

———. (1979) *West African Traders in Ghana in the 19th and 20th Centuries.* London: Longman.

Aronson, L. (1991) "African women in the visual arts." *Signs* 16, 3: 550–74.

———. (1995) "Women in the arts," in J. Hay and S. Stichter, eds. *African Women South of the Sahara.* Essex, UK: Longman.

"Ashé Natural. Natural hair and body care products." (2002) Ashé Natural online. http://www.ashenatural.com (21 October 2002).

"Aubrey Organics introduces new Swimmer's Shampoo and Swimmer's Conditioner." (1998) *Soap Cosmetics Chemical Specialties* 74, 5: 71.

Austin, R. (1987) *African Economic History.* London: James Currey.

Azarya, V., and Chazan, N. (1987) "Disengagement from the state in Africa: Reflections on the experience of Ghana and Guinea." *Comparative Studies in Society and History* 29, 1: 107–31.

Bailleux, N. (1996) *The Book of Chocolate.* New York: Flammarion.

Balle, J. (2002) "Vedr.: Shea market," personal correspondence (4 August 2002).

Barad, R. (1994) "Privatization of state-owned enterprises: The Togolese experience." in B. Grosh and R. Mukandala, eds., *State-Owned Enterprises in Africa.* Boulder, CO: Lynne Reinner.

Barham, B., Clark, M., Katz, E., and Shurmann, R. (1992) "Nontraditional agricultural exports in Latin America." *Latin American Research Review* 27, 2: 43–82.

Barth, F. (1966) "Models of social organization." *Royal Anthropological Institute Occasional Paper* no. 23. London.

Barth, H. (1890) *Travels and discoveries in North and Central Africa.* Philadelphia, PA: Keystone Publishing Co.

Bates, R. (1981) *Markets and States in Tropical Africa.* Berkeley, CA: University of California Press.

Bauer, P. T. (1954) *West African Trade.* Cambridge, UK: Cambridge University Press.

———. (1975) "British colonial Africa: Economic retrospect and aftermath," in P. Duigan and L. H. Gann, eds., *Colonialism in Africa*, vol. 4. Cambridge, UK: Cambridge University Press.

Bauer, P. T., and Yamey, B. S. (1957) *The Economics of Under-Developed Countries*, Cambridge, UK: Cambridge University Press.

Baumann, H. (1928) "The division of work according to sex in African hoe culture." *Africa* 1: 289–319.

"Beautyguide: Skin." (2000) *Essence* June: 36.

Beckman, B. (1981) "Ghana, 1951–1978: The agrarian basis of the post-colonial state," in J. Heyer, P. Roberts, and G. Williams, eds., *Rural Development in Tropical Africa.* London: MacMillan Press.

Beital, G. (1993) *In Danku the Soup Is Sweeter: Women and Development in Ghana.* Videocassette. New York: Filmmakers Library.

Bekure, Z., Donlan, M., Gordon, Y., and Thomson, J. (1997) *Local to Global: The International Market for Shea Butter.* New York: UNIFEM.

Bening, R. (1973a) "Indigenous concepts of boundaries and significance of administrative stations and boundaries in northern Ghana." *Bulletin of the Ghana Geographical Association* 15: 1–21.

———. (1973b) "The definition of international boundaries of northern Ghana, 1888–1904." *Transactions of the Historical Society of Ghana* 14: 229–61.

———. (1974) "Location of regional and provincial capitals in northern Ghana 1897–1960." *Bulletin of the Ghana Geographical Association* 16: 54–66.

———. (1975a) "Location of district administrative capitals in the northern territories of the Gold Coast." *Bulletin IFAN,* Series B, 37, 3: 646–66.

———. (1975b) "Foundations of the modern native states of northern Ghana." *Universitas* 5: 116–38.

———. (1975c) "Colonial development policy in northern Ghana, 1989–1950." *Bulletin of the Ghana Geographical Association* 17: 65–79.

———. (1977) "Administration and development in northern Ghana, 1898–1931." *Ghana Social Science Journal* 4, 2: 48–76.

———. (1983) "The administrative areas of northern Ghana, 1898–1951." *Bulletin de IFAN,* Series B, 45: 325–56.

———. (1999) *Ghana Regional Boundaries and National Integration.* Accra: Ghana Universities Press.

Benneh, G. (1987) "Land tenure and agroforestry land use systems in Ghana," in J. Raintree, ed., *Land, Trees and Tenure.* Nairobi, Kenya, and Madison, WI: ICRAF and the Land Tenure Center.

Berns, M., and Hudson, B. (1986) *The Essential Gourd: Art and History in Northeastern Nigeria*. Los Angeles: University of California Press.

Berry, S. (1985) *Fathers Work for their Sons*. Berkeley, CA: University of California Press.

———. (1986) "Social science perspectives on food in Africa," in A. Hanson and D. McMillan, eds., *Food in Sub-Saharan Africa*. Boulder, CO: Lynne Reinner.

———. (1988) "Concentration without privatization? Some consequences of changing patterns of rural land control in Africa," in S. Reyna and R. Downs, eds., *Land and Society in Contemporary Africa*. Durham, NH: University of New Hampshire Press.

———. (1989) "Social institutions and access to resources." *Africa* 59, 1: 41–55.

———. (1993a) *No Condition Is Permanent*. Madison, WI: University of Wisconsin Press.

———. (1993b) "Coping with confusion: African farmers' responses to economic instability in the 1970s and 1980s," in T. Callaghy and J. Ravenhill, eds., *Hemmed In: Responses to Africa's Economic Decline*. New York: Columbia University Press.

Bestor, T. (2001) "Supply-Side Sushi: Commodity, Market and the Global City." *American Anthropologist* 103, 1: 76–95.

Blackden, M., and Morris-Hughes, E. (1993) *Paradigm Postponed: Gender and Economic Adjustment in Sub-Saharan Africa*. Technical Note No. 13, World Bank, Human Resources and Poverty Division, Africa Technical Department, Washington, DC.

Bledsoe, C. (1980) *Women and Marriage in Kpelle Society*. Palo Alto, CA: Stanford University Press.

Boahen, A. (1962) "The caravan trade in the 19th century." *Journal of African History* 3, 3: 349–59.

Boateng, E. (1970) *A Geography of Ghana*. Cambridge, UK: Cambridge University Press.

Bohannan, P. (1955) "Some principles of exchange and investment among the Tiv." *American Anthropologist* 57: 60–70.

Bohannan, P., and Bohannan, L. (1968) *Tiv Economy*. Evanston, IL: Northwestern University Press.

Bohannan, P., and Dalton, G. (1963) *Markets in Africa*. Evanston, IL: Northwestern University Press.

Bonnano, A., L. Busch, W. H. Friedland, L. Gouveia, and E. Mingione, eds. (1994) *From Columbus to ConAgra: The Globalization of Agriculture and Food*. Lawrence, KS: University of Kansas.

Bortei-Doku, E., and Aryeetey, E. (1995) "Mobilizing cash for business in Ghana," in S. Ardener and S. Burman, eds., *Money Go-Rounds: The Importance of Rotating Savings and Credit Associations for Women*. Oxford, UK: Berg.

Boserup, E. (1966) *The Conditions of Agricultural Growth*. Chicago: Aldine.

———. (1970) *Women's Role in Economic Development*. London: St. Martin's Press.

Bourdier, J. P. (1996) *Drawn from African Dwellings*. Bloomington, IN: Indiana University Press.

Bourdieu, P. (1977) *Outline of a Theory of Practice*. Cambridge, UK: Cambridge University Press.

Bourret, F. M. (1960) *Ghana: The Road to Independence 1919–1957*. Stanford, CA: Stanford University Press.

Braimah, J. A. and Goody, J. (1967) *Salaga: The Struggle for Power*. London: Longmans.

Brenner, J. (1999) *The Emperors of Chocolate: Inside the Secret World of Hershey and Mars*. New York: Random House.

Brown, R. (1973) "Anthropology and colonial rule: The case of Godfrey Wilson and the Rhodes-Livingston Institute of northern Rhodesia," in T. Asad, ed., *Anthropology and the Colonial Encounter*. London: Ithaca Press.

Brown, R. (1998) "The natural way in cosmetics and skin care." *Chemical Market Reporter* 254, 2: FR8–FR9.

"Browned off on chocolate." (2000) *Daily Telegraph*, (UK) November 20.

Brozan, N. (1974) "Beating the high cost of cocoa beans." *New York Times*. July 22: 24.

Bruce, J. (1988) "Indigenous land tenure and land concentration," in S. Reyna and R. Downs, eds., *Land and Society in Contemporary Africa*. Durham, NH: University of New Hampshire Press.

Bryceson, D. F., ed. (1995) *Women Wielding the Hoe*. Oxford, UK: Berg.

Brydon, L., and Legge, K. (1995) "Gender and adjustment: Pictures from Ghana," in G. Emeagwali, ed., *Women Pay the Price: Structural Adjustment in Africa and the Caribbean*. Trenton, NJ: Africa World Press.

———. (1996) *Adjusting Society: The World Bank, the IMF and Ghana*. London: I. B. Tauris Publishers.

Burke, T. (1996) *Lifebuoy Men and Lux Women: Commodification, Consumption and Cleanliness in Modern Zimbabwe*. Durham, NC: Duke University Press.

Burton M and White, D. (1984) "Sexual Division of Labor in Agriculture," *American Anthropologist* 86,3:568–583.

"Business solutions to rural poverty." (2002) TechnoServe online. http://www.technoserve.org/home.html.

Callaghy, T. (1990) "Lost between state and market: The politics of economic adjustment in Ghana, Zambia and Nigeria," in J. Nelson, ed., *Economic Crisis and Policy Choice*. Princeton, NJ: Princeton University Press.

Callaghy, T., and Ravenhill, J., eds. (1993) *Hemmed In: Responses to Africa's Economic Decline*. New York: Columbia University Press.

Cardinall, A. (1920) *The Natives of the Northern Territories of the Gold Coast*. New York: E. P. Dutton.

———. (1927) *In Asanti and Beyond*. London: Seeley and Company.

"Cargill invests $50 m in Ivorian cocoa." (1999) *Africa Analysis* January 22.

Carney, J. (1994) "Contracting a food staple in the Gambia," in P. Little and M. Watts, eds., *Living under Contract*. Madison, WI: University of Wisconsin Press.

Carr, M., Chen, M., and Tate, J. (2000) "Globalization and homebased workers." *Feminist Economics* 6, 3: 123–42.

"Catalogue" (1995) The Body Shop.

"Catalogue" (n.d.a) The Body Shop.

"Catalogue" (n.d.b) The Body Shop.

"Catalogue" (n.d.c) L'Occitane.

Chalfin, B. (1996) "Market reforms and the state: The case of shea in Ghana." *Journal of Modern African Studies* 34, 3: 421–40.

———. (1997) "Centering the margin: The border zone economies of northeast Ghana." Paper presented at the African Studies Association annual meetings, Columbus, Ohio, November 13–16.

———. (1998) "Beauty and the beast: Natural cosmetics and the contradictions of late capitalism." Paper presented at the American Anthropological Association annual meeting, December, Philadelphia.

———. (2001) "Border zone trade and the economic boundaries of the state in north-east Ghana." *Africa* 71, 2: 197–224.

Chambas, M. (1980) "The politics of agricultural and rural development in the upper region of Ghana: Implications of technocratic ideology and non-participatory development." Ph.D. dissertation, Cornell University.

Chayanov, A. V. (1986) *The Theory of Peasant Economy*. Madison: University of Wisconsin.

Chazan, N. (1983) *An Anatomy of Ghanaian Politics: Managing Political Recession, 1969–1972*. Boulder, CO: Westview Press.

———. (1991) "The political transformation of Ghana under the PNDC," in D. Rothchild, ed., *Ghana: the Political Economy of Recovery* Boulder, CO: Lynne Rienner.

"Chocolate commission biding time on harmonisation of rules." (1995) *Agri Service International Newsletter* March 31, no. 415.

"Chocolate: COPAL fears introduction of 5% vegetable-fat rule in EU." (1993) *European Environment* December 14, no. 422.

"Chocolate directive: Background information." (2001) FEDIOL online. http://www.fediol.be/Subjects/CHOCOLATE.pdf.

"Chocolate directive: Cocoa producers critical of commission's position." (1998) *Agri-Industry Europe* May 29, no. 22.

"Chocolate: Draft directive believed ready for commission debate." (1995) *European Environment* February 7, no. 448.

"Chocolate: European parliament committee endorses minister's common position." (2000) *European Report* February 26, no. 2478.

"Chocolate: European parliament committee rejects rapporteur's opinion." (1997) *European Report* October 11, no. 2258.

"Chocolate-maker in hot water." (1997) *Daily News* (New York), December 7.

"Chocolate: Yet more delays for draft EU directive." (1996) *European Report* March 1, no. 2112.

Clapp, Jennifer. (1997) *Adjustment and Agriculture in Africa: Farmers, the State and the World Bank in Guinea*. New York: St. Martin's Press.

"Clarins targets dry skin." (1997) *Inside Cosmetics* January: 7.

Clark, G., ed. (1989) *Traders versus the State: Anthropological Approaches to Unofficial Economies.* Boulder, CO: Westview.

———. (1994) *Onions Are My Husband.* Chicago: University of Chicago Press.

———. (1999) "Mothering, work, and gender in urban Asante ideology and practice." *American Anthropologist* 101, 4.

Clark, G., and Manuh, T. (1991) "Women traders in Ghana and the structural adjustment program," in C. Gladwin, ed., *Structural Adjustment and African Women Farmers.* Gainesville: University of Florida.

Cleveland, D. (1980) "The Kusasi of Ghana," in S. Reyna, ed. *Sahelian Social Development.* Abidjan: Regional Economic Development Services Office, West Africa, USAID.

———. (1991) "Migration in West Africa: A savanna village perspective." *Africa* 61, 2: 222–45.

"Cocoa agreement." (1979) *Economist* January 27.

"Cocoa and coffee." (1980) *Economist* January 26.

"Cocoa: Belgium creates 'pure chocolate' quality label." (2000) *Africa News* October 28.

Cocoa Board (n.d.) *Educational Guide for Sheanut Farmers.* Ghana, 1980s.

"Cocoa/chocolate: CODEX committee postpones standards debate until 1998." (1996) *Agri Service International Newsletter* October 7, no. 448.

"Cocoa/chocolate producer states call for end to EU's vegetable fat derogation" (1995) *Agri Service International Newsletter* April, no. 416.

"Cocoa: CPA members demand more information on EU legislative plans." (1994) *Agri Service International Newsletter* November 18, no. 406.

"Cocoa: ICCO debates EU chocolate making rules and output targets." (1995) *Agri Service International Newsletter* December, 21 no. 431.

"Cocoa lobby to protest EU use of substitutes." (1995) *Journal of Commerce* April 3.

"Cocoa: Many obstacles to producer's cartel." (1980) *Latin America Commodities Report* April 25.

"Cocoa: Producers and consumers meet in Geneva." (1993) *Agri Service International Newsletter* June 18, sec. no. 375.

"Cocoa producers in new attack on chocolate directive." (1998) *European Report* February 21, no. 2293.

"Cocoa producers to coordinate bid to maintain high price." (1993) *Agence Press France* November 1.

Coe, S. (1996) *The True History of Chocolate.* New York: Thames and Hudson.

Cohen, A. (1969) *Custom and Politics in Urban Africa.* London: Routledge and Kegan Paul.

Collier, P. (1993) "Africa and the study of economics," in R. Bates, V. Y. Mudimbe, and J. O'Barr, eds., *Africa and the Disciplines: The Contributions of Research in Africa to the Social Sciences and Humanities* Chicago: University of Chicago Press.

Collins, J. (2000) "Tracing social relations in commodity chains," in A. Haugerud, P. Stone and P. Little, eds., *Commodities and Globalization: Anthropological Perspectives.* Lanham, MD: Rowan and Littlefield.

Collins, W. (1960) "Extension work in Kusasi, 1932–59." *Ghana Farmer* 4, 2: 64–71.

"Commodity Price Index." (1999a) *Economist* April 3.

———. (1999b) *Economist* June 26.

———. (1999c) *Economist* December 18.

———. (2000) *Economist* December 23.

Conlin, J. (1994) "Survival of the fittest." *Working Woman* February: 28.

Cook, I. (1994) "New fruits and vanity: Symbolic production in the global food economy," in A. Bonnano, L. Busch, W. H. Friedland, L. Gouveia, and E. Mingione, eds., *From Columbus to ConAgra: The Globalization of Agriculture and Food.* Lawrence, KS: University of Kansas.

Cooper, F. (1980) "Africa and the world economy." *African Studies Review* 24, 2/3: 1–86.

Cooper, F., and Stoller, A.L. (1997) "Between metropole and colony: Rethinking a research agenda," in F. Cooper and A. L. Stoller, eds., *Tensions of Empire: Colonial Cultures in a Bourgeois World.* Berkeley, CA: University of California.

Cowell, A. (2001) "Body Shop Talks." *New York Times* October 3.

"Currency trends: Ghana; key forecasts." (2000) *Business Africa* May 16–31: 7.

"Currency trends: Hedging against cedi devaluation." (2000) *Business Africa* July 16–31: 7.

Curtin, P. (1971) "Pre-colonial trading networks and traders: The Diahanke," in C. Meillassoux, ed., *The Development of Indigenous Trade and Markets in West Africa.* Oxford, UK: Oxford University Press.

————. (1975) *Economic Change in Precolonial Africa: Senegambia in the Era of the Slave Trade.* Madison, WI: University of Wisconsin.

Daaku, K. (1971) "Trade and trading patterns of the Akan in the 17th and 18th centuries," in C. Meillassoux, ed., *The Development of Indigenous Trade and Markets in West Africa.* Oxford, UK: Oxford University Press.

Dalzeil, J. (1937) *The Useful Plants of West Tropical Africa.* Great Britain: Watmoughs.

Davidson, A. (1996) "Anita Roddick." *Management Today* March: 42–6.

Davison, J. (1995) "Must women work together? Development and agency assumptions versus changing relations of production in southern Malawi households," in D. F. Bryceson, ed., *Women Wielding the Hoe.* Oxford, UK: Berg.

————, ed. (1988) *Agriculture, Women, and Land: The African Experience.* Boulder, CO: Westview Press.

De Vries, J. (1976) *Economy of Europe in an Age of Crisis, 1600–1750,* Cambridge: Cambridge University Press.

De Gregori, T. (1969) *Technology and Economic Development of the Tropical Frontier.* Cleveland, OH: Case Western Reserve.

Denham, M., and Clapperton, C. (1926) *Narrative of Travels and Discoveries in North and Central Africa: 1822–24,* vol. 2. London: John Murray.

Der, B. G. (1973) "Colonial land policy in the northern territories of the Gold Coast, 1900–1957." *Universitas* (Legon) 4, 2: 127–42.

————. (1987) "Agricultural policy in northern Ghana during the colonial era." *Universitas* (Legon) 8,1: 3–18.

Dettwyler, K. (1994) *Dancing Skeletons: Life and Death in West Africa.* Prospect Heights, IL: Waveland Press.

Devereux, S. (1993a) "Observers are worried," in S. Devereux and J. Hoddinott, eds., *Fieldwork in Developing Countries.* Boulder, CO: Lynne Rienner.

Devereux, S., and Hoddinott, J., eds. (1993b) *Fieldwork in Developing Countries.* Boulder, CO: Lynne Rienner.

Dickson, K. (1968) "Background to the problems of economic development in northern Ghana." *Annals of the Association of American Geographers* 58, 4: 689–96.

"Directive 74/241/EEC of the European Parliament and of the Council." (1973) *Official Journal of the European Communities* July 24, L 228, 16.

"Directive 2000/36/EC of the European Parliament and of the Council of 23 June 2000 relating to cocoa and chocolate products intended for human consumption." (2000) *Official Journal of the European Communities* August 3, L 197, 19; 20; 24–5.

Division of Agriculture (1962) "Crops other than cocoa and the diseases which affect them," in J. Wills, ed., *Agriculture and Land Use in Ghana.* Accra, Ghana: Oxford University Press for Ghana Ministry of Food and Agriculture.

"Do Cocoa Butter Equivalents (CBEs) affect the quality of chocolate?" (2002) Loders Croklaan online: Confectionary/Q&A/Chocolate formulations. www.croklaan.com/confectionary/en/content.html?tool_id+2andmenu_id=25.

Donham, D. (1990) *History, Power, Ideology.* Cambridge, UK: Cambridge University Press.

Douglas, M. (1967) "Primitive rationing: A study in controlled exchange." in R. Firth, ed., *Themes in Economic Anthropology.* London: Tavistock.

Drucker-Brown, S. (1988–1989) "Local wars in northern Ghana." *Cambridge Studies in Anthropology* 13: 86–106.

Dumett, R. (1971) "The rubber trade of the Gold Coast and Asante in the 19th century: African innovation and market responsiveness." *Journal of African History* 12, 1: 79–101.

Duncan, J. (1847) *Travels in Western Africa in 1845 and 1846.* London: Richard Bentley.

Dupre, G., and Rey, P. P. (1978) "Reflections on the relevance of a theory of the history of exchange," in D. Seddon, ed., *Relations of Production.* London: Frank Cass.

Dupuis, J. (1966) [1824] *Journal of a Residence in Ashantee.* London: Cass.

"Ébène: A line of 100% natural shea butter based products," (2002) Ébène online. http://www.ebenenaturals.com.

Edholm, F., Harris, O., and Young, K. (1977) "Conceptualizing women." *Critique of Anthropology* 3, 9–10: 101–30.

"Editors' picks: Spend small change or big bucks for these treats," (2001) *Essence* October: 44.

Elson, D. (1995) "Male bias in macro-economics: The case of structural adjustment," in D. Elson, ed., *Male Bias in the Development Process*. Manchester, UK: Manchester University Press.

Epstein, A. L. (1958) *Politics in an Urban African Community*. Manchester, UK: Manchester University Press.

"E. T. introduces new line of shea butter." (2002) *Drug Store News* June 17: 7.

"Ethnic hair care manufacturer Black & Beautiful." (2002) *Happi-Household and Personal Products Industry* 39, 3: 32.

Etienne, M. (1980) "Women and men, cloth and colonization: The transformation of production-distribution relations among the Baule (Ivory Coast)," in M. Etienne and E. Leacock, eds., *Women and Colonization*. New York: Praeger.

"EU/ACP: EU chocolate deliberations leave sour taste in ACP mouths." (1995) *European Report* November 4, no. 2081.

Fage, J. D. (1963) "Reflections on the early history of the Mossi-Dagomba group of states," in J. Vansina, R. Mauny, and L.V. Thomas, eds., *The Historian in Tropical Africa*. London: Oxford University Press.

Falconer, Julia. (1991) *Household Food Security and Forestry*. Rome: FAO.

"FEDIOL: EC Seed Crushers and Oil Processors Federation," (n.d.) Online. http://www.fediol.be/Subjects/CHOCOLATE.pdf.

Ferguson, G. E. (1974) *The Papers of George Ekem Ferguson*, ed. K. Arhin. African Social Research Documents, vol. 7. Leiden: Afrika-Studiecentrum.

Ferguson, J. (1988) "Cultural exchange: New developments in the anthropology of commodities," review of *The Social Life of Things*, ed. A. Appadurai. *Cultural Anthropology* 1, 3: 488–513.

Fieldhouse, D. K. (1978) *Unilever Overseas: The Anatomy of a Multinational*. Stanford, CA: Hoover Institution Press.

"Field report on shea nut industry." (1994) TechnoServe Office, Accra, Ghana.

Flint, J. E. (1976) "Economic change in West Africa in the nineteenth century," in J. F. A. Ajayi and M. Crowder, eds., *History of West Africa*. New York: Columbia University Press.

Fold, N. (2000) "A matter of good taste? Quality and the construction of standards for chocolate products in the European Union." *Cahiers d'Economie et Sociologie Rurales* 55/56: 92–110.

Food and Agriculture Organization (FAO) (1981) *Forest Resources of Tropical Africa Part II: Country Briefs*. Rome: FAO.

———. (1988) "Traditional food plants." *Food and Nutrition Paper* 42: 125–9.

"Foodstuffs: Ivory Coast lobbies against chocolate directive." (1997) *European Report* October 8, no. 2557.

"Foodstuffs: MEPS prepare for animated first reading on chocolate directive." (1996) *European Report* October 2, no. 2162.

"Foodstuffs: MEPS vote to restrict the scope for making non-traditional chocolate." (1997) *European Report* October 25, no. 2262.

"Foodstuffs: New draft compromise on chocolate directive." (1999) *European Report* May 13, no. 2407.

Forde, D. (1934) *Habitat, Economy and Society*. London: Methuen.

———. (1956) *Efik Traders of Old Calabar*. London. Oxford University Press.

Forde, D., and Scott, R. (1946) *The Native Economies of Nigeria*. London: H.M. Stationary Office.

Fortes, M. (1936) "Culture contact as a dynamic process." *Africa* 9. 1: 24–55.

———. (1945) *The Dynamics of Clanship among the Tallensi*. London: Oxford University Press.

———. (1949) *The Web of Kinship among the Tallensi*. London: Oxford University Press.

———. (1971) "Some aspects of migration and mobility in Ghana." *Journal of Asian and African Studies* 6, 1: 1–20.

Fortes, M., and Fortes, S. (1936) "Food in the domestic economy of the Tallensi." *Africa* 9, 2: 237–76.

Foucault, M. (1980) *Power/Knowledge*. New York: Pantheon.

———. (1984) *The Foucault Reader*, ed. P. Rabinow. New York: Pantheon.

Fox, C. (1986) "Undomesticated plants as food," in A. Hansen and D. McMillan, eds., *Food in Sub-Saharan Africa*. Boulder, CO: Lynne Reinner.

Frankel, C. (1998) "Compassion and business." *Yes: A Journal of Positive Futures* 1998: 50–3.

Freund, W. (1985) "Modes of production debates in African Studies." *Canadian Journal of African Studies* 19, 1.

Friedland, W. (1994) "The new globalization: The case of fresh produce," in A. Bonnano, L. Busch, W. H. Friedland, L. Gouveia, and E. Mingione, eds., *From Columbus to ConAgra: The Globalization of Agriculture and Food*. Lawrence, KS: University of Kansas.

"Full-bodied butters." (2000) Catalogue no. 18227. The Body Shop.

Gadsby, P. (2002) "Endangered chocolate." *Discover Magazine* 23, 8.

Gain, B. (1996) "Natural products gain favor." *Chemical Week* December 11, 158, 48: 35–7.

Gaye, M. (1999) "Africa '99: Globalisation in Africa after the failure of Seattle." *Africa News* December 28.

Geertz, C. (1983) *Local Knowledge: Further Essays in Interpretive Anthropology*. New York: Basic Books.

Gell, A. (1982) "The market wheel: Symbolic aspects of an Indian tribal market." *Man* 17: 470–91.

Gereffi, G., and Korzeniewicz, M., eds. (1994) *Commodity Chains and Global Capitalism*. Westport, CT: Greenwood.

Geschiere, P. (1985) "Applications of the lineage mode of production in African Studies." *Canadian Journal of African Studies* 19, 1.

"Ghana." (2000) *Business Africa* October 16–31, 9, 19: 6–7.

"Ghana backs withdrawal of 250,000 tons of cocoa." (2000) *Africa News* August 31.

"Ghana: Economic conditions." (1992) *Economist* August 22 324, 7773: 34.

"Ghana: Economic structure." (1996) *EIU Country Profile, Ghana* 9.

"Ghana: Economic structure." (2001) *EIU Country Profile, Ghana* 19.

"Ghana: Encourage use of shea butter—gov't told." (2001) *Africa News* November 8.

Ghana Export Promotion Council. (1998) Personal communication, Accra, Ghana.

"Ghana is one of West Africa's star performers." (1998) *Market Africa Mid-East* April.

Ghana Museums and Monuments. (1970) *National Musuem of Ghana Handbook*. Accra: Ghana Publishing Company.

Ghana Statistical Service. (1998) *Quarterly Digest of Statistics*. Accra, March 16, 1.

———. (2000a) "Ghana living standards survey, report of the fourth round (GLSS4)." *Quarterly Digest of Statistics*. Accra, October.

———. (2000b) "Poverty trends in Ghana in the 1990s." *Quarterly Digest of Statistics*. Accra, October.

"Ghana: Women want more control." (1986) *West Africa* February 10: 321.

Giddens, A. (1979) *Central Problems in Social Theory*. Berkeley, CA: University of California Press.

Gladwin, C. (1991) "Introduction," in C. Gladwin, ed., *Structural Adjustment and African Women Farmers*. Gainesville, FL: University of Florida.

Gluckman, M. (1961) "Anthropological problems arising from the African industrial revolution," in A. Southall, ed., *Social Change in Modern Africa*. London: Oxford University Press for the International African Institute.

Goheen, M. (1991) "The ideology and political economy of gender: Women and land in Nso, Cameroon," in C. Gladwin, ed., *Structural Adjustment and African Women Farmers*. Gainesville, FL: University of Florida.

Goldfrank, W. (1994) "Fresh demand: The consumption of Chilean produce in the United States," in G. Gereffi and M. Korzeniewicz, eds., *Commodity Chains and Global Capitalism*. Westport, CT: Greenwood.

Gonza, S. (1996) "Uganda northern women generate income from wild nut." *Africa News* June.

"Good but not at election time." (2002) *Economist* April 27, 363, 8270.

Goodman, D., and Watts, M., eds. (1997) *Globalizing Food: Agrarian Questions and Global Restructuring*. London and New York: Routledge.

Goody, E. (1982) *Parenthood and Social Reproduction: Fostering and Occupational Roles in West Africa*. Cambridge, UK: Cambridge University Press.

Goody, J., ed. (1958) *The Developmental Cycle in Domestic Groups*. Cambridge, UK: Cambridge University Press.

———. (1967) *The Social Organization of the Lowiili*. London: Oxford University Press for the International African Institute.

———. (1980) "Rice-burning and the green revolution in northern Ghana." *Journal of Development Studies* 16, 2: 136–55.

Gordon, J. (1970) "State farms in Ghana: The political deformation of agricultural development," in A. H. Bunting, ed., *Change in Agriculture*. New York: Praeger.

Gottlieb, A. (2000) "Luring your child into this life: A Beng path for infant care," in J. DeLoache and A. Gottlieb, eds., *A World of Babies*. Cambridge, UK: Cambridge University Press.

Green, M. (1941) *Land Tenure in an Ibo Village.* Monographs in Social Anthropology, no. 6. London: London School of Economics.

Green, P. (1999) "Spiritual cosmetics: No kidding." *New York Times* January 11: B7.

Green, R. (1994) "The structural adjustment of structural adjustment: Sub-Saharan Africa 1980–1993." *Bulletin of Institute of Development Studies* (University of Sussex) 25, 3.

Grier, B. (1981) "Underdevelopment, modes of production, and the state in colonial Ghana." *African Studies Review* 24, 1: 21–47.

Grishow, J. (1997) "Corruptions of development: Anthropology and Fabian colonialism in the northern territories of the Gold Coast, 1929–1957." Paper presented at the African Studies Association annual meetings, Columbus, Ohio, November 13–16.

Grosh, B., and Mukandala, R. (1994) "Tying it all together: What do we know," in B. Grosh and R. Mukandala, eds., *State-Owned Enterprises in Africa.* Boulder, CO: Lynne Reinner.

Guyer, J. (1980) "Household and community in African Studies." *African Studies Review* 24, 2/3: 87–137.

———. (1984). *Family and Farm in Southern Cameroon.* Boston University African Research Series, no. 15.

———. (1986) "Intra-household processes and farming systems research: Perspectives from anthropology," in J. Moock, ed., *Understanding Africa's Rural Households and Farming Systems.* Boulder, CO: Westview Press.

———. (1988) "The multiplication of labor." *Current Anthropology* 29, 2: 247–72.

———. (1989) "Local and colonial currencies." Paper presented at the Boston University African Studies Center Workshop on African Material Culture, Boston, MA.

———. (1991) "Female farming in anthropology and African history," in M. di Leonardo, ed., *Gender at the Cross-Roads of Knowledge.* Berkeley, CA: University of California.

———. (1995) "Women's farming and present ethnography: Perspectives on a Nigerian restudy," in D. F. Bryceson, ed., *Women Wielding the Hoe.* Oxford, UK: Berg.

———. (1997) *An African Niche Economy: Farming to Feed Ibadan 1968–1988,* London: Edinburgh University Press.

Guyer, J., and Idowu, O. (1991) "Women's agricultural work in a multimodal rural economy," in C. Gladwin, ed., *Structural Adjustment and African Women Farmers.* Gainesville, FL: University of Florida Press.

Guyer, J., and Peters, P. (1987) "Conceptualizing the household." *Development and Change* 18: 197–214.

Gyimah-Boadi, E. (1991) "State enterprise divestiture: Recent Ghanaian experience," in D. Rothchild, ed., *Ghana: The Political Economy of Recovery.* Boulder, CO: Lynne Reinner.

Hafkin, N., and Bay, E., eds. (1976) *Women in Africa: Studies in Social and Economic Change.* Stanford, CA: Stanford University Press.

Hailey, W. (1952) *Native Administration in the British African Colonies.* Liechtenstein: Kraus.

"Hair care gets natural accent." (1999) *MMR* 6, 13: 97.

Halperin, R. (1994) *Cultural Economies Past and Present.* Austin, TX: University of Texas.

"Handy work" (2001) *Soap, Perfumery and Cosmetics* 74, 4: 13.

Hannerz, U. (1987) "The world in creolization." *Africa* 57, 4: 546–59.

———. (1989) "Notes on the global ecumene." *Public Culture* 1, 2 (Spring): 66–75.

Hardt, M., and Negri, A. (2000) *Empire.* Cambridge, MA: Harvard University Press.

Hargreaves, J. (1966) *Prelude to the Partition of West Africa.* London: Macmillan.

Harsch, E. (2001) "Making trade work for poor women: Villagers in Burkina Faso discover an opening in the global market." *Africa Recovery* 15, 4: 6.

Hart, K. (1971) "Migration and tribal identity among the Frafra of Ghana." *Journal of Asian and African Studies* 6, 1: 21–36.

———. (1973) "Informal economic opportunities and urban employment in Ghana." *Journal of Modern African Studies* 11,1: 61–89.

———. (1974) "Migrations and opportunity structure," in S. Amin, ed., *Modern Migrations in Western Africa.* London: Oxford University Press for the International African Institute.

———. (1975) "Swindler or public benefactor: The entrepreneur and his community," in J. Goody, ed., *Changing Social Structures in Ghana.* Cambridge, UK: Cambridge University Press.

———. (1978) "The economic basis of Tallensi social history in the early twentieth century," in G. Dalton, ed., *Research in Economic Anthropology.* Greenwich, CT: JAI Press.

————. (1982a) *The Political Economy of West African Agriculture.* Cambridge, UK: Cambridge University Press.

————. (1982b) "On commoditization," in E. Goody, ed., *From Craft to Industry.* Cambridge. UK: Cambridge University Press.

————. (1986) "Heads or tails? Two sides of the coin." *Man* 21, 4: 637–56.

Haugerud, A. (1995) *The Culture of Politics in Modern Kenya.* Cambridge, UK: Cambridge University Press.

Heathcote, B. (2000) "Cocoa: Ghana's double game." *New African* 390: 40.

Hellman, E. (1948) *Rooiyard: A Sociological Study of an Urban Slum Yard.* Rhodes-Livingston Paper, no. 13. Capetown, South Africa: Oxford University Press.

Herbst, J. (1993) *The Politics of Reform in Ghana, 1982–1991.* Berkeley, CA: University of California.

Hill, P. (1963) *The Migrant Cocoa Farmers of Southern Ghana: A Study in Rural Capitalism.* Cambridge, UK: Cambridge University Press.

————. (1970a) *The Occupations of Migrants in Ghana.* Anthropological Papers, no. 42, University of Michigan Museum of Anthropology. Ann Arbor, MI: The University of Michigan Press.

————. (1970b) *Studies in Rural Capitalism in West Africa.* Cambridge, UK: Cambridge University Press.

Hilton, T. E. (1962) "Notes on the history of the Kusasi." *Transactions of the Historical Society of Ghana* 6: 79–86.

————. (1968) "Population growth and distribution in the Upper Region of Ghana," in J. C. Caldwell and C. Okonjo, eds., *The Population of Tropical Africa.* Fist African Population Conference, 1966, University of Ibadan. New York: Columbia University Press.

Hogendorn, J. (1975) "Economic initiative and African cash-farming: Pre-colonial origins and early colonial developments," in P. Duigan and L. H. Gann, eds., *Colonialism in Africa 1870–1960,* vol. 4. Cambridge, UK: Cambridge University Press.

————. (1976) "The vent-for-surplus model and African cash agriculture to 1914." *Savanna* 5: 15–28.

————. (1978) *Nigerian Groundnut Exports: Origins and Early Development.* London: Oxford University Press.

Holden, J. J. (1965) "The Zaberima conquest of North-West Ghana." *Transactions of the Historical Society of Ghana* 1, 3: 6–86.

Hopkins, A. (1973) *An Economic History of West Africa.* New York: Columbia University.

Howard, R. (1978) *Colonialism and Underdevelopment in Ghana.* New York: Africana Publishing Company.

Huq, M. M. (1989) *The Economy of Ghana: The First Twenty-Five Years since Independence.* New York: St. Martin's Press.

Hutchful, E. (1985) "IMF adjustment policies in Ghana since 1966." *Africa Development* 10, 1/2.

————. (1989) "From 'revolution' to monetarism in Ghana," in B. Campbell and J. Loxley, eds., *Structural Adjustment in Africa.* London: MacMillan.

Hyman, E. (1991) "A comparison of labor-saving technologies for processing shea nut butter in Mali." *World Development* 19, 9: 1247–68.

Iliasu, A. A. (1975) "The establishment of British administration in Mamprugu (Mamprusi), 1898–1937." *Transactions of the Historical Society of Ghana* 16: 1–28.

Imperial Institute. (1912a) "Shea nuts." *Bulletin of the Imperial Institute* 10: 132.

————. (1912b) "Shea nuts and shea butter." *Bulletin of the Imperial Institute* 10: 281–92.

————. (1927) "Shea butter." *Bulletin of the Imperial Institute* 25: 163.

————. (1930) "Shea nuts from Nigeria—I." *Bulletin of the Imperial Institute* 28: 123–31.

————. (1931a) "Shea nuts: Uganda." *Bulletin of the Imperial Institute* 29: 474–75.

————. (1931b) "Shea nuts from Nigeria—II." *Bulletin of the Imperial Institute* 29: 407–21.

————. (1932) "Shea nuts from the Gold Coast." *Bulletin of the Imperial Institute* 30: 282-93.

————. (1935) "Some African oil seeds." *Bulletin of the Imperial Institute* 33: 289–93.

Irvine, F. (1961) *Woody Plants of Ghana: With Special Reference to Their Uses.* London: Oxford University Press.

Issacman, A., and Roberts, R. (1995) "Cotton, colonialism and social history in sub-Saharan Africa," in A. Issacman and R. Roberts, eds., *Cotton, Colonialism and Social History in Sub-Saharan Africa.* Portsmouth, UK: Heinemann.

Jaffee, S. (1994) "Contract farming in the shadow of competitive markets," in P. Little and M. Watts, eds., *Living under Contract: Contract Farming and Agrarian Transformation in Sub-Saharan Africa.* Madison, WI: University of Wisconsin.

Jaffee, S., and Morton, J., eds. (1995) *Marketing Africa's High Value Foods: Comparative Experiences of an Emergent Private Sector.* Dubuque, IA: Kendall/Hunt for World Bank.

"J. F. Lazartigue introduces Nature L, new 7-product hair care line, in US." (1998) *Soap Cosmetics Chemical Specialties* 74, 3: 67.

Johnson, M. (1970) "The cowrie currencies of West Africa." *Journal of African History* 11: 17–49; 331–53.

Joseph, R. (1999) "The reconfiguration of power in late twentieth-century Africa," in R. Joseph, ed., *State, Conflict and Deomocracy in Africa.* Boulder, CO: Lynne Rienner.

Kaberry, P. (1952) *Women of the Grassfields: A Study of the Economic Position of Women in Bamenda, British Cameroons.* London: Colonial Research Publications no. 14. London: H.M. Stationary Office.

Kahn, A. "Fat chance it's real chocolate." (1995) *The Herald* (Glasgow) October 17: 16.

"Karlshamns," (1997) *Inside Cosmetics* March: 39.

Kassardjian, P. (1992) "Sheanut speech of Mr. P. Kassardjian—Accra." February.

———. (2002) "Ghana shea nut industry." Personal correspondence.

Kay, G. B. (1972) *The Political Economy of Colonialism in Ghana.* Cambridge, UK: Cambridge University Press.

Killick, T. (1978) *Development Economics in Action.* New York: St. Martin's Press.

Kimble, D. (1963) *A Potitical History of Ghana: 1850–1928.* Oxford, UK: Clarendon Press.

Kochan, N. (1997) "Anita Roddick: Soap and social action." *Worldbusiness* 3, 1: 46–7.

Konigs, P. (1986) *The State and Rural Class Formation in Ghana: A Comparative Analysis.* London: Routledge and Kegan Paul.

Kopytoff, I. (1986) *The African Frontier: The Reproduction of Traditional African Societies.* Bloomington, IN: Indiana University Press.

Krasner, S. D. (1974) "Oil is the exception." *Foreign Policy* 14, Spring.

Kraus, J. (1991) "The Political Economy of Stabilization and Structural Adjustment in Ghana," in D. Rothchild, ed., *Ghana: The Political Economy of Recovery.* Boulder, CO: Lynne Reinner.

Ladoucer, P. (1979) *Chiefs and Politicians: The Politics of Regionalism in Northern Ghana.* London: Longmans.

"La Source moisturising soap with shea butter." (2002) Crabtree and Evelyn online. http://store.crabtree-evelyn.com/las314420.html.

Leach, A., Mcardle, T. F., Banya W. A. S., Krubally, O., Greenwood A. M., Rands, C., Adegbola, R., De Francisco, A., and Greenwood, B. M. (1999) "Neonatal mortality in a rural area of The Gambia." *Annals of Tropical Paediatrics: International Child Health* March, 19, 1.

Lele, U. (1991) "Women, structural adjustment, and transformation: Some lessons and questions from the African experience," in C. Gladwin, ed., *Structural Adjustment and African Women Farmers.* Gainesville, FL: University of Florida.

Lewicki, T. (1974) *West African Food in the Middle Ages.* Cambridge, UK: Cambridge University Press.

"Lipids for care." (2002) Karlshamns online. http://www.karlshamns.com/other/oilsandfats/lipids.asp.

Lipp, M., and Anklam, E. (1998) "Review of cocoa butter and alternative fats for use in chocolate—part A: Compositional data." *Food Chemistry* 62, 1: 73–97.

Little, P., and Brokensha, D. (1987) "Local institutions, tenure and resource management in East Africa," in D. Anderson and R. Grove, eds., *Conservation in Africa: People, Policies, and Practices.* Cambridge, UK: Cambridge University Press.

Little, P., and Dolan, C. (2000) "What it means to be restructured," in A. Haugerud, P. Stone, and P. Little, eds., *Commodities and Globalization: Anthropological Perspectives.* Lanham, MD: Rowan and Littlefield.

Little, P., and Watts, M., eds. (1994) *Living under Contract: Contract Farming and Agrarian Transformation in Sub-Saharan Africa.* Madison, WI: University of Wisconsin.

Lonsdale, J., and Berman, B. (1979) "Coping with the contradictions: The development of the colonial state in Kenya." *Journal of African History* 20: 487–506.

Lovejoy, P. (1980) *Caravans of Kola: The Hausa Kola Trade, 1700–1900.* Zaria, Nigeria: Ahmadu Bello University Press.

———. (1986) *Salt of the Desert Sun.* Cambridge, UK: Cambridge University Press.

Lugard, F. (1922) *The Dual Mandate in British Tropical Africa.* London: Blackwood.

"Lush hour: Consume shoptalk." (2002) *Time Out* July 17: 31.

Lynn, C. W. (1937) *Agriculture in North Mamprusi.* Bulletin No. 34. Accra: Gold Coast Department of Agriculture.

MacGaffey, J. (1987) *Entrepreneurs and Parasites*. Cambridge, UK: Cambridge University Press.

Mackintosh, M. (1989) *Gender, Class and Rural Transition: Agribusiness and the Food Crisis in Senegal*. London: Zed.

"Magic of the Shea Tree." (1996) *L'Occitane*.

"Magic Shea Tree." (1992) *L'Occitane*.

Malcolm, C. (1994) "In search of rare essences for green-minded consumers." *Drug and Cosmetic Industry* 154, 5: 24–6.

Malcolm, S., and Soforawa, E. (1969) "Antimicrobial activities of selected Nigerian folk remedies and their constituent plants." *Lloydia* 32: 512–17.

Malinowski, B. (1922) *Argonauts of the Western Pacific*. London: Routledge.

Maliyamkono, T. L., and Bagachwa, M. S. D. (1990) *The Second Economy in Tanzania*. London: Currey.

Mamdani, M. (1991) "Uganda: Contradictions of the IMF programme and perspective." *Development and Change* 21: 427–67.

———. (1996) *Citizen and Subject: Contemporary Africa and the Legacy of Late Colonialism*. Princeton, NJ: Princeton University Press.

Manoukian, M. (1951) *Tribes of the Northern Territories*. London: International African Institute.

Marchand, D. (1988) "Extracting profits with a shea butter press." *International Development Research Center Reports* 17, 4: 14–15.

Marcus, G., and Fischer, M. (1986) *Anthropology as Cultural Critique*. Chicago: University of Chicago Press.

"Marketing news: Body Time." (2001) *Happi-Household and Personal Products Industry* 38, 3: 34.

"Marketing news: Desert Essence." (2001) *Happi-Household and Personal Products Industry* 38, 3: 34.

"Market pointers: North-South trade patterns." (2002) *Business Africa* March 1–15: 5.

Martin, S. (1988) *Palm Oil and Protest*. Cambridge, UK: Cambridge University Press.

Marx, K. (1967) *Capital, A Critique of Political Economy*, vol. 1: *The Process of Capitalist Production*. New York: International Publishers.

———. (1964) *The Economic and Philosophic Manuscripts of 1844*. New York: International Publishers.

"Master sculptors." (2000) *Soap, Perfumery and Cosmetics* 73, 1: 7.

McClintock, A. (1995) *Imperial Leather: Race, Gender and Sexuality in the Colonial Context*. New York: Routledge.

McKim, W. (1972) "The periodic market system in northeastern Ghana." *Economic Geography* 48, 3: 333–34.

McLeod, M. (1981) *The Asante*. London: British Museum.

McMichael, P. (1994) "Introduction," in P. McMichael, ed., *The Global Restructuring of Agro-Food Systems*. Ithaca, NY: Cornell University Press.

McPhee, A. (1926) *The Economic Revolution in British West Africa*. London: Routledge.

Meek, P. (1925) *The Northern Tribes of Nigeria*. London: Frank Cass.

Meena, R. (1991) "The impact of structural adjustment programs on women in Tanzania," in C. Gladwin, ed., *Structural Adjustment and African Women Farmers*. Gainesville, FL: University of Florida.

Meillassoux, C. (1971) "Introduction," in C. Meillassoux, ed., *The Development of Indigenous Trade and Markets in West Africa*. London: Oxford University Press.

———. (1972) "From production to reproduction." *Economy and Society* 1, 1.

———. (1973) "The social organization of the peasantry: The economic basis of kinship." *Journal of Peasant Studies* 1, 1: 81–90.

———. (1981) *Maidens, Meal and Money*. Cambridge, UK: Cambridge University Press.

Meredith, D. (1988) "The colonial office, British business interests and the reform of cocoa marketing in West Africa, 1937–1945." *Journal of African History* 29: 285–300.

Metcalfe, G. E. (1964) *Great Britain and Ghana: Documents on Ghana History*. London: P. T. Nelson and Sons.

Mikell, G. (1986) "Ghanaian females, rural economy and national civility." *African Studies Review* 29, 3: 67–88.

———. (1989) "Peasant politicisation and economic recuperation in Ghana: Local and national dilemmas," *Journal of Modern African Studies* 27, 3: 455–78.

———. (1991) "Equity issues in Ghana's rural development," in D. Rothchild, ed., *Ghana: The Political Economy of Recovery*. Boulder, CO: Lynne Reinner.

"Milking baby skincare." (2001) *Community Pharmacy* September, 3: 33.

Miller, P., and Rose, N. (1990) "Governing economic life." *Economy and Society* 19, 1: 1–31.

Minifie, B. (1989) *Chocolate, Cocoa and Confectionery: Science and Technology*. New York: Van Nostrand Reinhold.

Mintz, S. (1985) *Sweetness and Power: The Place of Sugar in Modern History*. New York: Viking.

"Missing ingredient." (1992) *Economist* August 22, 324, 7773: 34.

Mital, H., and Dove, F. (1971) "The study of shea butter." *Planta Medica* 20: 283–8.

Moley, T. (2001) "Chocolove introduces organic chocolate bars." Chocolove online. http://www.chocolove.com.

Moore, M. P. (1975) "Cooperative labor in peasant agriculture." *Journal of Peasant Studies* 2: 270–91.

Moore, S. F. (1987) "Explaining the present: Theoretical dilemmas in processual ethnography," *American Ethnologist* 14, 4: 727–36.

———. (1994) *Anthropology and Africa*. Charlottesville, VA: University Press of Virginia.

Morna, C. L. (1988) "The privatization drive." *Africa Report* November-December: 60–2.

Mosley, P., Harrigan, J., and Toye, J. (1991) *Aid and Power: The World Bank and Policy Based Lending in the 1980's*. London: Routledge.

Munn, N. (1977) "The spatiotemporal transformation of Gawan canoes." *Journal de la Societe des Oceanistes* 33, 54/55: 39–53.

———. (1986) *The Fame of Gawa*. Durham, NC: Duke University Press.

"Natural moisturizers; the benefits of shea butter." (1998) *Today's Black Woman* 4, 9: 13.

"Natural shea butter soothes, nourishes and protects your skin." (n.d.) Catalogue. Real Goods.

Newbury, C., and Schoepf, B. G. (1989) "State, peasantry and agrarian crisis in Zaire: Does gender make a difference?" in J. Parpart and K. Staudt, eds., *Women and the State in Africa*. Boulder, CO: Lynne Reinner.

"New cocoa agreement." (2001) *New African* 396: 15.

"New cosmetics and household products in Japan." (1997) *Business and Industry* April 15.

Northcott, H. P. (1899) *The Northern Territories of the Gold Coast*. War Office Intelligence Division. London: Harrison and Sons for H.M. Stationary Office.

Nugent, P. (1991) "Educating Rawlings: The evolution of government strategy towards smuggling," in D. Rothchild, ed., *Ghana: The Political Economy of Recovery*. Boulder, CO: Lynne Reinner.

———. (1995) *Big Men, Small Boys and Politics in Ghana*. London: Pinter.

O'Brien, S. (1991) "Structural adjustment and structural transformation in sub-Saharan Africa," in C. Gladwin, ed., *Structural Adjustment and African Women Farmers*. Gainesville, FL: University of Florida.

Okali, C. (1983) *Cocoa and Kinship in Ghana*. London: Kegan Paul.

O'Laughlin, B. (1973) *Mbum Beer-Parties: Structures of Production and Exchange in an African Social Formation*. Ph.D. dissertation, Yale University.

Ong, A. (1999) *Flexible Citizenship: The Cultural Logics of Transnationality*, Durham, NC: Duke University Press.

Oppong, C. (1967) "Local migration in northern Ghana." *Ghana Journal of Sociology* 3, 1: 1–16.

Oquaye, M. (1980) *Politics in Ghana*. Accra, Ghana: Tornado Publications.

Ortner, S. (1984) "Theory in Anthropology since the sixties." *Comparative Studies in Society and History* 26: 126–66.

Owusu-Ansah, D., and McFarland, D. (1995) *Historical Dictionary of Ghana*. New Jersey: Scarecrow Press.

Oyewole, D. (1997) "Sell 'A' quality shea butter." Northtown International Business Board. Online posting. http://www.northtown.com/wwwboard/messages/77.htm.

Paine, R. (1974) "Second thoughts about Barth's models," *Royal Anthropological Institute Occasional Paper* no. 32, London.

"Palmer's." (2002) EbonyLine.com online. http://www.ebonyline.com/skin-skin-by-brand-palmer-s.html.

Park, M. (1971) [1799] *Travels in the Interior Districts of Africa*. New York: American Press.

Parkin, D. (1972) *Palms, Wine and Witnesses*. San Francisco: Chandler Publishing.

———. (1980) "Kind bridewealth and hard cash: Eventing a structure," in J. Comaroff, ed., *The Meaning of Marriage Payments*. London: Academic Press.

Pearce, R. (1992) "Ghana," in A. Duncan and J. Howell, eds., *Structural Adjustment and the African Farmer*. London: James Currey.

Peiler, E. (1994) "Potentials and constraints of agroforestry in northern Ghana on the example of farmed parkland in the vicinity of Nyankpala Agricultural experiment station with special reference to the impact of *Butyrospermum parkii* and *Parkia biglobosa.*" Manuscript, Nyankpala Agricultural Experiment Station, Ghana.

Pellow, D. and N. Chazan (1986) *Ghana: Coping with Uncertainty.* Boulder, CO: Westview Press.

Perea, J. (1998) "Commodities: Cote d'Ivoire." *Interpress Service* March 27.

"Personal and beauty care: Newsbites." (1997) *Drug Store News* August 18: 17.

Plange, N. (1979) "Underdevelopment in northern Ghana: Natural causes of colonial Capitalism." *Review of African Political Economy* 15/16: 4–14.

Pobeda, M. (1999) "New industry trends are reviving interest in this natural ingredient." *Global Cosmetics Industry* April.

Podeba, M., and Sousselier, L. (1999) "Shea butter: The revival of an African wonder." *Global Cosmetic Industry* 164, 4: 34.

Polanyi, K. (1957) "The economy as instituted process," in K. Polanyi, C. Arensberg, and H. W. Pearson, eds., *Trade and Market in the Early Empires.* Glencoe, IL: Free Press.

"Power of nature." (1998) Holiday catalogue, Origins.

Pred, A., and Watts, M., eds. (1992) *Reworking Modernity: Capitalisms and Symbolic Discontent.* New Brunswick, NJ: Rutgers.

"Producers continue to press EU for 'pure cocoa' chocolate." (1995) *Agri Service International Newsletter* May 19, no. 418.

"Product alert." (1995) *Market Intelligence Service* June 19, 25, 25.

"Prospects: Ghana." (2000) *Business Africa* February 16–29: 12.

Public Ledger (1995) Ghana.

Raghavan, C. (1992) "Cocoa negotiations resume." *South-North Development Monitor* Geneva, November 2, Online. http://www.sunsonline.org/trade/areas/commodit/11031092.htm.

Raikes, P., and Gibbon, P. (2000) "'Globalisation' and African export crop agriculture." *Journal of Peasant Studies* 27, 2: 50–93.

Rathbone, R. (1978) "Ghana," in J. Dunn, ed., *West African States: Failure and Promise.* Cambridge, UK: Cambridge University Press.

Ravenhill, J. (1993) "A second decade of adjustment: Greater complexity, greater uncertainty in the 1970s and 1980s," in T. Callaghy and J. Ravenhill, eds., *Hemmed In: Responses to Africa's Economic Decline.* New York: Columbia University Press.

Rawlings, J. (1982) *A Revolutionary Journey: Selected Speeches of Flt.-Lt. Jerry John Rawlings Chairman of the PNDC,* vol. 1. December 31, 1981—December 31, 1982. Accra, Ghana: Information Services Department.

Read, M. (1942) "Migrant labor and its effects on tribal life." *International Labor Review* 45: 605–31.

"Relaxation of import rules prompts flood of exotic lotions." (1997) *New Cosmetic and Household Products in Japan* April 15.

Rey, P. P. (1975) "The lineage mode of production." *Critique of Anthropology* 3: 27–79.

Reyna, S. and Downs, R. E. (1988) "Introduction," in S. Reyna and R. Downs, eds., *Land and Society in Contemporary Africa.* Durham, NH: University of New Hampshire Press.

Richards, A. (1939) *Land, Labor and Diet in Northern Rhodesia.* London: Oxford University Press.

Richards, P. (1985) *Indigenous Agricultural Revolution.* London: Hutchinson.

———. (1988) "Response to Guyer." *Current Anthropology* 29, 2: 275.

Ridell, J. (1987) "Introduction," in J. Raintree, ed., *Land, Trees and Tenure.* Nairobi, Kenya, and Madison, WI: International Center for Agroforestry and the Land Tenure Center, University of Wisconsin.

Rimmer, D. (1992) *Staying Poor: Ghana's Political Economy 1950–1990.* Oxford, UK: Pergamon Press for the World Bank.

Roberts, P. (1988) "Rural women's access to labor in West Africa," in S. Stichter and J. Parpart, eds., *Patriarchy and Class: African Women in the Home and the Workforce.* Boulder, CO: Westview.

Robertson, A. F. (1983) *The Dynamics of Productive Relationships.* Cambridge, UK: Cambridge University Press.

———. (1984) *People and the State.* Cambridge, UK: Cambridge University Press.

Rocheleau, D. (1987) "Women, trees and tenure," in J. Raintree, ed., *Land, Trees and Tenure.* Nairobi, Kenya, and Madison, WI: International Center for Agroforestry and the Land Tenure Center, University of Wisconsin.

Roddick, A. (1991) *Body and Soul.* New York: Crown Publishers.

———. (1994) "Not free trade but fair trade." *Across the Board* 31, 6: 58.

Roncoli, M. C. (1994) "Managing on the margins: Agricultural production and household reproduction in Northeastern Ghana." Ph.D. dissertation. State University of New York at Binghamton.

Roseberry, W. (1988) "Political economy." *Annual Reviews of Anthropology* 17: 161–85.

———. (1996) "The rise of yuppie coffees and the reimagination of class in the United States." *American Anthropologist* 98, 4: 762–75.

Ross, D. (1974) "Ghanaian forowa." *African Arts* 8, 1: 40–9.

Rothchild, D. (1991) "Ghana and structural adjustment: An overview," in D. Rothchild, ed., *Ghana: The Political Economy of Recovery.* Boulder, CO: Lynn Rienner.

Rothchild, D., and Gymah-Boadi, E. (1986) "Ghana's economic decline and development strategies," in J. Ravenhill, ed., *Africa in Economic Crisis.* New York: Columbia University Press.

Safo, A. (1999) *African Business* February, 240: 38.

Sahlins, M. (1985) *Historical Metaphors and Mythical Realities.* Association for Social Anthropology in Oceania Special Publication, no. 1. Ann Arbor, MI: University of Michigan Press.

Sale, J. B. (1983) *The Importance and Values of Wild Plants and Animals in Africa*, part 1. Switzerland: International Union for the Conservation of Nature.

Sampson, M. (1956) "George Ekem Ferguson of Anomabu." *Transactions of the Historical Society of the Gold Coast* 2, 1: 30–45.

Sanik, S. (1996) "How 'bout a nice hot cocoa contract?" *Futures: News, Analysis and Strategies for Futures, Options and Derivatives Traders* 07462468, December, 25, 14.

Sarno, N. (1998) "Trade-development: EU cocoa directive threat to producer nations." *Interpress Service* February 19.

Sarris, A., and Shams, H. (1991) *Ghana under Structural Adjustment: The Impact on Agriculture and the Rural Poor.* IFAD Studies in Rural Poverty 2. New York: New York University Press.

Sassen, S. (1996) *Losing Control: Sovereignty in an Age of Globalization.* New York: Columbia.

———. (2000) "Spatialities and temporalities of the global: Elements for a theorization." *Public Culture* 12, 1: 215–32.

———. (2002) "Introduction" in S. Sassen ed., *Global Networks, Linked Cities*, New York, Routledge.

Saul, M. (1981) "Beer, sorghum and women: Production for the market in Upper Volta." *Africa* 51, 3: 746–64.

———. (1983) "Work parties, wages and accumulation in a Voltaic village." *American Ethnologist* 10, 1: 77–96.

———. (1986) "Development of the grain market and merchants in Burkina Faso." *Journal of Modern African Studies* 24, 1: 127–53.

———. (1987) "The organization of a West African grain market." *American Anthropologist* 89, 1: 74–95.

———. (1988) "Land tenure in Burkina Faso," in S. Reyna and R. Downs, eds., *Land and Society in Contemporary Africa.* Durham, NH: University of New Hampshire Press.

———. (1989) "Separateness and relation: Autonomous income and negotiation among rural Bobo women," in R. Wilk, ed., *The Household Economy:Reconsidering the Domestic Mode of Production.* Boulder, CO: Westview.

———. (2002) "Introduction: locating cities in global circuits," in S. Sassen, ed., *Global Networks, Linked Cities.* New York: Routledge.

Schaffer, R. (2002) *Understanding Globalization.* New York: Rowman and Littlefield.

Schapera, I. (1947) *Migrant Labor and Tribal Life.* London: Oxford University Press.

Scott, J. (1985) *Weapons of the Weak: Everyday Forms of Peasant Resistance.* New Haven, CT: Yale University Press.

Shafir, G., ed. (1998) *The Citizenship Debates: A Reader.* Minneapolis, MN: University of Minnesota Press.

"Sheabutter extraction methods." (1997) Teco Finance Export online. http://www.sheabutter.com/ExtractionMethods.htm.

"Shea butter family." (2002) Karlshamns online. http://www.karlshamns.com/other/shea_butter family.html.

"Shea butter: Karite Gold shea butter for healthy skin and hair." (2002) Karite Gold online. http://www.karitegold.com.

"Shea butter or Karite." (1997) Mode de Vie online. http://www.modedeviebodycare.com/md-vsheastory.htm.

"Shea butter range from L'Occitane." (2000) *Happi-Household and Personal Products Industry* 37, 11: 139.

"Shea butter: 'women's gold.'" (n.d.) L'Occitane.

Shenton, R. (1986) *The Development of Capitalism in Northern Nigeria*. Buffalo, NY: University of Toronto.

Shepherd, A. (1979) "Agrarian Change in Northern Ghana," in J. Heyer, P. Roberts, and G. Williams, eds., *Rural Development in Tropical Africa*. London: Macmillan.

"Shopping Wales: Stock take." (2002) *Western Mail* June 7.

"Shortfall in Ghanaian cocoa production." (2002) *Pan African News Agency* Daily Wire, July 12.

"Shortfall in Ghanaian cocoa production threatens jobs." (2002) *Pan African News Agency* July 12.

"Skin Care: 'Cream Cheese Cleanser HN' by The Body Shop." (1997) *New Cosmetic and Household Products in Japan* January 15.

Skinner, E. (1964) *The Mossi of Upper Volta*. Stanford, CA: Stanford University Press.

Smith, C. A. (1984) "Differentiation among petty-commodity producers in Guatemala." *Journal of Peasant Studies* 11.

Smith, C., Child J. and Rowlinson, M. (1990) *Reshaping Work: The Cadbury Experience*. Cambridge: Cambridge University Press.

Smith, D. A. (2001) "The politics of upper east and the 2000 Ghanaian elections," in J. Ayee, ed., *Deepening Democracy in Ghana: Politics of the 2000 Elections*, vol. 2, *Constituency Studies*. Accra, Ghana: Freedom Publications Ltd.

Smith, F. (1978) "Gurunsi wall painting." *African Arts* 12, 1: 36–41.

"Soap label." (n.d.) L'Occitane.

Southall, A and Gutkind, P. (1956) *Townsmen in the Making*. Kampala, Uganda: East African Institute for Social Research.

Stanford, L. (2000) "The globalization of agricultural commodity systems: Examining peasant resistance to international agribusiness," in A. Haugerud, P. Stone, and P. Little, eds., *Commodities and Globalization: Anthropological Perspectives*. Lanham, MD: Rowan and Littlefield.

Staudt, K. (1995) "The impact of development policies on women," in J. Hay and S. Stichter, eds., *African Women South of the Sahara*. Essex, UK: Longman.

Steffen, P. (1994) "The structural transformation of OPAM, cereals marketing agency," in B. Grosh and R. Mukandala, eds., *State-Owned Enterprises in Africa*. Boulder, CO: Lynne Reinner.

Stichter, S., and Parpart, J. L., eds. (1988) *Patriarchy and Class: African Women in the Home and Workforce*. Boulder, CO: Westview Press.

"Strategy and services." (2002) TechnoServe online. http://technoserve.org/strategy-1.html.

Sutton, I. (1981) "The Volta River salt trade: The survival of an indigenous industry." *Journal of African History* 22: 43–61.

———. (1983) "Labour in commercial agriculture in Ghana in the late nineteenth and early twentieth century." *Journal of African History* 24: 461–83.

———. (1989) "Colonial agricultural policy: The non-development of the northern territories of the Gold Coast." *International Journal of African Historical Studies* 22, 4: 637–69.

Swift, R. (1998a) "The cocoa chain." *New Internationalist*, August, 304: 7.

———. (1998b) "Deep roots in cocoa country." *New Internationalist* August, 304: 12.

———. (1998c) "Best of the best." *New Internationalist* August, 304: 20.

———. (1998d) "Chocolate saves the world!" *New Internationalist* August, 304: 30.

Swindell, K. (1985) *Farm Labor*. New York: Cambridge University Press.

Tabatabai, H. (1988) "Agricultural decline and access to food in Ghana." *International Labour Review* 127, 6: 703–34.

Tait, D. (1961) *The Konkomba of Northern Ghana*. Oxford, UK: Oxford University Press.

Talbot, J. (1994) "The regulation of the world coffee market: Tropical commodities and the limits of globalization," in P. McMichael, ed., *Food and Agriculture in the World Economy*. Westport, CT: Greenwood.

Tangri, R. (1991) "The politics of state divestiture in Ghana." *African Affairs* 90: 523–36.

Tannen, M. (1994) "Eco-yearnings." *New York Times Magazine* March 20: 66.

"TC Naturals: Take pride in your roots." (1994) *Pride* May/June.

Terray, E. (1974) "Long distance exchange and the formation of the state: The case of the Abron Kingdom of Gyaman." *Economy and Society* 3, 3: 315–45.

Terrio, S. (1996) "Crafting 'grand cru' chocolates in contemporary France." *American Anthropologist* 98, 1: 67–79.

Thomas, N. (1994) *Colonialism's Culture*. Princeton, NJ: Princeton University Press.

Thomas, R. G. (1972) "George Ekem Ferguson: Civil servant extraordinary." *Transactions of the Historical Society of Ghana* 13, 2.

——. (1973) "Forced labour in British West Africa: The case of the northern territories of the Gold Coast 1906–1927." *Journal of African History* 14, 1: 79–103.

——. (1975) "Military recruitment in the Gold Coast during the First World War," *Cahiers d'Etudes Africaines* 15, 1: 57–84.

Tomich, T., Kilby, P., and Johnston, B. (1995) *Transforming Agrarian Economies*. Ithaca, NY: Cornell University Press.

Tosh, J. (1980) "The cash-crop revolution in tropical Africa: An agricultural reappraisal." *African Affairs* 319: 79–94.

Toye, J. (1990) "Ghana's economic reforms, 1983–7: Origins, achievements and limitations," in J. Pickett and H. Singer, eds., *Economic Recovery in Sub-Saharan Africa*. New York: Routledge.

"Trade: Chocolate crazed Europe heedless of real costs." (1997) *Interpress Service* October 10, no. 23.

"Trade: EU chocolate rule endangers millions of cocoa farmers." (1997) *Interpress Service* October 10.

"Treatment cosmetics: The second dimension." (1998) *Soap Cosmetics Chemical Specialties* 74, 3: 30.

Tripp, R. (1981) "Farmers and traders: Some economic determinants of nutritional status in northern Ghana." *Journal of Tropical Pediatrics* 27: 15–22.

"Uganda shea butter: New vision." (2001) *Africa News* February 22.

USAID. "Export promotion." (1994) Trade and Investment Program. Mimeo. Accra, Ghana.

Van Binsbergen, W. M. J., and Geschiere, P., eds. (1984) *Old Modes of Production and Capitalist Encroachment*. London: Kegan Paul.

Van de Walle, N. (1994a) "The politics of private enterprise reform in Cameroon," in B. Grosh and R. Mukandala, eds., *State-Owned Enterprises in Africa*. Boulder, CO: Lynne Reinner.

——. (1994b) "Adjustment alternatives and alternatives to adjustment." *African Studies Review* 37, 3: 103–17.

Vaughn, J. (1973) "Kyagu as artists in Marghi society," in W. d'Azevedo, ed., *The Traditional Artist in African Societies*. Bloomington, IN: Indiana University Press.

"Vegetable fats for chocolate." (2002) Aarhus online. http://www.aarhus.com/aarhusolie/aarhusolie.nsf/links/FB28752EDCF75C87C1256AE200383626.

Von Braun, J., Hotchkiss, D., and Immink, M. (1989) *Non-traditional Export Crops in Guatemala*. Washington, DC: International Food Policy Research Institute.

Vreeland, C. (2000) "Organic chocolate market skyrockets." *Candy Industry* October.

WAIBL. (2003) *Monthly Newsletter*, February. http://www.ccawaible.com/homepage.php.

Wallerstein, I. (1979) *The Capitalist World Economy*. Cambridge, UK: Cambridge University Press.

——. (1980) *The Process of the World System*. Beverly Hills, CA: Sage.

Ward, W. E. (1957) *A Short History of Ghana*. London: Longmans.

"Watchdog: Hot shops." (2002) *Evening Mail* June 24.

Watherston, A. E. (1908a) "Trade possibilities in the northern territories of the Gold Coast." *Incorporated Chamber of Commerce of Liverpool Monthly Magazine*. October: 188–94.

——. (1908b) "The northern territories of the Gold Coast." *Journal of the African Society* 7, 28.

Watson, W. (1958) *Tribal Cohesion in a Money Economy*. Manchester, UK: Manchester University Press.

Watts, M. (1992) "Capitalisms, crises and cultures I," in A. Pred and M. Watts, eds., *Reworking Modernity*. New Brunswick, NJ: Rutgers University Press.

——. (1994) "Living under contract: Work, production, politics and the manufacture of discontent in a peasant society," in P. Little and M. Watts, eds., *Living under Contract: Contract Farming and Agrarian Transformation in Sub-Saharan Africa*. Madison, WI: University of Wisconsin Press.

Webber, P. (1996) "Agrarian change in Kusasi, North-East Ghana." *Africa* 66, 3: 437–57.

White, C. (2002) "The sweet smell of fast growth; but can L'Occitane retain its homegrown charm." *Business Week*. European Business: France, no. 3791, July 15: 32.

White, H. P. (1956) "Internal exchange of staple foods in the Gold Coast." *Economic Geography* 32, 2: 115–25.

Whitehead, A. (1984a) "Beyond the household? Gender and kinship-based resource allocation in a Ghanaian domestic economy." Unpublished paper presented at the workshop, Conceptualizing the Household: Theoretical, Conceptual and Methodological Issues, Harvard Institute for International Development.

———. (1984b) "Gender and famine in West Africa." Unpublished paper presented at the Development Studies Association Annual Conference, Bradford.

———. (1984c) "Men and women, kinship and property: some general issues," in R. Hirshon, ed., *Women and Property: Women as Property.* London: Croom Helm.

———. (1984d) "I'm hungry mum: The politics of domestic budgeting," in K. Young, C. Wolkowitz, and R. McCullagh, eds., *Of Marriage and the Market.* London and Boston: Routledge and Kegan Paul.

———. (1990) "Rural women and food production in sub-Saharan Africa," in J. Dreze and A. Sen, eds., *The Political Economy of Hunger,* vol. 1, *Entitlement and Well-Being.* Oxford, UK: Oxford University Press.

———. (1995) "Wives and mothers: Female farmers in Africa," in A. Adepoju and C. Oppong, eds., *Gender, Work and Population in Sub-Saharan Africa.* London: James Currey for the International Labour Office.

Wilck, J. (1997) "Baby boomers and natural ingredients life personal care." *Chemical Market Reporter* May 12, 251, 19: SR3–SR6.

Wilks, I. (1961) *The Northern Factor in Asanti History.* Legon: Institute of African Studies.

———. (1976) "The Mossi and Akan states, 1500–1800," in J. F. A. Ajayi and M. Crowder, eds. *History of West Africa.* New York: Columbia University Press.

Wilson, E. (1994) "The political-economy of economic reform in Cote D'Ivoire: A microlevel study of three privatization transactions," in B. Grosh and R. Mukandala, eds., *State-Owned Enterprises in Africa.* Boulder, CO: Lynne Reinner.

Wipper, A. (1995) "Women's voluntary associations," in J. Hay and S. Stichter, eds., *African Women South of the Sahara.* Essex, UK: Longman.

Wolf, E. (1982) *Europe and the People without History.* Berkeley, CA: University of California.

Wolpe, H. (1980) *The Articulation of Modes of Production,* London: Routledge and K. Paul.

World Bank (1981) *Accelerated Development in Sub-Saharan Africa.* Washington, DC: World Bank.

———. (n.d.a) "Ghana: Promoting growth, reducing poverty." Findings no. 52.

———. (n.d.b) "Ghana: Report 14111.GH."

"World cocoa beans production." (1996) Online. http://www.oardc.ohio-state.edu/cocoa/regions.htm.

Younger, S. D. (1989) "Ghana's economic recovery program: A case study of stabilization and structural adjustment in sub-Saharan Africa," in *Successful Development in Africa: Case Studies of Projects, Programs and Policies.* Washington, DC: World Bank Economic Development Institute.

Zeigler, G. "U.S. standards of identity." (2002) Personal communication.

Archival Sources

Ghana National Archives, Accra:

Adm. 56.1.126.

Adm. 56.1.152.

Adm. 56.1.158.

Adm. 56.1.275.

Adm. 56.1.513.

Adm. 57.5.4.

Adm. 57.5.9

Ghana National Archives, Tamale:

Report on the Mandated area of Kusasi for the year 1933.

Report on the Mandated area of Kusasi for the year 1936.

Bawku Subdistrict Diary for the Month of March, 1937.

Memorandum on the Kusasi, 1939.

Index